ROGUE ALLIES

ROGUE ALLIES

THE STRATEGIC PARTNERSHIP BETWEEN
IRAN AND NORTH KOREA

Bruce E. Bechtol Jr.
and Anthony N. Celso

UNIVERSITY PRESS OF KENTUCKY

Scholarly publisher for the Commonwealth,
serving Bellarmine University, Berea College,
Centre College of Kentucky, Eastern Kentucky University,
The Filson Historical Society, Georgetown College,
Kentucky Historical Society, Kentucky State University,
Morehead State University, Murray State University,
Northern Kentucky University, Spalding University,
Transylvania University, University of Kentucky,
University of Louisville, University of Pikeville,
and Western Kentucky University
All rights reserved.

Editorial and Sales Offices: The University Press of Kentucky
663 South Limestone Street, Lexington, Kentucky 40508-4008
www.kentuckypress.com

Cataloging-in-Publication data is available from the Library of Congress.

ISBN 978-1-9859-0212-1 (hardcover: alk. paper)
ISBN 978-1-9859-0217-6 (pbk.: alk. paper)
ISBN 978-1-9859-0215-2 (epub)
ISBN 978-1-9859-0214-5 (pdf)

Member of the Association
of University Presses

ASSOCIATION
of UNIVERSITY
PRESSES

Contents

Tables

Preface

Hamas's October 7, 2023, attacks on Israeli Gaza border communities threatened to ignite a war across the Middle East. The al-Aqsa Flood operation of Hamas and Palestinian Islamic Jihad (PIJ) killed over 1,200 people and wounded 7,000 others. Over 240 Israeli and foreign national hostages were taken by Palestinian "resistance forces."

Viewed as Israel's 9-11 moment, the assault was an example of Iran's forty-plus-year relationship with North Korea and the support that Pyongyang has proliferated to Shia and Palestinian terror or insurgent groups working with and for Iran. The North Korean arms traded, technical expertise provided, and military training conducted in the Middle East on behalf of Iran and its proxies constitutes a "rogue alliance" that is fortified by common enemies and similar anti-Western totalitarian ideology. Though neither was directly involved in the Hamas/PIJ attack, they provided financial, weapons, and technological support to the Hamas and PIJ militants who carried out the massacre.

Palestinian militias used Iranian financial support, training, and rockets and North Korean small arms and rockets to kill, burn alive, behead, rape, and sexually mutilate their victims. Israel's invasion of the Gaza Strip sparked tensions across the region. Iran's Lebanese proxy Hezbollah attacked Israel's northern border; the Islamic Revolutionary Guard Corps (IRGC) funded, trained, and armed Iraqi militias who attacked American troops stationed in the Middle East; and its Yemeni Houthi proxy assaulted Western cargo vessels transiting the Red Sea. The Gaza war thus risked igniting a larger military confrontation between the United States and Iran.

This book demonstrates that North Korea has supplied the missiles, rockets, small arms, ammunition, technology, and tunnel infrastructure that has enabled Iran to strengthen its "axis of resistance" proxy forces. Since its devastating war with Iraq in the 1980s, the Islamic Republic of Iran (IRI) has pursued a missile and proxy militia strategy to indirectly fight the United States, Israel, and Sunni Gulf Kingdoms. Tehran has spent billions of dollars to support Lebanese Hezbollah, Shia Iraqi Popular Mobilization Forces, Syria's Assad regime, the Yemeni Houthis, and Hamas/PIJ.

North Korea's transfer of rockets, missiles, small arms, and tunnel infrastructure assistance has allowed Iran and its proxies to project an Islamist arc of influence across the Middle East. Empowered by Iranian assistance and North Korean arms, Arab militias have killed thousands of Israelis and hundreds of American soldiers. Iran's sphere of influence stretches from Iraq to Lebanon, allowing its Islamic Revolutionary Guard Corps–Quds Force to fund, train, and transfer small arms, rockets, and missiles to aligned insurgent-terror groups.

We must always address North Korean military capabilities development (which is considered in an entire chapter of this book) as not just a threat to American interests in Northeast Asia or against the United States (via ballistic missiles) because of the proven threat of proliferation to volatile regions—in this case the Middle East. In this book, we specifically address North Korean military proliferation to Iran and its state and nonstate proxies. This threatens Washington's Arab allies in the region. It also, as we have seen in 2023 and 2024, poses an existential threat to the security and stability of Israel. North Korea's long and ongoing relationship with Iran has proved to be a key factor in the supply of weapons, training, and technical support to not only Iran but also those entities that Iran supports throughout the Middle East.

The issues addressed above raise certain questions. What role did North Korea play in the Syrian civil war? Is North Korea still playing a key role now that the war in Syria has wound down? Has North Korea supported Iran's nuclear weaponization program? How much of Iran's ballistic missile capability is due to North Korean support? And how has North Korea supported Iran's nonstate actor proxies (terrorists) in the region, such as Hezbollah, Hamas, and the Houthis? In this book, we answer all of these questions, as well as associated questions that address the North Korea–Iran relationship, in great detail.

The war in Gaza is but one example of an outcome shaped by Iran's hybrid warfare strategy that now threatens a major military conflagration with the United States. Tehran's warfare doctrine furthermore is underwritten by illicit financial, cyber, and criminal networks often working in tandem with

North Korean and Hezbollah networks that have for decades circumvented international sanctions. US policy has consistently failed to blunt Iran's military projection across the Middle East. Consternation over directly confronting the IRI has paralyzed American policy, allowing Tehran freedom to expand its regional influence.

This book aims to demonstrate how this "rogue alliance" has developed and how it threatens America's allies in the region. It suggests steps that American, Israeli, and international policymakers can take to weaken the North Korea–Iran partnership. So far, neither Republican nor Democratic presidential administrations have grasped the dangers posed by Tehran and Pyongyang's destructive alliance, nor have they devised an effective counterstrategy. We hope this book helps policymakers to understand how this rogue alliance works and suggests how to blunt its destabilizing consequences.

We wrote this book for a broad audience. We believe that the book will be useful for those who specialize in international security issues, regional specialists (for East Asia and the Middle East), scholars on North Korea and Iran, military planners, counterproliferation specialists, and anyone who has an interest in the compelling but seldom-addressed issues surrounding the Iran–North Korea political-military relationship. This work and the assessments that we offer will be useful to specialists and broader range analysts in the United States, the Middle East, and East Asia. Our goal in writing this book was not only to offer an accurate picture of the threat presented by the North Korea–Iran relationship but also to articulate predictive analysis that will be useful for policy and planning in the future. Thus, as with previous works both of us have produced, this book will hopefully be useful for not only those who have an operational or scholarly interest in these issues but also those who have a practical interest in seeing these challenges resolved.

The authors would like to thank Michael Rubin at the American Enterprise Institute; Foundation for Free Democracies analysts Emanuele Ottolenghi, Kristian Patrick Alexander, and Gina Bou Serhal at the Dubai Office for TRENDS Research and Advisory; and Khaled Almezaini, associate professor at Zayed University–Abu Dhabi, for interviews they granted during our research for this book. We would also like to thank William Newcomb, a retired former member of the State Department and a former member of the UN Panel of Experts, who was extremely helpful and offered very useful advice. Chun Seong Whun, a former presidential adviser in the Blue House in South Korea, was an excellent source of information and collaboration.

Greg Scarlatoiu, the current executive director of the Committee for Human Rights in North Korea, has been an excellent source for addressing sources and methods and seeking out resources for our research. We would like to thank Hugo Kim, our friend, our mentor, and a founding member of the International Council on Korean Studies; US general John Tilelli (retired); Andrew Scobell of the US Institute of Peace; former Congressional Research Service analyst Larry Niksch (now retired); author Gordon Chang; Jonathan Brewer, former coordinator of the 1540 group of experts at the UN; Enrico Carisch, former UN Security Council financial and natural resources monitor; Maiko Takeuchi, a former member of the UN Panel of Experts on North Korea; Hyun-Seung Lee, North Korean defector and current human rights activist in the United States; Tara O of the Hudson Institute; and Ssu-Ryong (David) Choe, retired South Korean intelligence official. The authors would also like to thank James Byrne, Giangiuseppe Pili, Gary Somerville from the Royal United Services Institute, and Tal Inbar of the Missile Defense Advocacy Alliance.

The responsibility for the writing and research of this work is solely our own. Thus, the views that we express in it do not necessarily reflect the policy or position of any US government agency or any university that we have been affiliated with. References to internet sites were accurate at the time of writing. As this book went into publication, all of the information included in it was up to date. Because North Korea and Iran are both moving targets, it is likely that events will continue to rapidly unfold. Nevertheless, the information contained in this work will remain relevant and provide value to scholars, students, the media, pundits, and the general public seeking to understand Iranian and North Korean strategies and activities. Neither the authors nor the University Press of Kentucky is responsible for websites that have expired or changed since this book was prepared.

1

Setting the Context

The Strategic Partnership between Iran and North Korea

Bruce E. Bechtol Jr. and Anthony N. Celso

North Korea has engaged in a highly profitable relationship with Iran for years. This partnership has received scant attention in policy and academic circles—unless a headline-grabbing incident occurs (such as Iran test launching North Korea–supplied ballistic missiles). In fact, some scholars have claimed the North Korea–Iran relationship has dissipated in recent years. This is clearly untrue. After the 1979 Revolution, Iran emerged as a pariah state, a revolutionary regime hostile to the United States and Israel. At the same time, North Korea's government, led by Kim Il-sung, saw the handwriting on the wall. They would soon need to find another way to finance their elite and their large military as Soviet subsidies were coming to a close (subsidies eventually totally ended in 1990). One of the ways to do this has proved to be profits from proliferation and other forms of economic cooperation with enemies of the United States and rogue states. This partnership has been robust and comprehensive. But it does not stop there.

North Korea and Iran have expanded their contact with nonstate actors Hezbollah, the Houthis, and Hamas into this important relationship that is destabilizing the Middle East (through proliferation) and East Asia (through illicit finance). Thus, this issue is important because it affects Middle East and East Asia security. In addition, the weapons of mass destruction (WMD) and related platforms (ballistic missiles) that North Korea continues to proliferate in the Middle East (largely through Iranian financing) present a danger that could threaten the United States and Europe. Questions about this alliance that have never truly been addressed in a public forum revolve around how this odd relationship was formed, how it has evolved over the years, how this partnership contributed to proliferation networks across the Middle East, how much money North Korea is making from this robust relationship, and finally how it can it be contained—or stopped.

Rogue nation-states armed with chemical and nuclear weapons, terrorists equipped with weaponry that threatens the daily security of citizens of our most closely allied countries (such as Israel and Saudi Arabia), and conventional weapons that continue to disrupt security and stability in the Middle East, where stability is already tenuous, are all aspects of this issue that make it an important one for both American foreign policy and that of US allies.

North Korea and Iran are linked by financial ties and common enemies. While some scholars have engaged in comparing and contrasting North Korea and Iran, almost no one has written in-depth scholarship on how this relationship works, how many other state and nonstate actors it affects, and what impact it has had on regional security all over the Middle East. In fact, some researchers have claimed this relationship has nearly shut down in recent years. This is untrue. To understand the relationship and its effects, one must examine the basis for the relationship and the policies that these nations enact because of it. The fundamental source of the North Korea–Iran bond is their shared status as rogue states, which aim to develop chemical and nuclear weapons, arm terrorists with weaponry that threatens key American allies, and employ conventional forces to disrupt security and stability around the globe—and especially in already volatile regions such as the Middle East.

The North Korea–Iran nexus seeks to undermine American strategic and economic interests in key regions across the world. It hopes to induce a US military disengagement from Asia and the Middle East. Tehran seeks the weakening of America's role in the Middle East, as it fortifies the "axis of resistance"—comprising Palestinian Hamas, Lebanese Hezbollah, and formerly, Syria's Assad regime—that aspires to undermine Israeli security. North Korea's export of weapons, trainers, technical experts, and dual-use technology assists Tehran's desire to destroy the Jewish state.

Despite their historical, cultural, and ideological differences, Iran and North Korea have united to combat what they consider to be pernicious American influence across the world and to ensure the survival of their respective regimes. Both governments see their behavior as an act of resistance against a hated America whose past political and military involvement in their affairs they resent. Tehran and Pyongyang aspire to upend the regional order and sow chaos to weaken their enemies. Beyond the destruction of Israel, Iran aspires to promote its brand of Shia revolutionary doctrine challenging Sunni Gulf States Saudi Arabia and the United Arab Emirates.[1] It has done so largely by financing, training, and arming proxy groups in Yemen, Iraq, Lebanon, and before the fall of the Assad regime in Syria to represent its influence.[2]

The funds that North Korea generates from its alliance with Iran serve to maintain the regime's ability to support its large military and to provide rewards to the small number of members in the elite who keep the governmental infrastructure running. It will be important for American policy, and key for decision-making processes, to determine not only how widespread and effective the end results of the North Korea–Iran nexus are but also how to effectively contain or shut down these activities—something that has not yet occurred, despite concerns in the United States, South Korea, Israel, and other allied nations. Therefore, American foreign policy must focus on targeting the "centers of gravity" in the Iranian and North Korean relationship and its vulnerability to American interdiction.

Research Methodology

The work will employ traditional research methods to address the following questions concerning the Iran–North Korea partnership:

1. How did the North Korea–Iran relationship begin, and why has it stood the test of time?
2. What are the common elements of rogue-state behavior shared by both states? Is this coordinated and planned, and is there a synergy of this behavior that threatens American national interests and the interests of our allies?
3. How do these two states team up to evade sanctions and other multilateral efforts to contain their illicit and rogue activities? How successful have their joint efforts been?
4. What ideological, financial, and environmental forces have led to the long-standing success of this alliance?
5. What are the specifics when it comes to proliferation, illicit finance, disruption of stability and security in the Middle East, and sanctions evasion? How much actual cooperation on all of these fronts can be proved?

6. How extensive is this alliance's support for terrorism and terrorist groups?
7. How involved is North Korea in supporting Iran's WMD programs?
8. How does this relationship affect stability in East Asia and the Middle East?
9. How has the North Korea–Iran alliance strengthened Hezbollah, Syria, the Houthis, and Hamas and endangered US and Israeli security interests in the Middle East?

We have used diverse sources to conduct the research necessary for this book. These sources include but are not limited to interviews, scholarship, and books by and from experts in East Asia, the Middle East, and the United States regarding North Korean military proliferation and the infrastructure that supports it; Iranian use of these weapons, systems, and training; and the collaboration in both financial and military networks between these two nations, as well as papers and presentations from conferences and symposia, analysis of speeches, press releases, press reports, and press conferences, interviews with defectors as well as current and former government officials in the United States, the Middle East (several nations), and South Korea, US, Middle Eastern, and South Korean government reports, white papers, and legislative testimony, declassified defector reports, speeches and statements by policymakers in the United States, the Middle East, and East Asia, and a study of papers, reports, and special releases by important think tanks, government agencies, public policy institutes, and universities. To provide further enlightenment on the sources used in this work, a comprehensive bibliography is included at the conclusion of the book.

A visit to Seoul has provided the authors the opportunity to collaborate with key defectors (we have collaborated with defectors—both Iranian and North Korean—in the past) in South Korea. It has also offered the opportunity to collaborate with fellow scholars in both policy and academic circles there. We have gone to where the important information is available—the Middle East, Europe, and the Far East (our travels included visits to Israel, Dubai, London, and South Korea). It will also be important to go where the money is being laundered. This, of course, applies to Dubai, known for laundering illicit and illegal Iranian funds—at least a portion of which go to North Korea (typically as hard currency or cryptocurrency). Visits to Israel and South Korea have revealed more information about the arms trade that Iran and North Korea continue to profit from and that supports American enemies, particularly in the Middle East. Our collaboration has included fellow scholars, law enforcement officials, military officials, and policymakers. We have each built an extensive network in some of these key areas and have been able to conduct in-depth research in the countries listed above. In addition, we have matched this research with context already formed from the book chapters, peer-reviewed journal articles, and books that we have each written on North Korean proliferation, Iranian support to state and nonstate actors in the Middle East, and the aspects of Pyongyang-Tehran cooperation that make all of this possible but that are seldom (or never) written about.

Importance of the Study and Existing Literature

The North Korea–Iran nexus involves weapons proliferation, political cooperation, money laundering, and robust support to state and nonstate actors in the Middle East. This strategic partnership has endured since the last years of the Cold War. It continues today, yet many still do not understand the largesse of these activities or the damage caused to stability in key regions important to American national security interests. There are some important reasons why Pyongyang's proliferation and illicit activities have not gained a lot of attention in the West or been placed as a top foreign policy priority in either Seoul or Washington.

On January 7, 2020, Iran attacked American bases in Iraq with missiles. At least one of the missile systems used to attack these bases was assessed to be the Qiam system, a missile based on the North Korean Scud C.[3] Thus, if one is to speak of North Korean proliferation to Iran directly affecting American forces in the Middle East, one has only to look at this example. This is no longer an abstract threat. The North Korean–supplied systems that Iran has are now a clear and present danger to American troops (and our allies) in the Middle East. A prudent unbiased analysis of the Iran–North Korea nexus and of ways to mitigate it as a threat will be of important use to both policymakers and academics alike in the United States.

This book offers writing based on groundbreaking research that looks at the strategic relationship between North Korea and Iran and a host of criminal and terrorist networks. The Iran–North Korea alliance has ominous consequences for Asian and Middle Eastern security. The book will provide new insights into the ideological, tactical, and strategic relationship between Iran and North Korea. Both are aligned to undermine Western interests. There is a synergy behind the relationship that few analysts have yet uncovered and whose rogue and destabilizing behavior is often difficult to comprehend from a Western prism. This book offers the reader the opportunity to explore the ideological, tactical, and strategic foundations of North Korea's partnership with Iran.

The nexus between criminal-terrorist networks and rogue states is furthermore explored in ways that have not yet been investigated. Both Iran and North Korea have extensively used front and shell companies to evade international sanctions. They have created an intricate network of criminal activities across the world. Iran's proxy Hezbollah is firmly embedded in drugs, money laundering, and arms smuggling across the world. It has launched terror operations against Jewish and American interests in South America, the Middle East, Africa, and Europe.

Iran and North Korea channel weapons across the world. Tehran is expanding its armament program to empower Shia and Alawi militias across the Middle East, exacerbating civil wars in Iraq, Syria, and Yemen. With North Korean assistance, Iran has developed Hezbollah into a formidable fighting force capable of offensive operations. Hezbollah forces in Syria have developed conventional capacity, and their military entrenchment in the country could portend a new round of warfare against Israel. Jerusalem faces threats on its northern and eastern frontiers.

The book provides a rare glimpse and offers insight into how rogue states and paramilitaries conspire to upend regional order. Though ideologically disparate, Iran and North Korea are united to sow discord across the world, preserve their regimes, and undermine Western security. Their alliance has endured for a generation, and it is worthy of scholarly exploration. Recent events are testimony that warrants further exploration of the armament nexus between Iran and North Korea.

The reimposition of US economic sanctions has put severe financial pressure on the Iranian regime. Hard-line conservative factions (especially Supreme Leader Ali Khamenei and the Council of Guardians) have clashed over the direction of Iranian national security policy with moderates in the presidency and the Parliament. Historically, conservative hard-liners have determined the parameters of Iranian national security policy.

Michael Eisenstadt's study of Iranian strategic culture notes that competition between extremist and pragmatic forces makes Iranian policy impossible to predict.[4] What is clear is that the regime aims to dominate the Persian Gulf and the Levant. The linchpin of this policy has been support for Shia and aligned forces across the Middle East. Assistance for Hezbollah has increased over time. With $700 million of support a year and an arsenal of hundreds of thousands of rockets of enhanced sophistication and accuracy,[5] Hezbollah is a formidable actor in the region. Suzanne Maloney argues that, since the 1979 Revolution, Iran's regional strategy has been to assist Shiite and aligned groups across the Middle East.[6] The 2003 US-led war in Iraq, moreover, empowered Shiite majorities who have dominated much of the country's post-Saddam governments. As Vali Nasr argues, the overthrow of Saddam Hussein's regime has expanded Iran's presence across the Middle East, catalyzing a "Shia revival."[7]

Iran's export of weapons technology, training, and expertise to proxies in Syria, Iraq, Lebanon, and Yemen has exacerbated political tensions across the region. Iranian- and North Korean–assisted underground missile factories in Lebanon and Yemen are a harbinger of future conflicts designed to undermine Western, Saudi, and Israeli security. Some fear that, faced with protests at home and an acute economic crisis, Tehran will use the American withdrawal from the Joint Comprehensive Plan of Action (JCPOA) as a pretext to accelerate its quest for nuclear weapons.[8] Iran has been steadily violating key provisions of the 2015 accord. Though Washington has equivocated about a preemptive military strike against Iran's nuclear facilities, Jerusalem stands ready to strike. Since Jerusalem previously destroyed Iraq's and Syria's nuclear facilities, few doubt its determination to eviscerate the threat of an Iranian nuclear weapons project.[9]

The dispersion of Iran's nuclear facilities, much of which are built underground with North Korean assistance, complicates such a military operation. Jerusalem's capacity to launch military strikes is bedeviled by the logistic and technological shortcomings of sustaining multiple bombing runs complicated by the lack of sophisticated bunker-busting bombs.[10] If Jerusalem did mount a military campaign, such an action would represent a nightmare scenario, and its consequences would further destabilize the region.

Past Iranian policy has veered between caution and risk-taking, making any forecast of future actions problematic.[11] Though few analysts doubt that

Iran would militarily retaliate, the scale of a response is difficult to gauge; Hezbollah's and Hamas's responses to an Israeli military strike are also diffi- cult to determine.[12] Few doubt that tensions across the region would increase to levels even higher than what the world has seen since October 7, 2023, and the Israeli Defense Forces (IDF) strikes against Hamas and Hezbollah. Though Israel has degraded Hamas and weakened Hezbollah and the Syrian regime of Bashar al-Assad has fallen to Islamist rebels, Iran still has consider- able military leverage in the region.

While there have been contributions to the scholarship regarding inter- national security and North Korea's illicit activities (to include proliferation), these contributions have been few and far between. The same applies to Iran. There are books that deal with Iranian issues, and there are books that deal with North Korean issues, but most of the scholarship addresses them as if they are both in isolation. It is our intention in this book to cover all aspects of the North Korea–Iran nexus, to include key nations and nonstate actors, the intertwining of their policy moves, the damage to the region that their ac- tivities cause, their methods of laundering their dirty money, the connections between their financial networks, and the role that these operations play in the infrastructure of both nations.

In *North Korea, Iran and the Challenge to International Order: A Comparative Perspective*, published in 2017, Patrick McEachern and Jaclyn O'Brien McEachern do a very good job of addressing some aspects of North Korea's government and policy—which are important to understanding the Democratic People's Republic of Korea (DPRK). They do not address North Korea's military, its activities overseas, or weapons proliferation abroad in any depth—including in Iran. Their book compares and contrasts Iranian and North Korean politics and policy, which is interesting and valuable. But their book does not address in depth how these two states are tied together in the numerous ways we will address in this book.[13]

Another interesting work regarding the North Korea–Iran nexus is also lacking in real evidence that can give analysts a chance to make assessments that can lead to policy recommendations. A book entitled *Inventing the Axis of Evil: The Truth about North Korea, Iran, and Syria* was published in 2006. This book was a collaboration of several scholars well known to those who specialize in North Korea and the Middle East. While interesting, the book appears to be written primarily to criticize George W. Bush's policy regarding Iraq and not to portray the real picture of the key relationship between North Korea and Iran or the policy challenges it presents—then and now.[14]

Two interesting works are relevant to anyone doing research on North Korea's involvement in proliferation in the Middle East. In *Warriors of God: Inside Hezbollah's Thirty-Year Struggle against Israel*, Nicholas Blanford describes many of the methods and tactics used by Hezbollah in their fight against Israel. Also useful in this work are the descriptions of tunnel building, small arms fire, and the use of rocket launchers. To anyone who has even slight knowledge of North Korean weapons and tactics, it should become obvious that Hezbollah has over the years received from the North Koreans not only a high number of weapons systems but also extensive training and adviser expertise that have inflicted casualties on the IDF and prevented casualties among Hezbollah "warriors." This work is quite interesting and helpful. The book addresses North Korea's relationship with Hezbollah and Iran. It is useful for any scholar who is pursuing research on North Korea's relationship with Hezbollah (and it was quite useful for our research) and, to a lesser extent, on Iran's support to terrorism.[15]

Another interesting work is a study published by the Congressional Research Service (CRS). Larry Niksch is a (now retired) widely respected scholar who worked for CRS for many years. In his study entitled *North Korea: Terrorism List Removal*, he takes the reader through a variety of issues that are important to understanding North Korea's support of both state and nonstate actors in the Middle East. Niksch also does a good job of explaining why North Korea was previously (before 2008) on the State Department's list of nations supporting terrorism—and why (this work was written in 2010) the DPRK should be placed back on the list (largely because of military proliferation to nonstate actors and states who support terror—which is why North Korea was placed back on the list in 2017). Niksch outlines exactly how North Korea provided support to Iran and its proxies and, perhaps as importantly, estimates how much money the DPRK made (up until 2010) by supporting both the Islamic Revolutionary Guard Corps (IRGC) and Hezbollah.[16] Unfortunately, since Niksch has retired from CRS, no one has done any research or writing that comes even close to the detail and analysis he provided (not just in this report but in many others as well).

An important theme in the works we reviewed here is that each of them was useful for certain aspects of understanding the North Korea–Iran nexus, but none of them offered comprehensive analysis of how it occurs, what effects it has on policy, and how it is integrated into Iranian and North Korean governmental infrastructures. What the scholarship in the fields of North Korean studies and Iranian studies needs is a work that addresses (1) what the basis and ongoing reasons are for the strong North Korea–Iran relationship, (2) what effects this long-term relationship has had and is likely to have on regional security, (3) how both North Korean and Iranian financial networks and front companies operate (in detail), which will aid in not just sanctions but sanctions enforcement, (4) how much money North Korea is making from all of this and how Pyongyang enables Iran's quest to become the hegemon in the Middle East, and (5) how this supports the government and maintains the Kim regime in power. To date, a literature review has shown that in fact there is no work that has yet accomplished this endeavor. We accomplish the above-stated goals in this book.

Chapter Outline

Chapter 2: North Korea's Military Capabilities:
Building Systems to Threaten and Sell

This chapter reviews North Korea's military proliferation efforts by discussing the capabilities and numbers associated with its WMD and conventional arms development and a significant new capability North Korea has—cyber. North Korea's nuclear weaponization program and its ballistic missiles have developed compelling capabilities that can potentially threaten the Middle East, Africa, and Europe when proliferated. Pyongyang also has formidable conventional ground and maritime forces with sophisticated arms. Though its proliferation of WMD and ballistic missile programs get most of the attention, North Korea's export of conventional arms and technical expertise has exacerbated conflicts across the Middle East and enhanced the lethality of terrorist groups like Hezbollah and Hamas. The security implications of North Korea's weapons proliferation activities present significant challenges for America and its allies in the Middle East.

Chapter 3: Iran's Military Capabilities: Becoming a Hegemon Thanks to Acquisition

The third chapter provides an overview of Iran's military capabilities (both conventional and asymmetric) and the role of North Korea in the modernization of Tehran's armaments industry. After reviewing the state of Tehran's nuclear weapons and ballistic missile capabilities, the chapter deals with Iran's growing conventional capability and the role of the IRGC in the development of Lebanese Hezbollah, Iraqi Popular Mobilization Forces (PMF), Yemeni Houthi rebels, and, formerly, the Assad regime in Syria. Many of these groups have been trained and equipped with North Korean arms by the IRGC elite Quds Force. In short, the North Korea–Iran nexus has enhanced the fighting capability of a host of Middle Eastern terror groups that threaten vital American security interests in the Middle East. The chapter ends by reviewing Iran's maritime capability, which threatens international shipping lanes in the Strait of Hormuz, and evaluating Tehran's growing cyber warfare capacity.

Chapter 4: The Ideological, Financial, and Environmental Forces Leading to the North Korea–Iran Rogue Alliance

The fourth chapter discusses the factors that led to the development of the "rogue alliance." Both Pyongyang and Tehran are considered revisionist powers hostile to the liberal global order. North Korea and Iran have been accused of significant human rights violations, and their autocratic character is inconsistent with the foundations of Western society. Historically, these regimes have been hostile toward the United States and its allies. United in their hatred toward the West and targeted by the international community for their support for weapons proliferation, Pyongyang and Tehran have forged a unique and highly profitable alliance. This partnership was formed as a marriage of convenience designed to evade international financial sanctions and undermine American interests in East Asia and the Middle East. Pressed by financial exigencies, Pyongyang has monetarily sustained its brutal regime by proliferating a maze of weapons and delivery systems that have enhanced Tehran's military modernization and facilitated its regional hegemonic ambitions. North Korean weapons and technical expertise have aided Tehran's capacity to develop regional proxy forces in Lebanon, Syria, Iraq, and Yemen that have destabilized the Middle East.

*Chapter 5: Rogue Allies and Pyongyang's Proliferation to
Iran: Russia and China Are Now Key Enablers*

The fifth chapter discusses North Korean weapons proliferation (conventional and unconventional) to Iran since the early 1980s. It has shipped nearly every kind of ballistic missile it builds, as well as sending related military advisers, engineers, technicians, and trainers to Iran. It has proliferated nuclear technology (likely), conventional weapons, and numerous spare parts to Iran and its regional proxy Hezbollah, along with other nonstate actors in the region. This has greatly enabled Tehran's efforts to fortify its proxy warfare capability and build an arms bridge stretching from Iran to the Mediterranean to threaten Israeli security. Of interest, this chapter also addresses how North Korea and Iran each work with both Russia and China. The evidence indicates that this is not happening in a vacuum. In fact, North Korea and Iran appear to be often collaborating or coordinating when it comes to their cooperation with Russia and China.

Chapter 6: Rogue Allies in Action: Proxy Wars in the Middle East

This chapter explores the history and strategic logic that drive Iranian foreign policy that reflects the regime's revolutionary ideology and its calculation that the West lacks the appropriate resolve to confront the Islamic Republic's regional ambitions. The historic origins of Iran's proxy hybrid warfare strategy are discussed, and the execution of its militia policy in Lebanon, Iraq, Syria, and Yemen is analyzed. This chapter concludes by looking at the impact of Israel's war against Hamas and Hezbollah after the Hamas's October 7, 2023, attacks against Israeli communities along the Gaza Strip. In the ensuing war, Hamas and Hezbollah have been weakened, and the Syrian regime of Bashar al-Assad has fallen to Turkish supported rebels. With North Korean assistance, Tehran has equipped its remaining Shia militia forces in Iraq and Yemen with a formidable military arsenal composed of sophisticated ballistic missiles and conventional arms. This development has serious security implications for America's regional allies.

Chapter 7: North Korean Support to Iran's Proxy Partners

The chapter details the role of North Korean weapons, delivery systems, and technical expertise among Iran's regional allies (formerly Syria, as well as Hezbollah, the Houthis, and Hamas)—starting during the Cold War and transitioning into the post–Cold War period. For years, North Korea has assisted the "axis of resistance" composed of Syria, Hezbollah, and Hamas, all of whom are committed to the destruction of the State of Israel. Pyongyang has proliferated chemical weapons, ballistic missiles, and conventional arms and sent advisers, trainers, engineers, and technicians for a variety of projects to Syria. Since the 1990s, the rate of proliferation has increased dramatically, fortifying Syrian president Bashar al-Assad's regime's ballistic missile and chemical weapons capability. The 2012–2020 Syrian civil war, moreover, expanded the Assad regime's need for all kinds of North Korean arms. Hezbollah's military intervention on behalf of the Syrian regime has also forced the Lebanese guerrilla movement and its Iranian patron to become increasingly dependent on North Korean weapons and expertise. Since this period, there have been astonishing developments. After Hamas's October 7 attacks, Israel has engaged in a yearlong effort to degrade Hamas and Hezbollah whose military capability has been devastated.

With Russia distracted in Ukraine, Hamas vanquished in Gaza, Hezbollah greatly diminished in Lebanon, Turkish supported Hayat Tahrir al-Sham, and the Syrian National Army overthrew the Assad regime by December 2024. Worried that Assad's military capability and chemical weapons would be acquired by Islamist rebel forces, Israeli Air Force eviscerated its Assad military and chemical infrastructure. Hoping to prevent terrorist penetration of its northern border, the IDF has expanded its territorial presence in Syria with two military bases overlooking strategic Mount Hermon.

With its proxy forces badly weakened, Iran will need North Korea to resupply its Iraqi, Hezbollah, and Yemeni proxies if it wishes to salvage its axis of resistance project.

Chapter 8: Rogue Allies and the Criminal Financial Networks That Support the Partnership

The eighth chapter examines how North Korea and Iran have evaded international economic and financial sanctions by supporting illicit financial networks composed of front companies, criminal mafias, and smuggling networks. Working with rogue criminal networks in Asia and the Middle East replete with sophisticated money-laundering schemes, North Korea and Iran have adapted to the financial rigors created by international sanctions. With the assistance of such illicit financial networks, Pyongyang and Tehran have facilitated their arms-for-money partnership.

Chapter 9: Conclusions and Policy Implications

The final chapter examines the study's main conclusions regarding why the strategic partnership between Pyongyang and Tehran was formed, how it has endured, and what dire security implications this rogue alliance presages for Asian and Middle Eastern security. The chapter assesses how financial sanctions can be strengthened to weaken the North Korean–Iranian weapons-for-money nexus and what the prospects are for future regime change. Without improved sanctions enforcement, the rogue alliance will likely persist.

North Korea's Military Capabilities

Building Systems to Threaten and Sell

Bruce E. Bechtol Jr.

North Korea remains a nation-state that continues to threaten the security and stability of its neighbors (particularly South Korea and Japan), proliferates military capabilities to countries around the globe (but particularly in the Middle East and Africa), and violates the human rights of its own people. But since the armistice to the Korean War was declared in 1953, the main concern for the international system and probably the key reason American troops remain stationed in South Korea has been the North Korean military threat. This threat not only continues to exist but continues to exacerbate security issues for the international system (and especially the United States) because North Korean military capabilities continue to evolve and modernize.

While North Korea has expanded its military capabilities over the past five years, this has been largely in the form of ballistic missiles, cyber, and continued work to upgrade its nuclear weaponization program. North Korea does in fact have a very large military (one of the largest in the world). But most of the upgrades in capabilities have been to the forces I addressed at the beginning of this paragraph. I will address the upgrades to conventional systems that have occurred since 2018. But for a more in-depth analysis of all of North Korea's major conventional systems, I recommend reading chapter 2 of my book *North Korean Military Proliferation in the Middle East and Africa*. There have been no major changes to conventional systems since that chapter was published, except for the examples that I will address in this book.[1]

As of the writing of this work, North Korea has not conducted a nuclear test since 2017. They have made moves as if they were making preparations, yet these never panned out. It is likely, however, that unless North Korea gets and responds to pressure from China, Russia, or both, they will conduct another nuclear weaponization test in the near future. Thus, it is important to examine and analyze North Korea's current nuclear weapons capabilities.

North Korea's ballistic missile capabilities have grown in leaps and bounds over the past five years. They have made improvements in range, ability to evade ballistic missile defense (BMD), accuracy, numbers, and lethality. Thus, it will be important for me to examine the current and rapidly growing North Korean ballistic missile threat.

While North Korea continues to maintain a big army and powerful missiles as well as a nuclear weapons program, before about seven years ago, very few people were addressing the threat that I must examine in this book—cyber. The North Koreans thus far have used cyber for a twofold mission. First, they have used it to disrupt and destroy command and control systems and communications systems, particularly in the United States and South Korea. Second, they now use their cyber capabilities to make money—a lot of it—for the regime. I will address these concerns and all that I have introduced thus far as we move through this chapter.

North Korea's Nuclear Weapons Programs

North Korea's nuclear weapons programs receive more focus than anything else in their threatening arsenal. There are two key reasons for this. First of all, North Korea is a rogue state that has historically refused to follow international norms and thus is a huge concern for policymakers in the United States, South Korea, and the international community as a whole. Second, the North Korean conventional military forces and their ballistic missiles are important issues, yet most in the academic community have very little context or knowledge of them. This leads many (who have been educated and trained only on geopolitics) to write about North Korea but mostly about the nuclear programs. Writing about conventional forces and ballistic missiles is simply done with methodologies that many in the academic community are not equipped to use. Geopolitics in East Asia is important, even vital, but it is only part of the international security picture. Having said all of that, North Korea's nuclear programs continue to grow in largesse and capabilities. In this section, I will address some key challenges and growth that we have seen in North Korea's nuclear weaponization program. These challenges and continued development continue to create a threat to the stability and security of Northeast Asia.

North Korea is now capable of weaponizing both plutonium and highly enriched uranium (HEU).[2] In fact, though the Bill Clinton administration was essentially silent about North Korea's HEU program all the way up until they left office in early 2001, officials and intelligence personnel already knew about and confirmed its existence during the late 1990s. Robert Gallucci, a State Department official during the Clinton administration, has publicly stated, "In addition, our intelligence community detected significant numbers of components for a gas centrifuge uranium enrichment program being transferred from Pakistan to the DPRK during the late nineteen nineties through the early part of this decade."[3]

North Korea's first underground test (2006) had a yield of one-half to one kiloton (according to many analysts), but in 2009, their second nuclear test yielded an estimated four kilotons.[4] North Korea's third nuclear test was assessed to yield six to seven kilotons.[5] According to sources in the press, Iranian VIPs attended North Korea's third underground nuclear test.[6]

In 2016, the North Koreans conducted two nuclear underground tests in one year. The first test that year (and the fourth overall) was in January. North Korea proclaimed to the world that the fourth test was of a "hydrogen bomb," but to date there has been no evidence to prove this assertion. Despite the bold claims from Pyongyang, the test was similar in size to North Korea's third underground nuclear test.[7]

In September 2016, the North Koreans conducted the second test that year—an unprecedented event (their fifth nuclear test). This test was unambiguously the largest yield the North Koreans had been able to achieve to that date. The majority of analysts who did estimates on the test assess its yield to be ten to twelve kilotons. Thus, the North Koreans in 2016 continued to advance the yield of their tested nuclear devices.[8]

North Korea conducted its most recent nuclear test—and its largest yield—in September 2017. There were many initial estimates of the yield, but many analysts agreed that it was likely more than one hundred kilotons. A research institute in Norway released scientific data estimating the yield to be 250 kilotons. The North Koreans claimed publicly that the test was of a thermonuclear device. Pyongyang also claimed that the test was of a hydrogen "bomb" capable of being mounted on a long-range missile.[9] Another study conducted by the American Geophysical Union and published in its *Journal of Geophysical Research: Solid Earth* asserts, "North Korea detonated a nuclear device in 2017 equivalent to about 250 kilotons of TNT, a new study estimates, creating an explosion 16 times the size of the bomb the United States detonated over Hiroshima, Japan, in 1945."[10] This is according to a press release by the scientific organization.

In 2015, the National Defense Commission (at the time the most important ruling body in the country) stated, "It is long since the DPRK's nuclear striking means have entered the stage of producing smaller nukes and diversifying them." The statement went on to say, "The DPRK has reached the stage of ensuring the highest precision and intelligence and best accuracy of not only medium and short-range missiles but long range ones." Despite this statement and other important evidence, the debate over whether or not North Korea can mount a nuclear warhead on a missile continues. In my opinion, it is more likely—much more likely—than not that they can. North Korea's HEU facilities have been confirmed to be both operational and located in several places since at least 2009 in open sources. There is a site at Sowi-ri, one at Kangson, and a plant at Pyongsan.[11] Yongbyon remains the main plutonium facility.[12]

During March 2022, North Korea was assessed to be restoring its underground testing facility at Punggye-ri. In April 2022, the UN Panel of Experts reported that, to keep up its nuclear capability, North Korea was continuing to acquire materials and technology while evading sanctions. In May 2022, it was reported that North Korea was literally working prisoners to death to rebuild the nuclear test site at Punggye-ri. Also in May 2022, senior South Korean officials revealed that North Korea had been observed testing a nuclear detonation device (likely a trigger mechanism). According to a report issued by the Council on Foreign Relations, "North Korea could have the material for more than one hundred nuclear weapons, according to analysts' estimates. It has successfully tested missiles that could strike the United States with a nuclear warhead."[13]

North Korea's Non-WMD Capabilities

North Korea has made what many consider to be amazing progress in its ballistic missile programs and, to a lesser extent, its multiple rocket launcher (MRL) programs. Indeed, Pyongyang has sought to improve and maintain both numbers and capabilities in the many ballistic missile tests it has conducted since 2018. If one were to conduct an analysis of North Korea's military developments in the six years after 2018, there can be almost no doubt that the North Koreans have radically improved their ballistic missile capabilities. This is not the only improvement though. Their MRLs have also clearly been upgraded (as I will discuss). There have been some minor upgrades elsewhere as well. In February 2021, the South Korean Defense Ministry reported that the North Korean military had expanded its missile units and "strengthened" its Special Operations Forces with modernized equipment and new types of exercises.[14] I will discuss improvements to non-asymmetric capabilities in this section. It is also important to note that North Korea continues to maintain the capabilities of its existing conventional forces.[15]

A key focus, particularly over the past five years, has been Pyongyang's obsession with testing and deploying longer-range MRLs. North Korea's 300mm MRL system began testing in 2013 and was reportedly formally integrated and deployed within its armed forces in 2020 (probably along the demilitarized zone with South Korea).[16] But the North Koreans have now also deployed a system with double the range and firepower. The 600mm system that the North Koreans possess began testing by at least 2019. It appears that the system was then supplied to the North Korean ground forces and fully deployed in combat positions by February 2023. This system carries "guided munitions," which means it can carry out more pinpoint attacks on key South Korean nodes that would never have been the focus of such attacks at such a distance in the past. These MRLs also appear to have a range of close to four hundred kilometers (or more). Of note, the North Koreans claim that the system is also capable of carrying nuclear weapons—though this has yet to be proved.[17]

The North Koreans have also made some significant developments in their armor capabilities. The Pokpung-ho IV tank has significant firepower. It has excellent guns onboard, including mostly Soviet-era munitions. Of note, one version of this tank carries two Bulsae-3 antitank missile launchers. This is a system similar to the Russian Kornet antitank launcher. These newer tanks also use a 14.5mm machine gun. While the tank is an upgrade over most of what the North Koreans have, it is still essentially an older design based on the Soviet T-62 tank, though it has likely included technology from other older Soviet systems as well.[18] In other armor developments, the North Koreans in 2018 revealed the newest version of their self-propelled howitzers. This version carries the 152mm gun and appears to be more capable than previous versions because of its mounted chassis (T-72) and some add-ons that make it a more effective artillery system.[19] The army's 152mm artillery is the bread and butter of North Korean combat units, and the system currently is being used a great deal by the Russians in the Ukraine conflict.

In September 2023, North Korea christened a new submarine. This submarine is quite large and is considered by most analysts to be a vessel based on the old Soviet Romeo-class submarine. The North Koreans are calling it a "tactical nuclear attack submarine." It is reportedly capable of launching ballistic missiles as the Sinpo-class submarine is, but this submarine can launch (and carry) more than one potentially nuclear-equipped missile. The Romeo-class submarine is noted for being both slow and noisy. It is unclear whether the North Koreans eliminated those two important issues, but it is clear that breaking out of local waters will be a challenge because of US and Republic of Korea antisubmarine tracking and destruction capabilities. Nevertheless, it is a new system with new capabilities, and the things it will do during upcoming training and exercises will certainly bear watching.[20]

All of the systems I have described in this section are new or relatively new and recently deployed. While they form relatively small pieces of the North Korean forces' capability, they show that Pyongyang continues to tweak and maintain the conventional capabilities of its forces. Those who study North Korean military issues would be wise to keep this in mind, as these systems will not only be used against the South; they can also be proliferated to places such as the Middle East, Africa, and Russia.

North Korean Ballistic Missile Capabilities

North Korea has engaged in test launches and actual unit deployments with a plethora of new ballistic missile systems, particularly since 2017. These systems largely fall into two basic categories: (1) short-range ballistic missile systems and (2) long-range ballistic missile systems—mostly intercontinental ballistic missiles (ICBMs). Pyongyang has also tested—several times—solid-fuel medium-range ballistic missiles using what is widely known as a Sinpo-class submarine to conduct the launches from underwater. With all these various types of missiles being tested and many deployed in a relatively short period, one must wonder if they have been completely researched and designed and if the North Koreans are getting foreign assistance, and if they are, who is providing it? I will address all of these issues in this section.

One short-range ballistic missile system, first test launched successfully on May 4, 2019, is remarkably similar to the Russian Iskander system. Russia has used this system in its current war with Ukraine and its past war with Georgia and has even proliferated it to other states, such as Armenia and Algeria.[21] A solid-fuel system, it gives North Korea accuracy and mobility that it has not had with previous systems such as Scuds. It has a range of nearly seven hundred kilometers and a payload of five hundred kilograms. Another system, which the North Koreans have tested successfully several times beginning in August 2019, is remarkably similar to the US ATACMS. This solid-fuel single-stage system is highly mobile and very accurate, with at least a four-hundred-kilometer range. Both of these systems present real challenges to allied defenses in South Korea.[22]

North Korea has also been experimenting with two new key capabilities. Beginning in 2021, one of the elite missile regiments conducted several launches of train-borne missiles. We had not seen this from Pyongyang before, and railways are yet another way to transport missiles before launching. Being able to actually launch a missile from a rail car appears to need more testing before the system is integrated into North Korean forces, but the tests appear to be largely successful thus far.[23]

As North Korea continues to develop new systems and experiment with them at a rapid rate—especially since 2017—another capability that Pyongyang appears to be putting through development and testing is a hypersonic missile. Such a missile reportedly can fly at a speed of Mach 10 or more. This is potentially a real threat to allied targets in the region. Another aspect of this new capability is that it makes BMD more vulnerable because it has the potential to maneuver once it is airborne. The North Koreans claim that this (liquid-fuel) system has already been demonstrated and is operational. While at least for now the system appears to be in the testing stage, a hypersonic capability is an advancement that most analysts and military planners had not anticipated before the test launches occurred.[24]

During the first week of April 2024, military officials in both the United States and South Korea confirmed that North Korea had conducted its second test of a solid-fuel, hypersonic, intermediate-range ballistic missile (IRBM). The test appears to have been successful. This was the second test that year of a solid-fuel hypersonic missile. During 2021, the North Koreans had conducted tests of a liquid-fuel hypersonic missile. This is rather advanced technology—though it is a capability that both the Russians and the Chinese have already used.[25] This raises several questions. What are the capabilities and differences between the new missile and the liquid-fuel hypersonic missile the North Koreans had tested previously? How will this change the way the United States and its allies conduct BMD in Northeast Asia? And perhaps as importantly as any question, how did the North Koreans suddenly come up with this capability?

An examination of this missile shows several fascinating factors. It is launched from a fourteen-wheel transport-erector-launcher (TEL). There is what some analysts have called a clamshell portion near the top of the missile. This clamshell device hides and some would say protects the boost-glide vehicle before the missile is actually launched. Based on what analysts saw when the test was conducted, it appears that this is a legitimate hypersonic missile—or at least a missile with that developing capability. According to a report in the *War Zone*, "After release, the boost-glide vehicle travels along a relatively shallow atmospheric flight path at hypersonic speeds, generally defined as anything above Mach 5, to its target. The vehicles are also designed to have a significant degree of maneuverability, allowing them to erratically change course and climb and descend along the way."[26]

If continued testing proves this missile to be capable and the North Koreans permanently include it in their inventory, they will have a liquid-fuel and a solid-fuel version of their hypersonic missiles. Maneuverability is the key aspect that makes hypersonic missiles more of a threat than typical ballistic platforms. The fact that this is a solid- instead of liquid-fuel missile also makes it easier to store and to transport safely. Some analysts have predicted that North Korea will now begin to phase out its liquid-fuel ballistic missiles in favor of using only solid-fuel missiles. I would say the chances of that are unlikely—at least for now. North Korea has a very large fleet of liquid-fuel missiles and at the very least is probably going to continue to use them, for proliferation at the very least.[27]

A big question for both policymakers and military planners is how this will change BMD in Northeast Asia. While the test conducted during the first week of April 2024 can most certainly be assessed to be at least partially successful, it has shown that the North Koreans remain a ways away from actually being able to produce a highly maneuverable hypersonic missile.[28] Nevertheless, the fact that Pyongyang is now testing both liquid-fuel and solid-fuel hypersonic missiles should be a wake-up call for BMD in Northeast Asia. At least in theory, the missile will have the range to target Japan, all of South Korea, and even Guam. Thus, developing advanced BMD capabilities on the ground and on the seas should now be a high priority for US and allied forces in the region. Washington, Seoul, and Tokyo should also make an increased focus on shared BMD capabilities a high priority. Failure to do so could be disastrous in time of war or conflict.

Another important question that arises is where North Korea got this capability. It is my assessment that there can be little doubt about this. North Korea has been proliferating military systems, ammunition, and even ballistic missiles to the Russians as Moscow prosecutes its war against Ukraine. Most analysts (including me) assess that the payment for these systems and ammunition has been largely in the form of foodstuffs and oil. But most analysts also assess (as do I) that the Russians have also agreed to provide technical assistance to North Korea for its military capabilities.[29] Key among these capabilities is of course more advanced ballistic missiles. As the war in Ukraine grinds on, we can also likely expect that Russia will continue to provide support for North Korea's military systems (including the missile addressed here). Thus, the advances for the solid-fuel hypersonic missile can be expected to be rapid and efficient if the North Koreans get the support from Russia that they will expect in return for providing vast amounts of arms and ammunition.[30]

North Korea continues to maintain and deploy its traditional Scud, No Dong, and Musudan missiles. There have been almost no new developments in these missiles, though, in the past ten years. For analysis on the capabilities and numbers of these missiles, I recommend to the reader that a review of my last book, *North Korean Military Proliferation in the Middle East and Africa*, will provide some important background and context (chapter 2).[31] Among newer systems that are being developed are the Pukguksong missiles. All of these missiles except for one (the Pukguksong-2) are submarine-launched ballistic missiles (SLBMs). All of these missiles also use the cold-launch system.

The Pukguksong-1 was the first North Korean SLBM system that was rolled out and was eventually launched from North Korea's Sinpo-class submarine—a craft that is capable of carrying and launching only one SLBM. After several failed launches, the Pukguksong-1 was successfully launched for the first time in 2016. It has an estimated range of twelve hundred kilometers. The land-based version of the Pukguksong-1 is the Pukguksong-2. It uses a TEL, making it highly mobile. It also uses the same cold-launch technology and has been successfully launched several times. The Pukguksong-3 is a longer-range system that reportedly has two stages—though it uses most of the same technology as its predecessors. The Pukguksong-4 and 5 have both been displayed in military parades and appear to be yet more capable than the previous versions. It should be noted that there have been several confirmed successful launches of Pukguksong systems since 2016, in 2019, 2021, and 2022. With the addition of a new, larger submarine that can carry more missiles, the North Koreans now are looking at (though they may not have it yet) a capability to legitimately threaten all of South Korea, Japan, and possibly even Hawaii or Guam—depending on whether or not the new submarine can get past sophisticated American antisubmarine warfare systems (a big challenge for the North Koreans).[32]

A major concern for the United States is of course North Korea's ICBM capability. This has grown in leaps and bounds since 2017. That was the year that North Korea first launched (successfully) the Hwasong-12, -14, and -15. The Hwasong-12 is an IRBM with a range of up to forty-five hundred kilometers. That means it can easily target US sovereign territory in Guam. The engine for the Hwasong-12 appears to be based on the Ukrainian RD-250 system, though it uses a single thrust chamber, whereas the RD-250 uses a double thrust chamber. This also appears to be what soon thereafter became the first stage of the Hwasong-14, a two-stage ICBM with the capability to hit Alaska and possibly parts of the US West Coast. Soon after the Hwasong-14 was successfully test launched, the North Koreans launched the Hwasong-15. The first stage of the Hwasong-15 appears to be powered by two thrust chambers, much like the original RD-250. This engine delivers eighty tons of thrust at sea level and gives this two-stage ICBM the capability to target all or most of the continental United States (an eight-thousand-mile range). There has been debate over the capability of these missiles to actually carry a nuclear warhead. There has also been debate over whether or not the Hwasong-14 or 15 can successfully reenter the earth's atmosphere without burning up. But the evidence from several tests is now fairly strong. I agree with those analysts who assess that these two missiles can in fact carry a nuclear warhead, and they have proved (several times) the ability to successfully reenter the earth's atmosphere.[33]

Yet another ICBM that North Korea has developed is the Hwasong-17. First seen in a military parade, this missile is larger than the often successfully tested Hwasong-15. It too can target the entire continental United States, but because of its size, it can carry a larger payload than the Hwasong-15. Perhaps exactly because of its size, the Hwasong-17 went through several unsuccessful tests before Pyongyang's technicians and engineers were able to figure out the issues associated with its launch. Nevertheless, the Hwasong-17 has now been success-fully test launched, and we are likely to see more launches in the future. That said, the reliability of the Hwasong-17 remains in question.[34] Thus far, the most reliable ICBM system the North Koreans have tested remains the Hwasong-15.

Perhaps the most compelling of the ICBMs that North Korea has test launched to date is the system they call the Hwasong-18. First test launched in 2023, this missile also has the capability to target nodes all over the conti-nental United States, but unlike the previous ICBMs addressed here, it uses solid-fuel technology to power its engines and is thus the most advanced of Pyongyang's long-range ballistic missiles.[35]

Research carried out by Theodore Postol for the Center for Strategic and International Studies (CSIS) indicates that North Korea's solid-fuel Hwasong-18 missile might be far more advanced, and present a much greater threat, than most analysts assessed from its early testing. Why? It seems likely the North Koreans developed this missile with direct Russian technical and engineering assistance. The Hwasong-18 shares a good number of character-istics with the Russian Topol-M ICBM (SS-27 Mod 2)—although the two are not exactly alike. The missiles have similar diameters, and they share com-parable capabilities and flight paths.[36]

But let's address this from a practical view as well. It is highly improbable that the North Koreans by themselves came up with the solid-fuel technology and designs for an ICBM. They had to get help from somewhere, and they had to get the technology from somewhere, too. The similarities between the North Korean Hwasong-18 and the Russian Topol-M suggest Moscow as the provider. Given how fast this North Korean system rolled out, it is also un-likely that rogue scientists or engineers were responsible, as was the case with the Musudan missile based on the Russian R-27/SS-N-6.[37]

Over the past five years, we have seen the North Koreans test and deploy several modern systems that elevate the threat on the Korean Peninsula. These include a North Korean copycat of the Iskander short-range ballistic missile and a weapon that in turn looks very much like the American MGM-140 ATACMS system. North Korea appears to be working to develop hypersonic capabilities for a ballistic missile, as well as long-range MRLs that use guid-ance systems and can cover large swaths of the Korean Peninsula.

Most of the systems North Korea has tested or deployed over the past five years are designed for combat on the Korean Peninsula. The new Hwasong-18 clearly is not. North Korea would likely use this ICBM to attack the United

States. Is it possible that North Korean leader Kim Jong-un asked his Russian allies to equip him both with tactical systems for use on the peninsula and with an ICBM that could credibly threaten the United States? If so, the North Koreans are pursuing serious measures to exacerbate the threat they pose to the United States, South Korea, and Japan.

Depending on how many ballistic capabilities the Russians provided to the North Koreans—if the Hwasong-18 is in fact a missile based on Russian technology—this development could completely change the way the United States, South Korea, and Japan conduct BMD. The Russian missile is capable of getting through US BMD with modern countermeasures. It can also launch multiple thermonuclear warheads. Finally, it is accurate enough to target specific neighborhoods.

Even if the Russians helped the North Koreans build a missile based on the Topol-M ICBM (SS-27 Mod 2), it remains unclear how many advanced capabilities the Hwasong-18 carries. But the North Koreans got this missile from somewhere, and it is highly unlikely they developed it on their own. This in itself may be the most troubling aspect of recent disclosures regarding its design and capabilities. The Hwasong-19 is essentially a newer, larger, upgraded version of the Hwasong-18.

The inevitable question is what to do about this. Sanctions, especially on Russian entities, are the obvious answer. But perhaps the best solution is to beef up BMD in the Asia-Pacific region. South Korea certainly needs to upgrade its current missile defense systems. It also needs closer integration with the United States and, if possible, Japan. Using BMD and other methods to shoot down these new North Korean systems or incapacitate them before they can do harm can and should be part of the focus of US, South Korean, and Japanese military planning, exercises, and acquisition in coming years. Failure to do so will allow the threat to grow.[38]

How Did North Korea Develop These Systems So Quickly?

Where did these systems suddenly appear from? It is very likely that most of them came from the Russians. In fact, a review of sanctions against Russian entities and individuals over the past three years reveals several sanctions that deal directly with proliferation to North Korea (though the systems involved are not specified).[39]

On January 12, 2022, the United States showed real evidence of Russian support to North Korea's ballistic missile programs. To quote the State Department document, "The United States has designated eight DPRK-linked individuals and entities under Executive Order 13382, which targets proliferators of weapons of mass destruction (WMD) and WMD delivery systems. The seven individuals and one entity designated today are all linked to the DPRK's weapons programs." The document goes on to say in part, "Specifically, the U.S. Department of State has designated one DPRK individual, one Russian individual, and one Russian entity that have engaged in activities or transactions that have materially contributed to the proliferation of WMD or their means of delivery by DPRK." Shockingly, the document says, "Between at least 2018 and 2021, Russia-based DPRK national O Yong Ho has procured and engaged in efforts to procure missile-applicable items from third countries on behalf of the DPRK's missile program, including aramid fiber, stainless steel tubes, and ball bearings on behalf of the Rocket Industry Department (aka Ministry of Rocket Industry), which is subordinate to the DPRK's UN- and U.S.-designated Munitions Industry Department."[40]

While the statements from the US State Department are quite compelling, there is still more. According to the document released by the State Department, "Between at least 2016 and 2021, O Yong Ho worked with Russian entity Parsek LLC and Russian national Roman Anatolyevich Alar, the director for development of Russian firm Parsek LLC, to procure multiple goods with ballistic missile applications, including Kevlar thread, aramid fiber, aviation oil, ball bearings, and precision milling machines controlled by the Nuclear Suppliers Group. Roman Anatolyevich Alar also provided O Yong Ho with instructions for creating solid rocket fuel mixtures." Also of key importance for the plethora of tests that have occurred since 2017, the document states, "The procurement and supply relationship between O Yong Ho, Roman Anatolyevich Alar, and Parsek LLC is a key source of missile-applicable goods and technology for the DPRK's missile program."[41] The statements above are unambiguous and clear. North Korea's ballistic missile programs received technology and support from Russian entities during the exact time frame that we saw a plethora of tests occur. In related evidence, according to press sources, the North Koreans have been using Russian satellite navigation systems, *instead of GPS*, for their missile launches.[42]

There is some evidence that China may also be supporting certain aspects of North Korea's ballistic missile programs. For example, there is evidence that China has supplied many of the mobile TELs that the North Koreans are using for their advanced missiles.[43] A document related to a secret plan the Chinese had for North Korea before its last nuclear test was obtained by well-known analyst and reporter Bill Gertz. The document was dated twelve days before North Korea's most recent nuclear test. According to the document, China would supply North Korea with a number of things if the isolated state halted nuclear tests. Among those things would be "more advanced mid- and short-range ballistic missiles, cluster munitions, etc."[44] There is no evidence to date that China has supplied North Korea with any ballistic missiles, but it certainly merits close watching and analysis should political conditions change.

Pyongyang's Cyber Capabilities: Kim Jong-un's New "All-Purpose Sword"

The cyber threat from North Korea is now sophisticated, diverse, and very real. North Korea in reality poses two important threats because of its cyber capabilities. The first threat is cyberattacks on military, business, and media entities in democratic states. The second threat is cyber theft from the international banking and business system. There is a third way that North Korea's cyber capabilities are an important concern for the United States and its allies: the transfer and laundering of cyber funds through what is now a sophisticated network. I will address the first two threats in this chapter and the laundering of funds more deeply in a later chapter. While North Korea has had cyber capabilities for at least fifteen years, the capabilities have really picked up in the level of sophistication, volume, and effectiveness since around 2018.

In October 2018, a breach of the computer systems of South Korea's agency that oversees weapons acquisition occurred. The breach included internal documents that contained information about sensitive military systems, including fighter aircraft. Pyongyang's cyber warriors also attacked government and corporate targets in South Korea in 2019. The breach is attributed to the North Koreans. During December 2018, North Korea was suspected to be the culprit in a malware attack that resulted in a delay in printing of several American newspapers, including the *Los Angeles Times*, the

New York Times, and the *Wall Street Journal.* By September 2019, the seriousness of the problem had become quite obvious as new US sanctions were imposed on North Korean cyber entities. The US Treasury Department at the time stated that Pyongyang had run operations across ten countries and stolen hundreds of millions of dollars, as well as stealing military secrets and destabilizing infrastructure. What would become the largest and perhaps most well-known group, the Lazarus Group, with its two subsidiaries, Bluenoroff and Andariel, had stolen $700 million during the previous three years, and other North Korean hacking groups had also accounted for $2 billion up to that time. According to Tonya Ugoretz, who at the time was the FBI's deputy assistant director of the Cyber Division, the financial burden of sanctions was (and it appears still is) the motivating factor behind North Korea's push for cyber capabilities.[45]

While the events described above were quite disturbing, perhaps even more disturbing was the unsurprising revelation by the Royal United Services Institute in the UK that in 2019 North Korea was using cryptocurrency to avoid sanctions and was also likely using it to fund WMD development. That same year, it was confirmed that a North Korean hacker group was using malware to record and steal data from ATM cards in India. Later in that year, another North Korean hacking group, identified as Kimsuky, mounted phishing attacks against North Korean human rights groups (nongovernmental organizations) that had sent a letter to then president Moon Jae-in requesting and pushing him to acknowledge North Korea's many human rights violations. But the attacks did not end there. In early 2020, Google reported that both North Korean and Iranian hackers were impersonating journalists in attempts to plant false stories in the press.[46]

A May 4, 2020, report highlighted among other things the skill and largesse of one of North Korea's key hacking groups—the Lazarus Group.[47] The Lazarus Group has now proved to be a key entity in helping North Korea to accomplish its cyber goals. In another report, according to Jason Bartlett in the *Diplomat,* "North Korea currently commands an estimated 6,000 cyber agents through four intelligence organizations scattered across the globe— one being the infamous Lazarus Group responsible for several major cyberattacks, including the 2017 WannaCry ransomware attack."[48] In October 2020, the Cybersecurity and Infrastructure Security Agency, an entity within the Department of Homeland Security, issued a warning that a North Korean hacking group was targeting "think tanks, experts, and government agencies." *Breaking Defense* stated, "The alert about North Korea's Kimsuky group comes just days after alerts about Iranian and Russian efforts, and a few weeks after an alert about potential cyber action from China." Thus, North Korea's hacking efforts against key entities are right up there with those of China, Russia, and Iran.[49]

According to Andrew Salmon in the *Asia Times* in February 2021, "North Korea, say experts who spoke to *Asia Times*, groups its cyber operatives under three arms of the state: The General Staff of the Korean People's Army; the State Security Bureau; and the Reconnaissance General Bureau, or RGB. The latter directorate oversees intelligence operatives and special forces units, and is tasked with both espionage and military operations." Salmon further goes on to say, "Some of the key sub-units identified, which are believed to operate under these various agencies have been dubbed Lazarus Group, APT38, Kim Suk Ki (aka Talium), D Track and Hidden Cobra Group." He then identified four key functions of these "cyber warriors," saying, "One is to gather foreign currency for a sanctioned, cash-strapped regime." He continued: "Another is to collect useful intelligence," and "another is to silence or threaten regime opponents or those who insult the dignity of the ruling Kim's." Finally, he added, "Yet another aim may be to showcase capabilities that awe the world—such as the infamous global Wannacry attack."[50]

By 2021, it had become obvious that North Korea was making billions off cyber theft and that this was among the most important priorities of North Korea's illicit activities. A 2021 report by Traders of Crypto, based in the UK, stated that North Korea had at the time stolen an estimated $1 billion in funds using financial hacking and had been the culprit in five of the last ten cyber theft incidents since 2011.[51]

By April 2022, it had become clear that the Lazarus Group, the best-known culprit among North Korea's spiderweb of cyber warriors, was continuing to successfully evade sanctions and was successfully laundering money from its crypto theft. As reported in the South Korean press, the coordinator for the UN Panel of Experts on North Korea, Eric Penton-Voak, "said the North has increasingly been relying on cyber activities for illicit income since 2017, noting a North Korean hacker group, known as Lazarus, was recently implicated in a US$625 million crypto hack against Axie Infinity, a play-to-earn online game." And the Treasury Department sanctioned a crypto service that helped North Koreans launder funds in May 2022. It appears that North

Korea increased its nefarious crypto activities—particularly crypto theft and crypto laundering of funds—once COVID-19 kicked in during mid-2020, and Pyongyang's activities became severely curtailed on the world illicit trade and proliferation scene. It should also be noted that, like all of North Korea's other illicit activities, including military proliferation, these activities are ultimately controlled by the infamous Office 39. Taking Office 39 out of operations would essentially throw a wrench in the works for all of Pyongyang's illicit activities—including crypto. But this has proved nearly impossible to do for many years.[52]

As 2022 moved into 2023, it became obvious that North Korea's cyber operations had not only become more active; they had become one of the largest, if not the largest, sources of illicit funds to help raise hard currency for the regime. Personnel from these operations came from units that were dispatched from the Munitions Industry Department, the Ministry of Defense, the Reconnaissance General Bureau, and the Ministry of State Security.[53] It is my assessment that the largest and most effective group of these dispersed personnel came from the Reconnaissance General Bureau.

The Lazarus Group appears to be behind a theft operation of deBridge Finance and an operation that hacked Harmony's Horizon Bridge and resulted in a rip-off of $100 million in virtual funds in 2022. In January 2023, it was revealed that the Lazarus Group was laundering their stolen funds using RAILGUN, a privacy protocol, and then sending the funds to virtual service companies while converting them to Bitcoin. In early 2023, it was reported that the Lazarus Group was disguising itself as Japanese and Vietnamese companies in its domains for operations. In a report also published in 2023, analysts from the cybersecurity firm Proofpoint allege that the North Koreans were successfully able to steal more than $1 billion in cryptocurrency and blockchain accounts in 2022 alone. Also in 2023, the firm Chainanalysis estimated that in 2022 the North Koreans had stolen $1.65 billion in cryptocurrency, or 43.4 percent of all crypto funds stolen in that year worldwide. In October 2023, the UN Panel of Experts confirmed that North Koreans had stolen nearly $1.7 billion in 2022, and assessed that the theft was a key source for funding Pyongyang's nuclear program. The amount of funds stolen, the ability to launder these funds (and all funds) effectively, and the attacks on governmental and associated entities worldwide all continue to be on the rise.[54] Of key concern for policymakers and international business, while estimates may vary, North Korea now appears to be making in the billions of dollars in cyber theft annually.

The evidence presented in this chapter should make it clear that the North Korean military threat continues to evolve, expand, and modernize. North Korea's armed forces now have ballistic missiles, tactical artillery, and special operations capabilities that they did not have even five years ago. All of this is exacerbated by evidence that for the first time since the end of the Cold War, Russia is again supporting Pyongyang's military capabilities development— particularly of ballistic missiles. North Korea's nuclear program remains in place, and the fact that platforms to carry it have advanced makes it even more of a threat. The relatively new threat from cyberattack and cyber theft continues to expand and presents a "dual-hatted" challenge for the United States and the international system. Not only is it a military threat to the many entities it can attack (and has attacked); North Korea is also now the world's largest cyber thief. Democratic states in the region and those with national interests in issues affected by North Korea's nefarious behavior should factor this into their foreign policy and military planning.

3

Iran's Military Capabilities

Becoming a Hegemon Thanks to Acquisition

Anthony N. Celso

This chapter assesses Iran's postrevolutionary military capacity. It has four sections. First, Iranian warfare doctrine and its dependence on foreign arms and military technology transfers are discussed. Second, Iran's nuclear program and diplomatic efforts to curtail Tehran's ability to develop atomic weapons are analyzed. Third, Iran's *asymmetric* and *conventional* military capabilities are assessed. Fourth, we discuss how Iran has used its military capability in past conflicts with its adversaries and how past behavior may shape Tehran's future actions.

Iranian Irregular Warfare and Tehran's Communist Bloc Military Alliances

The Islamic Republic of Iran's *way of war* is shaped by historic resentment over the military's prerevolutionary role. The army facilitated the Pahlavi family's dynastic rule from the early 1920s until the late 1970s. Reza Shah Pahlavi and his son Mohammad Reza Pahlavi viewed themselves as secular modernists in the mold of Turkey's legendary Kemal Ataturk.[1] In the 1920s and 1950s, army coups brought Reza Shah Pahlavi and Mohammad Reza Pahlavi to power as autocratic rulers who sought to transform Iran into a secular pro-Western regional power. The Pahlavis' connections to Anglo-American oil companies reinforced the antimilitary and anti-Western foundations of opposition to the shah's authoritarian rule.

Historically, Iran's clergy (ulama) resisted foreign interference in Iran's internal affairs. Clerical opposition to British cultural and economic imperialism enhanced the ulama's nationalist credentials among the Iranian public. The ulama led protests that forced the government to repeal concessions to British commercial interests over the tobacco trade in the nineteenth century. Past religious interference in state affairs would legitimate future clerical interference in state matters.

Russia's and Britain's occupation of Iran during World War II led to the removal of Reza Shah Pahlavi, whom they suspected of pro-Nazi sympathies. After the war, democratic elections resulted in a government dominated by the pro-Communist Tudeh Party, whose prime minister Mohammad Mosaddegh in the 1950s nationalized Anglo-American oil companies. Supported by the US Central Intelligence Agency, the army's 1953 overthrow of Mossadegh's regime led to Mohammad Reza Pahlavi's ascension. This event reinforced anti-Americanism as a unifying factor behind Communist and Islamist opposition to the shah's rule.[2]

US assistance in developing Iran's formidable military underscored the shah's reputation as an American lackey. Iran's army (the Artesh) retains antiquated American weapons systems (including F-14 fighters, AH-1 Cobra attack helicopters, and M60 tanks) bought by the shah's regime.[3] America's financial and military connections to the shah's dynastic rule left an indelible psychological resentment.

The shah's immunization from criminal prosecution of hundreds of US military advisers was criticized in Shia religious opposition circles. His 1963 White Revolution furthered religious and leftist resentment against Iran's capitalist secular modernization.[4] The shah's emulation of Ataturk's Turkish secular model enraged the Islamists who saw the regime as *heretical*. Prohibitions on Islamic dress, the licensing of liquor stores, and secular marriage and divorce laws catalyzed protests. Mohammad Reza Pahlavi's intent to resurrect Persia's imperial past combined with his secular modernization policy deeply upset the social and religious fabric of Iranian society.

The regime's usurpation of the historic role of Shia religious institutions in education, judicial affairs, and community welfare engendered the ulama's outrage. The shah's land reform policies, moreover, impoverished the peasantry, and the regime's preferential treatment of multinational capital and large enterprises incensed the bazaar commercial classes.

Iran's prerevolutionary military was strengthened by American and Israeli assistance, which only furthered the regime's credentials as a neocolonial anti-Islamic force in the Middle East. At its height, the Artesh numbered over four hundred thousand men, making it one of the most powerful militaries in the region.[5] The army's role as a pillar of the shah's regime and its association with the West invited anger and resentment. Cultural resistance to the shah's modernization program was defined by religious and clerical opposition to the government's reforms.

Government domestic policy exacerbated societal anger, and revolutionary opposition to the shah's rule built throughout the late 1970s. Mohammad Reza Pahlavi's White Revolution unchained social, religious, and economic turmoil that furthered oppositional unity. A Communist-Islamist coalition formed the bedrock of the revolutionary movement that gained some liberal middle-class support.[6] United in their hostility toward the regime, these groups conspired to bring an end to the shah's reign.

Ayatollah Ruhollah Khomeini's decades-long opposition to the shah's regime personified societal and religious grievances. His critique of the regime's secularization and economic policies proved a galvanizing force. The charismatic cleric agitated for an Islamic Third Way and an ulama-led state based on the rule of the jurisprudent (velayat-e-faqih) that gave supreme authority to religious authorities.[7] Exiled to Iraq for his opposition to the shah's rule, Khomeini condemned the regime, thereby encouraging religious opposition among the peasanty and the bazaar commercial classes. Khomeini's incendiary speeches against the regime were smuggled clandestinely into Iran on audio, making him a popular opposition leader.[8]

By the late 1970s, Khomeini integrated Marxist analysis into his activist religious worldview, dramatizing foreign capitalist exploitation of the devout peasantry and the working class. Taking their cue from Khomeini, Iranian religious conservatives addressed social and economic grievances within an Islamic socialist caste. Ali Shariati's theological opposition to the shah's regime, for example, fused past Shia oppression with revolutionary proletariat aspirations.[9] Dominated by religious conservatives and Marxists, the protest movement agitated for Islamic social and economic justice.

The shah's unpopularity and his regime's repressiveness undermined American support. The 1978 killing of Ayatollah Khomeini's son by the shah's SAVAK intelligence service increased Khomeini's standing in the opposition. The Jimmy Carter administration pressured the shah's regime to end repressive measures, limiting his ability to check powerful protests. The ruler's advanced cancer, moreover, proved distracting and hindered his ability to counter revolutionary forces. Increasingly isolated and devoid of Western support, the shah exiled himself.

His regime was toppled by Islamo-Communist revolutionary forces. The postrevolutionary chaos resulted in the purging of the shah's state bureaucracy, military, and political party. In classic fashion, the radical phase of the revolution *devoured its children* as religious conservatives consolidated power and violently repressed Communists and liberals. Condemned by ulama-directed courts, thousands were executed. Underscoring the revolution's legacy, Iran's current president, when he was the regime's deputy prosecutor, took a lead role in judicial processes that led to the death of thousands of political prisoners in the late 1980s.

Like its Communist predecessors, the Iranian Revolution had a Leninist stage resulting in the consolidation of power by the ulama and their religious students. Once they seized power, the clerics hoped to preserve their rule through a cultural revolution that would undo the Pahlavi era's secularization policy.

Iran's clerical purging of the judiciary, the universities, and the state has been described as a *postmodernist* reaction to Western secularization.[10] The ulama's religious reforms became Iran's equivalent to Mao Zedong's Cultural Revolution. The desecularization of Iranian society reinforced conventional religious morality, resulting in Sharia law regulating social, cultural, political, and economic relations. After the US Embassy's 1979 seizure by regime-backed religious students who took the embassy staff hostage for over four hundred days, relations between Tehran and Washington deteriorated.

The revolutionary regime's desire for societal transformation fell acutely on the armed forces. Resentment against the Artesh's support for the shah's regime led to the eradication of the army's high command and the professional officer corps. Morale and membership in the armed forces decayed. The reorganization of the military eroded its status within Iranian society and hindered its capacity to function during the Iran-Iraq War.

Distrust of the armed forces encouraged the growth of the revolutionary militias as a counterweight to the Artesh. The army's poor performance and the revolutionary *martyrdom* of the new militias during Iran's war with Iraq between 1980 and 1988 reinforced the distrust of conventional military tactics.

It is difficult to overstate the impact of the Iran-Iraq War on Tehran's development of an asymmetric warfare strategy. The Islamic Republic's missile and militia strategy was born from this chaotic tragic period. The human and economic damage done by the war coupled with the Iranian military's failure to achieve a decisive victory left significant psychological scars. Iran's cities were devastated by Iraqi missiles that killed thousands.

During the conflict, militia forces used mass suicidal wave attacks to clear Iraqi minefields. Grisly trench warfare and the indiscriminate bombing of civilian population centers dominated the fighting. The Islamic Republic's fixation on missile technology was inexorably shaped by this terrible experience.

Iraq used chemical weapons against Iran's civilian population, elevating the psychological and material toll of the war. Relying on imported North Korean, Chinese, and Russian missiles, Iran retaliated against Saddam Hussein's army with a concerted bombardment campaign that brutalized Iraq's cities.

The revolutionary fervor of these groups, who were hastily dispatched to the war's battlefront with little training, contributed to the regime's survival in a devastating conflict that produced over two hundred thousand dead Iranians. These populist militias became the forebears of the Islamic Revolutionary Guard Corps (IRGC) and the Basij, whose valor and effectiveness were juxtaposed with the Artesh's failure to defend the country.

The inefficacy of conventional military campaigns applied equally to naval warfare. Iran's efforts to close the Strait of Hormuz through missile and mining operations were impaired by a militarily superior and technologically savvy US Navy. Iran's use of naval frigates to combat American antimining operations resulted in the destruction of or extreme damage to several of its larger vessels. Tehran's inability to derail America's antimining Operation Praying Mantis during the tanker war led to greater use of swarm operations by light patrol boats, and the lessons derived from failed conventional efforts inform today's Iraqi naval strategy, which relies on small vessels, mines, antiship missiles, and coastal defense batteries.[11]

By 1988, Tehran's military position was untenable and faltering. Having steadfastly refused diplomatic efforts to end the war, Ayatollah Khomeini relented. Despite viewing the peace deal as a *poisoned chalice*, Iran's supreme leader saw it as a necessary measure to preserve his regime.[12]

Since the war, Tehran has prioritized the IRGC's professionalization. The corps plays a multifaceted role within the Islamic Republic.[13] First, it preserves and defends the Islamic Republic against internal and external enemies. The IRGC's Basij militia has crushed protest movements throughout the Islamic Republic's history. Second, the IRGC serves as a vehicle to propagate the regime's ideology and indoctrinate its members with a messianic vision committed to the supreme leader. The corps' recruitment practices prioritize religious indoctrination, propagate a martyrdom cult, and inculcate hatred of Americans and Jews. IRGC manifestos present the Islamic Republic as a vigilant defender of Shia religious values against the onslaught of a demonic *Zionist-Crusader-Wahhabi* world order.[14] Third, the corps' Quds Force is committed to the projection of the Islamic Republic's military force throughout the Middle East, which aims to *liberate* Jerusalem.

Created by the supreme leader in 1988, IRGC–Quds Force (IRGC-QF) has extended Iranian military influence across the Middle East. The Quds Force is the vehicle for Tehran's asymmetric warfare model. The force's evocation of unconventional military tactics is, moreover, buttressed by religious and historical forces.[15] IRGC-QF advocacy of guerrilla tactics is presented within a theological caste that references the wartime practices of Mohammad and his companions, which emphasized stealth, speed, and surprise attacks by small bands.

Shia narratives of martyrdom and military valor emphasize the life, guerrilla war tactics, and death of the Prophet's cousin/son-in-law Ali and his son Hussein, who are considered Mohammad's legitimate successors unjustly denied and killed by treacherous and villainous (Sunni) forces. The Shia religious holiday of Ashura commemorates Hussein's death at the seventh-century Battle of Karbala, and IRGC members see themselves as carrying forth Hussein's legacy.

The corps prioritizes protecting Shia shrines, grave sites, and religious architecture in Iraq and Syria.[16] IRGC ideological indoctrination emphasizes the glory of past Shia caliphates and the ignominy of the sect's past persecution. Combined with Iran's Persian imperial past, Islamist martyrdom and militarist narratives drive the Quds Force ambitions to fulfill the supreme leader's quest to create a Shia imamate in the Middle East. The pan-Shia vision provides a powerful ideological impetus for Iran's *asymmetric* way of war.

Born from the calamitous Iran-Iraq War, the Islamic Republic's missile and militia strategy has evolved. Denied access to Western arms by international sanctions, Tehran has acquired Russian, Chinese, and North Korean weaponry and armaments technology that have enabled the Islamic Republic's regional hegemonic ambitions. Originating during the Cold War, Tehran's relationships with these regimes have strengthened over time.

Iran's Postrevolutionary Military Alliances

After the 1979 Revolution, Iran became an anti-Western outlaw regime. Labeled the Great Satan by Ayatollah Khomeini, Washington is the Islamic Republic's chief rival and number one security threat. American military and economic support for Israel is viewed as furthering Washington's neo-imperial project in the Middle East. Given Western opposition to the regime, Tehran outreach to Communist bloc nations is unsurprising. Iran's war with Iraq forced the Islamic Republic to rely on foreign weapons transfers.

Russia, North Korea, and China were eager to supply weapons systems to Tehran's beleaguered regime. Needing to access Iranian oil and funds, cash-strapped Moscow, Pyongyang, and Beijing provided missiles, weapons platforms, and conventional arms to the Islamic Republic. Iran's cooperation with Communist bloc nations was driven by transactional considerations, common enemies, and compatible strategic interests that aspired to weaken America's military position in the Middle East.

Most of Tehran's missile architecture is based on foreign technological blueprints that have been adapted by Iranian technicians. Iran's al-Shahab missile series, for example, is based on North Korean No Dong designs. Foreign expertise and weapons systems were an indispensable lifeline that allowed Tehran to compete against a militarily superior Iraq, and since this time, they have played a pivotal role in the Islamic Republic's missile arsenal, which is estimated to be the Middle East's largest.

Foreign-source technology empowers Tehran's asymmetric missile and militia war strategy designed to ensure regime survival and project its military influence abroad. Communist bloc expertise, capital, and technological assistance have allowed Iran to develop a national defense and aerospace industry. Tehran, moreover, has utilized North Korean technology, advisers, and weapons systems to develop missile assembly plants run by Hezbollah in Lebanon and has financially underwritten Pyongyang's assistance to the Assad regime's weapons of mass destruction program.

The Islamic Republic's involvement in the Syrian conflict aspires to recreate its successful development of a missile development infrastructure run by its proxy groups elsewhere. Though they have been impaired by hundreds of Israeli air strikes in Syria, Iran's efforts to proliferate weapons and assembly plants have not stopped. Syria is also a vital connection between Tehran and

Moscow, whose military intervention in the country's civil war has allowed the Assad regime to survive.

Moscow's arms transfers are reinforced by energy and trade links.[17] Geographically connected by the oil-rich Caspian Sea, Moscow and Tehran have engaged in joint energy projects. Though weapons procurement began during the Cold War, arms transfers and military cooperation between the two countries have increased dramatically under Vladimir Putin's regime. Moscow's transfer of technology and weapons to Iran weakens the US military standing in the Middle East.[18]

Hoping to weaken the American-dominated regional and international order, Moscow's technology and weapons transfers have augmented Tehran's missile and submarine warfare capability. Iran's Soumar and Quds-1 land-based cruise missiles are based on Russian AS-14 designs, and Tehran purchased three Russian-made Kilo submarines in the 1990s.[19] Russia has facilitated Iran's progressive development of a sophisticated missile defense system capable of downing advanced combat aircraft.[20] Tehran's 2016 purchase of the SA 20 C air defense system augments its arsenal of surface-to-air missiles managed by the Islamic Republic of Iran Air Defense Force, which is designed to protect the regime's critical military infrastructure.

The Islamic Republic, moreover, is poised to purchase Russian-made SA-400 antiaircraft missiles. In October 2020, UN prohibitions on Iranian arms imports and exports ended up giving Tehran ample opportunities to strengthen its military capability—a fact underscored by Tehran and Beijing's signing of a $400 billion twenty-five-year defense and economic cooperation agreement that will enhance the Islamic Republic's military capability.[21]

Starting in 2022, these historic allies have reversed operational roles. The February 2022 Russian invasion of Ukraine has dissipated Moscow's vast arsenal of precision-guided missiles and armed drones. Putin's military struggles in Ukraine have forced Moscow to rely on hundreds of Iranian drones that the Russian Air Force has used in an ongoing air campaign to impair Kiev's energy grid and water supply system. Reportedly, the Russians have purchased thousands of Shahed-136 and 133 loitering drone munitions and have also purchased ballistic missiles.[22]

Such an unprecedented Iranian commitment to Moscow's war effort is dramatic proof that the Russo-Iranian alliance has grown appreciably. US intelligence officials estimate that Moscow is in return assisting the Islamic Republic's nuclear program and missile development program. Once the limits on Iranian ballistic missile development enacted by the Joint Comprehensive Plan of Action (JCPOA) ended in 2023, Tehran and Moscow began rapidly expanding their scientific, economic, and military cooperation. Russia is not alone among Tehran's revisionist allies.

Shrouded in secrecy, the accord advances Beijing's and Tehran's efforts to carve out a dominant position in the Middle East.[23] It is the full maturation of a bilateral relationship that has endured since the Islamic Republic's founding. China has fortified Iran's military capacity by providing it conventional weapons, missiles, and delivery platforms.

Much of Iran's coastal antiship and cruise missiles were fabricated on Chinese C802 and CSSC missile 2 and 3 series designs.[24] IRGC-Navy forces, moreover, are dependent on Chinese-constructed patrol boats, which are a critical component of their maritime defense.

North Korea is the single most significant contributor to Tehran's ambitious weapons acquisition policy. Pyongyang's export of missiles, weapons platforms, and conventional arms to Iran and its proxies strengthens Iran's asymmetric and conventional warfare capabilities. Iran's midget submarine fleet, for example, is based on North Korean engineering Yono-class designs.[25]

Tehran's *axis of resistance* strategy and its regional *forward defense system* are predicated on the cultivation of Shia proxy forces in Lebanon, Iraq, and Yemen and on the preservation of the Assad regime. Hezbollah's military entrenchment in Lebanon has been furthered by Iran's financial underwriting of North Korean rockets, missiles, and underground tunnel facilities that allowed the group to survive a monthlong war with Israel in the summer of 2006. Since this period, Hezbollah has augmented its vast stockpiles of North Korean rockets and missiles that Tehran is equipping with precision-guided systems.[26]

IRGC-QF trainers work with Iraqi, Lebanese, Bahraini, and Syrian militias who employ North Korean rockets, missiles, and conventional arms against US, Israeli, and Sunni Gulf forces and aligned groups. North Korea, moreover, has been a critical node in Iran's quest to develop a nuclearized intercontinental ballistic missile (ICBM). Tehran's successful launching of a space satellite in 2020 was based at least partially on North Korean No Dong missile technology. Pyongyang's history of violating arms control agreements to augment its weapons of mass destruction program is an invaluable precedent indicating how outlaw regimes can scam the international system through subterfuge, deception, and military provocation.

Iran's lack of transparency over its nuclear ballistic missile program and its circumvention of some limits imposed by JCPOA were likely influenced by North Korea's past actions.[27] Concern over Iran's weaponization of its nuclear program has increased dramatically with the JCPOA's collapse. Reacting to covert Israeli actions that sabotaged its Natanz reactor's centrifuge uranium enrichment capacity, the Islamic Republic has systematically violated the 2015 agreement. Responsible for overseeing the agreement's enforcement, the International Atomic Energy Agency (IAEA) reports that Iran has vastly exceeded uranium enrichment levels mandated by the 2015 accord.[28]

Despite the Trump administration's intent to revise the accord, negotiations between Washington and Tehran remain tenuous. Discussions over the deal, moreover, are complicated by Iran's delivery of armed drones to Russia, which has resulted in the previous Biden administration sanctioning Iranian unmanned aerial vehicle supply chains.[29] Tehran's brutal crackdown on Iranian protests over the religious police's killing of a Kurdish woman for the improper wearing of her hijab have furthermore impeded any real progress in the JCPOA's resumption.

Past diplomatic efforts to prevent North Korea's development of nuclear weapons suggest that multilateral initiatives to contain Iran's weaponization of its nuclear program will flounder. The international system's previous efforts to restrict the Islamic Republic's ballistic missile development provide ample evidence that future endeavors are problematic.

Iran's Nuclear Program and the JCPOA's Precarious Status

Iran began its nuclear program under the shah. Ironically, French and American financing and technology facilitated the construction of Iran's nuclear reactors throughout the 1960s. The shah's ambitious program envisaged the creation of dozens of nuclear reactors to diversify Iran's economy and reduce its dependence on oil exports.[30] To allay concerns over the military implications of its nuclear program, Tehran in 1970 signed the Nonproliferation Treaty.

The program's development was derailed by Iran's postrevolutionary turmoil and by its war with Iraq. Ayatollah Khomeini's declaration that nuclear weapons were "un-Islamic" may have influenced Tehran's suspension of the program. His death in 1989 and the ascension of Ayatollah Ali Khamenei as the country's supreme leader were instrumental in the resumption of Tehran's nuclear reactor program.[31]

The devastation inflicted on Iran's cities by Saddam Hussein's missiles, coupled with Tehran's international isolation, also influenced the program's reactivation. Though Khamenei issued a fatwa prohibiting the country's development of nuclear weapons, suspicion over the country's quest for atomic weapons capability endured.

Of particular concern was weapons-related scientific experimentation conducted by Tehran's Physics Research Center from 1989 to 2003. Supervised by then leading nuclear physicist Mohsen Fakhrizadeh, the facility conducted experiments centering on the weaponization of atomic energy. Iran's involvement in the A. Q. Khan network, which proliferated nuclear weapons technology across the world, was seen as especially troubling.[32]

Despite Tehran's participation in treaties banning chemical and biological weapons, similar concerns have been raised about Iran's possession of these armaments.[33] Though Western intelligence agencies believe Iran terminated its nuclear weapons program in 2003, the Israeli government is convinced Tehran has a covert program. An Iranian dissident group's 2011 disclosure of clandestine nuclear reactors at Natanz and Fordow increased the international community's angst over Tehran's weaponization plans.

Based on a FDD (Foundation for Defense of Democracies) report, the Islamic Republic seeks to develop the technological capacity to produce nuclear weapons.[34] The regime's motivations for pursuing a nuclear option are driven by multiple calculations that range from ensuring the Islamic Republic's survival to furthering its *axis of resistance* project.

There are, however, more sinister suspicions. The Islamic Republic's eschatological worldview that sees the supreme leader as a custodian of the twelfth imam, whose future release from occultation will trigger an apocalyptic war, leads some to argue that Iran will be driven by messianic religious imperatives to use nuclear weapons.[35] Israeli security analysts, moreover, argue that Tehran's quest for nuclear weapons is motivated by its desire to eradicate the Zionist presence in Palestine. Israeli prime minister Benjamin Netanyahu has argued that Tehran's development of nuclear weapons is a red line that Jerusalem will never allow the Islamic Republic to cross.[36]

Punishing Iran for violating the Nonproliferation Treaty, the international community has used economic sanctions and diplomatic measures to derail Tehran's weaponization program. Such efforts culminated in the Barack Obama–era 2015 JCPOA. Negotiations over curtailing Tehran's nuclear program have been long, complex, and arduous.

Starting in 2003, French, British, and German authorities negotiated an interim accord with Iran that swapped trade concessions in return for Tehran limiting its uranium enrichment capability. Iran's violation of the agreement led to a renewed round of diplomatic contracts between the international community and the Islamic Republic. America's 2006 involvement in multilateral discussions with Tehran signaled a renewed interest in using economic sanctions to force Iranian compliance with mandated uranium enrichment thresholds. Passed by the United Nations Security Council in 2010, Resolution 1929 imposed far-reaching economic sanctions on Iran's nuclear reactor program and sought to abolish its ballistic missile development program.

Suffering from debilitating sanctions, Tehran struck a 2013 interim agreement with the United States, Britain, France, Russia, China, and Germany. Under the terms of the accord, Iran would restrict uranium enrichment at its nuclear reactors in return for sanctions relief. Iran's failure to implement the agreement led to renewed diplomatic efforts.

By 2014, the Obama administration believed that Tehran was a few months away from producing enough weapons-grade fissile material to empower a nuclear weapon. Working with the French, British, German, Chinese, and Russians, the US imposed sanctions on Iran's economy and weapons industry hoping to convince Iran to sign an agreement that would demilitarize its nuclear program. By 2015, international sanctions had sharply reduced Iran's oil exports leading to Tehran's signing of an agreement called the JCPOA. This concession proved controversial for it merely restricted Tehran's uranium enrichment activities for a limited duration. After the deal's expiration in 2030, for example, all restraints on Iran's nuclear capacity will be removed.

After securing Iran's agreement to the JCPOA, the UN Security Council made any sanctions relief contingent on the Islamic Republic's fidelity to the accord's terms. Among the JCPOA's main provisions are that it

1. requires Iran to export highly enriched material overseas that would be diluted and returned to it at lower levels,
2. limits uranium enrichment at the Natanz reactor to a level of 3.67 percent,
3. requires the decommissioning of Iran's heavy water reactor at Arak,
4. mandates that it convert its Fordow nuclear reactor into a research center,
5. requires IAEA inspections of declared and suspected Iranian nuclear technology development sites,
6. limits the Islamic Republic's nuclear ballistic development program until 2023,
7. limits Iran's research and development of advanced centrifuge technologies until 2024, and
8. bans Iranian arms imports and exports until 2020.[37]

Though the agreement prohibits Iran from developing ICBM capability to carry nuclear weapons, it does not limit the Islamic Republic's conventional ballistic missile development. Critics were further incensed by the accord's refusal to penalize Iran for its support for terrorism and for its cultivation of violent Shia Islamist militias across the Middle East.

Iran abided by the 3.67 percent uranium enrichment threshold during most of the agreement's duration; however, IAEA inspectors were denied access to Iran's suspected military nuclear sites. Israel, American conservatives, and Sunni Gulf counties heavily criticized the accord. The expansion of Tehran's missile precision project and its military interventions in Iraq, Syria, and Yemen reinforced critics' assertions that the JCPOA financially underwrote Iran's destabilizing policies in the Middle East.[38]

Such concerns convinced the Donald Trump administration in 2018 to end American involvement in the agreement. The US government reimposed sanctions related to Iran's missile development and expanded sanctions to include Iran's financial and energy sectors. The Trump administration hoped to use its maximum-pressure policy to force Iran into a new, more comprehensive treaty that restricts Tehran's ballistic missile development and curbs its support for proxy forces.

Trump's maximum-pressure policy was rejected by the JCPOA's other signatories, who sought to maintain the agreement by cushioning the impact of the American sanctions. As Iran's economy steadily deteriorated, tensions in the Persian Gulf and the Middle East rose. Backed by Iran, Iraqi militias launched rocket and mortar attacks against US troops in the country and harassed their resupply convoys. Tehran's underwriting of these attacks prompted American military retaliation.

Hostilities reached a critical threshold when the Trump administration killed Qasem Soleimani and Kataib Hezbollah leader Abu Mahdi al-Muhandis in a January 2020 air strike at Baghdad International Airport. Iran retaliated with ballistic missile strikes against US air bases in Iraq, prompting fears of a major escalation.

Pushed to the brink of war, Washington and Tehran have engaged in limited military clashes between US forces and Iranian-backed militants in Iraq and Syria. The Biden administration aimed to calm tensions between the United States and Iran. This new administration's prime objective was to resume American participation in the 2015 agreement and reach a new accord that restricted Iran's missile and militia strategy.

By seeking a more comprehensive agreement, the Biden administration tacitly acknowledged many of the JCPOA's weaknesses.[39] Hoping to arrive at interim agreements that exchange sanctions relief for Iranian compliance with uranium enrichment limits, ongoing negotiations in Geneva have failed to make progress.[40]

It is possible that a new JCPOA consensus will never be reached. Beginning in 2020, Iran has increased its uranium enrichment capacity. IAEA inspectors have been denied access to military sites implicated in advanced centrifuge technology research. Responding to a concerted Israeli sabotage campaign against its Natanz uranium enrichment facility, Iran has restarted its Fordow nuclear reactor, introducing advanced gas centrifuges capable of enriching uranium at 60 percent levels.

Once it attains this threshold, Iran shortens its breakout time to produce nuclear-weapons-grade fissile material. By some estimates, Iran by September 2021 was only months away from developing weapons-grade fissile material.[41] One 2022 study by Michael Eisenstadt suggests that Iran seeks nuclear threshold capacity while retaining the option of developing atomic weapons.[42] He reckons that Tehran's attainment of nuclear threshold state status is consistent with the regime's calculated ambiguity that underlines its historic grand strategy and that if Iran does eventually develop, it will be driven by the need for regime preservation.[43]

The Islamic Republic's JCPOA violations portend a future conflict where Iran will continue to use the hybrid warfare and conventional capabilities that it has effectively employed in past gray-zone conflicts.[44]

Iran's Asymmetric and Conventional Hybrid Warfare Military Capabilities

The DIME (diplomatic, intelligence, military, and economic) model is often used as an analytical tool to look at a country's full-spectrum use of its instruments of national power.[45] Employing this model, we can differentiate between *hard power* (military) and *soft power* (diplomacy). Among revisionist nations, Iran is unequaled in its integration of hard and soft power designed to achieve its strategic objectives. Historically, it has been relentless in ensuring the regime's preservation and the projection of its influence across the Middle East. What follows is a brief survey of its full-spectrum use of diplomatic, intelligence, and economic measures that has abetted its hard-power military strategy.

Iranian diplomacy is intimately tied to Tehran's propaganda war against the West and presents itself as an *axis of resistance* defender of Palestinian and Shia groups. Iranian foreign policy perpetuates Islamic martyrdom and victimization narratives to justify an armed resistance policy against the United States and Israel. Tehran furthermore evokes Shia and Islamic suffering to legitimate its military involvement in Syria, Lebanon, Iraq, Yemen, and the Palestinian occupied territories.

The Islamic Republic's diplomacy reflects the regime's strategic ambiguity that oscillates between feigned accommodation with and fanatical resistance to Western power. Iran disingenuously uses diplomacy to conceal its hegemonic ambitions and often relays a desire for coexistence with Western powers.[46] In accepting the JCPOA, Tehran has used the accord to facilitate its ballistic missile program and used sanctions relief to finance its proxy militias across the Middle East.

Iran's maximalist interpretation of the accord's ambiguous provisions allows it to pursue missile development while disingenuously claiming fidelity to the JCPOA. This exemplifies the Islamic Republic's use of taqiya (dissimulation), which conceals its true intentions. Tehran has parlayed its diplomacy with economic assistance.

Soft power for Iran facilitates its Shia imamate project. The Islamic Republic's financing of Shia clerics, mosques, education centers, television and radio networks, community welfare agencies, and charities in Iraq, Lebanon, and Syria are intimately connected to its militia project.[47] Recruitment in Iran-connected Arab militias is buttressed by social welfare benefits that are accompanied by intense religious indoctrination.

Iranian involvement in the Levant is justified by its religious obligation to preserve Shia shrines and burial sites threatened by Sunni jihadi groups and is presented as a humanitarian project to assist endangered Shiite and aligned religious groups. Iran's use of soft power undergirds its military strategy by creating a robust militia presence to project political influence. Parliamentary groupings tied to Hezbollah and the Iraqi Popular Mobilization Forces (PMF), for example, often shape government policy in Lebanon and Iraq.

Lebanon's political paralysis is a consequence of Hezbollah resistance to forming a parliamentary majority and the unwillingness of the Lebanese army to challenge the group's military supremacy. With Iranian support, Hezbollah has constructed a parallel state that compromises Lebanon's sovereignty and hinders its effective governance.

Political factions tied to the Iraqi PMF militias, moreover, are important players in the Iraqi legislature. Tehran's financing and arming of the Syrian National Defense Forces and its positioning of Hezbollah in Syria similarly give it an important voice within the Assad administration.

The network of mosques, community centers, health clinics, and financial institutions associated with Iran-sponsored Shia charities in the Levant makes Tehran a formidable economic presence in the economies of Lebanon, Iraq, and Syria. Since the 1979 Revolution, the Islamic Republic has adroitly parleyed economic assistance and religious propaganda to advance its hard-power militia project across the region.

Iran synchronizes diplomatic, information, and economic instruments of national power to buttress its hybrid warfare doctrine. Tehran has invested considerable resources to advance its proxy project. Since 2012, the Islamic Republic has spent $16 billion to prop up the Syrian regime and its aligned surrogates.[48] This includes $700 million a year for Hezbollah, billions for the Assad regime, and some $100 million a year split between Hamas and Palestinian Islamic Jihad (PIJ).

Iranian intelligence services coordinate their operations with proxy forces to conceal Iran's role in attacking its adversaries. Iran's long-game approach to warfare is tantamount to a death-by-a-thousand-cuts strategy designed to weaken stronger adversaries and exhaust their ability to resist the Islamic Republic's regional policy.[49] IRGC-QF trained and armed Iranian proxies in South Lebanon and in Iraq who have killed thousands of Israeli soldiers and hundreds of American service members. Tehran's mastery of irregular warfare in gray-zone conflicts has been crafted over a generation.

Since the 1979 Revolution, the IRGC has dominated the country's defense planning. Iran prioritizes the IRGC by allocating two-thirds of the defense budget to the group.[50] IRGC financing also comes from its dominant position in Iran's economy, patronage networks, and its control over community welfare funds.[51]

Within Iran, the IRGC plays multiple roles. The IRGC and its domestic Basij militia protect the revolutionary state and propagate its ideological message, and the corps' expeditionary Quds Force acts as a trainer, armer, and catalyst for its regional forward defense militia and missile strategy.[52]

With their own army, navy, and air force, the IRGC, Basij, and Quds Force have substantial offensive capabilities.[53] The IRGC's influence within Iran's military and command structure is preeminent, for it plans and coordinates Tehran's defensive and external military policy. Favored by Supreme Leader Ayatollah Khamenei, the IRGC has created a deep state within Iran buttressed by financial and personal connections to the country's banking, construction, aerospace, and defense industries.[54]

As seen in table 3.1, Iran's military chain of command is hierarchical and multilayered. Under Iran's Constitution, the Shia religious doctrine of *velayat-e-faqih* establishes the absolute authority of the supreme leader. Ayatollah Khamenei determines the main goals of Iran's security doctrine. As directed by the supreme leader, the Supreme Council for National Security (SCNS) is responsible for fashioning national security and foreign policy strategy to realize the supreme leader's chief objectives. Chaired by Iran's president, the SCNS is composed of key executive, legislative, and military leaders who are tasked with developing and coordinating the Islamic Republic's military policy.

Iran has a trimodal military structure composed of IRGC air, land, and naval special forces; its domestic Basij militia; and Artesh conventional military forces. Each unit has a specialized niche, but their responsibilities

Table 3.1. Central Command System and National Security
Policymaking Apparatus

Actor	Responsibilities
Supreme leader	Iranian head of state who has absolute authority to determine national and defense policy priorities and guides the development of national security strategy. Appoints commanders to guide the AFGS and the KCHQ's execution of Iran's foreign and defense policy.
Supreme Council for National Security (SCNS)	Chaired by the country's president, the SCNS is composed of senior military commanders and key cabinet and legislative members and is charged with formulating national defense and foreign policy strategy as guided by the supreme leader.
Armed Forces General Staff (AFGS)	Senior military body that implements the country's foreign defense policies. AFGS's commander is determined by the supreme leader.
Khatam al-Anbiya Central Headquarters (KCHQ)	Iran's principal command and control center that coordinates IRGC and Artesh implementation of the country's foreign and defense strategy. KCHQ's commander is determined by the supreme leader.
IRGC and Artesh Headquarters	Command and control bodies that oversee the application of IRGC asymmetric and Artesh conventional air, naval, and land forces per the guidance of the supreme leader.
al-Ghadir Missile Command and the Islamic Republic of Iran's Air Defense Force (IRIADF)	IRGC-Aerospace directs the al-Ghadir Missile Command governing the use of missile forces. The Artesh's IRIADF directs the country's air defense systems.
IRGC–Quds Force (IRGC-QF)	Responsible for Iran's militia strategy and foreign asymmetric strategy.

Source: Defense Intelligence Agency, "Iran's Military Power: Ensuring Regime Survival and Securing Regional Dominance," 2019, https://www.dia.mil/News-Features/Articles/Article-View/Article/2020456/.

overlap. Chosen directly by the supreme leader, an IRGC commander chairs the Armed Forces General Staff (AFGS), which contains the senior leaders of Iran's special and conventional forces to establish time frames for the implementation of national security policy.

The AFGS works closely with Khatam al-Anbiya Central Headquarters (KCHQ) to ensure proper coordination between the IRGC and the Artesh in the provision of naval, air, and territorial security. Established in 2016 as a separate command, the KCHQ has the authority to direct the lower echelons of Iran's military bureaucracy. Within its strategic purview are the activities of the al-Ghadir Missile Command and the Islamic Republic of Iran's Air Defense Force (IRIAD) that control the Islamic Republic's missile project.

Iran is estimated to have the largest ballistic missile force in the Middle East. Though precise numbers are hard to determine, *Iran Watch* estimates that the country by March 2020 had between twenty-five hundred and three thousand short- and medium-range ballistic missiles at its disposal, some of which could strike targets up to twenty-five hundred kilometers away.[55] This formidable arsenal is buttressed by significant numbers of cruise missiles, surface-to-air missiles, and rockets.

Run by the IRGC–Aerospace Force, the al-Ghadir Missile Command Center guides the development of Tehran's precision missile project, which is in the vanguard of the nation's territorial defense and its regional power projection. By constructing a large missile force, the Islamic Republic hopes to deter aggressors, transfer select systems to its proxy militias, and intimidate its enemies.

Buttressed by sophisticated Russian-made SA-20 missile defense systems, the Artesh's IRIAD is designed to protect the Islamic Republic's critical military, scientific, and economic infrastructure from the superior airpower of its adversaries. The strategic importance of Tehran's missile project is further underscored by the activities of the IRGC-QF.

Created in 1988, the Quds Force is the Islamic Republic's vehicle to create a forward defense system composed of Shia and aligned militias across the Persian Gulf and the Levant. Personal ties between the late Qasem Soleimani and Ayatollah Khamenei elevated the Quds Force's role in developing Iran's regional proxy policy.

Tasked by the supreme leader, Soleimani ran the Quds Force as his own fiefdom, establishing personal connections with militia leaders. He also cultivated the Islamic Republic's relationship with other *revisionist* powers. Soleimani traveled to Moscow in 2015 to convince Russian president Vladimir Putin to intercede in the Syrian civil war. Tehran's construction of a pan-Shia militia movement allows it to attack its adversaries, maintain plausible deniability, and reinforce its forward defense deterrence architecture.

The Quds Force's transfer of missiles as well as conventional arms achieves the Islamic Republic's deterrence and regional power projection aims—strategic aims that are, furthermore, reinforced by a large conventional land, naval, and air force.

IRGC and the Artesh

Iran's military blends asymmetric and conventional capabilities. Table 3.2 outlines the responsibilities and capabilities of these forces. Counting reserves, Iran's conventional and special forces number over half a million people. Within this force's structure, the IRGC's domestic Basij militia protects the country from internal subversion. The Basij crushed 2009 protests over the result of a disputed presidential election, and in 2018, it repressed demonstrations against Iran's regional policies and stagnant economy. Its members undergo intense ideological indoctrination. Basij membership is often a pathway into the IRGC.

IRGC's land force has over one hundred thousand members, and it is the country's elite force to protect it from invasion. Trained in asymmetric warfare techniques, IRGC has joined the Quds Force in expeditionary operations in Lebanon, Syria, Iraq, and Yemen. Its members undergo intense ideological and religious indoctrination that matches and at times exceeds their fighting skills.

The IRGC's commanders dominate Iran's major national security policy-making apparatus, and its influence with the supreme leaders vastly exceeds that of Iran's Artesh conventional force. Along with its Basij domestic militia, it cooperates with the nation's intelligence and law enforcement to preserve internal order.

The IRGC-Navy is responsible for maritime and airspace defense. The naval force protects the Persian Gulf and the strategic Strait of Hormuz. Numbering twenty thousand members, the IRGC-Navy controls hundreds of patrol boats equipped with antiship missiles, commands dozens of North Korean–designed Yono-class midget submarines, and has five thousand mines and hundreds of coastal and cruise missile batteries at its disposal. It specializes in swarming tactics employing light vessels that can easily navigate the Gulf's shallow waters and hide along its rugged coast. The IRGC's naval contingent is especially gifted at mining operations against commercial tanker traffic, a tactic it has employed against Sunni and Israeli shipping in the Gulf.

The IRGC–Aerospace Force is responsible for the development of, control over, and use of the Islamic Republic's missile precision project. The Aerospace Force's 2020 launching of a satellite puts the Islamic Republic on the cusp of developing ICBM capability. Much of Iran's missiles and rockets

Table 3.2. Iranian Asymmetric and Conventional Capabilities

Armed forces branch	Islamic Revolutionary Guard Corps (IRGC), Quds Force (QF), and Basij militia	Artesh
Responsibilities	Protection of Islamic Republic from internal subversion and external attack. QF responsible for the projection of Iranian overseas asymmetric power. IRGC and Basij militia committed to the defense of the Iranian homeland, the preservation of the Islamic Republic, and the propagation of its revolutionary values.	Protection of Islamic Republic from external military attack. No internal security functions or propagandistic functions.
Land capability	100,000 IRGC members, 5,000 IRGC-QF personnel, and 100,000 Basij militants. IRGC-QF responsible for weapons transfers and the training of overseas proxy forces, including the provision of antitank missiles and rockets.	350,000 personnel. Conventional force designed to protect the Iranian homeland from external threats.
Air force responsibilities	IRGC-Aerospace responsible for missile program and missile defense systems. IRGC-QF oversees and coordinates rocket, drone, and missile transfers to overseas proxy forces. No estimates of IRGC-Aerospace member composition.	Iranian air force comprises 30,000 members. Oversees the maintenance of conventional combat aircraft and drones.
Naval force responsibilities	IRGC-Navy has 20,000 members that oversee coastal defense and the projection of Iranian naval capability in the Persian Gulf and the Red Sea.	Naval forces comprise 18,000 members. Responsibilities overlap with Iran's Artesh naval branch in the protection of Persian Gulf and projection of Iranian power in the Red Sea. Projection of conventional naval power in the Caspian and Mediterranean.
Weapons System Control and Command Structure	Joint headquarters with control over IRGC and Artesh; reports directly to the Supreme Leader. IRGC-Aerospace al-Ghadir Missile Command responsible for missile defense, missile development, and offensive capability. Shares responsibility with Khatam al-Anbiya Air Defense Headquarters, which oversees surface-to-air missiles. Control over ballistic, cruise, antiship, and coastal defense missile batteries. IRGC-Navy responsible for patrol boats, fourteen North Korean-made midget subs, and use of 3,000–5,000 naval mines.	Control over conventional forces that include some 1,650 tanks, 330 combat aircraft, artillery batteries, larger naval vessels including four corvette destroyers and three Kilo submarines.

Source: Congressional Research Service, "Iran's Foreign and Defense Policies," 12–16.

Table 3.3. Iran's Rockets and Missiles (Ranges, Technology
Sources, and Proxy Transfers)

Iranian weapon system	Missile range	Adaptations of foreign-source technology	Transfer to proxy
Fajr rocket	40 miles	Chinese WS-1	Hezbollah and Hamas
al-Shahab-1,2, and Qiam short-range ballistic missiles	150–400 miles	North Korea Scud series	Hezbollah, Iraqi PMF, and Houthis
Shahab-3 (Meteor) and variant medium-range missiles	600 miles	North Korea No Dong series	No evidence of transfer
Soumar and Quds-1 land-based cruise missile	1,200 miles	Russian Kh-55 series	Houthi rebels
Noor, Ghadir, and antiship and coastal defense missiles	Up to 2,500 miles	Chinese C802 and CSSC missile 2 and 3 series	Hezbollah and Houthis
BM-25 intermediate range missile	Up to 2,500 miles	North Korean Musudan missile technology	No evidence of transfer to proxy groups
ICBM Capacity	February 2020 successful launch of Qased space launch vehicle and placement of satellite in space	North Korea No Dong liquid-fuel engine	Potential for transfer

Source: Defense Intelligence Agency, "Iran Military Power: Ensuring Regime Survival and Securing Regional Dominance."

are based on North Korean, Chinese, and Russian designs that have been progressively developed by Tehran's industrial defense infrastructure. Table 3.3 sketches Iran's ballistic and rocket missile forces in terms of their aerial ranges, source technology, and transfer to aligned groups across the Middle East.

The al-Ghadir Missile Command Center controls Tehran's formidable missile arsenal. Iranian intermediate-range ballistic missiles have projected ranges of over two thousand kilometers, allowing them to hit targets across the Persian Gulf, the Middle East, and southeastern Europe. These weapons augment the Aerospace Force's short-range and cruise missiles, which are an integral part of the country's coastal and air defense system.

The Aerospace Force has the capacity to strike all of Israel's major cities and strategic military assets. Though no US service members were killed in Iran's reprisal attacks following America's killing of IRGC-QF commander Qasem Soleimani, dozens of Iran's ballistic missiles successfully hit American and Iraqi military installations. The accuracy and lethality of Iran's precision missile project have improved over time.

The IRGC's air wing was pivotal in the development of Tehran's combat drone program, which has supplemented cruise missile attacks on Saudi oil and airport facilities. Tehran's December 2019 attacks against the kingdom's Aramco oil facility were devastating. Iran's cruise missiles, for example, halved the country's oil exports for a day. IRGC–Aerospace Force, moreover, is the primary agent that transfers missiles, rockets, and drones to the foreign operations Quds Force.

IRGC-QF's five-thousand-member force is Tehran's main expeditionary agent responsible for arming, financing, training, and advising Shia and aligned militias across the Middle East. With the Quds Force's prominent role in Iran's ambitious regional militia and missile strategy, it is difficult to overestimate its significance. Under Soleimani's development, Iran created a panethnic Shia militia numbering 190,000 members.

The Quds Force's transfer of domestic and foreign-made rockets, missiles, drones, and conventional arms (see table 3.3) to advance its proxy militia project has facilitated these groups' armed capability. They are a vital conduit to realize Tehran's ambitious land bridge linking Iran-supported militias from Baghdad to Beirut. The Quds Force secured the Assad regime's military survival by recruiting and deploying hundreds of thousands of Lebanese, Iraqi, Syrian, Afghan, and Pakistani militia members to combat antigovernment rebels.

The Quds Force's dominance in foreign policymaking has bred contention within Iran's government.[56] Despite the historic role the IRGC has played in defense planning, Iran has recently prioritized the enhancement of its conventional force capacity.[57] Chronically underfunded with antiquated shah-era heavy weapons, the Artesh is a formidable military force. Organized into a brigade structure, the Iranian army numbers over 350,000 soldiers, controls some 1,650 tanks, and has thousands of artillery pieces and mortars at its disposal.

Iranian defense doctrine views the Artesh as a conventional and a guerrilla force. Should the army fail to repulse an invasion, it is trained to revert to asymmetric insurgent tactics to exhaust a foreign invasion force. Artesh's special forces would organize popular resistance to foreign occupation.

Buttressing the Artesh's land capability are a deepwater navy, combat aircraft, and missile defense systems. Numbering eighteen thousand sailors and air members, the Iranian navy has four corvette destroyers and three Kilo submarines, and it is tasked with the projection of conventional sea power in the Red and Caspian Seas as well as the mounting of operations in the Mediterranean.

Iran's navy has engaged in joint naval exercises with the Chinese and Russian navies and could very well benefit from Tehran's 2021 $400 billion security agreement with Beijing. Though much attention has been given to the Iranian air force's thirty-three thousand antiquated French, Russian, and American combat aircraft, the Artesh's air command is an important player in the country's missile defense system.

Its Khatam al-Anbiya Air Defense Headquarters oversees the use of surface-to-air missiles. This includes the management of the sophisticated Russian SA-20 system that is a vital asset in the country's defense against air strikes against its nuclear weapon infrastructure. It is one of the few areas where the Artesh exercises a critical defense responsibility.

There are, moreover, signals that Tehran is emphasizing its conventional military. Units of the Artesh were deployed to Syria to assist the Assad regime's reconquest of Aleppo from rebel forces. Comments by the supreme leader in 2016 prioritized upgrading conventional forces.[58]

Critics have argued that Tehran's light mobile forces, asymmetric tactics, and proxy militias would be infective in war against the American military.[59] The supreme leader's remarks may be an acknowledgment that Iran cannot exclusively rely on the IRGC and its aligned militias to adequately defend the nation. By strengthening the Artesh, Iran may also be planning for a future conflict with the United States in the post-Soleimani era.

Conflict Scenarios: Past, Present, and Future

How Iran will respond if attacked by Israel or the United States preoccupies Western security experts.[60] Analysts speculate that attacking Iran could have destabilizing consequences throughout the Persian Gulf and the Middle East.[61] On the basis of past military clashes, however, the last few years do offer clues to Iran's potential retaliatory actions.

For over forty years, Tehran has waged a concerted proxy terrorist and in-surgent campaign to undermine Israeli security across the world. Iran-directed Hezbollah terrorists have killed Jews in Argentina, India, and Bulgaria.[62] The Islamic Republic's hatred of Israel reflects religious, geo-military, and polit-ical considerations. Tehran views Israel as an occupier of Muslim territory that includes Jerusalem's al-Aqsa Mosque, the third-holiest site in Islam.[63] As a self-declared defender of the *ummah*, the Islamic Republic campaigns for Jerusalem's reconquest and the annihilation of the Jewish state. Annually, the Islamic Republic celebrates al-Quds Day, underscoring the regime's determi-nation to reimpose Islamic rule over Jerusalem.

In the 1980s, Iran created the *axis of resistance*, embracing the Palestinian cause by providing weaponry, finances, and technical expertise to Islamist Hamas and PIJ, whose principal aim is the liquidation of the Zionist state. By appropriating the Palestinian issue, Tehran hoped to overcome Sunni re-sistance to its Shiite imamate project.

Within Israel's occupied territories, PIJ's ideology, finances, and tactics are squarely aligned with Tehran's regional aims.[64] PIJ is the Islamic Republic's main Palestinian proxy force, and unlike Hamas, it is not conflicted over be-ing supported by a Shiite regime. Its late founder Fathi Shikaki was an admir-er of Khomeini's Islamic Third Way, seeing it as a bridge across the Muslim confessional divide.

Tehran is the PIJ's sole financial patron (expending $30 million annually) and weapons provider.[65] Because of its financial leverage over the group, it has been able to stifle any internal resistance to its directives. Along with Hamas, PIJ has waged a concerted terrorist and insurgent campaign against the Jewish state since the 1980s. Without Iranian support, it is unlikely that Hamas and PIJ would have been able to launch over four thousand rockets in the first week of their May 2021 conflict with Jerusalem.[66]

Tehran's annihilationist goal toward Israel is also driven by Shia escha-tological beliefs, some of whose adherents see the destruction of Israel as a precursor to the hidden imam's return and humanity's liberation from satanic evil.[67] During his two terms as Iranian president, Mahmoud Ahmadinejad denied the Holocaust, vowed to destroy the Zionist state, and connected Israel's liquidation with the Mahdi's reappearance.

Iran created Hezbollah in the 1980s to expel American and French peacekeepers from the country and undermine Israeli military operations in Lebanon. Forty years of Islamic Republic military and economic patronage have made the Party of God a quasi state whose weaponry and training eclipse the Lebanese army's capabilities. Its sponsorship of Hezbollah martyrdom attacks during Israel's occupation of southern Lebanon cost the Jewish state over a thousand soldiers.

Hezbollah has moreover been transformed into a potent expeditionary force whose entry into the Syrian civil war is credited with the Assad regime's preservation. Under IRGC direction, Hezbollah coordinated operations with the Russian military and operated as a conventional force. The Islamic Republic views Syria as a third front against Israel and as a vital transit point to resupply its Hezbollah proxy with precision-guided weapons and conventional arms in Lebanon. With the Assad's regime's overthrow in December 2024, this third front is no longer available.

Tehran's military entrenchment in Syria has been frustrated by Israeli countermeasures. Jerusalem's air strikes against IRGC and Hezbollah weapons supply convoys, military installations, and missile development sites have hampered Iran's plan to convert Syria into a third battlefront. Israel's *mabam* (war between the wars) campaign prevented Iran from using Syria as a base of operations to launch precision-guided missiles against the Jewish state.[68]

On October 7, 2023, Palestinian Hamas and Palestinian Islamic Jihad (PIJ) attacked Israeli border communities killing twelve hundred people. Israel's subsequent invasion of Gaza to destroy Hamas's military infrastructure ignited a shooting war with Hezbollah along Jerusalem's northern border. Israel's military campaigns against Hamas and Hezbollah have unraveled Iran's resistance project.

Much has changed since Israel's military campaign against Iran's proxy forces after Hamas's October 7 attacks. With Hamas vanquished, Hezbollah weakened, and the Assad regime overthrown by Turkish-backed rebels, Iran's resistance project is in serious jeopardy.

The Islamic Republic will be forced to rely on Iraqi and Yemeni proxies and depend more on its own military forces to protect its weakened position in the Middle East. Hezbollah's diminished armed capability requires more Iranian arms. Iran will need to augment and improve its own ballistic missile offensive and defensive capabilities.

Israeli defense planners have employed countermeasures against Iran's missile and militia strategy. Jerusalem has improved its Arrow and Sling missile defense capability to offset the IRGC-Hezbollah Lebanese missile-rocket arsenal.[69] Acting in solidarity with Hamas and Hezbollah after the October

7 attacks, Iran's April and October 2023 missile and drone attacks were neutralized by Israeli defensive measures. Israel's sophisticated underground bunker and tunnel seismic detection equipment allow it to identify and destroy subterranean transit sites along its Lebanese, Syrian, and occupied territory borders.

Iran's retaliation against Israeli strikes in Syria, Lebanon, and the Gaza Strip has failed. Though Tehran employed drone operations and missile fire against Israeli forces, these efforts have netted only one down fighter jet. Its cyber campaign against an Israeli desalination plant failed to yield significant damage. The Islamic Republic has even resorted to having its tankers spill oil on Israel's coast.

Syria, the Gaza Strip, and Lebanon are not the only battlegrounds where Iranian and Israeli forces have clashed. Jerusalem has sabotaged the Islamic Republic's nuclear enrichment facilities at Natanz and assassinated scientists working on its precision missile project, including Mohsen Fakhrizadeh, who is considered the architect of Tehran's nuclear weapons program.

The last few years (post–Arab Spring [2011–2024]), moreover, have witnessed a dramatic escalation. Israel is suspected of undermining Iran's advanced centrifuge program at its Natanz enrichment research center through covert bomb attacks and cyber warfare. Though Tehran has vowed to avenge Israel's actions against its nuclear program, it has yet to launch any major military operations against the Jewish state.

Should covert operations and cyber measures fail to derail the Islamic Republic's nuclear weapons program, Israel is prepared to attack Iran's nuclear facilities with a concerted bombing campaign. Enforcing the Begin Doctrine, named after the late prime minister's authorization of a 1981 Israeli air strike against Iraq's nuclear reactor, Israel bombed a North Korea–assisted construction site for a nuclear reactor facility in Syria in 2007.[70] Iran's atomic weapons program may be next in line.

Equipped with laser-guided JBU-28 bunker-busting bombs, Israeli fighter jets would attempt to penetrate the Islamic Republic's reinforced concrete underground nuclear complexes. Logistically, Israeli military strikes against Iran's nuclear program would be complex and risky.[71] The Israeli Air Force would have to fly thousands of miles over foreign territory, navigate past Iran's air defense system, and launch multiple strikes against dozens of heavily fortified Iranian facilities. At best, Israeli defense planners estimate that Jerusalem could degrade but not destroy Tehran's atomic program.

Underscoring Iran's intent to eradicate the Zionist presence in Palestine, the Islamic Republic in January 2021 passed legislation calling for Israel's liquidation.[72] Israel and Iran have clashed in the Persian Gulf. In what is characterized as a *shadow naval war*, Jerusalem and Tehran mine each other's commercial and military traffic in the Persian Gulf.[73] Hezbollah's plots to attack Israeli interests in African countries have been foiled by joint Israeli-Ethiopian and Sudanese intelligence operations. Matthew Levitt notes that recent Iranian terror operations against Israeli interests in Thailand and India have yielded more failure than success.[74]

Tehran has, however, been more effective in attacking US and Sunni Gulf interests.[75] The Islamic Republic–backed PMF has used rocket and mortar attacks against US bases in Iraq. Iran was instrumental in the 2019 storming of the US Embassy in Baghdad. Iran-supported Iraqi militias have killed US soldiers and contractors.

Iran's strikes against US positions in Iraq forced Washington's hand. In January 2020, the United States killed IRGC-QF commander Qasem Soleimani and Iraqi Kataib Hezbollah leader Abu Mahdi al-Muhandis at Baghdad International Airport. The Trump administration's assassination of the second most influential player in Iran's national security apparatus produced shock and outrage in the Islamic Republic. Soleimani's killing was a potent message to Iran that it can no longer kill Americans with impunity.

Shocked by his killing, Iran initiated a hard-revenge retaliatory campaign that was more rhetorical than militarily substantive. Though it launched ballistic missiles against US air bases in northern and central Iraq, Tehran's advanced warning to the Iraqi government was relayed to American military commanders, allowing the targeted troops to protect themselves in underground bunkers.

The percussive force of Iran's missile bombardment did produce brain trauma for hundreds of US troops but failed to yield one American fatality. The Islamic Republic's ineffective retaliatory campaign was magnified by its air defense downing of a Ukrainian passenger jet that it mistakenly believed was an American attack plane.

Iran's response to Soleimani's killing demonstrates its fear of confrontation with a militarily superior and technologically advanced US military. The Islamic Republic has, however, mounted devastating attacks against the Saudi kingdom's economic installations via its missile and drone support for Houthi rebels in Yemen.

Throughout the Yemeni civil war, IRGC trainers and advisers have shipped precision-guided missiles, advanced combat drones, and conventional weapons to the Shia Houthi rebels fighting against Saudi-UAE-supported government.[76] Today the Houthi insurgents are in control of much of the country. As reported in a 2022 study by Michael Knights, the Houthis have created a centralized command and control system mirrored on the Hezbollah model that has sufficient flexibility to give its regional commanders significant autonomy to mount offensive operations against Saudi- and UAE-backed forces.[77]

Tehran's Houthi rebel proxies have conducted dozens of missile and drone attacks against Saudi Arabia, including assaults against its oil and airport facilities. Iran, moreover, has used cyberattack operations against Saudi petroleum and finance corporations in retaliation for the kingdom's support of the Trump administration's maximum-pressure campaign against the Islamic Republic.[78]

Though the Biden administration relaxed sanctions enforcement in a failed effort to secure Iran's assent for a reconstituted JCPOA, Tehran's Iraqi and Syrian proxies continued their rocket and drone attacks against US troops in Syria and Iraq. These attacks increased after the October 2023 Israel-Hamas-Hezbollah war and American support for the actions of the Israeli Defense Forces in Gaza and South Lebanon. Cognizant of American military superiority, Tehran has carefully calibrated its actions.

Iran cautiously attacks US and Israeli interests but appears less risk averse when striking against America's Arab Gulf allies. With its foreign reserves dwindling, its oil export capacity debilitated, and its Central Bank denied credit from international financial markets, Tehran has escalated its military activities in the Persian Gulf.

Iran-backed PMF forces continue to harass US bases and support convoys in Iraq. IRGC patrol boats routinely threaten US warships in the Gulf. Should the incoming Trump administration aggressively pursue economic sanctions against the Islamic Republic, military escalation in the Persian Gulf and the Middle East could occur. Under such a scenario, Iran is likely to hit Saudi oil facilities and significantly increase its mining and patrol boat operations against tanker commercial traffic. Attacks against US forces stationed in Iraq by the Iran-backed PMF would likely be more severe.

Since October 2023, Iran's Middle East system of alliances has been significantly degraded. Israel's dismantling of Hamas's military structure in

Gaza, Hezbollah's weakened position in Lebanon, and the fall of the Assad re-gime in Syria have forced Tehran to rely more on its Iraqi and Yemeni proxies. It will also be forced to rely more on its own military forces to counter what could be a more aggressive Trump administration whose plans for the Middle East have yet to be unveiled.

It is easily imaginable that American military force will be used more sig-nificantly in the Persian Gulf and the Middle East if Iran attempts to develop nuclear weapons or use its Yemeni and Iraqi proxies against the US and allied interests in the region. What is clear is that further instability and warfare will likely continue and may escalate.

4

The Ideological, Financial, and Environmental Forces Leading to the North Korea–Iran Rogue Alliance

Bruce E. Bechtol Jr. and Anthony N. Celso

Despite the objections from some academics and pundits—many of whom either are uninformed or have a political agenda—the long-standing relationship between North Korea and Iran has been ongoing almost since the very beginning of the theocratic government in Tehran was formed after the fall of the shah. Thus, it will be the goal of this chapter to examine, analyze, and assess why this relationship began, what it has involved, and how it has evolved over the years leading up to the state of affairs as it exists today.

As we move through the background, context, and operations of this important and evolving relationship, we will discuss the formulation of the heart of many of these activities—Office 39. We will then address what started the arms trade that is a pillar of this relationship that began in the 1980s because of Iran's international isolation during the Iran-Iraq War. The relationship continued into the 1990s, which was an important period. During the 2000s, North Korea continued to support Iran with both new weapons systems (by North Korean standards) and military advisers.

Beginning in 2011, a quickly evolving series of events known as the Arab Spring occurred, and because Syria was an ally supported by both Iran and North Korea, it set off a large-scale set of increased proliferation activities—often from North Korea to Iran and Syria or from North Korea to Syria and paid for by Iran. We believe the Joint Comprehensive Plan of Action (JCPOA) agreement that Iran entered into with the United States and European nations had important similarities to North Korea's Agreed Framework signed in 1994, and we will analyze this. While many analysts know of the numerous missile sales deals from North Korea to Iran, the latest missile deal, of the most powerful missiles ever, has received little attention—but it will in this chapter. We will also provide assessments of North Korea's suspected support to Iran's nuclear program and new developments that involve China.

In the remainder of the chapter, we will proceed to examine Iran and North Korea as revisionist powers. The ideological, transactional, and strategic drivers of Iran's deadly alliance with North Korea are detailed. The destabilizing geostrategic consequences of this revisionist partnership are felt across the Middle East. North Korean assistance for Iran's missile and militia strategy advances Tehran's efforts to become a dominant regional power. Despite varying approaches, no administration has effectively contended with the geo-military challenges this partnership portends.

The Formulation of Office 39

North Korea experienced moderately successful economics and stability during the Cold War when it served as a satellite of the USSR. The Soviet Union was responsible for almost completely subsidizing the North Korean economy. As the Cold War ended, Moscow ceased North Korean subsidies.[1] This caused the economic collapse and starvation that began in the early 1990s and continues to a lesser extent today. The effects of no longer being a Soviet satellite were immediate and profound. Food, electricity, fuel, and nearly all societal needs were drastically reduced.[2] Because of this, there has always been the odd question of how Pyongyang could keep such a large military and even proliferate its weapons all over the world despite numerous sanctions and (what was largely) a failure to join the international system.

Though it has remained mostly unknown for many years, North Korea continues to survive economically largely because of what is known as Office 39. Kim Il-sung formed Office 39 in 1974 because the leadership of the Democratic People's Republic of Korea (DPRK) realized that their economy was helpless without Soviet subsidies and needed a way to become more self-supportive. To lead this new entity, Kim Il-sung chose his young (at the time) son, Kim Jong-il. Office 39's mission is quite simple: to generate funds for the regime.[3] Thus, beginning with its founding in 1974, this entity oversees all operations that raise money for the regime—some of them quite astounding. The DPRK is a proven counterfeiter of US money (called su-pernotes because they are so well done) and cigarettes and undertakes many other activities such as using North Korean workers overseas (as Office 39 takes most of their salaries). These are all interesting and money-raising op-erations. But the operation that makes the most money for North Korea is now and traditionally has been military proliferation. The largest customer is Iran.[4]

Office 39 maintains direct control over what can be accurately described as a slush fund for the Kim family and ultimately the regime. The money generated for Office 39 comes from places all over the world. The funds must then be laundered illegally in banks and front companies, placed in a variety of locations worldwide (but in Asia more than anywhere), and used for the regime. Annually, some of these funds are used in the purchase of luxury items, such as expensive European cars, liquor, jewelry, and clothing used by the Kim family and the elite in North Korea. But of even more importance to regional and global security, a large portion of these funds is also used to advance and maintain North Korea's weapons of mass destruction (WMD) programs and to support the military.[5]

North Korea has an incredibly diverse set of front companies, set up in a weblike network in places like China, Malaysia, Singapore, and even nations in sub-Saharan Africa and the Middle East. But all of these entities (and there are hundreds of them) answer in one way or another to Office 39. The office comes directly under Kim Jong-un. According to several reports, Kim Jong-un's sister, Kim Yo-jong, now has the chief responsibilities for running Office 39. So, getting back to how North Korea survives despite a basket case economy and heavy sanctions, there can be no doubt that it is because of the country's sanctions-busting illicit activities—activities that flourish because of the expertise and international corruption of Office 39. A North Korean defector who spoke to the press in 2018 stated that illicit activities make up around 40 percent of North Korea's real economy.[6]

North Korea has seen sanctions against the regime increasing gradually—especially since 2006, when Pyongyang detonated its first nu-clear weapon. In response to this, the operations of Office 39 have evolved and often undergone rapidly changing tactics, techniques, and procedures.

The UN's declaration of Resolution 1718 (2006) started the ball rolling on sanctions that made it increasingly difficult for North Korea to conduct international trade of any kind around the world. Thus, it was rather disappointing when the first report released publicly by the UN Panel of Experts (2010) stated, "The Democratic People's Republic of Korea also employs a broad range of techniques to mask its financial transactions, including the use of overseas entities, shell companies, informal transfer mechanisms, cash couriers and barter arrangements. However, it must still, in most cases, rely on access to the international financial system to complete its financial operations. In structuring these transactions, attempts are made to mix illicit transactions with otherwise legitimate business activities in such a way as to hide the illicit activity."[7]

The UN Panel of Experts continued to actively observe, analyze, and recommend actions to be taken by member states to contain or destroy North Korea's illicit and illegal activities. Despite these efforts, the DPRK has not ceased its widespread military proliferation and acquisition of everything from luxury goods to badly needed oil. Even more importantly, North Korea continues to launder the funds "earned" from illicit activities, maintaining them and depositing them in banks and front companies all over Asia, the Middle East, and Africa to maintain the regime and pad Kim Jong-un's slush funds. As stated in the UN Panel of Experts' report from 2021, "The Democratic People's Republic of Korea continues to access international banking channels in violation of United Nations sanctions, mainly by using third-party intermediaries. It continued illegally to acquire virtual currencies and to conduct cyberattacks against global banks to evade financial sanctions. Designated entities such as the Reconnaissance General Bureau and the Munitions Industry Department are actively seeking to obtain fiat currencies and virtual assets by illicit means, the former through hacking and the latter by illicitly dispatching information technology workers abroad."[8] The evidence continues to show that though the international community is now better informed about North Korea's proliferation, sales of illegal goods, counterfeiting, and money laundering and despite the credible assessment that these activities provide funds used for the military (including the nuclear program)[9] and the regime, it still appears that the actions taken to prevent North Korea from bypassing sanctions have been too little and too late.

DPRK-Iran Arms Trade Begins in the 1980s: The Iran-Iraq War

North Korea was heavily subsidized by the Soviet Union throughout most of the Cold War. The Soviet Union was rewarded for this with the DPRK sending troops, weapons, and military support to war zones such as Angola and Syria.[10] Pyongyang also made large-scale arms transfers to countries and nonstate actors all over the Middle East and Africa. The bill was of course paid by Moscow. North Korea's activities during the Cold War included proliferation, arms transfers, and sending military advisers.[11] Typically, the countries and nonstate actors receiving support did not pay money (or anything else), and the USSR footed the funding (including paying North Korea for providing this assistance).

This began to change in the mid-1980s and ended completely in the 1990s. Countries such as Syria and Ethiopia that had been receiving their arms and advising for free no longer got that special privilege. The same applied to North Korea. They now had to pay for everything from the Soviet Union. That meant that arms deals completely financed by Moscow no longer occurred. But this was also a glass-half-full scenario. Because of the connections built up with these state and nonstate actors, North Korea could now continue to conduct arms deals. Only this time, it would be on a cash-and-carry basis or by a trade in commodities.[12]

The case with Iran was different. Iran was an ally of the United States until the fall of the shah. It was then that Iran basically became a pariah. Iran was no longer an ally of the United States, but the Persian nation was also not an ally of the USSR. This meant that in case of a war or major conflict, Iran would be badly in need of arms and advisers. Enter North Korea. While Iran was essentially a theocracy and North Korea a Communist state, they basically had two things in common: (1) a deep hatred of the United States and (2) a mutual need to buy and sell arms and all of the factors that go with that. Then and now it should be clear. Iran was the buyer and North Korea was the seller.

North Korea was still in the Soviet sphere of influence, and the Cold War was still on during this time frame. But it appears that arms deals with Iran were only with North Korea (not the USSR), and the two dealt with each other exclusively. Of course, the Iran-Iraq War exploded in the 1980s. Iran was badly in need of arms and training. North Korea was badly in need of money (and it would get worse). Thus, during the Cold War, because of a desperate need for arms, the North Korea–Iran relationship was born. Both states largely remain pariahs, and both states continue to profit from this relationship. Regarding how North Korea supported Iran during its war with Iraq, between 1980 and 1985, Iran got $4 billion worth of arms from Pyongyang. By the end of the war, there were reportedly more than three hundred North Korean military advisers on the ground.[13]

The JCPOA, the Arab Spring, and the Agreed Framework

It is of some importance to mention the Agreed Framework and to compare and contrast it with the JCPOA that the United States and other nations signed with Iran. The Agreed Framework was signed in 1994, and while the agreement had many details, the main focus was that North Korea froze but did not dismantle its plutonium nuclear program at Yongbyon north of Pyongyang. The agreement essentially came apart when the United States realized that North Korea was violating the agreement by developing a highly enriched uranium program with Pakistan's assistance. After a confrontation, both Pyongyang and Washington declared the agreement null and void, UN monitors were sent home, and North Korea began again processing plutonium at the Yongbyon facility. Thus, the history of the Agreed Framework shows us that when a nation—by agreement—freezes but does not dismantle a WMD program, when things go sour, that nation can simply unfreeze the program and go right back to developing and maintaining the weapons that will create instability in the international security environment.[14]

With North Korea, the Agreed Framework ended up being a complete failure. That is why it is so surprising that the Obama administration was so intent on the JCPOA. In fact, there was nothing comprehensive about the JCPOA, and it did not dismantle Iran's nuclear program. To make things worse, it only froze Iran's nuclear program for ten years. When Donald Trump became United States president, he declared the JCPOA null and void—which was his constitutional right since the agreement was not a treaty. But during the Obama administration, as billions of dollars of Iranian-owned hard currency were unfrozen in American banks and sent to Iran as cash, Tehran used unfrozen funds to support its steady supply of arms purchases to Syria and nonstate actors such as the Houthis, Hezbollah, and Hamas.[15] All of this increased during the Arab Spring. Thus, during the Arab Spring, North Korea experienced a real boon for its military-industrial complex (such as it is). North Korean small arms, big-ticket items such as tanks and artillery, chemical weapons, ballistic missiles, and military trainers all flowed into the Middle East as billions of dollars of profits from these efforts went to Office 39. Now we will turn to why and how Iran is involved in this important strategic relationship.

Iran as Revisionist Power (1979–2021)

Iran's grievances against the Western global order reflect ideological, nationalistic, and strategic motives.[16] Resentment over US and Israeli military support for the shah's autocratic secular regime remains. This facilitates the Islamic Republic's popular mobilization of anti-Western hatred. Tehran's animosities, moreover, extend to US-aligned Sunni Gulf States that have historically repressed their Shiite minorities.

Iran's hostility toward Washington and its Middle East allies drives its efforts to develop a Shia imamate across the Arab Middle East.[17] Preconditions of this are the exodus of American military forces in the region, the quelling of Sunni Gulf States, and the liquidation of the Zionist presence in Palestine.

The Iranian regime's Islamic Revolutionary Guard Corps–Quds Force (IRGC-QF) exemplifies Tehran's determination to destroy Israel and reclaim Jerusalem as a Muslim city. Iran's size, ample resources, and strategic Persian Gulf location make it a formidable and natural power in the region. Here Persian imperialism, shaped within a Shia revolutionary caste, drives Iran's ambitions to become a regional hegemonic power.

The Islamic Republic's forty-plus-year export of Shia militancy and terrorism represents the consecration of late Ayatollah Ruhollah Khomeini's desire to create a Shia-dominated Islamic *ummah* uncontaminated by Western influence.[18] The building blocks of Tehran's revolutionary state reflect religious and strategic interests, regime preservation, and imperialistic imperatives. Guided by Iran's supreme leader Ayatollah Ali Khamenei, the IRGC-QF is the institutional vehicle to impose the Islamic Republic's interests on the region.[19]

The grand design for Iran is a pan-Shia state stretching from the Persian Gulf to the Levant. Since the 1979 Revolution, the Islamic Republic's regional ambitions have unfolded opportunistically. Iranian foreign policy has adjusted to the shifting winds of Middle East conflict and has been indelibly shaped by the sectarian passions laid bare by the wars in Iraq, Syria, and Yemen.[20] Iran's export of its revolutionary doctrine has sought to balance Islamic ecumenicalism with the projection of Shia influence across the Arab Middle East.

Tensions between these two goals were initially overcome by Sunni Arab hostility toward Israel and by Tehran's support for the Palestinian cause. For decades, Iran's anti-Zionist *axis of resistance* with Shia Hezbollah and Sunni Hamas successfully navigated the sectarian religious divide.

Tehran's support for Hezbollah's insurgency against Israel's 1983–2000 occupation of southern Lebanon provided a source of unity between anti-Zionist Shia and Sunni groups. Iran's 1979 Revolution and the 1989 Afghan mujahidin defeat of Soviet forces, moreover, were interpreted as heralding a period of *Islamic rebirth*. So significant were these events that terrorism expert David Rapoport viewed them as ushering a *fourth wave* of modern religious terror.[21]

The Islamic Republic's efforts to overcome Sunni-Shia tensions exploited Judeophobic sentiments across the Arab Middle East to build support. Shia and Sunni jihadi groups saw Israel as a European neocolonial presence whose existence in formerly Islamic land denied Allah rightful sovereignty (*hakimiyah*) of his territorial domain. United by religious antipathy against Jews, Iran worked actively with Hamas, Hezbollah, the Assad regime, and Palestinian Islamic Jihad to undermine Israeli security in Lebanon, the West Bank, and the Gaza Strip.

Iran's *ecumenical moment* reached its apogee when Hezbollah resisted Israel's superior military might in the 2006 war, an outcome that won it the admiration of the Sunni Arab World. Tehran's export of rockets, mortars, and missiles (many with North Korean designs) and DPRK assistance in the construction of underground tunnels were instrumental in facilitating Hezbollah's ability to withstand Jerusalem's monthlong bombing campaign and territorial combat operations.[22]

Though anti-Zionism remains a pillar of Iranian foreign policy, it has, since the 2003 Iraq War, succumbed to a renewed sectarian emphasis that has damaged Tehran's reputation across the Sunni world. The Arab Spring's stimulation of sectarian tensions across the Middle East has strained Iran's ecumenical project.

Tehran continues its dual policy, often making opportunistic adjustments. Ironically, the fulcrum of Iran's ecumenical strategy has turned out to be a major sectarian albatross for the Islamic Republic. The preservation of the Assad regime was critical for the consummation of Iran's hegemonic ambitions to destroy Israel and forge its pan-Shia imamate. Historically, Syria was a key conduit for Iranian arms moving to Sunni Palestinian factions, an outgrowth of its Lebanon policy and its use of Hezbollah as a major military force in the region. Before the Arab Spring, Tehran's patronage of Palestinian jihadi groups worked to bridge the Sunni-Shia divide.

The 2011 Arab Spring protest movement, however, had the opposite impact. The movement's weakening of the regional state system accelerated sectarian tensions in religiously stratified Syria, Iraq, and Yemen. Sunni-dominated revolts against the Iranian-aligned Iraqi and Syrian regimes inflamed confessional fault lines across the Middle East.

Since the US-led 2003 toppling of Saddam Hussein's regime in Iraq and the empowering of the Shia majority, Iran's military footprint across the Middle East has grown. Iraqi Popular Mobilization Forces (PMF) backed by Iran are the power behind Baghdad's throne. Hezbollah, moreover, is a key power broker in Lebanon. With a pronounced military presence across the region, Iran and aligned Shia militias have sparked Sunni Arab resistance.[23]

The civil wars in Syria and Yemen threaten Shiite-aligned minorities. Syria's hosting of Shiite religious shrines and Sunni jihadist attacks against heterodox Muslim minorities have altered the foundation of Tehran's regional strategy. By 2015, the Sunni revolt against the beleaguered Assad regime threatened vital Iranian interests, triggering IRGC and Hezbollah military intervention.

IRGC-QF was instrumental in the recruitment and resettlement of tens of thousands of Shiite Afghan and Pakistani fighters into Syria in support of the Assad regime.[24] Such measures have damaged Tehran's relations with Palestinian Hamas and led to widespread anti-Shiite resentment across the Arab world.

Al-Qaeda and Islamic State ideological discourse, for example, evokes a nefarious Zionist-Crusader-Iranian complex intent on the destruction of Sunni Islam.[25] The confessional antagonisms of the Syria conflict sparked an unprecedented flight of foreign Shiite and Sunni fighters into the country. Shia and Sunni Islamic eschatology sees sectarian discord in the Levant as a harbinger of the Mahdi's return laying the basis for an apocalyptic war and Muslim global conquest.[26] Driven by end-time visions, Sunni and Shiite jihadists butcher each other in the sectarian killing fields of Iraq, Syria, and Yemen.

Iran's decades-long efforts to form a Shia *arc of influence* stretching from Tehran to Lebanon are largely complete. Under the guidance of the late IRGC-QF commander Qasem Soleimani, Tehran created Arab Shia militias that wield veto power over the Iraqi and Lebanese governments, assisted in the Assad regime's preservation, and facilitated Houthi domination in Yemen.

Undergirding Soleimani's militia doctrine of asymmetric warfare was the Islamic Republic's export of tens of thousands of rockets, missiles, conventional weapons, improvised explosive devices, weapons platforms, and drone technology to aligned groups. With North Korean assistance, IRGC-QF trainers provide the technological expertise that allows these militias to construct missile assembly plants in Lebanon, Iraq, Syria, and Yemen.[27]

Tehran's regional dominance may irrevocably damage the Islamic Republic's ecumenical appeal. Long a difficult balancing act in a sectarian-prone Middle East, Iran's transethnic Shia militia strategy and weapons transfer programs have undermined its call for pan-Islamic unity. Anti-Shiism has become so pronounced in the region that Sunni nations work with Israel to frustrate Iranian ambitions.

The 2020 Abraham Accords establishing diplomatic relations among Israel, the United Arab Emirates (UAE), and Bahrain were forged in part by shared hostility toward Iran's increased influence in the Middle East. The Islamic Republic's ability to harmonize its *ecumenical* and *sectarian* projects is now compromised. Prospects for future equilibrium will be challenging. Having failed to navigate the Shia-Sunni divide, Iran's militia and missile strategy has reinforced the sectarian focus of its foreign policy.

Faced with Saudi-UAE opposition, American resistance, and Israel's determination to prevent its military entrenchment in Syria, Iran has strengthened its alliances with North Korea, Russia, and China. Tehran's fifty-year oil-and-cash-for-weapons alliance with Pyongyang has paid handsome dividends.

The Rise of the Revisionists and the Return of Great Power Competition

Once thought vanquished by globalization, the emergence of great power competition is now recognized in US national security documents.[28] This is a struggle that analysts argue the United States is ill prepared to manage. Rising *revisionist powers* hoping to upend the global and regional order designed and dominated by the United States is now seen as America's top security problem.

Since no one revisionist power has the political and economic wherewithal to directly challenge American interests, they have done so through cooperation with other regimes who have vested interests in the weakening of America. Collectively, they have pursued hybrid warfare strategies in gray-zone conflicts designed to maximize their geo-military position.

Iran's military cooperation with Russia in Syria, for example, has tried to assure the Assad regime's preservation; that was a critical node ensuring Moscow's and Tehran's regional influence.[29] Moscow's bombing campaign worked with IRGC-QF units, the Syrian army, and Hezbollah to quell the Sunni-dominated rebel insurgency. The Islamic Republic's alignment with Russia, China, and North Korea has been carefully cultivated and managed over a generation.

If anything, these alliances have strengthened as America seeks to extricate itself from costly interventions in the Middle East and central Asia. Tehran and Beijing's March 2021 $400 billion economic and military cooperation agreement, for example, provides the Islamic Republic with the financial means to pursue its regional agenda.[30] America's disastrous exodus from Afghanistan will hasten Russian and Chinese leverage in the war-torn country and is likely to result in good relations between Beijing, Moscow, and the victorious Taliban regime.

Despite their different cultures and politico-economic systems, revisionist powers have common strategic and transactional interests. Russia,[31] China,[32] and North Korea cooperate with Iran to fortify Tehran's military and economic capability. Collectively, they have assisted the Islamic Republic's efforts to become a rising power in the Middle East. Historically, these countries have cooperated in illicit activities designed to circumvent international sanctions imposed on Iran's nuclear weapons development programs. Criminal smuggling networks assist Iran's capacity to trade oil and money for advanced weaponry, the platforms that carry them, and dual-use technology related to WMD development. The concealment of North Korean weapons and spare parts in reflagged commercial shipping tankers aids Pyongyang's efforts to clandestinely export arms to the Middle East. Such proliferation is highly lucrative.[33]

At the same time, weapons proliferation serves as a critical financial lifeline for the North Korean regime. By some accounts, the DPRK earns $2–3 billion a year on sales to Iran and its proxies alone.[34] Like other revisionist powers, Iran scams the system by exploiting international clandestine networks. Criminal smugglers operating throughout the Gulf allow Tehran to violate UN resolutions aimed at curtailing its quest to develop a nuclear-armed ICBM.

Since the early 1980s, Iran's development of short-, medium-, and long-range missiles has been assisted by North Korea. Having successfully circumvented the international community's efforts to hamper its own development of nuclear weapons, Pyongyang is uniquely situated to assist Tehran's quest to develop WMD capacity. The majority of Iran's liquid-fuel ballistic missile series are based on North Korea's Scud, No Dong, and Musudan designs.[35] North Korean technicians and advisers play instrumental roles in assisting the progression of Iran's ballistic missile development programs, which are hidden in fortified underground bunkers built with Pyongyang's assistance. Forged by common ideological, transactional, and strategic interests, Iran's North Korean alliance has endured for over a generation.

The Iran–North Korea Partnership: The View from Tehran

The Iran–North Korea alliance reflects the convergent interests of revisionist powers aiming to undermine American influence across the globe. The strategic and transactional drivers of this policy (see table 4.1) have been shaped by anti-American sentiment. Both nations share a history of conflict with the West.

American intervention in the Korean conflict in the early 1950s and Washington's support for the shah's repressive regime have been utilized by Pyongyang and Tehran to instill hatred of the United States among their populations. Anti-Americanism represents a central pillar of North Korean Communism and Iranian Islamism. Both are revolutionary regimes intent on thwarting US geopolitical interests and America's alliances in the Middle East and Asia. Collectively, they seek America's regional military disengagement.

American-led efforts to isolate the Iranian and North Korean regimes, furthermore, provide sufficient incentives for cooperation. The Tehran-Pyongyang alliance assists their mutual survival and facilitates their military and economic capability. Reinforcing their antipathy toward Washington are America's alliances with hated regional adversaries.

American support for Japan, Israel, and Sunni Gulf Kingdoms exacerbates Pyongyang's and Tehran's anti-Western hatred by reinforcing historical resentments. Past Japanese atrocities on the Korean Peninsula, Jerusalem's military and economic cooperation with the shah's regime, and the Sunni-Shia conflict converge to reinforce hostility and paranoia toward American allies.

America's partnership with disliked regional adversaries reinforces conspiratorial thinking within the Iranian and North Korean governments. IRGC manifestos and pamphlets evoke a nefarious US, Zionist, and Saudi/UAE alliance intent on Iran's destruction.[36] Such sentiments echo the Kim regime's evocation of a diabolical US-Japan conspiracy that is presented as an existential threat to the regime's survival.[37]

The international community's efforts to curtail Pyongyang's and Tehran's nuclear weapons programs through economic sanctions have disrupted their economies. Faced with daunting military and economic problems, Tehran and Pyongyang have forged a partnership that facilitates their survival and furthers their regional policies.

Reinforcing this alliance is a similar totalitarian worldview. The ideational convergence between the two regimes is multifaceted. Collectively, their regimes reify supreme leaders, embracing a communitarian worldview that sharply restricts political and economic freedoms.

Within the Shia Twelver tradition, Iran's supreme leader is viewed as the earthly representative of the twelfth imam, who, once released from occultation, will usher forth an apocalyptic war resulting in global Islamic domination. Since he is the embodiment of divine rule, the supreme leader's decisions in North Korea cannot be challenged. Despite its secular ideology, North Korean Communism has imbued its leadership with quasi-divine qualities that are quite similar to the religious deference given to Iran's supreme leader. North Korea's system of *suryong* consecrates the guided-leader absolutist position in a rigidly stratified social and political order.[38]

Both regimes are dominated by leadership cults where absolutist power is undergirded by a formidable military and powerful security services who imprison, punish, and execute regime dissidents. North Korea's slave labor camps are notorious for their human rights abuses and economic predation. The DPRK's *songbun* classification system condemns most of the population

Table 4.1. The Strategic, Ideological, and Transactional Drivers of the Iran–North Korea Alliance

Revisionist power	Iran	North Korea
Anti-Western regimes seeking to project regional influence	Three-prong strategy: (1) (Ecumenical) Muslim unity against US and Israel by the appropriation of Palestinian Issue. (2) (Sectarian) 2003 Shia arc of influence across the Middle East to contain Sunni state groups and isolate Israel. (3) Work with other revisionist powers to attain regional dominance.	Tripartite foundation: (1) Regime survival and the preservation of the Kim dynasty via the development of WMD programs. (2) US military disengagement and Korean unification under Northern dominance and influence. (3) WMD proliferation policy designed to provide financial security for the Kim regime's preservation and assist revisionist Iranian and aligned groups committed to the weakening of American interests in the Middle East.
Socialistic anti–free market and private property	IRGC control over key strategic industries related to national defense and aerospace.	Socialist command economy (juche) and military-party control over strategic industries (Songun and Ch'ongdae).
Deference to and reification of omniscient autocratic leaders	Supreme leader and the cult of personality.	Chairman Kim and cultish devotion to the Kim family's dynasty rule. North Korea's "guided leader" (suryon) doctrine sanctifies the leader's absolute authority in a rigid stratified (songbun) social order.
Extremist conspiratorial/ paranoid worldview	Zionist-Crusader-Sunni Gulf conspiracy aiming to eradicate the Islamic Republic.	Diabolical US and Japan alliance committed to North Korea's destruction.
Common military doctrine	Asymmetric tactics, missile precision, and the Shia militia projects.	Develop and export WMDs to enhance regime preservation and provide support for insurgent/terror groups linked to other revisionist powers. Reorientation toward special forces' operations and asymmetric warfare techniques.
Victimization narratives	Shia martyrdom and exaltation of the impoverished classes.	Oppressed Asian proletariat/capitalist exploitation at the hands of American and Japanese imperialists.
Deep state and their clientele network	Supreme Leader Ali Khamenei's alliance with IRGC, IRGC-QF, and Basij conspires to weaken presidential, legislative, and administrative constraints.	Kim's extended family and military elites circumvent party, legislative, and bureaucratic restrictions.

Sources: Michael Eisenstadt, "The Strategic Culture of the Islamic Republic of Iran," MES Monographs 1, Washington Institute for Near East Policy, August 2011, https://www.washingtoninstitute.org/policy-analysis/view/the-strategic-culture-of-the-islamic-republic-of-iran-religion-expediency-a; Saeid Golkar and Kasra Aarabi, "The View from Tehran: Iran's Militia Doctrine," Tony Blair Institute for Global Change, February 2021, https://institute.global/sites/default/files/2021-02/Tony%20Blair%20Institute%2C%20The%20View%20From%20Tehran%2C%20Iran%27s%20Militia%20Doctrine%20%28February%202020%29.pdf; Takashi Sakai, "North Korea's Political System," Japan Digital Library, March 2016, https://www2.jiia.or.jp/en/pdf/digital_library/korean-peninsula/160331_Takashi_Sakai.pdf; Robert Collins, Marked for Life: Songbun, North Korea's Social Classification System (Washington, DC: Committee for Human Rights in North Korea, 2012).

to economic servitude and misery.[39] Iranian jails house hundreds of thousands of dissidents, and the Islamic Republic has one of the highest execution rates in the world.[40] Here totalitarian personality cults, strict censorship, and military power act synergistically to advance regime survival.

North Korea and Iran are united in their rejection of liberalism, which they see as threatening to their autocratic one-party regime's survival. Liberalism's emphasis on democratic rule and individual rights is the antithesis of Iran's and North Korea's totalitarian worldviews, which reify dynastic cults and prioritize collective interests. Khomeini's Islamic Third Way and Kim Il-sung's *juche* (self-reliance) were cast as autonomous revolutionary movements at war with the West.

The Kim family's successful monopolization of political and economic power reflects the regime's integration of Stalinist and Confucian principles, imbuing the state with a mandate to protect the popular classes.[41] Under Kim Jong-il, the Communist Party's military-first doctrine (*Songun*), which prioritized the modernization of the armed forces and continued the focus on a guided-leader personality cult, was initiated.[42]

A parallel dynamic has occurred in Iran, where Supreme Leader Ayatollah Ali Khamenei has accelerated the IRGC's influence over the country's national defense and industrial scientific complex.[43] With some seven hundred companies under its management, the IRGC is estimated to control up to 40 percent of the Iranian economy.[44]

At the epicenter of the IRGC's economic empire is the engineering consortium *Khatam al-Anbiya Construction Headquarters* (GHORB) and its 812 affiliated companies. Run by a former IRGC commander and high-level regime officials, GHORB gets preferential access to government contracts. Cronyism, corruption, and clientele networks have fed GHORB's growth for decades. The consortium is embedded in Iran's banking, aviation, armaments, mining energy, and telecommunications sectors.

The supreme leader's strong personal relationship with the late Qasem Soleimani led to the development of the IRGC-QF, which has been in the vanguard of Iran's regional missile and militia strategy. Khamenei's favoritism toward IRGC and its domestic Basij militia has sidestepped legislative and presidential controls, creating a highly personalistic form of decision-making. Tehran's and Pyongyang's *deep-state* concentration of power has furthered their strategic partnership free of outside controls.

Iranian Islamism has strong socialist foundations that emphasize the fight against social and economic oppression. Throughout the shah's regime, Shia clerics worked with the Iranian Communist Party to undermine the US-supported regime.[45] The revolutionary movement that toppled the Pahlavi dynasty integrated Shia religious discourse with a significant socialist component. Historically, the Shia religion has embraced the cause of social justice and retribution for past wrongs and railed against the economic oppression of popular classes.

Some leading clerics in the prerevolutionary period spoke of a religious mandate to create an *Islamic form of socialism.* After the 1979 Revolution, Supreme Leader Ayatollah Khomeini nationalized much of the economy and sought to redistribute resources toward the workers and impoverished peasantry. Tehran's embrace of the impoverished classes extends to the liberation of oppressed Shia populations across the Muslim world.[46]

Shia historical narratives of past victimization and martyrdom mesh well within a Marxist-Leninist theory of capitalist oppression of the proletariat. It provides a key ideological tie to Tehran's cooperation with North Korean Communist regimes. The ideological synthesis between Iran and North Korea is furthered by their ambitious foreign policies to remake the regional order free of American military and economic influence.

Ideological ties and hatred of America and its allies are buttressed by common strategic and transactional interests. North Korea has been paid handsomely with Iranian oil and cash for its weapons technology transfers and scientific expertise that have equipped Iran and its regional proxy forces with a formidable arsenal of missiles, conventional arms, and underground tunnel complexes.[47] With North Korean assistance, Tehran's regional influence stretches from the Gulf to the Levant.

North Korean weapons transfers and other forms of military-scientific assistance have allowed Iran to fortify its missile and militia strategy, which has given it de facto control over the Iraqi, Lebanese, and Syrian regimes. Having formed a panethnic Shia force comprising 190,000 militia members, Tehran is poised to strike across the Middle East.[48] Iran's military expansion in the Levant and the Gulf jeopardizes US, Israeli, and Sunni Gulf security interests and escalates the violence driving the Syrian and Yemeni civil wars.

North Korea, moreover, has a long history of weapons transfers to the Assad regime. As will be described in more detail in chapter 7, Pyongyang played a pivotal role in Syria's development (with Iranian funds) of a plutonium nuclear reactor that, had it not been destroyed by a 2007 Israeli air strike, could have produced enough fissile material to develop a nuclear weapon.[49] The Syrian regime's chemical weapons program was built with North Korean materials, infrastructure assistance, and technical expertise to deadly effect. Syrian military artillery and ballistic missile strikes employing sarin nerve agents against rebel forces in 2013 killed over a thousand people.[50]

Even after his December 2024 downfall, the status of Assad's remaining chemical weapons arsenal is unclear. Though UN officials oversaw a 2014 Russian-Syrian program to dismantle Assad's chemical weapons supplies, stockpile verification was based on regime weapons declarations.[51] Assad's subsequent use of chemical weapons calls into question the veracity of the regime's disclosures.

North Korea's arms pipeline and advisory assistance are integrated with Tehran's hybrid guerrilla warfare strategy. Faced with overwhelming American conventional military capability, Tehran and Pyongyang have crafted an asymmetric warfare strategy designed to maximize their regional influence and impair direct American military retaliation. The IRGC training and strategy borrow from Communist guerrilla doctrine developed by Mao and Che Guevara. Pyongyang, moreover, has greatly augmented its asymmetric military assets and has significantly increased its emphasis on special forces operational capability.

The DPRK doctrine of *Ch'ongdae* (gun philosophy) sees military mobilization and modernization as indispensable for the revolutionary regime's survival.[52] Iranian and North Korean military doctrine and weapons technologies converge to compromise Western interests. The Iran–North Korea partnership has proved highly destabilizing to American and allied interests in Asia and the Middle East.

The Destabilizing Impact of North Korea's Support for Iran's Missiles and Militia Strategy

The alliance between Iran and North Korea is fortified by convergent political and economic interests. Individually, these nations can ill afford to directly confront American military superiority. Acting in unison, however, their combined efforts in gray-zone conflicts significantly threaten America and its allies in Asia and the Middle East.

The Iran–North Korea partnership has proved particularly vexing. Despite decades of international economic sanctions and diplomatic isolation, Tehran and Pyongyang have circumvented the pressures meant to force them to abandon their missile development and nuclear weaponization programs.

Their forty-plus-year alliance buttresses their military capacity, ensures their survival, and furthers their ambitious regional agendas. Much of Iran's formidable arsenal of conventional and missile weaponry (much of it based on North Korean designs) has with Pyongyang's assistance been transferred to Tehran's regional proxies in Syria, Iraq, Lebanon, Yemen, and the occupied Palestinian territories. Iranian and North Korean assistance has fortified the axis of resistance creating a vast technological and scientific infrastructure for enhanced missile and conventional weapons development.

Many of these weapons development factories are placed in populated areas in Lebanon, making any US or Israeli military strikes problematic.[53] North Korean–assisted tunnel construction and underground weapons depots allow Iran, Hezbollah, and Hamas the ability to shield further weapons development from the international community. Even with hundreds of Israeli air strikes against IRGC and Hezbollah armaments depots, weapons development factories, and arms convoys, Jerusalem did not prevent Tehran military entrenchment in Syria during the prior Assad regime.[54]

The Islamic Republic's formation of a coastal defense system of cruise missiles, drones, swarm boats, and submarines (some manufactured by North Korea) threatens oil tanker shipping in the Persian Gulf and gives it the capacity to strike at Saudi refining capability.[55] Iran's drone and missile support has assisted Houthi rebel attacks striking airports and oil operations across Yemen's Saudi border.[56] Having launched space satellites, Iran's missile precision project is progressively moving into developing an ICBM capable of carrying nuclear weapons. Pyongyang's export of conventional arms to Syria and Yemen has prolonged the intensity of their civil wars.

Though Iran experienced debilitating financial and oil sanctions under the Trump administration's maximum-pressure policy, its regional policy has been furthered by clandestine Asian, African, Latin American, and Middle Eastern criminal networks that have allowed the Islamic Republic to export its missile and militia strategy across the region. Abetted by Hezbollah's clandestine criminal smuggling syndicates, Iran has used front companies, Iranian and Lebanese expatriates, and aligned regimes to acquire sanctioned military hardware and dual-use technologies.

The Iran Threat Network's sanctions evasion strategy has increased over time. Its expansion has been driven by the need to finance its ambitious missile and proxy militia agenda in the Middle East. Hezbollah's costly 2006 war with Israel and the IRGC and aligned militia intervention in the Syrian, Iraqi, and Yemeni civil wars have expanded the Iran Threat Network's need for increasingly sophisticated weapons and dual-use technologies.

The IRGC-QF Unit 190 is responsible for smuggling weapons and other forms of support to Iranian proxies in Lebanon, Iraq, and Yemen.[57] Unit 190's pipeline smuggling weapons, oil, and dual-use technology to Syria is actively coordinated with Hezbollah Business Affairs Component's Unit 108 to support the Assad regime and aligned militia efforts to defeat opposition forces.[58] Working with these specific units, IRGC-QF and Hezbollah have created shell companies to mask Iranian transfers of oil, weapons, and funds to its proxies.

The same network of front companies conversely permits the Islamic Republic to gain access to sanctioned weapons and dual-use technology and to make illegal foreign payments to creditors. Comparable networks exist in Iraq, Bahrain, and Yemen to channel weapons to Tehran's proxy militias. Iran's capacity to evade international sanctions has been assisted by North Korea's front companies and by smuggling networks controlled by Hezbollah, the Syrian National Defense Forces, and the Iraqi PMF.

These clandestine networks are a critical modality that permits these regimes to survive and thrive. North Korean and Iranian resiliency has destabilized the Middle East and Asia. Despite increased international attention, the global community appears to have little will to roll back the influence these malign states exert on the world stage. The Biden administration's efforts to diplomatically engage Iran and North Korea were as unsuccessful as previous attempts.

North Korea has what Iran wants: nearly every kind of weapons system that Iran can use in striving to become the hegemon in the Middle East. Iran has what North Korea needs: hard currency and oil. Together, these two rogue states have cemented this useful relationship (for the past forty years) in a way that shows that mutual interests, no matter how lacking in ideals, can make nations work together. Culturally, North Korea and Iran have next to nothing in common. The Iranian and North Korean regimes, however, share an autocratic style of governance run by deep-state interests whose desire to survive comes at the expense of their subjugated populations. Both nations, as a matter of doctrine, have an obsessive hatred of the United States—and that is what they most have in common. As we look to the future, we can expect to see this mutually beneficial relationship continue, expand, and flourish.

Rogue Allies and Pyongyang's Military Proliferation to Iran

Russia and China Are Now Key Enablers

Bruce E. Bechtol Jr.

On January 7, 2020, Iran launched ballistic missiles at American bases located in Iraq. One set of the missiles launched was in the Qiam series, missiles based on the North Korean–built (and proliferated to Iran) Scud C system—and likely enhanced with North Korean assistance as well.[1] But this is only the latest example of North Korea's deep involvement with and support of Iran's ballistic missile programs, an activity that has been ongoing since the 1980s, although it was wrongly assessed by some poorly informed analysts to have "declined" after the 1990s,[2] and it poses a very real threat that continues with the likely presence of North Korean advisers and technicians in Iran today.[3] But the threat is probably more compelling than most analysts realize.

North Korea has either developed or assisted with the development of the majority of Iranian liquid-fuel ballistic missile systems. In fact, the majority of Iran's ballistic missile systems can trace their genesis back to North Korean proliferation or technical assistance. Some key examples include several Scud systems, the No Dong series, the Musudan series (now seen in the Khorramshahr), the Safir satellite launch vehicle (the first stage is a No Dong), and Unha technology—now seen in the Iranian Simorgh. The first stage of the Unha rocket is a cluster of four No Dong engines—which is also the first stage of the Simorgh.[4] Iranian technicians were reportedly present at both the 2009 and 2012 Unha launches.[5] But there is more, and this now involves both intermediate-range ballistic missile (IRBM) and intercontinental ballistic missile (ICBM) advances in North Korea (and of course a new rocket).[6]

North Korea has also provided important advances in IRBM and ICBM technology and ballistic missile parts as well as technical support to Iran—ongoing since at least 2013.[7] But this is only the tip of the iceberg and a factor in North Korean proliferation to Iran that is often overlooked. There is evidence that North Korea has provided support to Iran's nuclear weaponization program. There is also a broad swath of evidence proving that since the early 1980s, North Korea has provided a wide variety of conventional weapons and training to both Iran and its proxy partners. Further, there now appears to be a nexus that involves both North Korea–Iran–China and North Korea–Iran–Russia. I will address all of these aspects of the North Korea–Iran military cooperation description—a description that is now more than forty years in the making, a constant source of regional instability, and a scenario that is ongoing today.

North Korean Proliferation to Iran: A Long and Profitable History

North Korea's initial support for Iran's military began after the fall of the shah in Iran. Tehran was no longer able to rely on the United States for its military systems, its training, or its acquisition. Enter North Korea. Iran was a pariah state that many states simply refused to trade militarily with (at least openly). This was not a problem for North Korea. In addition, the governments of both Iran and North Korea have a genuine hatred for the United States and all that it stands for. While this was not the dominating factor, it certainly added to the motivations that led to this important and long-lasting military proliferation relationship. Thus, beginning in the early 1980s, North Korea started the cycle of military proliferation to Iran that continues today.

It is important to understand the prime motivating factor behind North Korea's long-standing and broad-based military proliferation to Iran. During the Cold War, North Korea supported Communist rebel groups (as well as nations) in Africa and nations such as Syria and Egypt (as well as nonstate actors such as Hezbollah) in the Middle East. But during this time frame, North Korea was heavily subsidized by the Soviet Union.[8] By the 1980s, it had become obvious that North Korea was completely incapable of surviving economically on its own. Thus, Kim Il-sung had begun to look for ways to bring in money that augmented the vast subsidies of the USSR. In this light, Iran was the first cash-and-carry military proliferation relationship that North Korea engaged in. After the collapse of the Soviet Union (and of the huge subsidies North Korea had been receiving) in the early 1990s, North Korea's many proliferation relationships (largely in the Middle East and Africa) all became sales based on either hard currency or barter (such as oil or other resources). But with Iran, that is how the military assistance (proliferation) relationship worked from the very beginning. In other words, the primary reason for North Korea's initiation of this relationship was (and is) money, and Iran's primary motivation was that North Korea would militarily proliferate to them when most other states would not.

North Korea has truly engaged in military proliferation with Iran in two key areas: (1) conventional weapons and (2) WMDs and the platforms that can potentially carry them. As the years have gone by, the capabilities of the systems have advanced, and the geopolitics of the region Iran sits in have changed. But the thing that has not changed is the nature of the relationship between Pyongyang and Tehran. It is also important to note that in this relationship, North Korea is the seller and Iran is the buyer. Thus, discussions regarding the military cooperation between these two pariah states should evolve on the basis of that premise.

During the Iran-Iraq War, Iran got much of its supply of arms and training from China and North Korea. To quote Anthony Cordesman in his book titled *The Lessons of Modern War*, volume 2, *The Iran-Iraq War*, "Iran's military problems during the course of 1988 do not seem to have been the result of a shortage of arms, although Iran was having growing problems in getting Western parts, ammunition, and replacement systems. Iran obtained roughly $1.5 billion worth of arms, and got 60–70% of its arms from the PRC and North Korea, 20% more from Eastern Europe, and 20% from the rest of the world." Cordesman further describes the proliferation: "North Korea sold another $400 million worth of arms in 1987, including artillery, fast patrol boats, and Soviet-designed Scud surface-to-surface missiles. New North Korean arms shipments, including Scud and Silkworm missiles arrived in January, 1988."[9]

To quote an excellent interview in a work titled "Saddam's War: An Iraqi Military Perspective of the Iran-Iraq War," "Moreover, the Iranians relied on the expertise of the North Koreans. As a result, their engineering methods, as far as tactical bridges and floating bridges and pipelines they built on the

Shatt al-Arab, all came from the Korean experts who worked with them. Iran received military support and advice from North Korea as well as the Pakistanis, the latter especially for the air force, but the most came from the North Koreans."[10] During the Iran-Iraq War—which started the long-standing relationship—the North Koreans were heavily involved in supporting Iranian military forces. Indeed, throughout the conflict the North Koreans reportedly provided advisers in addition to trainers and equipment such as antiaircraft systems, antitank weapons, self-propelled artillery, and a variety of small arms.[11]

The flow of conventional weapons systems, advisers, and trainers to Iran from North Korea did not stop at the end of the Iran-Iraq War. In fact, some of the systems that Tehran acquired from Pyongyang are quite interesting. A report to Congress by the CIA in 2001 concluded, "Iran continues to seek and acquire conventional weapons and production technologies, primarily from Russia, China, and North Korea."[12] Another interesting example of conventional weapons that North Korea proliferates to Iran is the Yono-class submarine, a system noted for its sinking of a South Korean corvette naval vessel in 2010. The submarine is called the Ghadir in Iran, and the Iranians have acquired fourteen of them from the North Koreans, according to open-source reporting.[13] Iran actually conducted a cruise missile test using this submarine in 2017.[14] The submarine is now being "indigenously" produced in Iran in a factory the North Koreans built. If past precedent holds true, the North Koreans will continue to be involved in the project and provide parts and technicians.

North Korea continued the flow of conventional weapons to Iran until recently, and it actually ticked up during the Syrian civil war. The reasons for this are simple. Iran has acted as a conduit for North Korean weapons flowing to Hezbollah and other nonstate actors in the Middle East who used North Korean arms during the Syrian civil war. I will address this more in a later chapter, but suffice to say that the conventional weapons flowed to and through Iran's shipping routes during the Syrian civil war.[15] Iran also likely financed many of these transactions, as Tehran has heavily subsidized groups such as Hezbollah while also providing support for the Syrian state.[16] But it should also be noted that many of these weapons likely went directly to Iran, as it is well known that Iran sent a large number of fighters to conduct combat operations for Assad during the Syrian civil war.[17]

As stated earlier, it is not an exaggeration to say that Iran owes most of its liquid-fuel ballistic missile fleet to proliferation and assistance from North Korea. To summarize the main North Korean systems deployed, they include several Scud systems (B, C, D, ER), the No Dong series (including the Ghadir and Emad missiles),[18] the Musudan series (now seen in the Khorramshahr),[19] the Safir satellite launch vehicle (the first stage is a No Dong),[20] and Unha technology—now seen in the Iranian Simorgh. The first stage of the North Korean Unha rocket is a cluster of four No Dong engines—which is also the first stage of the Simorgh.[21] Iranian technicians were reportedly present at both the 2009 and 2012 Unha launches.[22] In short, as the North Korean ballistic missile programs advance their capabilities, these new developments are often then proliferated to Iran. As Israeli missile expert Tal Inbar has stated, "If you see it in North Korea today, you will see it in Iran tomorrow."[23] There is more than this dizzying amount of proliferation going on from North Korea to Iran, and it involves IRBM and probably ICBM technology. I will address it in the next section.[24]

Of note, on April 14, 2024, Iran launched what can only be described as an overwhelming attack on Israel. More than three hundred drones, cruise missiles, and ballistic missiles targeted Israel. While the attack was quite large, it was also quite ineffective. According to press sources and both the US and Israeli military spokespeople, 99 percent of the systems launched at Israel did not make it through. Both Israeli and American missile defense worked effectively, along with support from other allies, including Jordan. In fact, the Israeli ballistic missile defense system may be the best in the world at protecting its homeland. Nevertheless, of the roughly 120 ballistic missiles that Iran used, about 50 percent either failed to launch or crashed in flight (and almost all of the rest were shot down).[25] Thus, only half of the ballistic missiles used actually flew the way they were supposed to. While this is still a large number of missiles that would have damaged Israel were it not for superior ballistic missile defense, it also shows systems that are anything but well made. Where did the Iranians get the technology for these long-range ballistic missile systems that worked "fairly" well? The answer is, unquestionably, North Korea.

According to pictures and descriptions from reporting in the region, many of the ballistic missile systems used in the Iranian attack were what Tehran calls the Emad. Of course, the Emad is a medium-range ballistic missile based on the Shahab-3. The Shahab-3 is nothing more than a copycat of the No Dong missile. The Shahab-3 (No Dong) has a range of 1,300–1,500 kilometers, but the Emad has a range of about 1,700 kilometers, which gives it the definitively longer range to "effectively" target Israel.[26]

Going back to where this started, the North Koreans conducted a live test of the No Dong for the Iranians and the Pakistanis in 1993. After the test, both Tehran and Islamabad placed orders for dozens of these missiles (including launchers).[27] After the delivery of these missiles to both nations, at Iran's request, North Korea helped build a fabrication facility for the No Dong (now called the Shahab-3 in Iran) for Tehran.[28] But the Iranians still needed technical support and parts for the missiles they were now "indigenously" producing.

After the successful integration of the Shahab-3 (No Dong) into the actively tested Iranian ballistic missile force, the Iranians almost immediately began work on a follow-up missile based on the same design but with a longer range. And thus was born the Emad. The Emad was publicly announced as a "new" long-range missile by the Iranians in 2015. The Emad has been legitimately tested (at least according to the Iranians) to a range of seventeen hundred kilometers—and the system shot down near the Dead Sea in Israel also probably proves that to be true. Again, according to the Iranians, the Emad is significantly more accurate than other missiles in the Iranian inventory. This has not been proven to be true.[29] While this system is uniquely Iranian, there can be almost no doubt that the North Koreans provided assistance in adding to its range.[30] But even if they did not (which is unlikely), since the Emad is really nothing more (despite the hyperbole) than a "souped-up" version of the Shahab-3, and since the Shahab-3 is a copy of the original No Dong missiles North Korea proliferated to Iran, this means that in the attack on April 14, 2024, the Iranians had missiles with the range to target Israel thanks to proliferation and technical assistance from the North Koreans. Of this there can be no question, as the evidence clearly proves.[31] The Iranians attacked Israel again during the first week of October 2024. On that occasion, nearly two hundred ballistic missiles were launched. Again included in the inventory of missiles launched were many Emad systems. The damage to Israel in the second attack (despite the higher number of ballistic missiles fired) was minimal.[32]

North Korea's nuclear weaponization proliferation relationship with Iran is much more challenging to analyze than are its definitive conventional weapons and ballistic missile sales. Nevertheless, there is evidence that such a relationship has existed since the early 2000s. *Los Angeles Times* reporter Douglas Frantz reported in 2003, "North Korean military scientists recently were monitored entering Iranian nuclear facilities. They are assisting in the design of a nuclear warhead, according to people inside Iran and foreign intelligence officials. So many North Koreans are working on nuclear and missile projects in Iran that a resort on the Caspian coast is set aside for their exclusive use." Frantz further stated, "In addition to China and Russia, Pakistan and North Korea have played central roles in Iran's nuclear program, according to foreign intelligence officers and confidential reports prepared by the French government and a Middle Eastern intelligence service."[33]

According to the Congressional Research Service (which cited *Jane's Defence Weekly*), the North Koreans constructed underground nuclear facilities for the Iranians. To quote the Congressional Research Service:

> Two other forms of North Korean–Iranian nuclear collaboration have been reported recently. At least one involved direct North Korean–IRG collaboration. In 2005, the Iranian leadership is reported to have initiated a huge project to develop underground bunkers and tunnels for Iran's nuclear infrastructure, estimated to cost hundreds of millions of dollars. The project reportedly includes the construction of 10,000 meters of underground halls for nuclear equipment connected by tunnels measuring hundreds of meters branching off from each. Specifications reportedly called for reinforced concrete tunnel ceilings, walls, and doors resistant to explosions and penetrating munitions. The IRG implemented the project. North Korea is said to have participated in the design and construction of the bunkers and tunnels. In early 2005, Myong Lyu-do, a leading North Korean expert on underground facilities, traveled to Tehran to run the program of North Korean assistance.[34]

In 2011, according to an article by Reuters, the North Koreans were supplying the Iranians with software that could simulate neutron flows—technology important for the development of nuclear weapons. As Reuters reported, "Such calculations, linked to identifying a chain reaction, are vital in the construction of reactors and also in the development of nuclear explosives."[35] And in November 2011, the *Washington Post* reported, "Iran relied on foreign experts to supply mathematical formulas and codes for theoretical design work—some of which appear to have originated in North Korea, diplomats and weapons experts say."[36] While all of the evidence is anecdotal regarding North Korea's nuclear weaponization proliferation of technology (and perhaps more) to Iran, it remains troubling. The developments I have discussed above, while troubling, have received almost no comment (at least officially) from the US government. It is also unclear whether North Korea has or has not continued this assistance. That said, as often as not, where there is smoke, there is fire. This is certainly an issue that rates continued analysis and monitoring.

Ongoing North Korea–Iran Military Cooperation

The history of North Korean military proliferation to Iran is long and profitable for Pyongyang. But there are some analysts who would have us believe that this cooperation has become more limited in recent years. Clearly that is not the case. Thus, this section will summarize key aspects of North Korea–Iran cooperation in recent years. Though it is likely true that COVID-19 limited military shipments going from North Korea to the Middle East for at least a year, the relationship never faltered, and according to key sources, numerous shipments of technology and equipment, as well as deployments of technicians and engineers, resumed quickly thereafter.

Ballistic missiles are the most documented and arguably the most important export that North Korea makes to Iran; thus, it will be best to discuss the most recent and compelling news and analysis on those systems. As discussed earlier in this chapter, North Korea began to assist Iran with the development of an eighty-ton rocket booster (presumably for an ICBM) as early as 2013.[37] In 2015, further developments were revealed in the press, when it was disclosed that several shipments of the aforementioned rocket from North Korea to Iran had occurred even as Joint Comprehensive Plan of Action (JCPOA) talks were ongoing.[38] In 2016, after the conclusion of the JCPOA talks, the US Treasury Department imposed sanctions on Iranian companies and individuals for violations of sanctions imposed on North Korea. To put a finer point on it, North Korean and Iranian officials had visited both nations. This was done so that Iran could procure an eighty-ton rocket booster for a missile that North Korea was developing at the time. The names and companies (including front companies) involved are in the Treasury Department document.[39]

In 2017, North Korea tested what they called the Hwasong-12. This missile is an IRBM with a range of forty-five hundred kilometers (or more). It turns out that the Hwasong-12 is powered by a rocket engine reportedly based on an engine procured from the Ukrainians (according to the Ukrainians, illegally, under the table, and unknown to officials, or not at all), known as the RD-250. The RD-250 is powered by two thrusters, giving it eighty tons of thrust at sea level. The Hwasong-12 has only one thruster, thus giving it forty tons of thrust at sea level.[40] Later in 2017, North Korea tested two ICBMs. The first, the Hwasong-14, is assessed to be capable of hitting Anchorage in Alaska, while the second, the Hwasong-15, is assessed by many analysts to be capable of hitting the East Coast of the United States. The Hwasong-12 is powered by a large single-rocket motor, which, though it appears to be based on the RD-250, is not exactly like it as the RD-250 is powered by two thrusters. The Hwasong-12 appears to be the first stage of the Hwasong-14 two-stage ballistic missile. The Hwasong-15 appears to use a much more powerful engine as its first stage—one that looks very much like the actual RD-250 rocket motor with two thrusters (instead of the one-thruster unit used by the Hwasong-12 and -14). This engine has eighty tons of thrust at sea level.[41] This is probably the system with the eighty-ton rocket booster that the North Koreans are collaborating on with the Iranians.

What does this mean? It appears that North Korea collaborated on and then proliferated a system to Iran that was then tested in 2017—first as an IRBM and then (using the rocket from the first test as the first stage of an ICBM) as two separate ICBM systems. If this is the case—and it appears that it is—this means that North Korea has proliferated an IRBM (based on the RD-250 engine) to Iran, and if they have also proliferated the associated technology from the Hwasong-14 and 15, they have now given Iran both an advanced IRBM capability and an ICBM capability. It also means that when it comes to ballistic missile technology, North Korea has now proliferated Scud, No Dong, Musudan, Unha, and Hwasong-12, -14, and -15 technology to Iran—updating Iran's missile capabilities as they updated their own. We can probably expect to see tests of this system and perhaps associated systems in Iran within the next two to five years.[42]

While not gaining much attention in the American press, other important information has come to light in recent years regarding the North Korea–Iran strategic relationship.

In August 2018, Iran's foreign minister, Mohammad Javad Zarif, welcomed a group of North Korean officials led by Ri Yong Ho. The officials reportedly talked about "bilateral relations and regional issues in the Middle East."[43] According to press reports in 2019 citing the UN Panel of Experts, "The presidents of top North Korean regime arms firms, KOMID, which exports equipment for ballistic missiles and other weapons, and Green Pine, which sells conventional arms, recently traveled to Iran, according to air passenger documents cited by the report by the U.N. panel. A U.N. member state informed the panel that the two North Korean arms firms—which are both blacklisted by the United Nations—are 'extremely active in Iran now,' Hugh Griffiths, coordinator of the U.N. panel assessing sanctions on North Korea, told NBC News in an exclusive television interview."[44]

On September 21, 2020, the US Treasury Department sanctioned several entities and individuals active in Iran's nuclear and ballistic missile programs. Among them was Seid Mir Ahmad Nooshin, who was "key to negotiations with the North Koreans on long-range missile development projects."[45] Perhaps related to the aforementioned sanctions by the US Treasury Department, in 2021 it was disclosed that according to the UN Panel of Experts, North Korea had resumed actual shipping of technology and parts to Iran for long-range missile projects. The information in 2021 stated, "Citing information from a member state, the U.N. report noted that the cooperation included 'the transfer of critical parts,' with the most recent shipment taking place in 2020."[46] It appears that if there was a lull in North Korean military cooperation and assistance to Iran, it did not last for very long. But there is more to this picture. North Korea appears to currently be cooperating with Iran when it comes to both China and Russia.

The North Korea–China–Iran Nexus: Old Wine in New Bottles?

The connection between North Korea, China, and Iran certainly has not been a constant. In fact, after the end of the Cold War, very little is known about any dealings that North Korea has had with the Middle East that involved China though it is reported that Pakistani flights shuttling highly enriched uranium materials to North Korea and No Dong missile parts back to Pakistan were allowed to fly through China and refuel at Chinese air force bases. This was stopped in 2002.[47] When it comes to Iran, though, there has been no reporting (at least in unclassified sources) regarding cooperation among North Korea, China, and Iran since the end of the Iran-Iraq War.

During the Iran-Iraq War, it was a very different story. As we discussed earlier, North Korea was a large supplier of many things to Iran, from advisers and trainers to ballistic missiles and a plethora of conventional weapons that were used throughout the war. But according to many sources, China also used North Korea as a go-between to shuttle arms to Iran during its long and bloody war with Iraq. According to a *Washington Post* report from 1984, "Peking has kept the weapons deals with Iran secret to avoid alienating the Arab world and to protect it from charges of prolonging the 3½-year conflict, sources said. Publicly, China backs mediation efforts and denies selling arms to either side." The article further articulates, "China is believed to have sent its first large arms shipment through North Korea last summer after a high-level Iranian military delegation visited Peking in April and concluded the $1.3 billion deal."[48] China reportedly continued to funnel military equipment and complete systems to Iran through North Korea throughout the Iran-Iraq War.[49]

But the lull in North Korea and China's collaboration to assist Iran with its military programs has apparently ended. In October 2020, the long UN embargo on Iranian weapons trade ended. According to press reports, this has now opened the way for the military component of the already-announced "Twenty Five-Year Deal" between China and Iran, starting in November 2020. It now appears that as part of the military component of China's new deal with Iran, North Korea will reportedly also provide weapons and technology to Tehran. They will be paid for these services with Iranian oil—something, of course, that North Korea badly needs. Of note, North Korea is reported to be providing among its weapons and technology support the aforementioned Hwasong-12 missiles and also the development of liquid-powered rocket engines for ICBMs. This confirms what (if one is to connect the dots) has been ongoing since the JCPOA talks (2013). But now, it appears that a more long-term deal on these and other systems is being brokered—with Chinese support.[50]

The liquid-powered rocket engines for ICBMs are most likely the first stage of what is known as Hwasong-15, and the Hwasong-15 uses what looks very much like an RD-250 engine as its first stage. While Iran may call their "new" system a "space launch vehicle," because we have already seen it deployed as an ICBM, we know that at the very least it will in reality be a dual-use system that can easily be converted to an ICBM. Thus, according to press sources and other sources that at least for now remain anonymous, what we are now seeing is a triangular, long-term deal involving Iran, China, and North Korea.

What does this mean? The long-term arms sales relationship between North Korea and Iran has been ongoing and well known since the early 1980s. But now it appears that this relationship will once again involve China—for the long term. One would have thought that with China (and perhaps Russia) openly being willing to sell sophisticated military systems to Iran, this would push North Korea out as Tehran's major military arms benefactor. Instead, it appears that China's new and profitable relationship with Iran will actually enable continued North Korean arms sales to Tehran. While China (and Russia) are likely to be selling things such as sophisticated aircraft, upgraded tanks, and modernized command and control systems, North Korea will probably still be proliferating things such as small arms, military training for both Iranians and the proxy groups they support, and, of course, ballistic missiles.

Iran will thus have even more resources to continue its quest to become the hegemon in the Middle East, with all of the violence, instability, and terrorism that it will entail. China will gain a solid foothold in the Middle East and the hard currency and energy resources that Beijing needs (about half of China's oil exports either come from nations in the Persian Gulf region or transit the Suez Canal). North Korea will be able to continue its long and profitable relationship with Iran (now also coordinated with the Iran-China "Twenty-Five-Year Deal"). In short, all three of these nations have nefarious plans for the future that will enable violence, create instability, and perhaps even create more rogue regimes in the Middle East.[51]

New Relationship for the Future?
The North Korea–Russia–Iran Nexus

Ten years ago, no one would have thought that China would be openly blocking key actions against North Korea on the UN Panel of Experts or that Russia would be doing the same. Not only are Russia and China blocking important sanctions initiatives at the UN; they both now are routinely violating sanctions against Pyongyang.[52] Of course, as documented above, China has entered into a formal deal with Iran that includes North Korea as a key player and arms supplier. It is, of course, also interesting that Russia is now working with both North Korea and Iran to get badly needed arms it is using in its war against Ukraine.

The timeline of North Korea's provision of assistance to Russia is relatively fast, and it also involves Iran. In June 2022, North Korean diplomats reportedly attended meetings at the Russian Foreign Affairs Ministry, where they discussed their role in eastern Ukraine. Pyongyang's representatives reportedly wanted access to Western weapons seized by Russian troops in the war and also offered up manpower (of course).[53] In August 2022, North Korea selected "workers" to be dispatched to eastern Ukraine. Also in August 2022, North Korea reportedly offered Moscow "100,000 volunteers."[54]

In September 2022, US government officials disclosed to the press that Russia was buying millions of artillery shells and rockets from North Korea.[55] In November 2022, the US government released to the press its accusation that North Korea was covertly shipping a "significant number" of artillery shells to Russia. John Kirby, the National Security Council (NSC) spokesman, said he did not know if the munitions had reached Russia at that time. He added, "Our information indicates that they're trying to obscure the method of supply by funneling them through other countries in the Middle East and North Africa."[56] This is the likely Iran connection. Iran is (and was) already supplying Russia with drones, so why not ship North Korean munitions through Iran into Russia and ultimately into combat zones? In December 2022, imagery was released in the public domain that revealed that North Korea was also likely making shipments to Russia using the railway that runs between the two nations starting at the Russia–North Korea border.[57] By that time, the North Koreans were shipping weapons and receiving Russian barter payments using at least two methods—through the Middle East (likely Iran) and through the railway system.

In December 2022, the White House confirmed that North Korea had made its initial arms shipment to the Wagner Group (Russian mercenaries) and that more military equipment was to be delivered.[58] In January 2023, White House spokesman John Kirby stated to the press that North Korea continues to provide ammunition to Russia, and the NSC at the White House even released imagery of Russian railcars delivering weapons.[59] In

February 2023, satellites showed that rail traffic between North Korea and Russia had increased significantly.[60] North Korea reportedly received Russian oil, gas, and flour in exchange for its initial arms deliveries.[61] In August 2023, the US Treasury Department invoked sanctions against several entities and individuals in Russia accused of working with the North Koreans to get arms into Russia for the fight in Ukraine. Reportedly, the individuals and entities sanctioned have organized the acquisition of over two dozen kinds of weapons and munitions, with goods being used for payment.[62]

In October 2023, the White House released information stating that North Korea had delivered "more than 1,000 containers of military equipment and munitions to Russia for its ongoing war in Ukraine." White House NSC spokesman John Kirby also stated, "In return for support, we assess the Pyongyang is seeking military assistance from Russia including fighter aircraft, surface to air missiles, armored vehicles, ballistic missile production equipment, or other materials and other advanced technologies."[63] In some excellent research reported by James Byrne, Joseph Byrne, and Gary Somerville of the Royal United Services Institute, they, using imagery, showed how Russian ships were essentially operating in a cycle of moving containers (likely carrying munitions and arms) from Rajin, North Korea, to the Russian port of Dunai. The Russian ships conducting these movements had already made several runs back and forth by the time the study was released. To quote the study, "The final destination of these shipments appears to be a munitions depot in the Russia town of Tikhoretsk, approximately 200 km from the Ukrainian border."[64] This appears to be the third method used during the early operations to get North Korean systems and ammo to the Russian troops fighting on the battlefields of Ukraine. While there is no way of knowing for sure, it is certainly possible that North Korea will use more methods and routes to get these weapons where the Russians need them—including through Iran if necessary.

As of December 2023, the shipments using the third method of transfer were ongoing from the North Korean port of Rajin to the Russian port of Dunai. According to press reports, the South Korea National Intelligence Service (NIS) estimated at the time that there had been at least ten shipments totaling as much as one million artillery rounds. According to military analyst Joost Oliemans, these deliveries reportedly consisted of "120 millimeter mortars, 122 mm and 152 mm artillery shells and 122 mm rockets."[65] The large number of shipments and the ammunition that was delivered was no doubt an important boost for Russian forces fighting in Ukraine.

A fourth method that appears to be used occasionally is transport by air. For example, during March 2024, sanctioned Russian aircraft made runs between North Korea and Vladivostok and between North Korea and China. The method of using aircraft to transport arms, technology, or technicians and engineers appears to be used for higher-value systems or for systems and capabilities that are needed quickly by either North Korea or Russia.[66]

On July 20, 2023, the US State Department sanctioned several Russian entities and also sanctioned a North Korean arms dealer for enabling North Korean arms shipments to the Wagner Group in Russia. To quote the State Department document, "Yong Hyok Rim (Rim) is designated pursuant to section 1(a)(vi)(B) for having materially assisted, sponsored, or provided financial, material, or technological support for, or goods or services to or in support of, Yevgeniy Viktorovich Prigozhin, a person whose property and interests in property are blocked. Rim, a North Korea national, has assisted or provided support for Prigozhin and has facilitated shipments of munitions to the Russian Federation."[67] According to a UN Panel of Experts report from 2019, Rim previously was the deputy head of the infamous North Korean front company KOMID, in Syria.[68] This is the likely Middle East connection.[69] Also of interest, the confirmation that the systems and ammunition had reached the battlefields of Ukraine and were being used could not have been more glaring when, in December 2023, reports began to filter out of the region that some of the ammunition supplied by the North Koreans to the Russians was of low quality and had created issues during combat.[70]

In January 2024, both the South Korean government and the NSC from the US White House confirmed that important wrinkles had occurred in the growing North Korea–Russia arms supply relationship. Reports revealed that North Korea had transferred several dozen short-range ballistic missiles (reportedly most likely the North Korean KN-23, as it is called by the Pentagon, which appears very similar to the Russian-made Iskander), as well as a number of launchers for the missiles. John Kirby of the White House confirmed that these missiles had already been in combat against Ukrainian targets—once in late December 2023 and then again during the first week of January 2024. In what is unlikely a coincidence, reports also indicated that Iran was in the process of providing missiles to the Russians for the fight in Ukraine. By February 2024, the Iranians had reportedly proliferated at least four hundred short-range ballistic missiles to Russia. The fact that the transfer of missiles from North Korea and Iran occurred in nearly the same time frame means that collaboration between the two was likely. To quote Latvia's foreign minister Krisjanis Karins, speaking to the press, "There is a rather clear triangle with Russia, Iran and North Korea. Both Iran and North Korea supplying weapons and ammunition to Russia, which is then using these weapons and ammunition to try to destroy Ukraine. So that is a very real cooperation, which is a great concern to everyone." By January 2024, the list of arms North Korea had transferred to Russia had grown considerably and included short-range ballistic missiles, antiaircraft missiles, and antitank missiles. In addition, North Korea had by this time transferred rifles, rocket launchers, rockets, mortars, and shells, along with a great deal of ammunition.[71]

As of February 27, 2024, according to a press briefing by South Korean defense minister Shin Won Sik, at least 6,700 containers had been shipped from North Korea to Russia containing munitions, most of them assessed to be 152mm artillery shells and 122mm rockets. He also stated that North Korean factories producing these munitions for Russia were "running at full swing."[72] According to a fact sheet the US State Department distributed to the press earlier in the month and later reported on in the South Korean press, "Since September 2023, the DPRK has delivered more than 10,000 containers of munitions or munitions-related materials to Russia."[73] By February 2024, it was obvious not only that large-scale shipments of important weapons systems and munitions were going from North Korea to Russia to be used on the battlefield but that these shipments were likely to continue as long as the war in Ukraine lasted.

On February 23, 2024, the State Department issued a sanctions update with compelling information. To quote the report, "Since September 2023, the DPRK has delivered more than 10,000 containers of munitions or munitions-related materials to Russia." It further states, "Russia has imported shipping containers carrying military-related cargo from the DPRK through Vostochny Port for use in the Ukraine conflict since early October 2023. Specifically, more than 7,400 containers of munitions and munitions-related materials have been delivered to Russia through the VOSTOCHNAYA STEVEDORING COMPANY LLC (VSC)–owned terminal at Vostochny Port. Containers of munitions and munitions-related materials have also been delivered to Russia through the nearby DUNAY PROBABLE NAVAL MISSILE FACILITY." On Iran's links to this proliferation, the report said, "The Department remains focused on highlighting and disrupting the ongoing military cooperation between Iran and Russia to further Russia's war efforts against Ukraine. In December 2022 and October 2023, we designated numerous Russian and Iranian entities for their involvement in the prolifer-ation of arms including transfers of UAVs from Iran for Russia's use against Ukraine, conventional arms and related materiel from Iran to Russia, and major weapons systems from Russia to Iran, including the Yak-130 combat aircraft."[74]

On October 4, 2024, the Times (of the UK) reported (citing western intelligence sources) that about half of the shells being used by the Russians in the war against Ukraine were being supplied by North Korea. That amounts to approximately three million shells a year.[75] On October 15, 2024, sources in the Ukrainian press revealed that up to 10,000 North Korean troops were being deployed to the war in Ukraine to fight either with or alongside Russian troops.[76] While that number appears to be relatively small, especially given the high number of Russian casualties, it is also a number that is likely to grow if reports are accurate. According to Reuters, by September 2024, the North Koreans had shipped 16,500 containers of "munitions and related materials" to Russia since September of the previous year.[77] In other words, in one year, the North Koreans reportedly shipped 16,500 containers of military cargo to Russia for its fight in Ukraine—a staggering number. On October 18, 2024, the South Korean press reported that according to the NIS—the South Korean equivalent of the CIA, "approximately 1,500 North Korean soldiers were transported during the first phase, using four amphibious landing ships and three escort vessels owned by Russia."[78] According to Radio Free Asia on October 18, 2024, "The NIS said that 1,500 North Korean troops have already moved to Vladivostok, Russia, and that four brigades of the 11th Corps, North Korea's elite special operations force and the so-called Storm Corps, a total of about 12,000 troops are expected to be deployed to the war in Ukraine."[79] The Eleventh Corps is the headquarters for all North Korean light infantry brigades. Thus, the combat troops deployed to the fight with Ukraine were light infantry. This, of course, does not include other reported North Korean elements on the ground in the war at the time, including engi-neers, missile technicians, and artillery adviseors.

In late December 2024, press reports indicated that North Korea had provided up to 60 percent of Russia's artillery shells used in the war against Ukraine. In addition, the reports indicated that North Korea had made more than $6 billion in profits from its arms sales and troop deployments to the Russians for the conflict being prosecuted against Ukraine, and the figures have continued to rise since that time. The Russians also continue to provide technical support to North Korea's military programs.[80]

In April 2024, Russia vetoed the mandate at the UN Security Council (UNSC) to renew it for the UN Panel of Experts. The Panel of Experts has been the most credible unbiased source for making recommendations to the UN about North Korea's illicit activities and sanctions violations. But now, many of those violations include large-scale arms sales to Russia and other Russia-enabled illicit activities. Thus, Russia vetoed an entity that would have been able to shine light on its rogue-state behavior in the UN. Now that the UN Panel of Experts will no longer exist, it will be more difficult to monitor sanctions violations and to make recommendations to the UNSC.[81]

North Korea continues to have an important and compelling military relationship with Iran. This relationship now also includes a deal cut with China in 2020 and likely even includes collaboration and possibly transshipment of North Korean military cargo through Iran into Russia. There is more. As we will examine in a chapter on illicit activity and sanctions evasion, the Iranians are now also working with North Koreans to launder their cryptocurrency and other illicit funds. In yet another chapter, we will address how North Korea sells its arms, training, and advisers to Iranian proxies (largely financed by Iran) such as Syria, Hezbollah, and the Houthis. Yes, when it comes to involvement, financial intertwining, weapons development, and collaboration with other state and nonstate actors, North Korea and Iran remain joined at the hip, creating disruption and instability in the Middle East, and now in Ukraine as well.

6

Rogue Allies in Action

Proxy Wars in the Middle East

Anthony N. Celso

America's killing of Islamic Revolutionary Guard Corps–Quds Force (IRGC-QF) Commander Qasem Soleimani and Iraqi Kataib Hezbollah leader Abu Mahdi al-Muhandis represents a seismic change in US policy, indicating that Iran cannot hide behind its regional militia strategy.[1] Since the 1980s, America has exercised extreme caution allowing Iran's Shia militias impunity to attack, kill, and kidnap Americans in Lebanon and Iraq.

Such inaction emboldened an Iran content to hide behind its proxies. Washington was eager to accept Tehran's denials of responsibility, fearing escalating conflict with Iran.[2] The Islamic Republic's Middle East expansion is, moreover, a consequence of military interventions made by its enemies and state failures in the region. Israel's incursion into Lebanon, the US invasion of Iraq, and Syria's civil war have allowed Iran and its aligned militias an opportunity to expand their geopolitical influence.[3]

In this chapter, we explore the strategic logic that drives Iranian foreign policy. We discuss Iran's proxy war and missile proliferation strategy in three stages. First, we analyze the origins of Iran's proxy hybrid warfare approach. Second, we examine the execution of its missile and militia policy; and finally, we assess Iranian-Hezbollah military entrenchment in Syria and Yemen and discuss how this development contributed to Hamas and Hezbollah's attacks against Israel that have the potential of leading to a region-wide war.

Iranian Strategic Culture and the Historic Origins of Its Proxy Warfare Approach

Iran's militia and missile strategy was shaped by Tehran's calamitous eight-year war with Iraq.[4] The Islamic Republic's chaotic formative years exacted fear of direct warfare. Such anxieties, however, had to be reconciled with Iran's desire for Middle East domination.

Proxy warfare and missile proliferation resolved this dilemma. This strategy, however, was hard to execute. Tehran has struggled against formidable external challenges. Despite these impediments, the Islamic Republic has capitalized on the missteps of its enemies, exploiting the resulting opportunities.[5]

Iran's postrevolutionary period was characterized by mass executions of former allies (mainly Communists and liberals) who joined the revolution against the shah.[6] Dominated by clerics and religious students, the new government tried and executed thousands of political opponents. The supremacy of Islamist forces is hardly surprising given Iran's history of religiously inspired violence.[7] Led by Ayatollah Ruhollah Khomeini, the revolutionary movement toppled the shah's regime.[8]

Within the insurrectionary movements, religious students and clerics sought to replace the shah's regime with a theocratic state. These revolutionaries embraced the leadership doctrine of *velayat-e-faqih* (government by Islamic jurists). After the shah's overthrow, clerical elements dominated the new government. Theocratic rule is exemplified by the regime's Assembly of Experts and the Guardian Council responsible for the selection of the country's supreme leader. Collectively, they determine Iran's foreign and national security strategy.

Enforcing theocratic rule were revolutionary brigades that contributed to the IRGC's foundation and shaped the development of its elite Quds Force. The IRGC and its expeditionary Quds force are responsible for safeguarding the revolution at home and promoting the regime's overseas interests. Regime ideology, moreover, reflects the messianic Shia Twelver tradition—an eschatological movement that reveres twelve imams (religious scholars) associated with Ali's genealogical line.[9] Adherents believe that the last imam remains in a state of occultation until the final days of humanity. Released from his state of suspension, this revered figure becomes a central protagonist in Islam's future rejuvenation.

Referred to as the Mahdi in Islamic apocalyptic literature, this figure confronts satanic forces in a final battle that results in Islam's conquest of the world. Driven by religious beliefs, the Islamic Republic views the country's supreme leader as the Mahdi's custodian responsible for the protection of regional Shia interests.[10] These religious convictions shape Tehran's ambitions to confront American and Israeli power that they view as "demonic."

Iran's regime embraces a culture of martyrdom rooted in Shia narratives of past repression and victimization. The killing of the Prophet's grandson Husayn and his followers at the Battle of Karbala in 680 is venerated in the ritualistic practice where worshippers beat themselves with whips during the high holy period known as Ashura. Such sentiments led the Islamic Republic to embrace the cause of Shiite communities across the Middle East and support aligned rebel movements fighting Israel and Sunni Arab states.

Iran's pan-Shia project has brought it into conflict with Sunni Gulf Arab states that fear the projection of Tehran's power. The Middle East is a sectarian tinderbox with historic tensions between Sunnis and Shiites. These religious antagonisms drive civil wars in Iraq, Syria, and Yemen. Iran's backing of Lebanese Hezbollah, Iraqi Popular Mobilization Forces (PMF), Shiite/Alawite militias in Syria, and Yemeni Houthi rebels pits the regime against Sunni jihadist networks.[11]

These conflicts evoke religious symbolism that exalts martyrdom, vengeance, and jihad. The deaths of Ali and Husayn and the Prophet's granddaughter Zynab, who symbolized resistance to Sunni oppression, are used by the regime to inspire future martyrs.[12] The commemoration of Shia suffering and the quest for revenge drive Tehran to expand Shia influence across the region. This religious narrative is a critical facet in Iran's soft-power projection across the Arab Middle East.[13]

Such theological ambitions, however, had to be reconciled with the regime's fear of direct war with powerful enemies—a trepidation rooted in the internal revolutionary upheaval later magnified by the carnage of the Iran-Iraq War. Iran's revolution and subsequent war with Iraq shaped the regime's hybrid warfare strategy, which has been refined for over a generation.

One cannot overstate the psychological impact of Tehran's destructive war with Saddam Hussein's Iraqi regime. That war began when Iraq tried to seize the disputed territory along its frontier with Iran. Eight years of trench warfare and missile exchanges resulted in over a million deaths. Underscoring the martyrdom culture of Iranian Shiism, soldiers and children suicidally marched into minefields along the Iraqi border.

Throughout the conflict, Iran's major cities were struck by Iraqi missiles. With their economies devastated and armed forces weakened by conflict, Tehran and Baghdad agreed to end hostilities.

Seeing the costs of conventional war against a formidable adversary, Iran was forced to develop indirect combat strategies.[14] This has involved the development of proxy forces operating overseas to ensure the realization of Tehran's regional objectives and shield the Islamic Republic from retaliation. Connected to this strategy are the progressive development of Iran's missile capability at home and the transfer of these weapons to aligned militias.

The Islamic Republic began its ambitious missile strategy during its war with Iraq by utilizing Libyan-made delivery systems.[15] Tehran began to import missile systems from Russia, China, and especially North Korea.

> One 2023 study of Iran's missile arsenal states: "Over the four past decades Iran has procured at least three whole ballistic missile systems from North Korea. Pyongyang reportedly developed Iran's first nuclear-capable medium range missile system ballistic missile (MRBM) known as the Nodong-A, which Tehran produced under the Shahab-3 and first tested in the late 1990's. Today the Shahab-3 is the bedrock of several liquid propellant MRBM. . . . In the early 2000's Pyongyang provided yet another liquid propellant nuclear capable ballistic missile that may be the foundation of an intermediate-range ballistic missile (IRBM) capability."[16]

Iran's missile strategy initially involved the transfer of entire weapons systems to its regional allies, then progressed to the delivery of spare parts, and ultimately laid the basis for missile factories in Lebanon and Yemen.[17] Here the Islamic Republic's relationship with Lebanese Hezbollah was pivotal in the development of its hybrid war strategy. Tehran's efforts to undermine the Zionist state were facilitated by Israel's 1982 invasion of Lebanon. By launching an incursion into Lebanese territory, Jerusalem hoped to destroy the military infrastructure of the Palestinian Liberation Organization (PLO). Though it succeeded in driving the PLO from the country, Israel unintentionally created an ever more formidable adversary.

Lebanon's significant Shiite minority assisted Tehran's efforts to attack Israeli forces. Iranian military advisers, money, and weapons flowed into Lebanon to organize resistance first against Israeli forces and then later against international peacekeepers whose mission was to secure the evacuation of the PLO's forces. The UN's Franco-American peacekeeping contingent afforded Tehran an opportunity to kill Westerners.

Throughout the 1980s, Shiite militias launched attacks against Israeli and international forces. Such assaults were spearheaded by suicide bombers, whose martyrdom operations resulted in the deaths of hundreds of American and French peacekeepers. Dozens of US and European citizens were kidnapped for ransom by Shia insurgent groups. Some of these hostages were killed.

Unable to counter Shiite terrorist attacks, Paris and Washington in 1984 withdrew their forces. Western disengagement from Lebanon emboldened Iran's efforts to harass Israel's forces in South Lebanon. During this period, Iran sent military trainers, funds, and weapons to develop Hezbollah, whose guerrilla operations and suicide bombers killed over a thousand Israeli soldiers. After eighteen years of occupation, Jerusalem evacuated its forces, allowing Hezbollah to militarily entrench its forces along Lebanon's border with Israel.[18]

Iran's hybrid warfare strategy uses information warfare to complement its kinetic actions. As Tehran's key regional proxy force, Hezbollah has been presented by the Islamic Republic as a resistance force against Zionist oppression of the Muslim *ummah* (community).

Tehran's embrace of the Palestinian cause committed the Islamic Republic to liberate Jerusalem. Iran's support for Hamas and Palestinian Islamic Jihad is presented as an opening salvo in a war of annihilation against the Zionist regime. The Islamic Republic's financial and weapons pipeline to Palestinian resistance forces in the West Bank and Gaza Strip (ferreted through North Korean–assisted underground tunnels) allowed Tehran to claim leadership over the struggle against the Zionist state. Its association with the Palestinian movement and its success against Israeli forces in Lebanon are hailed by Hezbollah's and IRGC's media operations.

Having vanquished Western and Israeli forces in Lebanon, Iran and Hezbollah created a military infrastructure in South Lebanon. Since 2005, Iran has invested $700 million annually, supplied 130,000 missiles and rockets, and transferred conventional weaponry to Hezbollah.[19] Tehran has created an arms pipeline across aggrieved Shiite communities stretching from Iraq to Lebanon. The Islamic Republic refers to its regional arms corridor as *Imam Ali Province*, underscoring the religious significance.[20]

Iran hopes to mount a resistance project against Washington's allies across the region. Partnership with Shiite "resistance militias" became the fulcrum for the development of IRGC-QF and its experimental hybrid warfare strat-egy.[21] This strategic alliance serves as a model for Tehran's expeditionary war-fare policy later exported to Iraq, Syria, and Yemen. Though the growth of Iranian power in the region is a natural trajectory of the regime's expansionist policy, it has been abetted by events beyond Tehran's control. As was seen in the previous chapter, North Korea has served as a vital conduit for arms, technology, and expertise in the development of this resistance project. It continues to do so today.

The 2003 American-led war to overthrow Saddam Hussein's Baathist re-gime and Washington's incubation of a fragile democratic system politically empowered the Shia majority, which propelled Iranian influence across the country. The development of close ties between Baghdad and Tehran did not surprise Sunni Gulf States, which were unanimous in their opposition to the 2003 war.[22] These states feared that Iran could use Iraq as a base for future destabilization by supporting Shia militant groups in Saudi Arabia, Bahrain, and Yemen. The course of subsequent events proved these fears to be prescient.

Iran's border with Iraq and the close religious and cultural ties between their Shia communities made Tehran a natural economic and political part-ner.[23] The Shia clerical establishments in these countries were moreover inex-tricably linked. Many Iraqi clerics trained in Iran, and thousands of Iranian pilgrims visited Iraq's revered religious sites.[24]

The presence of thousands of American troops as an occupation force provided a strategic opening for Iran's IRGC-QF to strike against Western coalitional forces. After Hussein's fall, Tehran financed, trained, and armed Shia militant groups. Using its Lebanese Hezbollah model as a basis, Tehran created dozens of Shia militias, which in turn spawned a vast network of char-itable and political organizations. Today such groups as PMF are a backbone of Iraq's security forces not directly under Baghdad's control.[25] Militias like Kataib Hezbollah have been directly trained by IRGC-QF. In a recent study, Michael Knights estimates that pro-Iranian militias in Iraq number some six-ty thousand people.[26] Their allegiance is to Tehran, not Baghdad.

They have mounted attacks against US military bases in Iraq and are a potent force to be used at Tehran's discretion. During the Iraq War, the most dangerous Shia militia to Western troops in Iraq comprised the brigades associated with the cleric Muqtada al-Sadr. His Jaysh al-Mahdi, or Mahdi Army, was a vital part of the Iraqi Shia resistance to coalitional forces battling them throughout the US occupation of the country[27]. Hundreds of American troops and thousands of Shia militia members died in these battles.[28] By calling his political-paramilitary force the Mahdi Army, al-Sadr evoked apocalyptic images of a prophesied redeemer who would vanquish injustice and advance the Islamic conquest of the world.

Iraqi democratization created a dysfunctional precedent that contributed to the Arab Spring's upheavals years later. Though the Iraq War may have aggravated populist resentment against regimes in Tunisia, Egypt, Libya, Yemen, and Syria, it pales in comparison to internal forces in these countries. Government oppression, economic stagnation, corruption, state illegitimacy, and youth unemployment drove the 2011 populist protests that toppled governments in Tunisia, Egypt, Libya, and Yemen.[29]

Israel's withdrawal from Lebanon in 2000 gave Hezbollah the ability to fortify its position in South Lebanon. This development set the stage for the next round of conflict with Israel six years later. In this regard, North Korean assistance has been vital in enhancing Hezbollah defensive and offensive capability. Pyongyang has played a critical role in Hezbollah's evolving missile project and the construction of its formidable and complex tunnel system.

Syria served as a conduit for Iran's provision of North Korean weapons to Hezbollah. This continued well into 2006 as it became obvious the North Koreans had aided Hezbollah in building a huge underground network in South Lebanon—a network that made it challenging for the Israeli forces to pinpoint and attack Hezbollah positions.[30] Another shipment of thirty-five tons of conventional arms was caught on its way to the Middle East in 2009. Israeli officials publicly assessed that the shipment was bound for Hezbollah and Hamas.[31]

Proxy Warfare in Action (Lebanon, Syria, Iraq, and Yemen)

Lebanon

Central to Iran's axis of resistance project was Tehran's ability to run its weapons through Syria, whose Alawite-dominated government and refusal to sign a peace accord with Israel made it a natural sectarian and strategic partner. Iranian and Syrian support allowed Hezbollah and Palestinian Hamas to launch 2006 attacks on and kidnap Israeli troops along the Lebanese border and the West Bank. Israel launched retaliatory attacks.

The war proved to be a publicity boon for Hezbollah and its Iranian patron. The Shia militia's capacity to survive a war with Israeli forces contrasted
strikingly with past Arab military defeats against the Zionist state. Fearing a
protracted land war against a determined enemy and the prospect of heavy
casualties, Israeli prime minister Ehud Olmert hoped to bomb Lebanon into
submission, convinced that Beirut would exert pressure on Hezbollah to re-
lent. The damage done to Lebanon's civilian population and international
efforts to end the conflict did not permit Jerusalem sufficient time to follow
through with its war aims. Hezbollah's al-Manar television network drama-
tized civilian deaths associated with the Israeli bombing campaign.

Its media operations also broadcast images of a burning Israeli frigate hit
by Hezbollah rockets. These images left an impression that Hezbollah was
winning the propaganda war. Though Hezbollah took heavy losses and did
not *win*, it survived, earning the admiration of the Arab world.[32] Israel's failure to achieve a significant blow against Hezbollah, contrastingly, was interpreted as an embarrassing *defeat*. Since the war, Israeli strategic planners have
devised alternative strategies to combat Hezbollah's asymmetric operations.[33]
These include efforts to destroy the organization's network of tunnels, targeted offensive operations, and general improvements in Jerusalem's missile
defense system.[34]

The 2006 war had consequences. First, Hezbollah and Iran expanded
their financial and armaments relationship. Iran has strengthened Hezbollah.
Since the war, Iran has fortified Hezbollah's offensive capability, which com-
prises 130,000 short-, medium-, and long-range rockets.[35] This arsenal allows
Hezbollah the capability of launching some 1,500 rockets a day into Israel
in a future war.[36] Tehran's supply of rockets (some designed and provided by
North Korea) has given Hezbollah the capacity to reach all of Israel's major
cities.[37] More alarmingly, there is evidence that Iran has assisted Hezbollah
in the development of precision-guided missiles that, combined with massive
rocket attacks, could overwhelm Israeli missile defense systems.[38]

With its IRCG-QF training, Hezbollah has also developed conventional
capabilities to complement its guerrilla tactics. The Army of God militia,
moreover, has established a preeminent military position in Lebanese society,
relegating the nation's army to a subordinate position. Hezbollah's monopolization of power in the country is reinforced by its political wing's representa-
tion in Parliament; it has veto power over governmental formation and policy.

Until Assad's December 2024 overthrow, the alliance among Iran, Syria, and Hezbollah grew. Damascus's refusal to sign a peace treaty with Jerusalem established its bona fides as a resistance force against Zionist aggression. Assad supplied Hamas, Hezbollah, and Palestinian Islamic Jihad with arms, logistic support, and funds. The strategic role that Syria previously played as a partner in the *axis of resistance*, however, was threatened by anti-Assad protests during the 2011 Arab Spring upheaval. North Korean assistance has greatly helped Syria's government to survive a debilitating civil war.

The Syrian Civil War

Civil disobedience in Syria after the Arab Spring was met with severe repression. President Bashar al-Assad responded with a brutal crackdown, converting a nonviolent protest movement into a violent revolutionary force. The regime's murder of four young graffiti artists in March 2012 resulted in a mass oppositional movement. Hundreds of protesters were arrested.[39] Many were tortured and killed. Faced with little prospect of peaceful change, the rebellion became increasingly violent.

Syria's volatile ethno-sectarian complexion and Damascus's repression have triggered a violent Sunni insurgent movement. By late 2012, rebellion against the Assad regime had spread across the country.

Syria's eastern frontier with Iraq was largely abandoned, allowing rebel forces to capitalize on the resulting power vacuum. Having captured territory in northwestern Iraq in 2013, Islamic State (IS) forces came across the border and displaced other rebel groups. IS forces came to govern the region, with the Euphrates town of Raqqa serving as its administrative capital.[40] During the civil war, Damascus withdrew its military from Kurdish dominated areas along Syria's border with Turkey. This contributed to the rise of the Syrian Democratic Union Party (PYD) and its People's Protection Units (YPG) military branch.

By 2013, the Assad regime was reeling under the strain of fighting a rebel movement supported by the Sunni majority. Assaults by secular and Islamist rebel groups supported by the West, Turkey, and Arab Gulf States were beginning to take their toll. So desperate was the regime to survive that it resorted to the use of chemical weapons that killed over a thousand people.[41] Despite the American warning that the use of chemical weapons would spark a military response, the Obama administration failed to retaliate.

The Obama administration's failure to enforce its warning sent a signal to other regional powers that they could intercede in the Syrian civil war with little fear of American countermeasures.[42]

Iran and Hezbollah's historic alignment with the Assad regime as an *axis of resistance* against Israel convinced them to intervene in the conflict. IRGC-QF combat personnel and thousands of Lebanese Hezbollah militia members defended the regime, reversing rebel gains and stabilizing Assad's position in major cities and coastal Latakia. At the height of its military intervention, Hezbollah is estimated to have had some six thousand fighters in Syria.[43]

Since 2012, Iran has spent some $16 billion in the region and deployed two thousand of its advisers and combat soldiers in Syria.[44] Tehran, moreover, recruited and armed some forty thousand Iraqi, Pakistani, and Afghan Shia "volunteers" to defend the regime.[45] Combined with Hezbollah, this Shia expeditionary force strengthened the regime's army and militia units. Augmented militarily, the regime secured key regions. The summer 2013 offensive by the Syrian army and Hezbollah dislodged rebel forces from Qusayr and secured supply lines linking Damascus, Aleppo, and coastal Latakia.[46]

Despite Iranian and Hezbollah assistance, the regime's security forces experienced severe manpower shortages. By summer 2015, rebel groups were making advances in Latakia, Idlib, and Hama Provinces. Worried about the prospect of the Assad regime's fall and the weakening of the axis of resistance, Tehran sent IRGC-QF commander Qasem Soleimani to Russia hoping to convince Moscow to accelerate its support for the beleaguered Syrian government. His entreaties were instrumental in Moscow's expanded military presence in Syria.

In September 2015, Russia increased its military involvement by launching air strikes against Syrian rebels fighting Assad's regime. Hoping to abate the regime's deterioration, Russia deployed its armed forces in Syria. With two thousand support personnel, Moscow became an active participant in Syria's civil war.[47] Though Putin justified his military intervention as part of the international anti-IS military campaign, his strategic goals in Syria lay elsewhere.[48]

The Kremlin reinforced the Assad regime's military position and fortified the Iranian-Shiite regional arc of power to blunt Western interests. Its Syrian policy sought to reinvigorate Russia's Mediterranean presence and weaken America's regional dominance.[49] Even more pressing was Moscow's need to prevent thousands of Russian Islamic terrorists in Syria from returning to their homeland and to preserve its Tartus naval base.

This commitment is not surprising. Syria and Russia's relationship dates back to the Cold War. Since Moscow's entry into the civil war, hundreds of air strikes have targeted anti-Assad rebels, helping the regime to retake towns and villages near Aleppo and Latakia. Most Russian bombs dropped were against Western-backed *moderate* rebels. The Institute for the Study of War reports that 90 percent of Russia's air strikes were concentrated in northwestern Syria outside areas controlled by IS.[50] Government forces in 2016 encircled rebels in Aleppo, forcing a negotiated withdrawal of their remaining forces.

The recapture of rebel-held Aleppo in 2017 was a turning point in the civil war.[51] The government's offensive to create a corridor linking Damascus, Aleppo, and Alawite northern coastal bastions succeeded. Assisted by Hezbollah, IRGC units, and Iraqi, Afghan, and Pakistani Shiite militias, Assad's regime has strengthened. Damascus furthermore ensured its survival through merciless brutality. Government forces eviscerated rebel-supported neighborhoods in Aleppo, killing thousands of civilians by dropping barrel bombs packed with gasoline and nails. The war has featured the use of chemical weapons that have killed thousands.[52] By 2018, close to half a million people had died in the civil war, which has left eleven million displaced.[53]

Central to Damascus's previous success was its brutality; it targeted civilians by bombing hospitals, schools, and community centers, whose efforts to shield noncombatants mattered little to Syria's Iranian and Russian supporters. Iran-Russia-Hezbollah and Syria's effectiveness in using indiscriminate force against jihadist insurgents challenges the strategic logic that drives current American counterinsurgency doctrine aimed at winning hearts and minds.

One also must recognize the importance of Pyongyang's assistance to Assad's beleaguered regime. North Korea's shipments of conventional and unconventional arms into Syria fortified Damascus's ability to fend off Western-supported rebels. As confirmed by reports in 2018, each year North Korea was proliferating hundreds of millions of dollars' worth of conventional and unconventional weapons to Syria, thus facilitating the regime's military advances.[54]

Coordinating with Russia and IRGC-QF, Hezbollah and the Syrian army regained more than 50 percent of the country. Ankara petitioned the North

Atlantic Treaty Organization (NATO) to support its Syrian policy while simultaneously threatening to flood Europe with the nearly three million refugees it was currently hosting.[55] Though many had thought that the Syrian conflict was not amenable to a military solution, Iran, Russia, and Hezbollah have proved these critics wrong.[56] Though Assad was not able to consolidate control over Kurdish areas and was stymied by a Turkish security zone in Idlib Province, his regime survived for nine more years.

Iran's success in executing its hybrid warfare model has been carefully honed across the Middle East. Relying on its IRGC-QF and Shiite militias, Tehran has capitalized on the missteps of its adversaries. Wars in Iraq, Lebanon, and Syria have provided it with enhanced capabilities that Tehran hopes to utilize in future conflicts. A 2020 report estimates that Iran's partner forces across the Middle East comprise some 190,000 Shiite militia members.[57]

One, moreover, must recognize the role of late IRGC-QF commander Qasem Soleimani in developing Tehran's partnership with Shiite militias across the Arab Middle East. He, more than any other regime figure, established a personal relationship with militia commanders, patching together a formidable network of Iranian proxy groups across multiple countries transferring invaluable expertise, arms, and weapons.[58]

Working through Hezbollah and Iraqi PMF, Tehran wields enormous influence over Beirut's and Baghdad's policies. Its goal of establishing a power base in the Arab Middle East to undermine American and Israeli security has been achieved.

Acting through the IRGC-QF, Hezbollah, the former Assad regime, and aligned Shiite/Alawite militias, Iran (with North Korean help) has developed a military infrastructure composed of missiles and underground tunnels in Syria and Lebanon to prepare for a new round of military escalation against Israel. Responding to Tehran's regional policy, the Israelis launched thousands of strikes against Iranian and Hezbollah military developments in Syria, hitting IRGC installations and militia convoys.

Jerusalem's main intent was to frustrate Iran's ambitious arms project running across Iraq, Syria, and Lebanon.[59] The fall of Bashar al-Assad's regime to Islamist rebels in December 2024 allowed Israel to expand its military presence on the Syrian side of the Golan Heights border.

Fearing that Sunni jihadists would acquire Assad's chemical arms and military capability, the Israeli Defense Forces (IDF) conducted air strikes that destroyed much of this military infrastructure. The collapse of the Assad regime presents a major strategic challenge for the Islamic Republic and forces it to recalibrate its diplomatic and military efforts in the Middle East. It will take years for Iran to rebuild its shattered series of alliances in the region.[60]

Iraq and Yemen

Tehran has also moved into Iraq.[61] Shiite militias financed and armed by Iran wield de facto control of Iraq's government, mirroring Hezbollah's position in Lebanon.[62] Among the core groups that have substantial connections to IRGC-QF are Asaib Ahl al-Haq, Kataib Hezbollah, Kataib Sayyid al-Shuhada, and Harakat Hezbollah al-Nujaba.[63]

Iran has also capitalized on the unmooring of the Yemeni state after the Arab Spring. Like Syria, Yemen is a sectarian tinderbox convulsed by shadow wars between Iran and Saudi Arabia. Popular protest in 2011 led to the exile of President Abdullah Saleh and invited a power struggle between Shia-affiliated Houthi rebels and the new fragile regime supported by the West and Sunni Gulf States. By 2014, Iranian-assisted Houthi rebels dominated much of the country's North, including the capital, Sanaa, and were marching south, threatening access to the Bab el-Mandeb Strait, from which it could easily attack oil tankers.

Alarmed that Iran would be able to carve out a sphere of influence, Saudi Arabia and United Arab Emirates (UAE) militarily intervened, attempting to prevent a Houthi-dominated Yemen. Since 2015, Yemen has been mired in an intractable civil war with no victor in sight. Tehran, however, has used the country as a base of operations ferreting IRGC advisers, missiles designed and fabricated by North Korea, antitank-guided missiles, drone technology, and conventional arms to the Houthi rebels. The UN Panel of Experts, for example, reported that North Korea had supplied missiles that the Houthis likely were using to target Saudi Arabia and the UAE.[64]

From Yemen, Iranian-assisted Houthis have attacked Saudi airports, oil facilities, and military installations along the border.[65] The Iranian supply of drone and missile technology was vital in the success of the Houthi attacks and is designed to punish the Saudis and the UAE for their support for the Yemeni regime.

Like Hezbollah in Lebanon, the Houthis have developed into a formidable fighting force that controls over half the country. Assisted by IRGC-QF and Hezbollah, the Houthis' Jihad Council has centralized military operations while employing a hybrid warfare strategy that gives regional commanders significant autonomy to carry out armed actions against Saudi-backed government forces and their tribal allies.[66]

A 2023 study by the Foundation for Defense of Democracies indicates that the Houthis have received more ballistic missile systems than any of Tehran's other regional proxies, indicating the group's centrality in the Islamic Republic's plans.[67] Given Yemen's long Persian Gulf coastline, the Houthis have attacked oil tankers and maritime shipping, impairing the kingdom's ability to export oil.

Under financial pressure from American sanctions, Tehran, by equipping Houthi rebels with advanced missiles, hopes to make Saudi Arabia and UAE pay a substantial price for supporting US policy in the region. The Houthis are a potent force that can be used at Tehran's discretion to disrupt maritime traffic and strike across Yemen's border with Saudi Arabia.

After Israel's military campaign against Hamas after the group's October 7 attack, the Houthis attacked maritime shipping in the Red Sea. Acting in solidarity with Hamas, the Houthis attacked Israel with drones and missile strikes. The Israelis retaliated with air strikes against Yemeni ports and oil-refining infrastructure. Along with Hezbollah and Hamas, the Houthis became a key proxy in Iran's axis of resistance project.

Iran's Support for Palestinian Groups

For over forty years, Iran has waged a concerted proxy terrorist and insurgent campaign to undermine Israeli security across the world. Iranian-directed Hezbollah terrorists have killed Jews in Argentina, India, and Bulgaria.[68] The Islamic Republic's hatred of Israel reflects religious and political considerations. Ayatollah Khomeini decried Israel as *Little Satan*, and Tehran views Israel as an occupier of Muslim territory that includes Jerusalem's al-Aqsa Mosque, the third holiest site in Islam.[69] As a self-declared defender of the umma, the Islamic Republic campaigns for Jerusalem's reconquest and the annihilation of the Jewish state.

Iran created the axis of resistance in the late 1980s, embracing the Palestinian cause by providing weaponry, financing, and technical expertise to Islamist Hamas and the Palestinian Islamic Jihad (PIJ), who campaigned to liquidate the Zionist state. By appropriating the Palestinian issue, Tehran hoped to overcome Sunni resistance to its Shi'ite Imamate project. Tehran spent $100 million supporting Hamas.[70] Though a Sunni fundamentalist group, Hamas's stated objective, emblazoned in its 1988 founding charter, is Israel's destruction.

With Iranian financial support, Hamas improved its missile production capability. Based on Iranian and North Korean designs, the Palestinian resistance's arsenal of rockets and missiles grew. Hamas's electrified underground tunnel system was a vital supply route for criminal contraband and weapons. Described as the *Gaza Metro* by Israel defense experts, this elaborate subterranean network was a critical node in Hamas's resistance strategy for it permitted its al-Qassam military wing to store, smuggle, and deploy weapons. Hamas had some fifteen hundred antitank weapons supplied by North Korea via Iranian conduits to counter an Israeli invasion force.[71]

Hamas constructed sea tunnels running underneath the Mediterranean to transport Iranian-supplied arms dropped in the sea by "fishing vessels." The Palestinian militia used hundreds of underwater divers to transport arms through sea tunnels linked to its Metro underground system. In 2020, Israel destroyed what it suspected was a Hamas port to transfer maritime arms traffic to its underground system.[72]

In past wars with Hamas, Israel had prioritized the destruction of the Palestinian resistance's tunnel system. During the May 2021 military confrontation between Hamas and Israel, Palestinian resistance forces launched more than forty-three hundred rockets in eleven days from the Gaza Strip— four times more than in last 2014 conflict.[73] Many of these rocket systems were based on North Korean prototypes replicated by Tehran and exported to Hamas via illicit channels. Though most of these rockets were intercepted by Israel's antimissile system, Iranian support improved Hamas and PIJ military capability.

Within Israel's occupied territories, PIJ's ideology, finances, and tactics were squarely aligned with Tehran's regional aims.[74] The PIJ was the Islamic Republic's most direct Palestinian proxy force, and unlike Hamas it was not conflicted over being supported by a Shi'ite regime. Its late founder, Fathi Shikaki, was an admirer of Khomeini's Islamic Third Way, seeing it a bridge across the Muslim confessional divide.

Tehran was the PIJ's sole financial patron (expending $30 million annually) and weapons provider.[75] Because of its financial leverage over the group,

Tehran has been able to stifle any internal resistance to its directives. Along with Hamas, PIJ waged a concerted terrorist and insurgent campaign against the Jewish state. Without Iranian support, it was unlikely that Hamas and PIJ would have been able to launch over four thousand rockets in the first week of their May 2021 conflict with Jerusalem.[76]

The 2023 Gaza Crisis, the 2024 Israel-Hezbollah War, and the Limits of Iran's Asymmetric Warfare Capabilities

After the 2021 war, Israel mistakenly believed that Hamas and PIJ were contained by its border security measures along the Gaza Strip. Hamas and PIJ's assault on Israeli border communities and kibbutzim along the Gaza Strip on October 7, 2023, shattered Jerusalem's efforts to manage its Gaza problem.

After deactivating Israeli communication towers through drone attacks, Hamas overwhelmed the Jewish state's Iron Dome missile defense system by launching thousands of rockets. Having disrupted Israel's border command and control system, Hamas breached Jerusalem's security fence, allowing thousands of Hamas and PIJ militants to storm across southern Israel, sacking towns and kibbutzim, killing twelve hundred, and taking over two hundred hostages. Hamas's ethnic cleansing campaign included summary executions, rape, burnings, and beheadings.[77] The Islamic Resistance Movement's October 7 pogrom amounted to the greatest single day of loss of Jewish life since the Holocaust.

It took days for Israeli security services to push Hamas and PIJ militants back to their Gaza stronghold. Some sixteen hundred Palestinian fighters died in these battles. After the October 7 attack, Israel launched thousands of air strikes against Hamas and PIJ military installations and invaded Gaza. The IDF took Gaza City and Khan Younis in a bloody military campaign.

Israel's military campaign in Gaza showed demonstrable results in weakening Hamas. The first ten months of attritional warfare killed eighteen thousand militants, eradicated 80 percent of its senior military leadership, and degraded three-quarters of its armed brigades.[78] Ido Levy (2024) reported that the IDF had decimated much of Hamas's midlevel brigade and battalion commanders and that its military wing was badly degraded.[79]

Senior Hamas leaders Yahya Sinwar, Ismail Haniyah, Marwan Issa, Rawhi Mushtaha, Saleh al-Arouri, and Mohammad Deif were killed. Hamas's critical tunnel infrastructure, munition factories, and arms depots were degraded. In May 2024, the IDF seized the Philadelphia Corridor, which served as a critical Gazan-Egyptian hub to resupply Hamas with Iranian-supplied arms and material support.[80]

By August 2024, the IDF had disabled 150 Hamas underground tunnels that ran from Rafah to the Egyptian border. Israel had largely finished its military campaign in Gaza. Hamas's military and political organization had unraveled.

Starting in September 2024, Israel began to focus its military operations against Hezbollah along its northern border with Lebanon. After the October 7 attack, Israel battled both Hezbollah along the Lebanese border and Hamas in the Gaza Strip. Such a development made good on Iran's threat to use its axis of resistance to support Hamas.

As Iran's premier proxy force, Hezbollah was best positioned to combat Israel. When Israel started its military campaign in Gaza, Hezbollah began daily rocket and missile attacks against the Jewish state. Jerusalem countered with air and artillery strikes against Hezbollah rockets in South Lebanon. Fearing Hezbollah military operations against its northern border communities, Israel uprooted sixty thousand of its inhabitants and moved them to more secure locations in the country's central region.

Israel's war with Hezbollah dramatically escalated in mid-September 2024 when the IDF and Mossad intelligence branch launched attacks disabling Hezbollah communication and military command systems. Israeli intelligence clandestinely sold Hezbollah-linked contractors explosively charged pagers and radios that the network used for close to year.[81] Fearing that Israel could monitor its cell phone traffic, Hezbollah resorted to using pagers and radios to communicate within its organization. Between September 17 and 18, Israel activated its explosively charged devices, killing dozens and wounding thousands of the Party of God's members.

Having disabled Hezbollah's communication systems, Israel next focused on air strikes to assassinate Hezbollah senior leadership including its legendary chairman Hassan Nasrallah. IDF bombing raids degraded missile and rocket delivery systems. By one estimate, Israel's air campaign destroyed 50 percent of Hezbollah rocket and missile infrastructure.[82]

Starting in October 2024, Israel invaded South Lebanon to destroy Hezbollah's tunnel system, which shielded its missiles and rockets, and to prevent the militant network from clandestinely entering the Jewish state's northern territory.

Supporting its Hamas and Hezbollah proxies, Iran launched two failed missile and drone strikes against the Jewish state on April 13 and October 1, 2024. Both assaults were precipitated by Israel's killing of senior Hamas, Hezbollah, and IRGC commanders. Despite launching some four hundred missiles, the Islamic Republic failed to kill one Israeli and inflicted only minor material damage.[83] Working with the United States and its Arab allies, Jerusalem's Arrow missile defense system interdicted most of Iran's missiles.

Israel's military retaliation for the October 1 attack was delivered twenty-four days later. On October 25, IDF warplanes struck twenty Iranian missile and drone production facilities, disabling their defense systems and inflicting damage on these locations.[84] The Israeli Air Force concentrated its attacks on Iran's Parchin and Khojir military complexes, which featured advanced nuclear weapons research as well as drone and missile production sites.[85] With the armed capabilities of Hezbollah, Hamas, and Iran crippled by the IDF military actions, the Assad regime in Syria fell. Russian military redeployment to the Ukraine and a weakened Hezbollah prevented the Syrian government from countering Turkish-backed anti-Assad Islamist rebels. Backed by Ankara, the jihadist Hayat Tahrir al-Sham captured the country's central and coastal regions forcing Assad's exile to Russia.

Since October 7, 2023, Iran's axis of resistance project has collapsed forcing the Islamic Republic to recalibrate its regional approach. Iran's Middle East strategy is badly compromised. It will take Tehran years to rebuild Hezbollah.

By destroying Hamas, weakening Hezbollah, and attacking Iran's missile defense systems, the IDF has the ability to strike deep into Iranian territory. Netanyahu's government has warned Tehran that any future attacks against Israeli territory would be met with a massive response that could target the Islamic Republic's energy and nuclear facilities—a prospect furthered by a new Trump administration that pledged to support Israel's military campaign against Iran and its remaining Yemeni and Iraqi proxies.

Though the Houthis have attacked Israel, Yemen's geographic distance from the conflict and its weakened position from years of civil war, draught, famine, and financial crisis restricted its military capabilities. The Houthis' previous cruise missiles and drones attacks against Israel were neutralized by Jerusalem's Arrow missile defense system. Israeli counterattacks have degraded the Houthis' military and transport infrastructure.

Faced with an emboldened IDF and the prospect of a more aggressive Trump administration, the Islamic Republic of Iran can ill afford the risks that a wider war would bring. Iran's beleaguered economy had bred internal political grievances toward the regime. The country's severe recession, devalued currency, and heightened inflation limited Tehran's war-fighting capability. Economic atrophy bred political resentment.

The Gazan, Syrian, and Lebanese crises exemplified Tehran's corrosive regional influence. Iran's axis of resistance project bred decades of regional crises and civil wars.[86] Though Iran exploited these tragedies to expand its influence, it faced the consequences and disastrous ramifications of its actions.

With its surrogates vastly diminished, Iran could accelerate its push to develop nuclear weapons and intensify its defense relationships with North Korea, Russia, and China. With its large arsenal of nuclear weapons and scientific expertise, Pyongyang is uniquely positioned to assist Tehran's drive to develop nuclear weapons capability.

Faced with a crumbling proxy network, Iran will likely accelerate its nuclear weapons project. Since the collapse of the Joint Comprehensive Plan of Action in 2019, Tehran has expanded its stockpiles of enriched uranium.[87] It currently has enough fissile material to fabricate several nuclear weapons. The Islamic Republic has further conducted satellite launches, metallurgical experiments, and computer modeling simulations—all measures consistent with the advancement of a nuclear weaponization program.[88]

The Islamic Republic needs to rebuild Hezbollah degraded capabilities. With Israel's occupation of Gaza, it is doubtful the Iran can reconstitute Hamas or PIJ. Having expended four hundred of its own missiles in failed April and October 2024 strikes against Israel, Tehran has to replenish its own diminished stockpiles. Ever more reliant on its Yemeni Houthis and Iraqi Shia militias, they, too, will need to be refortified. Here, North Korea is uniquely positioned to assist Iran's rearmament efforts.

North Korean Support to Iran's Proxy Partners

Bruce E. Bechtol Jr.

In the previous chapter, we addressed rogue allies in action—Iran's hybrid wars in the Middle East. This rather unusual but in many ways successful form of aggression has become possible because of the several state and non-state actors in the Middle East who are now supported (some would say sub-sidized) either partially or mostly by Iran.[1] As a follow-up, it is important to note that these proxy partners have also long been provided arms, training, technology, and advisers by North Korea. In some cases (Syria is a key exam-ple), North Korea has provided support for these state and nonstate Iranian proxy partners even longer than Iran.[2] For several years now, North Korea has provided many of the capabilities that these entities need in order to be effec-tive fighting forces in the ongoing violence in the Middle East—sometimes through Iran, sometimes directly, and sometimes using a hybrid of each. But because North Korea provides nothing for free, this support is largely paid for by Iran.[3]

As we read the results of Iran's hybrid wars in the Middle East and the Syrian civil war, the death and destruction that has occurred—particularly since 2011—is quite compelling. But what is less well known is how long North Korea has been supporting the forces that are creating this violence. Thus, we will look at North Korean support given to Syria, Hezbollah, and even Palestinian splinter groups during the Cold War. This was largely (if not completely) subsidized by the USSR, as North Korea was itself serving as a proxy for the greater "socialist cause."[4] Soviet subsidies to North Korea ended in the very early 1990s, and thus, the deals that North Korea had with state and nonstate actors changed from ideological partnerships to a strictly cash-and-carry business.[5] It also meant that someone else was (and is) footing the bill (in other words, paying North Korea for this military support)—Iran. In the post–Cold War period since 1991, North Korea has continued providing large-scale military support to Syria (originally paid for by Syria, eventually largely subsidized by Iran),[6] to Hezbollah, to both Hamas[7] and Palestinian splinter groups, to Yemen (before the Houthis took over), and then later to the Houthis.

We will look at the kind of support that North Korea has provided and continues to provide to these entities. We will look at the amount of money this has generated for Kim Jong-un's slush funds, and we will look at how the military proliferation, support, and advice have paid off in the form of violence and threats to America's allies in the region. Understanding how North Korea was able to take Cold War relationships and turn them into cash-and-carry proliferation agreements is not only interesting; it informs us about what is going on now in the region and what we can expect in coming years.

North Korean Proliferation during the Cold War: Syria

Syria's relationship with North Korea during Damascus's historically bloody civil war is now a matter of record. For several years now, this relationship has been well documented not only by respected press sources but by equally credible sources such as the UN Panel of Experts. While this relationship was extremely important to the survival of Syrian forces in combat and to North Korea's military-industrial complex (which is largely based on antiquated Soviet technology but is extremely useful in providing fighting forces with arms as they encounter equally primitively armed rebel forces in the civil war that Damascus fought since 2011), it would surprise many analysts to learn that this relationship is nothing new. In fact, North Korea and Syria had a long-standing and robust relationship throughout much of the Cold War, largely because both nations were considered surrogates of the Soviet Union at the time and were often the subjects of large-scale subsidies, especially for arms and related training and advisers. Thus, in this section we will address how the relationship evolved during the Cold War, what North Korea brought to the party when it came to conflicts with Israel, and in which specific roles and missions North Korea was involved.

North Korea and Syria established formal diplomatic relations in 1966.[8] This was not surprising at the time as nation-states such as Egypt and Syria were considered to be in the Soviet "sphere of influence,"[9] albeit in a far less dominant way than Warsaw Pact states or even states such as Cuba and North Korea, which were totally dependent on the USSR for basic economic and political survival (or so it seemed at the time). The diplomatic relationship that North Korea and Syria established in 1966 existed until late December 2024—and remains important. At the time, the funding for military aid, advisers, equipment, and training was completely subsidized by the Soviet Union—a situation that would remain in existence right up until the very early 1990s.[10]

In a Stimson Center publication, North Korean scholar Alexandre Mansourov highlights many key aspects of the North Korea–Syria relationship that began in full bloom in 1967. In that same year, Pyongyang sent twenty-four pilots to Syria in the midst of the Six-Day War. But there is much more. According to the report:

> In 1970, the DPRK dispatched 200 tank crewmen, 53 pilots, and 140 missile technicians to Syria. During the October 1973 Arab-Israeli War, the DPRK dispatched 30 pilots to Egypt and Syria, who provided training for Syrian pilots to fight against Israel. Moreover, the North Korean Air Force pilots themselves flew the Soviet-made Egyptian and Syrian airplanes during some key air battles. In 1975 and 1976, Pyongyang sent 75 Air Force instructors and 40 MIG pilots to Damascus, respectively. In 1982, during the Lebanese civil war, the DPRK government dispatched SOF (special operations forces) servicemen to Syria to provide training for guerrilla operations, some killed by the Israeli military.[11]

Mansourov also states, "Beginning in the late 1970s through the 1980s, the DPRK supplied Syria with various conventional weapons such as rifles, guns, mortars, ammunition, bombs, armored vehicles, antitank missiles, radars, and even military uniforms. In particular, in 1978, the DPRK sold 300 recoilless guns to Syria. In 1982, when the civil war broke out in Syria, the Syrian military killed 20,000 civilians by firing 'BM-11, 122mm MLRS (Multiple Launch Rocket System),' the weapon system imported from the DPRK. The Israel military snatched the notorious 'BM-11' from Syria during the Lebanon war in 1982, killing 25 KPA soldiers who serviced it."[12]

Clearly, during the Cold War, during conflicts starting with the Six-Day War, North Korea was knee-deep in helping its ally Syria to prepare its armed forces to fight Israel. In fact, as indicated in the documented evidence above, North Korean military personnel actually appear to have participated in combat operations—both on land and in the air. This relationship was also dominated early by the presence of Kim Kyok-sik (now passed away), who played a large role in maintaining a robust North Korea–Syria military relationship. Kim Kyok-sik was considered a close confidant of both Kim Il-sung and Kim Jong-il and served over a decade in Syria—a factor that undoubtedly led to Pyongyang's large contributions of manpower, training, and equipment.[13] The Cold War relationship between Pyongyang and Damascus laid the baseline for a relationship that was to come into play after the Soviet Union's collapse in the early 1990s. But the North Koreans do nothing for free, and they never have. In 1991, with Soviet subsidies gone, North Korea and Syria would have to find new ways to fund their mutually beneficial relationship. This proved to be far less difficult than one would initially imagine.

North Korean Proliferation during the Cold War: Hezbollah

Hezbollah is an organization that is well known for being both violent and well trained. Hezbollah is also well known for not hesitating to use terrorism (repeatedly) as a tool of policy. The group has been a part of the Iranian proxy plan since the later stages of the Cold War. In fact, though Hezbollah gets financial support from largely illicit activities overseas and expatriate remittances, the group would be unable to maintain its powerful status without patronage from both Syria and Iran and without financial support to the tune of at least $100 million a year from Tehran.[14] Iran has been providing this support to Hezbollah since the Cold War still existed (Syria played its role since that time as well). What makes this situation even more dangerous is that, beginning in the Cold War (which is what we will discuss in this section), North Korea has provided both arms and training to Hezbollah—typically paid for by Iran and supported by Syria.

During the Cold War (and largely now in a much more sophisticated way), North Korea supported Hezbollah in two key ways: improved versions of rocket systems, such as 122mm or 107mm multiple rocket launchers, and specialized training for Hezbollah commando units and commanders of these units. Of course, this was often—then and now—very difficult to analyze because as Carl Anthony Wege states, "Iran simply uses a complex of shell companies, vendors, multiple purchases, and transfer modalities to acquire arms and other prohibited materials under for itself and its proxies such as Hizballah."[15] In other words, Iran acquires systems for itself from North Korea and also supplies them to proxy groups such as Hezbollah, Hamas, and the Houthis. For Hezbollah, this has been ongoing since the 1980s. Thus, during the Cold War, North Korea provided arms to Hezbollah through Iran, sometimes through Syria, and sometimes through Iran and then Syria (since sometimes arms would go to Iran and then be transshipped to Syria and then to Hezbollah), and sometimes North Korea even cut separate deals with Hezbollah as funds from the group's illicit activities began to kick in.[16]

As any Israeli could tell you, the Hezbollah rocket attacks into the Jewish state have been quite effective at inflicting casualties and, perhaps just as importantly, creating an unstable environment. The range and accuracy of these weapons have been as effective as they have been in past years—beginning in the Cold War—at least in part thanks to the proliferation from the North Koreans.[17] Of course, the Iron Dome system has greatly cut into the effectiveness of these rockets, as recent warfare with Hezbollah has proven.[18] But in the Middle East, as in Africa and elsewhere, the North Koreans also were quite prolific at proliferating military capabilities by conducting training, largely in unconventional warfare methods. During the 1980s, Hezbollah leaders visited North Korea to learn special warfare techniques.[19] While this is the first known instance of North Korean Special Operations Forces training Hezbollah fighters, it certainly was not the last. But it laid a baseline for more training that would occur later and become significant in Hezbollah operations against Israel.

Much like Syria, Hezbollah now has a relationship with North Korea that spans generations. Starting its baseline in the 1980s with the proliferation of what proved to be effective rockets and important commando training, the relationship has now expanded to a level of sophistication not normally expected of nonstate actors. A key reason for this has been the financing of Iran and the support (from and for) Syria. As long as there is instability in the Middle East created largely by Iran, North Korea will be there to supply the weapons and training. But there is more than we have addressed thus far. The post–Cold War era brought in even more violence and destruction.

North Korean Proliferation during the Cold War: Palestinian Groups

Hamas is an organization that has often used terrorism against Israeli citizens. It also has fired numerous rockets into Israeli cities—especially Tel Aviv.[20] But Hamas came to primacy after the Cold War was over. Long before the Cold War ended, beginning in the 1960s, North Korea had a relationship with Palestinian groups who considered themselves to be "warriors" against the state of Israel. It was during this Cold War period that North Korea (through these relationships) laid the baseline for a later relationship that Pyongyang would form with Hamas. Thus, I will address how North Korea supported terrorist groups comprising Palestinians during the Cold War. This period allowed Pyongyang's military forces to gain a reputation as a group capable of providing weapons and training—both of which these Palestinian entities would use against Israel.

The Kim Il-sung–Yasser Arafat relationship began in 1966. North Korea began supplying arms and training to not just the Palestine Liberation Organization (PLO) but also the Popular Front for the Liberation of Palestine (PFLP) and the Democratic Front for the Liberation of Palestine (DFLP) in the very early 1970s, and this continued at least to the end of the 1980s.[21] In 1970, PFLP founder George Habash visited North Korea to seek arms and training. Subsequently, PFLP leader Wadi Haddad recruited three Japanese Red Army terrorists for a terrorist mission into Israel at the Lod Airport in 1972 (North Korea also supported the Japanese Red Army).[22] According to documents from the Congressional Research Service, North Korea provided both arms and training to the PLO beginning in the late 1970s.[23] Reportedly, in 1972, thirty Palestinians (guerrillas) were trained by seventy to eighty North Korean instructors. Palestinian guerrillas continued to conduct military training in North Korea until at least 1975.[24]

If one wonders why North Korea has been able to establish what appears to be a continuing relationship with Hamas, one has only to look at the long-standing arms and training relationship that Pyongyang had in the Cold War, not only with the PLO but with splinter groups who conducted violent terrorist acts against Israel and others as a matter of policy. It was this proven capability, along with North Korea's close cooperation with Iran—which has often served as a benefactor to Hamas—that led to Hamas being yet another customer, along with the several state and nonstate actors in the Middle East that Pyongyang currently serves. Hamas has proved itself to be a formidable post–Cold War enemy of Israel, and one that will rate discussion later in this chapter. Suffice to say, today the big difference is where the money is coming from—Iran, not the Soviet military (which ultimately subsidized North Korea so that it could remain deeply involved in these Cold War antics).

North Korean Proliferation to Syria: Post–Cold War

During the Cold War, the Middle East, along with the rest of the world, existed in a bipolar paradigm. That is to say, much of the conflict worldwide simply comprised small proxy wars fought between allies of either the United States or the Soviet Union. In the Middle East, Soviet benefactors often attacked US allies and US interests in the region, but they were simply acting as proxies for Moscow, which paid for these acts of violence in the form of both military aid and economic subsidies.[25] In 1991, after the end of the Gulf War, it became obvious that the well had run dry and the Soviet Union was well on its way to collapse. Certainly countries like Syria had more of an interest than simply being a proxy of the Soviet Union when it came to confrontations with Israel. But the military aid and economic subsidies that came in certainly helped their cause.[26] With the end of Soviet aid and subsidies during the very early 1990s, it became obvious that Syria would have to seek other means to finance a military it continued to need—at least in the minds of those who ruled the Alawite regime. This would allow them to purchase arms from the North Koreans and to fight their next war.

After the end of the Gulf War in 1991, Syria was awarded several billion dollars from Saudi Arabia for the role Syrian troops played in the war. This was gratuitous because it occurred soon after military aid and other subsidies from the Soviet Union ceased. Syria used a portion of this money to place an order with the North Koreans for Scud C missiles—reportedly hundreds of them. The North Koreans would later build a Scud C fabrication facility in Syria. This facility—like most North Korean fabrication facilities that exist in the Middle East and Africa—was likely unable to function without North Korean parts and North Korean technical assistance.[27] Later, the Syrians reached a deal with Pyongyang to purchase Scud D missile systems. During the early stages of and throughout the Syrian civil war, North Koreans were still on the ground in Syria, assisting Syrian forces in upgrading the Scud D systems.[28]

An important component to all of this is understanding how a poor country like Syria was able to get through tough economic times and still manage to rebuild and upgrade its military. The answer is Iran. By the late 1990s, it had become obvious that Iran was at least partially financing Syria's military and also providing economic subsidies. This was extremely important at the time because North Korea—then and now—does nothing for free. Thus, Syrian entities required Iranian money to develop and upgrade Syria's military capabilities, many of them coming from and being developed by North Korea.[29] Perhaps the most striking of these military subsidies was Tehran's reported financing of Syria's nuclear reactor, built with North Korean assistance (destroyed by Israeli forces in 2007). This is described in detail in my book *North Korean Military Proliferation in the Middle East and Africa*.[30]

As the Syrian civil war hit full swing in 2011, military aid and economic subsidies from Iran radically increased, as the Alawite government in Damascus was literally in a fight for its life. The Syrian civil was an economic boon for the primitive yet effective military-industrial complex that existed (and still exists) in North Korea. When a nation-state fights a war, it uses up artillery and rocket systems, it loses armor in battle, it needs to replace ballistic missiles that have been fired in combat or simply destroyed by rebel forces, and it needs to rapidly beef up the small arms of many kinds that its conventional forces use in combat (North Korea provided all of this, with Iran largely footing the bill). And if the nation-state is a country like Syria, it needs help maintaining and resupplying its military forces with chemical weapons that will strike fear and desperation into enemy forces that might otherwise carry out completely successful military campaigns. This is where North Korea came in and became a much-needed partner in Syria.[31]

It is important to note that most (if not all) of the bill for the upgrade and maintenance of Syrian military during the bloody civil war was paid for through direct purchases, economic subsidies, or large loans from Iran.[32] As this money came in, the sanctions on North Korea, Iran, and Syria seemed to have no effect on the seemingly endless shipments of both conventional and unconventional arms from North Korea into Syria.

In 2016, reports showed evidence that North Korea had supplied Syria with several types of artillery systems, light machine guns, and antitank-guided missiles, as well as refurbishing older Syrian Soviet-era tanks. They also supplied the Syrians with man-portable air defense systems (MANPADS).[33] Also in 2016, the North Koreans reportedly had two Special Operations Forces battalions conducting combat missions in support of the Syrian army. The units were known as Chalma 1 and Chalma 7.[34] In the end, by 2018, it became obvious that North Korea was proliferating hundreds of millions of dollars' worth of conventional and unconventional weapons per year to Syria during the infamous civil war.[35]

As the Syrian civil war continues to die down and the rebel forces' ability becomes almost nonexistent (or at least much less of a threat), the refurbishment and upgrade of Syrian military forces becomes very important. North Korea also helped Syria with similar efforts in the 1970s after the Six-Day and Yom Kippur Wars.[36] Thus, since it must happen, Iran will most likely be the benefactor helping to rebuild and refurbish Syrian military forces. Can there be any doubt that North Korea will play a major role in this? In fact, the North Koreans reportedly sent eight hundred new workers to Syria as early as the fall of 2019. The North Koreans were also on the ground even before that occurred, assisting Syrians with missile systems.[37] It is likely that most if not all of these workers deployed to Syria to reconstruct military facilities and support Syrian combat systems.

North Korea continued to supply Syria even as the Assad regime was supporting Hezbollah following its attacks on Israel from October 7, 2023, and continuing into December 2024, when the Assad regime collapsed and a new rebel government took over. The new government clearly did not want the support of Iran, Russia, or North Korea.[38] In what was clearly a defensive move, the Israeli Air Force destroyed what they called strategic sites following the fall of Assad's government. This took away any opportunities the new government would have to attack Israel with Assad's old weapons. Included in the weapons systems targeted in the attacks were ballistic missile facilities and facilities housing chemical weapons—both supplied by North Korea.[39]

North Korean Proliferation to Hezbollah: Post–Cold War

The relationship between North Korea and Hezbollah has spanned a generation. It remains intact and robust today. The reasons for this are quite simple: Hezbollah has been involved in violent conflict nearly every day of its existence, and thus the need for arms is nearly unending. Iran has been a Hezbollah sponsor since the earliest days of the 1980s. And North Korea, one of the key suppliers of arms to Hezbollah, has maintained a constant and useful (for both parties) military proliferation relationship with Iran for over forty years.[40] Since Iran is Hezbollah's most important benefactor (especially financially), the arms and the training keep flowing for this nonstate actor that has been so effective at creating violence and instability in the Middle East. In this section, we will examine North Korean proliferation to Hezbollah during the post–Cold War days and the challenge its existence poses to the national security interests of the United States and its allies.

During the 1990s, Hezbollah continued to operate as an effective and lethal organization. During this period, Syria and Iran cooperated in supporting the organization.[41] In fact, Syria often served as a conduit for Iran when North Korean weapons were coming in for Hezbollah from Iran.

The world watched Israel go into Lebanon with ground forces during the last week of September 2024, and it is important to understand that this would not have been necessary had Hezbollah not had a vast network of tunnels (their second one) that prevented destruction from purely air power. To destroy or degrade Hezbollah's military ability to continue attacking Israel's citizens, the IDF had to send in land forces to attack them underground. This military paradigm shift, which started in the 2006 war and then was on steroids for the latest conflict, would not exist were it not for North Korea's expertise, engineering (including special equipment), advisors, and technicians. Hezbollah paid Pyongyang's Korea Mining Development Corporation (KOMID) $13 million to build this forty-five-mile-long tunnel network. Now we have seen it in combat thanks to North Korean military proliferation and Hezbollah's unending appetite for launching rockets into towns in northern Israel.

Numerous reports following the 2006 Israel-Hezbollah war provide evidence that Hezbollah's underground facilities were constructed under North Korean supervision and advice in 2003–04. The constructed tunnels contained, among other things, dispensaries, arms dumps, and food stocks.[42] This significant tunnel network was far more robust than Israeli forces anticipated as they prosecuted combat operations against Hezbollah in 2006. To quote an article in the Israeli press, "Hizbullah's military bases, armories, bunkers, and communications networks were much more extensive than Israel's intelligence services estimated on the eve of the 2006 war."[43] Other reporting based on testimony from a former IRGC officer states, "With the assistance of several Iranian engineers and technicians, as well as North Korean experts, who traveled to Lebanon disguised as servants for the Iranian embassy and its officers, Hezbollah has successfully built a 25km long underground belt, with 12-meter openings along it, the officer added. Every four openings are connected to one another through an easily accessible passageway."[44] But this system Hezbollah used in 2006 was only the beginning.

In 2021 a very important report from the Alma Research Center in Israel revealed Hezbollah had built another larger tunnel system—with the assistance of the North Koreans, and of course, the Iranians. Hezbollah agreed to a $13 million deal with KOMID (North Korea's primary proliferation front company) to build a forty-five-kilometer tunnel system connecting several key nodes in Lebanon and reportedly much longer and more sophisticated than the first tunnel system. The North Koreans had already been paid $6 million by 2013, and the tunnel system appears to have been completed by 2021. As the Alma Research Center articulates in the report, "In our estimation, the cumulative length of all the tunnels in the 'Land of the Tunnels' can reach up to hundreds of kilometers. Hezbollah tunnels, like Hamas tunnels, contain underground command and control rooms, weapons and supply depots, field clinics and specified designated shafts used to fire missiles of all types (rockets, surface-to-surface missiles, anti-tank missiles and anti-aircraft missiles). These shafts are hidden and camouflaged and cannot be detected above ground."[45]

What the evidence presented above shows us is that Hezbollah had been building up in anticipation of its next conflict with Israel. Clearly they were enabled in this process by support from North Korea and Iran. It is also important to note that these tunnels were a key factor, perhaps *the* key factor, in Israel's decision to bring ground forces into the conflict with Hezbollah in Lebanese territory in 2024. The tunnels gave Hezbollah not only longer sustainment but the ability to move forces and equipment from combat zone to combat zone without being seen by IDF aircraft or other intelligence-collection methods. Thus, North Korea has been a key aspect of Hezbollah's military capabilities and logistical flexibility, including in the present day. There is quite simply no other way of going after attacking Hezbollah forces except to take out this extensive sophisticated tunnel system—and that takes ground troops.[46]

In 2009, a shipment of over thirty-five tons of military equipment on a plane leased by the North Koreans (and carrying North Korean military equipment) was caught in Thailand where it had landed to refuel. The weapons on board included small arms, rocket-propelled grenades, and other weapons that one would expect to go to a force like Hezbollah. The Israeli foreign minister at the time stated that these weapons were bound for Hezbollah and Hamas.[47] These are just two compelling examples of North Korea's constant supply of weapons to Hezbollah, which has remained a constant in the post–Cold War era.

Perhaps the most important role that Hezbollah's fighting forces have played in the Middle East has been what we have seen in the Syrian civil war.[48] As we described earlier, North Korea has actively supported both Iran and Syria throughout Damascus's struggle for continued power. The many arms shipments into both Syria and Iran have often contained weapons that could be used by not just Iranian and Syrian troops but Hezbollah fighters as well. As Hezbollah's role has become more important, it has also become more sophisticated. Thus, the weaponry, command and control, and training for Hezbollah have become more and more like those of a traditional military organization. With this, of course, has come North Korean assistance and arms. In fact, according to several reports, Syrian forces have even supplied Hezbollah with Scud D missiles—which they obtained from the North Koreans.[49] According to a Syrian defector, his former army had also supplied Hezbollah forces with chemical weapons components—also originally supplied to the Syrians by North Korea.[50] According to reports in the Israeli and American press, by November 2022, Hezbollah had moved hundreds of rockets with chemical munitions to a warehouse near the border with Syria. The missiles were reportedly equipped with thionyl chloride with the assistance of North Korean experts and in collaboration with Iranian chemical weapons specialists.[51]

As conflict and violence continue to flourish in the Middle East, Hezbollah remains a key player. They may be the most trusted proxy of the Iranian regime. Their role in the region is important and compelling. Thus, the proliferation of arms and training that North Korea continues to provide (for a price, of course) is vital. Much if not most of this continues to be financed or transported by Iran (or Syria) as a conduit for North Korean arms that eventually get to Hezbollah. Thus, North Korea plays an important role in supporting—both directly and indirectly—one of Iran's key proxy bene-factors in its ongoing war to be the hegemon in the Middle East.

North Korean Proliferation to Palestinians: Hamas after the Cold War

North Korean cooperation with Palestinian groups has been ongoing for a very long time, as was addressed earlier in this chapter. Since the end of the Cold War, however, North Korea has essentially focused on supporting Hamas more than other groups. The reasons for this are important. Hamas has had an on-again, off-again relationship with Iran that involved millions of dollars when it actually occurred. When this relationship was "off again," it gave North Korea an opportunity to sell arms to Hamas without "Iranian involvement," thus allowing Tehran to delay relations and aid to Hamas for reasons I will describe later. In addition, North Korea has a long history of selling rockets (largely 107mm and 122mm) to Hezbollah, Iran, and Syria. Hezbollah has had and continues to have a relationship with Hamas that has included aid and training provided to the Palestinian group—thus allowing North Korea to gain a foothold in supporting military operations.[52]

According to the US Institute of Peace, between 1990 and 2000, Iran donated $20 to $50 million annually to Hamas. Iran also provided arms and training. At a meeting during 2006, Iran reportedly pledged to donate $250 million more to Hamas. During the 2008 Hamas-Israel war, Iran donated rockets, at least some of which likely came from North Korea. The outbreak of the Syrian civil war triggered a break in the very profitable (for Hamas) relationship between the Gaza-based organization and Tehran. The Iranians backed Assad while Hamas backed the mostly Sunni opposition. Thus, in 2012, Iran cut off financial assistance to Hamas. This gap in the relationship was exacerbated in 2015 when Hamas openly expressed support for the Saudi fight against the Houthis. In 2017, after a meeting involving Iranian offi-cials and the Hamas second-in-command, the relationship (and aid) became "on again."[53] So there was a five-year time frame (2012–2017) during which Hamas reportedly received no aid from Iran. Enter the North Koreans.

Back in 2021, I wrote a piece for the *National Interest* in which I outlined arms deals that reportedly occurred between North Korea and Hamas and resulted in rockets, upgrades to technology, and other military capabilities.[54]

At the time, Hamas was launching thousands of rockets into Israel, but most were destroyed by the Iron Dome system, and the Israeli people largely considered themselves safe from attack.

Fast forward to October 2023. Things had changed. The threat from Hamas proved to be so horrifying that most agreed it needed to be completely destroyed. The terrorist attacks against civilians and civilian communities in Israel were carried out with a level of brutality rarely seen since medieval times. In the footage the whole world has seen, Hamas "fighters" used weaponry from several sources—and shockingly to some, an analysis of weapons used thus far shows several systems with North Korean origins.

The world first took notice of North Korean arms that ended up in the hands of Hamas in 2009, when arms shipments consisting largely of rockets and rocket-propelled grenades were interdicted in Thailand and the UAE. The Israeli government at the time stated that these shipments were both probably bound for Hamas and Hezbollah.[55] North Korea's go-between to these two entities was almost certainly Iran. Since interdicted shipments are often only the tip of the iceberg, this is quite disturbing.

According to reporting in the *Telegraph* during July 2014, North Korea had entered into a deal with Hamas to sell the terrorist organization both rockets and communications gear (more on the "communications" gear later). The deal is said to have been worth several hundred thousand dollars, so it likely involved the sale of thousands of North Korean rockets to Hamas. The deal was reportedly brokered through a Lebanese front company with ties to Hamas, located in Beirut. In addition, by the time the article was published, a down payment had already been made,[56] so it is likely that the shipment of rockets and communications gear occurred sometime in late 2014.

In 2018, Fadi al-Batsh, a Palestinian and reported Hamas operative, was assassinated in Malaysia. Malaysia was for many years (including during that time frame) a location that North Korea used to operate many of its front companies for arms deals all over the world, particularly in the Middle East and Africa, as well as to launder the money from those deals. According to press reporting, intelligence officials from the West and the Middle East had evidence Batsh was part of negotiations with the North Koreans for arms deals being run out of Malaysia (as many of Pyongyang's arms deals were at the time), including for communications components used in rocket guidance systems. According to Egyptian officials, a shipment of North Korean communications components used for guided munitions that they captured in 2018 was destined for Gaza.[57]

And what of the actual capabilities that North Korea has contributed to Hamas? According to sources within the South Korean Joint Chiefs of Staff, "Some of the multiple rocket launchers found near the Israel border that Hamas militants reportedly used had 'Bang-122' written in Korean." The official further remarked, "Lately, we have repeatedly detected North Korea exporting various weapons to Middle East countries and militant organizations, including the 122-millimeter multiple rocket launchers found along the border near Israel." The official said, "We believe these weapons were used by Hamas or an organization that supports Hamas." The F-7 North Korean–made rocket-propelled grenade was also photographed in the possession of Hamas fighters attacking Israel on October 7, 2023.[58]

Israeli and South Korean intelligence later confirmed that fuses of an F-7 system recovered from Hamas had Korean characters on them. And according to the Associated Press, as confirmed by numerous photos, "Hamas propaganda videos and photos previously have shown its fighters with North Korea's Bulsae guided anti-tank missile."[59] The Bulsae is a laser-guided anti-tank-guided missile that has the potential to be effective against Israeli armor as it moves through a ground campaign in Gaza.

Finally, back in 2014, according to reporting from the *Telegraph*, "Israeli military commanders supervising operations against Gaza believe North Korean experts have given Hamas advice on building the extensive network of tunnels in Gaza that has enabled fighters to move weapons without detection by Israeli drones, which maintain a constant monitoring operation over Gaza."[60] In November and December 2023, as the IDF in Gaza began to uncover more Hamas tunnels, it became obvious that many of these tunnels were much bigger and wider than had previously been assessed by most analysts. In fact, the new tunnels uncovered were big enough for sophisticated facilities and even a rail line. According to Daphné Richemond-Barak, a tunnel warfare expert at Reichman University in Israel, "These tunnels look a whole lot like the tunnels North Korea has dug into South Korea. I see something at a much higher level of sophistication. We are talking about tunnel warfare at a different level. I see in addition to the inference of North Korea, . . . I also see the hand of Iran here."[61] These tunnels have been a major challenge to the IDF in Gaza.

North Korean Proliferation in Yemen:
It Is About the Money, Not the Ideology

The situation in Yemen is a confusing one in relation to North Korea. The North Koreans (as evidenced throughout this chapter) have a long history of backing separatist movements, Communist nations, and terrorist groups. But it would still come as a surprise to many that North Korea sent sophisticated weapons to the government in Yemen yet now is a confirmed supplier of weapons and training to the Houthis—who overthrew the previous government and now are locked in an ongoing civil war with no end in sight.

North Korea supplied conventional arms and advisers as well as missiles to the previous government in Yemen, going back to the 1990s. In 2002, Yemen took shipments of Scud C missiles from North Korea. In fact, one of the shipments was intercepted by Spanish Marines, and the president of Yemen actually called the White House to ensure he got back "his missiles." Yemen was allied with the United States in the war on terror at the time and was considered an important ally. But the government in Yemen did make a promise to cease its arms relationship with North Korea (and Yemen got its North Korean missiles back). Thus, during the 1990s and into the early 2000s, North Korea provided military support (for a price) to the government of President Ali Abdullah Saleh.[62]

As the civil war in Yemen raged on and ravaged an already very poor country, the tide shifted, and the Houthis (a Shiite group backed by Iran) became the dominant force in the country. It was at this point that North Korea apparently decided it would be much more profitable to support them than to support a government that had publicly stated it no longer wanted to work with Pyongyang. In 2015, South Korean intelligence confirmed that North Koreans had supplied missiles that were now being launched into Saudi Arabia. Saudi officials assessed that the missiles had been supplied to the Houthis by Iran—which is probably at least partially true.[63] According to a UN Panel of Experts report from 2019, North Korea was in a deal to sell ballistic missiles to the Houthis (likely improved versions with longer ranges than the original Scud C).[64] No report mentions anything about North Korean trainers or advisers on the ground assisting the Houthis—but someone has to have done this. Thus, it is likely that the Iranians (as alleged by the Saudis) were playing this role. Iranians have been heavily involved in Houthi decision-making.[65] The North Koreans also reportedly have been supplying the Houthis with a variety of conventional weapons. To quote Open Democracy, an independent, global media association, "The weapons intended for Yemen range from light weapons such as Kalashnikovs through general-purpose machine guns, anti-tank missiles and shoulder-launched anti-aircraft missiles right up to tanks and ballistic missiles. The transit route has been primarily through a Syrian-registered company, the Consulting Bureau for Marketing, headed by a Syrian arms trader, Hussein al-Ali."[66]

The Houthis fired a missile at Israel on October 31, 2023. The missile was shot down over Jordan, and fragments of the missile were later recovered. Based on analysis conducted on the ground at the time, Hangul characters (Korean writing) were clearly written on the engine cover. It is not clear if this missile was first proliferated to Iran and then passed on to the Houthis or if the missile came directly from the arms deal that reportedly occurred during 2019, as addressed above. What is clear is that the Houthis were now using North Korean technology in their missiles and probably conventional weapons as well.[67]

North Korea has proved that ideology has little to do with its arms sales and military support. Yemen is an important case study in this. The previous government to which Pyongyang provided missiles was actually an ally of the United States. Pyongyang's current ally in Yemen, the Houthis, is often thought of as a surrogate for Iran.[68] Is Iran paying for the military support that North Korea is supplying to the Houthis? I think that of that there can be no doubt. If they are not paying for all of it, then it is a very big portion. In addition, Iranian advisers and North Korean specialists are also likely working on the ground (or have in the recent past) in Yemen. It would be nearly impossible to conduct the missile mission without doing so. Thus, the Houthis are just one more aspect of Iran's hybrid warfare that has been and likely will continue to be supported by the North Koreans.

Watching North Korea's actions in the Middle East is a long and fascinating endeavor. The North Koreans used their Cold War connections to enable relationships that would be very profitable for North Korea in the post–Cold War era—especially with countries like Syria. The benefactor changed. The Soviet Union was replaced by Iran as the financial powerhouse for military and terrorist action once the Cold War ended. North Korea's most profitable and compelling relationship in the Middle East is with Iran. But Iran's hybrid warfare involves extensive use of proxy state and nonstate actors. It also involves giving a great deal of financial support to these proxies. Because North Korea is providing much of the military support to these entities, this has been a significant boost to North Korea's military-industrial complex, which consists largely of copies of old Soviet-era weaponry. This is perfect for fighting a hybrid war—and North Korea has been able to use it for its full financial and military advantage.

What does all of this mean? First of all, North Korea will sell anything to anybody—including terrorist groups. Second, the governments of Israel and the United States must consider North Korea's military proliferation an existential national security threat, and more proactive means of thwarting it must immediately commence. Third, North Korea's strong ties to Iran also equate to strong ties to proxy state and nonstate actors supported by Iran. Thus, the road to destroying North Korea's illicit arms networks in the Middle East runs through Iran.[69]

Rogue Allies and the Criminal Financial Networks That Support the Partnership

Bruce E. Bechtol Jr. and Anthony N. Celso

The Islamic Republic of Iran has for decades been subject to US and international economic sanctions that aim to punish the regime's malign behavior.[1] This includes Tehran's support for terrorism and its domestic human rights violations. For decades, its nuclear and ballistic missile programs have been targeted by UN-supported international sanctions.[2] Though nuclear-program-related sanctions were eased during the JCPOA's 2016–2017 implementation, America's 2018 withdrawal from the accord led to expanded US sanctions that have restricted the Islamic Republic's ability to access the global financial system and impaired its oil exports.

Between 2018 and 2020, the Trump administration imposed sixteen hundred sanctions against Islamic Revolutionary Guard Corps (IRGC)-connected individuals, companies, and insurgent groups to force the Islamic Republic's acquiescence to greater international controls over its nuclear program.[3] It failed. Despite America's and the international community's efforts to rein in Tehran's nuclear and missile development programs, the Islamic Republic has mitigated their effect through sanctions evasion. Aided by North Korean support, Iran's partnership with Hezbollah's clandestine smuggling operations has enabled it to finance its missile and militia strategy, which has destabilized the Middle East.[4]

This cooperation is widely recognized. The UN Panel of Experts' 2018 report indicated that North Korea used Syrian Hussein al-Ali's arms-trafficking company to cut an arms deal with IRGC-supported Houthi rebels in Yemen.[5] This in microcosm illustrates the relationship between North Korean–

supported and Iranian-supported proxy forces. It is one of many cases that we address in this book.

Capitalizing on illicit trade, the Islamic Republic has survived at the expense of the Iranian people. They, not the regime, bear most of the pain that sanctions have created. Massive street demonstrations in 2019, for example, were driven by economic duress. Faced with 2022 protests against the morality police's murder of a Kurdish woman for improperly wearing her hijab, the regime has resorted to even greater repression.

Abetted by criminal finance, the Iran Threat Network composed of Islamic Revolutionary Guard Corps–Quds Force (IRGC-QF) and its proxy forces have since the 2003 Iraq War been on the ascendant across the Middle East.[6] This chapter first examines Iran's illicit activities that aim to preserve the regime and facilitate its regional policy. It does so in two parts. First, it develops a theoretical framework to explain Iran's sanctions evasion strategy and the way it works across the world. In this section, we discuss the constituent components of Iranian and Hezbollah smuggling networks in Latin America, Africa, Europe, and the Middle East that comprise a mix of criminals, rogue states, diplomats, insurgent groups, and diaspora communities that provide a financial and weapons lifeline to the regime. Second, we assess the IRGC's role in devising a global smuggling network designed to finance Tehran's militia and missile strategy. The third part of this chapter examines the role that North Korea plays in the fortification of the Iran Threat Network and the ways in which these rogue actors' sanctions evasion systems overlap and diverge. This part will also discuss North Korea's sanctions evasion strategy and the way it works—particularly with Iran. We conclude that Tehran and Pyongyang have successfully evaded sanctions by the international community and that their partnership continues to fuel conflict across the Middle East and Africa.

Based on past evidence, the Biden administration's efforts to rejoin the JCPOA, if they had been realized, are likely to provide more resources enabling Tehran's destabilizing missile and militia strategy. One 2022 Foundation for Defense of Democracies study estimates that Iran rejoining the accord could result in $1 trillion of sanctions relief within the decade.[7] Like its North Korean ally, the Islamic Republic has taken every opportunity that diplomatic engagement offers to achieve its strategic aims. It has done so by enmeshing the IRGC and its proxy Hezbollah in a complex world of criminal finance to underwrite its strategic ambitions.

Iran's illicit financial networks and proliferation modus operandi bear striking similarities to North Korea's system. We believe that North Korea has set a precedent for Iran's future behavior. These regimes have created a deep-state apparatus committed to the realization of a totalitarian ideology. Tehran and Pyongyang have specialized administrative units (Unit 190 and Office 39, respectively) committed to organizing and coordinating sanctions evasion across the world. These offices oversee a bewildering maze of front and shell companies aimed at sanctions evasion, money laundering, drug smuggling, weapons procurement, and proliferation.

As in North Korea's case, the Islamic Republic's populism provides an ideological cover to mask the regime's true motives. Iran has two objectives behind its clandestine sanctions evasion and weapons proliferation network: (1) regime survival and (2) the fortification of a regional forward defense strategy based on the arming of Shiite proxy groups across the Persian Gulf and the Levant.[8] Iran's sanctions evasion and weapons procurement channels assist its funding and weaponization of Shia and regime-aligned militias across the Middle East. By illicitly transferring small arms, missiles, and drone technology to insurgent proxies, Iran is funding terrorism and promoting regional instability. North Korea has provided many of these conventional arms, weapons platforms, rockets, and missiles.

Iran's clandestine weapons procurement program requires a sophisticated strategy of forging connections between insurgent-terrorist groups, other anti-Western states, and the criminal world. The Islamic Republic's clandestine procurement channels are run by Iranian and Lebanese criminal syndicates with connections to the IRGC-QF and Hezbollah.[9] Like North Korea, Tehran has undertaken significant efforts to evade sanctions and fund its regional hegemonic missile and militia project.

These attempts, however, have been vigorously challenged by tightened American sanctions and by multinational criminal investigations against Iran's facilitators. Sanctions, legal actions, cargo seizures, and kinetic measures have restricted but not successfully derailed Iran's illicit procurement channels. Iran, however, has made significant progress in the pursuance of its foreign policy objectives.

It has done so by partnering with Hezbollah, which is a key conduit for its regional ambitions and has been implicated in Iranian policy across the Middle East. Hezbollah involvement in the Syrian civil war is a manifest example of how the group has become Tehran's premier expeditionary force.

The Islamic Republic's insertion of IRGC-QF arms and trainers in Iraq and Yemen offers further evidence of its commitment to creating a Shia imamate whose expansion has been hastened by sectarian civil wars in the region.

This effort has been facilitated by a clandestine criminal network whose operations span Latin America, Asia, West Africa, the Middle East, and Europe. The Islamic Republic's strategic culture blends ideological and pragmatic motives whose central vision is driven by its religious obsession to preserve its faith, which for centuries has been persecuted by Sunni extremists and regimes.[10]

Tehran aspires to create across the Middle East a Shia imamate that threatens Israeli, American, and Sunni Gulf security.[11] This grand plan is predicated on procurement channels to circumvent oil, weapons, and financial sanctions against Iran and aligned groups. This requires an international network that links criminalized states, diaspora communities, transnational criminal networks, insurgent groups, and entrepreneurial facilitators.[12]

Iran exploits lax passport laws to enable Lebanese and Iranian expatriates to create overseas shell companies to procure sanctioned materials.[13] Since the 1980s, Iran has created an international criminal network to finance its state-sponsored terrorism aimed at killings Jews and Americans. Iranian-linked attacks have killed hundreds of Americans and thousands of Israelis, and they portend continued efforts to threaten American citizens and Jews across the world.

Tehran's most successful attacks were the byproduct of joint ventures between IRGC and Hezbollah. These assaults have featured trucks laden with explosives and suicide bombers that killed hundreds of American and French peacekeepers in Lebanon. The global expanse of the Iran-Hezbollah terror network was dramatically underscored by its 1992 Israeli Embassy bombing in Buenos Aires, which killed dozens, and by its 1994 Asociación Mutua Israelita Argentina (AMIA) Jewish community center, which killed eighty-five and wounded over three hundred people in Argentina's capital.[14]

Acting as a diplomatic cultural representative in Tehran's Buenos Aires Embassy, Mohsen Rabbani worked with two Hezbollah-linked agents who planned, financed, and executed the community center attack. Hezbollah criminal procurement networks in South America's Tri-Border Area (TBA) purchased the explosives used in the operation, and Rabbani rented a van that was packed with explosives, which Hezbollah agents parked next to the target. Before the attack, Rabbani's phone records crisscrossed the globe, directly implicating Hezbollah agents in the TBA, where Argentina, Paraguay, and Brazil meet, and IRGC offices in Tehran. One day after the AMIA bombing, a Hezbollah-trained suicide bomber brought down a Panamanian passenger plane, killing twenty-one passengers, including some Israeli citizens.[15]

Working under Iranian guidance, Saudi Shia terrorists in 1996 attacked the Khobar Towers US Air Force housing complex in Dhahran, Saudi Arabia, killing nineteen American airmen. Sixteen years later, a Hezbollah suicide bomber killed five Israeli tourists traveling on an airport bus in Bulgaria.[16] Not all of Iran's efforts, however, have been successful. Some plots against the United States were disrupted by police and intelligence services. Planned attacks targeting Israeli and Jewish interests in Peru, Kenya, and Thailand were foiled before they could reach fruition.[17]

Iran's failed effort to assassinate the Saudi ambassador to the United States during a lunch at a prestigious Italian restaurant in Washington, DC, underscores Iran-Hezbollah's connections to the drug world. A Drug Enforcement Administration (DEA) sting operation arrested an Iranian agent who attempted to recruit what he believed to be a Mexican cartel hit man but who instead worked for the American narcotics control agency.[18] The intersection between crime and terror is at the heart of Iranian sanctions evasion across the world.

Iran's proxies have historically been subject to American and increasingly European sanctions because of their reliance on illicit finance for the procurement and proliferation of weapons. Despite receiving over $700 million annually from Iran, Hezbollah has a global clandestine network with specialized operations in drug running, money laundering, sex trafficking, and arms smuggling.[19] In 1997, the US Department of State designated Hezbollah as a foreign terrorist organization.[20] Working with Hezbollah's criminal operators, the Islamic Republic has spawned a vast clandestine network.

Iran also relies on aligned criminal states. Throughout Latin America, the Middle East, Asia, and West Africa, the Islamic Republic has assisted criminalized states like North Korea, Venezuela, Lebanon, Iraq, Sudan, and Syria that provide protection and support for its proxy forces.[21] Iran has adroitly capitalized on destabilizing events like the 2003 US-led war in Iraq and the 2011 Arab Spring that have facilitated its weapons and financial pipeline to proxy groups in Lebanon, Syria, and Yemen. Iranian patronage of these groups has resulted in an arms and proxy land bridge stretching from Tehran to Beirut. The Islamic Republic effectively exploited the JCPOA nuclear agreement that provided a substantial cash infusion, enabling the expansion of its militia and missile strategy.

Tehran, moreover, has relied on preexisting networks and new initiatives to offset the injurious effects of Trump-era sanctions. This clandestine system involves criminal facilitators, insurgent groups, criminalized states, and Lebanese expatriates across the globe whose money-laundering and criminal enterprises have netted Iran and Hezbollah significant economic remuneration.

In the next section, we address the actors that constitute Iran's global money-laundering, illicit-trade, and weapons procurement networks.

Iran's Criminal-Terrorist Financial Pipeline

The nexus between terrorism and criminality is well recognized.[22] Connections between the terrorist and criminal groups are facilitated by actors whose financial, ideological, and political interests overlap. Network analysis is often employed to determine interrelationships between criminalized states, transnational criminal organizations, insurgents, terrorist groups, and entrepreneurs. Interconnections between these groups can be fluid and unstable.[23] Terrorist-criminal pipelines and the interconnections between criminal and insurgent groups often depend on entrepreneurial facilitators working in border areas notorious for smuggling operations. Criminalized states either are unable to impose sovereignty on lawless border areas or voluntarily surrender their control to capitalize on the highly profitable criminal opportunities these regional trading hubs offer.[24]

Some Latin American, Middle Eastern, Asian, and West African states protect insurgent-criminal networks in return for bribes. In some cases, the state is directly involved in criminal activity. Venezuela, Liberia, North Korea, and Sierra Leone, for example, are widely seen as criminalized states who have lucrative relations with drug runners, cross-border insurgents, and terrorist groups. Hezbollah connections to Lebanese diaspora communities in Latin America and West Africa, some of whom are involved in black market smuggling of arms, drugs, human traffic, and money laundering, serve as an invaluable conduit for the Iran Threat Network's financial enrichment. In South America's TBA, where Argentina, Paraguay, and Brazil meet, the Lebanese diaspora population numbers over thirty thousand people, facilitating Hezbollah recruitment, fundraising, indoctrination, and mobilization of clandestine activity.[25]

Lebanese dual nationals are used by Hezbollah to procure sanctioned materials and run front companies across the world. Many of these expatriates have ideological and familial connections to Hezbollah's leadership core. The Party of God's weapons procurement network is composed of money launderers, drug traffickers, and criminal facilitators, agents, and expatriates. The Islamic Jihad Organization (IJO) within Hezbollah is responsible for weapons and dual-use equipment procurement.

IJO's first leader was Imad Mughniyeh, the mastermind behind attacks against Western peacekeepers in Lebanon who is blamed for attacks against the Israeli Embassy and for AMIA attacks in Buenos Aires. After its destructive 2006 war with Israel, Hezbollah needed to replenish its supply of weapons across its clandestine procurement network. This weapons procurement effort extended to the United States.

The Federal Bureau of Investigation's 2007 Operation Flash Drive disrupted plans by the insurgent group to procure vast quantities of antiaircraft and antitank weapons in Philadelphia.[26] Hezbollah's Business Affairs Component (BAC) oversees its global money-laundering and drug-smuggling operations. BAC's early operations were run by Abdullah Safieddine, cousin of Hezbollah's secretary-general Hassan Nasrallah, and Adam Tabaja, his associate, to finance weapons procurement for the Lebanese militia. Hezbollah's drug-running and money-laundering operations in Latin America serviced the Colombian cartel Oficina de Envigado.

The BAC has created specialized bodies to oversee its criminal operations. Managed by Mohammad Qasir, Hezbollah Unit 108 is the organizational core of this clandestine network.[27] Hezbollah drug and money-laundering operations are assisted by family and personal connections between Lebanese diaspora communities and the group's operators in Lebanon. These expatriates run lucrative money-laundering operations along lawless borders that are critical nodes that assist in financing and transferring weapons to terrorist and transnational criminal groups.[28] Displaced by the country's disastrous 1976–1990 civil war, tens of thousands of Lebanese refugees settled in Latin America and West Africa and have become a dominant economic minority whose financial dynamism provides a critical economic resource to the local and regional economy. Some of them have served Iran and Hezbollah as a conduit for financial support, recruitment, and weapons proliferation. Table 8.1 examines the key actors involved in Iranian and Hezbollah smuggling

Table 8.1. Pro-Iranian and Aligned-Group Smuggling Networks

Actors and conditions that facilitate Iran's criminal-insurgent network	Lebanese diaspora communities in Latin America, North America, Europe, and West Africa engaged in illicit activities in support of Iran and its proxies	Lawless border territories in Latin America and West Africa that allow for the flow of clandestine trade through permissive policies and corruption	Criminalized states (Lebanon, Syria, Sudan, North Korea, Venezuela, and Sierra Leone) who willingly surrender state sovereignty for criminal purposes	Shia and pro-Iranian insurgent groups (Hezbollah, Houthis, Iraqi PMF, Syrian Alawite/Shia militias, Palestinian Hamas, and Islamic Jihad)	Nonaligned criminal facilitators Insurgent and criminal networks in Latin America and West Africa that profit through smuggling and assist sanctions evasion
Contributions and impact	Global network of supporters motivated by ideological, personal, familial, and financial interests	Ungoverned territories that facilitate criminal smuggling, money laundering, and sanctions evasion	State support for sanctions evasion and facilitation of criminal smuggling to advance regime preservation and propagation of regional policy	Insurgent-criminal groups that fortify Tehran's strategic policy aimed at regime preservation and expand Iran's regional policy aimed at undermining Israeli and Western security in the Middle East	Facilitates Iranian and aligned-group smuggling and sanctions evasion policies designed to finance weapons procurement for the regime

Sources: Douglas Farah, "Terrorist-Criminal Pipelines and Criminalized States: Emerging Alliances," *Prism* 2, no. 3 (January 2013): 1–32; Robert Killebrew, "Criminal Insurgency in the Americas and Beyond," *Prism* 2, no. 3 (January 2013): 33–52; Emanuele Ottolenghi, *The Laundromat: Hezbollah's Money-Laundering and Drug-Trafficking Operations in Latin America*, Midest Security and Policy Studies 194 (Ramat Gan: Begin-Sadat Center for Strategic Studies, Bar-Ilan University, 2021), https://besacenter.org/wp-content/uploads/2021/07/194web.pdf.

networks that have become a cash cow for the Islamic Republic and its militias.

This configuration of actors is seen across the world but is particularly pronounced in lawless territories that serve as strategic hubs linking criminals, insurgents, and terrorist groups. One of the most significant of these areas is South America's TBA, which connects Argentina, Paraguay, and Brazil. The region is notorious for its largely unregulated criminal smuggling activities.[29]

Drug transfers, human trafficking, counterfeiting, passport fraud, embezzlement, the sale of pirated goods, and money laundering run through the regional economy. Corrupt, poorly led and financed security forces, unregulated markets, and lax enforcement intersect to create an ideal environment for transnational criminal-insurgent and terrorist groups to prosper. They are linked by enterprising *regional businessmen* who are critical nodes assisting connections between myriad groups.[30]

The relationship is especially tight between Islamist and leftist groups whose ideological affinity and visceral anti-Americanism unify them. Hezbollah, al-Qaeda, and the Colombian Communist insurgent group Fuerzas Armadas Revolucionarias de Colombia (FARC; Revolutionary Armed Forces of Colombia) use the area for drug and arms shipments. Lebanese, Russian, and Chinese Mafias and Latin American transnational criminal organizations also operate in the area.[31]

Criminal syndicates run by expatriates dominate the local economy. The Arab population in the region has become a politically powerful and economically prosperous minority who clandestinely transferred billions of dollars of laundered drug money to Hezbollah financial accounts in Lebanon. Criminalized elites within local Lebanese and Palestinian communities have facilitated clandestine trade in the region, where Paraguay's Ciudad del Este is the critical financial node in the criminal-terrorist pipeline.

That city hosts hundreds of currency exchange houses laundering criminal funds through external financial accounts linked to Hezbollah-dominated banks.[32] Run by Iranian and Hezbollah-appointed clerics, mosques and charities operating in the region also have an important source of terrorist financing, indoctrination, and recruitment.[33]

Hezbollah operatives charge prosperous Arab businesspeople residing in Brazil's Foz de Iquaçu, Paraguay's Ciudad del Este, and Argentina's Puerto de Iquazu a *war tax*, nonpayment of which results in violent action against the offending party.[34] Those few police officers and prosecutors who crack down on Ciudad del Este's clandestine markets end up murdered or are coerced to end their investigations. By some estimates, illicit activities generate $18 billion a year for the local economy.[35]

The TBA is an important node in a trade-based money-laundering scheme where cocaine is shipped to Europe via Hezbollah's West African networks. Cash couriers are sent from West Africa to Lebanon to transport drug money through Hezbollah-controlled ports of entry. Lebanese criminal syndicates linked to Hezbollah use illicit proceeds to launder drug profits through its West African used-car sales network. Most of the cars sold in West Africa come from North America and are invoiced at inflated prices. The cash proceeds from these car sales are laundered through Lebanese banks and remitted back to overseas cartel accounts.

Hezbollah-linked criminal operators in Asia use drug money to purchase often pirated Chinese, Japanese, and South Korean luxury goods, whose re-sale in Latin America provides remittances for cocaine traffickers. Hezbollah's trafficking of blood diamonds and gems shipped from Africa to Europe and Lebanon is also used to mask cartel drug money.

Hezbollah-connected criminal operators use cutouts and front companies to ferret money to Iran and its proxies. Beirut's Lebanese Canadian Bank (LCB) became the epicenter of a global money-laundering system with ties to Hezbollah. The Ayman Joumaa criminal syndicate laundered $200 million a month at 20 percent commission (netting some $480 million a year) through its Beirut Chams Exchange Company.[36] The laundered money then was deposited in the LCB accounts. Given that LCB's US correspondent banks made overseas payments to cartel linked financial institution, US Treasury Department was forced to move against the Beirut-based financial institution in 2011. Treasury actions forced the Lebanese government to reorganize and sell LCB assets to competitor banks. Those banks that have absorbed LCB's Hezbollah-connected accounts continue to service the Party of God's clan-destine activities.[37]

Given the commissions made by its front companies, Hezbollah earns between $500 million and $1 billion a year.[38] This makes up between 20 and 30 percent of the organization's budget. Combined with the $700 million from Iran the organization gets annually, this makes Hezbollah the world's most prosperous terrorist-insurgent group. The Party of God is also a power-ful and influential force in Lebanon. Hezbollah controls the country's ports and dominates security at Beirut International Airport, allowing it to get a cut from clandestine smuggling entering the country. This dramatically facilitates the group's capacity to profit from illicit finance.

Hezbollah's Laundromat includes couriers, shell companies, financial institutions, and financers who clean money made from drugs and organized crime.[39] The BAC launders drug money through the Black Market Peso Exchange network in the TBA. Hezbollah's linked import and export business in *Ciudad de Este* facilitated the transfer of tens of millions of dollars into Hezbollah-linked financial accounts in Lebanon.[40] The BAC's criminal operations run by IJO member Assad Barakat in Ciudad de Este's Galeria Page mall were targeted by the DEA's Operations Titan and Cassandra, which aimed at breaking up its global smuggling network.[41]

Under scrutiny for its TBA criminal operations, Hezbollah's operatives and associates have shifted some of their operations to other Latin American locales.[42] Assisted by Venezuela's criminalized state, Hezbollah-linked criminal facilitators operate along the country's border with Colombia and in the Bolivarian Republic's Margarita Island in the Caribbean.

Venezuela is a key conduit for Iranian-Hezbollah illicit finance.[43] By some estimates, two hundred metric tons of cocaine annually transit from its territory, two-thirds of which is shipped to North America.[44] The Bolivarian Republic's lax passport laws and rampant corruption allow Lebanese expatriates easy dual citizenship and unregulated use of government transport facilities. Venezuela's army provides security for the Colombian drug syndicate Cartel de los Soles, symbolizing the country's degeneration into a criminalized state. Government leaders like former vice president Tareck El Aissami and former military intelligence chief Hugo Carvajal Barrios, moreover, are linked to Hezbollah-FARC arms and drug-trafficking networks.[45]

Politically connected Venezuelan-Lebanese crime families use the country for drug running, oil smuggling, arms shipments, and money laundering along the Colombian and Ecuadorian borders. The region has become notorious for its transshipment of drugs and pirated goods throughout the world.

This underscores the link between illicit finance and criminalized states who for ideological and opportunistic purposes partner with the Iran Threat Network. This relationship reflects the global expanse of the Iranian-Hezbollah smuggling network and the decisive importance of expatriates who support Tehran's criminal activities.

Hezbollah's West African operations are another critical vector in its global criminal enterprise. Sierra Leone and Liberia are *criminalized states* that prosper from clandestine arms, drugs, human trafficking, mineral trading, and pirated goods.[46] As in the TBA, Lebanese expatriate communities are dominant players in these countries' robust black market economies.

Hezbollah uses these nations' transport infrastructure to ship arms, cash, and drugs to Lebanon, where it controls the country's seaports, precluding any seizure of contraband. The flow of illicit wealth into the Lebanese financial system has had dire economic consequences.

The movement of clandestine funds to Lebanese banks has undermined the financial integrity of the country's banking system.[47] Given US and European sanctions against the Lebanese terrorist-insurgent movement, many of the country's financial institutions have been targeted. Today Beirut faces an unprecedented financial collapse.

The US Treasury Department has sanctioned Lebanese financial institutions linked to Hezbollah, including Jamal Trust Bank and its eight subsidiaries and currency trading establishments. Lebanon's negotiations with the International Monetary Fund have been undermined by the government's dependence on Hezbollah's political support.

Given the country's political problems, few are optimistic that Lebanon can successfully navigate its economic travails, which are exacerbated by the 2020 Beirut Port explosion and the COVID-19 pandemic.[48] Any rescue package is severely compromised by the lack of transparency within the Lebanese banking system, which is rife with illicit enrichment. The inconclusive 2022 parliamentary elections have left no faction capable of forming a legislative majority, adding an obstacle to any effective resolution of the country's problems.

Iranian-Hezbollah criminal networks in Latin America and West Africa are illustrative of the Islamic Republic's need to circumvent American and European sanctions arrayed against the IRGC, its Quds Force, and its Hezbollah ally.[49] Sanctions evasion financially underwrites Tehran's missile and militia strategy spearheaded by the IRGC, which controls key sectors of Iran's economy that are adversely affected by international sanctions.

Working with Hezbollah, Iran has used supporters within Lebanese diaspora communities across the world who have created front companies and currency exchange houses involved in clandestine markets to channel resources back to the Islamic Republic's financially pressed economy. Without such resources, IRGC's deep state is unlikely to survive and Tehran's quest for Middle East dominance will collapse.

Sanctions evasion is a critical lifeline for the regime, whose unpopularity was made clear by the public's massive abstention in its 2021 presidential election. With the election of regime loyalist Ebrahim Raisi, whose blood-thirstiness as a Tehran executioner is widely admired by the supreme leader, Iran is likely to escalate its clandestine networks even further. A recent analysis of Raisi's cabinet by the Foundation for Defense of Democracies finds that a high percentage of its members have been sanctioned by US, UN, and European agencies for drug smuggling, support for terrorism, human rights violations, and illegal weapons proliferation schemes.[50]

The Strategic Role of the Iranian Deep State in Tehran's Sanctions Evasion System

The IRGC and the Office of the Supreme Leader control vast segments of Iran's economy.[51] Both groups benefited from Tehran's privatization and liberalization policy in the 1990s. During Mahmoud Ahmadinejad's administration, the IRGC prospered from insider deals that allowed it to purchase state-owned assets at artificially low prices, and IRGC-controlled firms disproportionately profit from generous state contracts. With some seven hundred companies under its management, the IRGC is estimated to control up to 40 percent of the Iranian economy.[52]

At the epicenter of the IRGC's economic empire is the construction and engineering consortium Khatam al-Anbiya Construction Headquarters (GHORB) and its 812 affiliated companies. Run by a former IRGC commander and high-level regime officials, GHORB gets preferential access to government contracts. Cronyism, corruption, and clientele networks have fed GHORB's growth for decades. The consortium is embedded in Iran's banking, aviation, armaments, mining, energy, and telecommunications sectors.

The Office of the Supreme Leader is another important player in Iran's deep-state political economy.[53] It guides a vast complex of pension systems, scholarships, universities, seminaries, and veterans' and orphans' charities. Since his 1989 ascent, Ayatollah Ali Khamenei has directed the Office of the Supreme Leader to support and advance IRGC-QF's priorities. Controlling over $200 billion of economic assets, Khamenei's management of the Office for the Execution of Imam Khomeini's Order, Mostazafan, and Astan Quds Razavi strongly influences state economic policy.

Acting in concert with the supreme leader, the IRGC has parlayed its preeminent economic and political role in advancing Iran's missile and militia expansion strategy across the Middle East.[54] Preserving its dominant status within Iran's economy and supporting Iran's regional policy are predicated on a thriving IRGC-directed global sanctions evasion network.

Many IRGC-linked firms are under American and European sanctions for their involvement in Iran's nuclear program, human rights violations, sponsorship of terror, and promotion of sanctioned insurgent groups. Firms connected to the IRGC and Office of the Supreme Leader account for 23 percent capitalization on the Tehran Stock Exchange and were badly hit by international sanctions imposed by the UN between 2010 and 2015.[55] Faced with a potential economic calamity, the IRGC and the Office of the Supreme Leader pioneered a variety of illicit schemes to circumvent sanctions.

The Islamic Republic has been targeted by US and international sanctions denying it legitimate access to global financial and energy markets. After the 1979 Revolution and seizure of the US Embassy and its staff, America forbade US companies and banks from conducting trade and financial relations with Iran. Though American sanctions were lifted after the return of the embassy personnel, they were reimposed after Iranian-linked Hezbollah attacks against US military forces in Lebanon in the 1980s.

Driven by concerns over Iran's nuclear weapons development, the United Nations imposed sanctions against Iranian oil exports and limited the Islamic Republic's ability to use the global financial system between 2010 and 2015.[56] The adverse economic impact of global sanctions on Iran's financial, missile, defense, nuclear, and oil sectors pressured the regime into negotiating limits to its nuclear development and research program. Though many international sanctions were lifted with Iran's signing of the JCPOA between 2016 and 2018, the American withdrawal from the accord led to tightened American financial, oil, defense, and aviation sanctions, jeopardizing Tehran's capacity to export oil and gain access to international financial markets.

Faced with economic isolation, the Islamic Republic created a global network to circumvent American and international sanctions. Abetted by Hezbollah's clandestine criminal smuggling syndicates, Iran has used front companies, Iranian and Lebanese expatriates, and aligned regimes to acquire sanctioned military hardware and dual-use technologies.

The Iran Threat Network's sanctions evasion strategy has increased over time. Its expansion has been driven by the need to finance its ambitious missile and proxy militia agenda in the Middle East. Hezbollah's costly 2006 war with Israel and the intervention of IRGC and aligned militia in the Syrian, Iraqi, and Yemeni civil wars have expanded the Iran Threat Network's need for increasingly sophisticated weapons and dual-use technologies. Many of these weapons and dual-use technologies (as will be seen later in this chapter) have been supplied by North Korea, underscoring Pyongyang's role in Iran's sanctions evasion system. Like North Korea's Office 39, Tehran has created a specialized unit to direct its sanctions evasion and illicit activities.

The IRGC-QF Unit 190 is responsible for smuggling weapons and other forms of support to Iranian proxies in Lebanon, Iraq, Yemen, and Syria.[57] Unit 190's pipeline smuggling weapons, oil, and dual-use technology to Syria is actively coordinated with the Hezbollah BAC's Unit 108 to support the Assad regime and aligned militia efforts to defeat opposition forces.[58] Working with these specific units, IRGC-QF and Hezbollah have created shell companies to mask Iranian transfers of oil, weapons, and funds to its proxies.

The same network of front companies conversely permits the Islamic Republic to gain access to sanctioned weapons and dual-use technology and make illegal foreign payments to creditors. Comparable networks exist in Iraq, Bahrain, and Yemen to channel weapons to Tehran's proxy militias. Table 8.2 sketches some notable examples of how Tehran circumvents sanctions. What follows are some case illustrations of the Iranian and Hezbollah sanctions evasion system.

Faced with American, European, and international sanctions during significant periods of its history, the Islamic Republic found ways to exploit maritime trade and get US dollars in foreign exchange markets.[59] Given that 90 percent of international commerce is transported by sea and most transactions are conducted in dollars, Iran's financial lifeline depends on its mastery of clandestine shipping methods and ability to get American hard currency.

Iran uses diverse methods to facilitate the flow of sanctioned military hardware and dual-use technologies to IRGC firms and its regional proxy forces. The volume of maritime trade (estimated to be $14 trillion in 2019) shipped by over one hundred thousand vessels makes interdicting the sanctioned commerce problematic.[60] Iran uses third-party carriers navigating across international ports, hides sanctioned cargo through fraudulent invoices, changes the shipping registries of its vessels frequently, reflags vessels, and makes ship-to-ship transfers to evade sanctions.

Table 8.2. Iranian and Hezbollah Clandestine Networks to Circumvent
Sanctions

Objectives	Case illustrations	Impact
Regime preservation by evading sanctions aimed at denying Iranian access to financial, weapons, energy, and dual-use technologies that have a military application	Use of currency exchange houses in the United Arab Emirates to access dollar-denominated assets for the IRGC Use of Turkish banks and fraudulent accounts to make foreign payments for the Iranian oil industry Mahan Air front companies to acquire planes and aviation parts for sanctioned Iranian air carriers	Transfer of illicit funds to IRGC accounts and payment to weapons procurement and dual-use technology front companies
Fund and proliferate weapons to proxies	Use of Iraqi banks and fraudulent accounts to funnel funds to Hezbollah IRGC weapons-smuggling networks in Bahrain and Oman to support Houthi rebels	Furtherance of Iran's regional policy of hegemonic domination
Support aligned states	Clandestine smuggling of sanctioned oil and weapons to Syria and Venezuela	Support for Iranian-aligned criminalized states complicit in Tehran-Hezbollah illicit smuggling networks

Sources: Peter Kirechu, "Iran's Currency Laundromats in the Emirates," *CTC Sentinel* 14, no. 5 (June 2021): 26–31; "Under the Shadow of Illicit Economies in Iran," Global Initiative against Transnational Organized Crime, October 2020, https://globalinitiative.net/analysis/under-the-shadow-illicit-economies-in-iran/; "Outlaw Regime: A Chronicle of Iran's Destructive Activities," May 2018, https://www.state.gov/wp-content/uploads/2018/12/Iran-Report.pdf; John P. Caves and Meghan Peri Crimmins, "Major Turkish Bank Prosecuted in Unprecedented Iran Sanctions Case," Wisconsin Project on Nuclear Arms Control, March 2020, https://www.iranwatch.org/our-publications/articles-reports/major-turkish-bank-prosecuted-unprecedented-iran-sanctions-evasion-case; Emanuel Ottolenghi, Ann Fixler, and Yaya J. Fanusie, "Flying under the Radar: Evasion in the Iranian Aviation Sector," Foundation for Defense of Democracies, July 2016, https://s3.us-east-2.amazonaws.com/defenddemocracy/uploads/documents/Ottolenghi_Fixler_Fanusie_Aviation_Sanctions_Evasion.pdf.

Such techniques hide the end user delivery of sanctioned commerce to Iran, complicating the international community's ability to disrupt Tehran's clandestine maritime network. The many front shipping companies change ownership frequently, fly under different national registries, and at times turn off their vessels' automatic identification system (AIS) to disguise navigation routes and delivery to Iranian ports. With most trade conducted in dollars,

Iran needs to acquire hard currency to facilitate its illicit trade and pay off its third-party front companies. Without access to restricted US dollars, Iran's entire sanctions evasion system could not be sustained.

Working with IRGC-linked firms and traders, the Central Bank of Iran (CBI) has given these entities preferential exchange rates for the conversion of the rial into dollars.[61] Preferential currency exchange rates allow IRGC-linked traders greater access to dollars to finance their clandestine weapons and dual-use technology procurement channels. The CBI has exploited United Arab Emirate (UAE) currency exchange houses to acquire dollars to enhance IRGC's finances.[62] Under this scheme, the CBI issues cash to money couriers to convert Iranian rials into dollars through UAE currency houses. These financial institutions are loosely regulated, have lax disclosure laws, and often engage in fraudulent transactions. Once dollars are obtained at preferentially high exchange rates, they are transported back to Iran by couriers or wired through fraudulently created UAE bank accounts.

The UAE serves as a key smuggling route for Iran.[63] Over four hundred thousand Iranian expatriates live in the UAE, and it is estimated that this diaspora population owns over ninety-five hundred businesses.[64] Many of these companies are involved in the import-export trading sector that specializes in clandestinely serving the Islamic Republic's need for sanctioned military and dual-use merchandise. Dubai's free trade zones, moreover, permit complete foreign ownership, and the entire economy is lightly regulated.

Dubai's large Iranian expatriate community and economically permissive environment are enhanced by the UAE's long coastline and geographic proximity to the Islamic Republic. The UAE borders the Strait of Hormuz, which is infamous for its nighttime small-boat smuggling of clandestine merchandise to Iran. Dubai's position as a preeminent regional financial, shipping, and banking hub provides a critical lifeline for the Islamic Republic.

Iranian expatriates in Dubai who operate currency houses and import-export front companies linked to IRGC firms have allowed Iran to surreptitiously acquire dollars and sanctioned goods. Iran's UAE currency fraud network was exposed in December 2014 when American and Emeriti authorities closed some exchange houses linked to the Iranian currency manipulation scheme.

The Treasury Department's Office of Foreign Assets Control enforced sanctions against dozens of designated Iranian nationals and commercial enterprises operating out of the UAE for currency fraud and manipulation.[65]

Among the sanctioned individuals and trading concerns were Asadollah Seifi and Teymour Ameri, who used Rashad Exchange and Belfast Trading Company to illegally send dollars to Iran.

Beyond currency manipulation, IRGC forces have engaged in counterfeiting operations to finance their regional proxies. The IRGC-QF in 2017 used German front companies to acquire printing equipment and paper to print fake Yemeni banknotes to finance the Houthi rebels.[66] German authorities closed the operation. Such capabilities reflect the network's presence in Europe and its use of expatriates for clandestine activity.

Since the disruption of Iran's currency manipulation and money counterfeit schemes, Tehran's foreign currency reserves have dramatically fallen under Trump-era financial and energy sanctions. The collapse of Iran's external accounts makes acquiring dollars urgent. Tehran has historically relied on illicit networks in Turkey, some of which are directly supported by the Turkish government to illegally engage in dollar-denominated foreign transactions.

One of these cases involved a money-laundering scheme run through the state-owned Turkish Halkbank.[67] Masterminded by Iranian-Turkish businessman Reza Zarrab, the ruse involved laundering Iranian oil funds deposited in Halkbank disguised as gold and food transactions to permit Tehran the ability to pay its weapons procurement front companies. It is estimated that before his arrest in the United States, Zarrab laundered $20 billion in Iranian oil proceeds between 2012 and 2016.

Zarrab bribed Halkbank's former deputy manager to illegally transfer Iran's oil proceeds from frozen state accounts to private accounts held by IRGC-linked private financers, who then transferred the funds to Zarrab's front companies in the UAE and Turkey, who through gold sales and fraudulent food transactions made payments on behalf of Iran.

Facilitating the gold and food transaction schemes were loopholes in US sanctions legislation that permitted private sector transactions in gold between Iranian nationals and foreign financial institutions and exempted food sales for humanitarian reasons. Zarrab used the gold sales and fictitious food transactions made by his UAE and Turkish front companies to make illegal dollar-denominated payments to overseas IRGC front companies.

The US Treasury Department and Turkish police closed the illegal gold operation after two years. It is estimated that Zarrab's front companies used the gold sales to acquire $900 million between 2012 and 2013 to pay Iran's foreign obligations. Zarrab's bribery of key Turkish officials prompted his release from prison, resulting in a resumption of Halkbank's money-launder-ing scheme that disguised payments made from Iranian oil proceeds as fraud-ulently invoiced food transactions. Only Zarrab's 2016 arrest in the United States for money laundering and sanctions evasion put an end to Halkbank's clandestine financing of Iranian debts. By all accounts, the Turkish president, Recep Tayyip Erdoğan, was complicit in facilitating the illegal gold and food transactions.

Beyond the UAE and Turkey, Iraqi financial institutions have assisted the illegal transfer of IRGC funds. Working in concert with IRGC-QF, CBI ex-ecutives created fraudulent accounts at Iraq's al-Bilad Islamic Bank that wired funds to Hezbollah-linked financial institutions.[68] Iran's ability to use Iraq as a conduit to support its overseas militia project is no great surprise. Having played a formidable role in arming Shia militias in Iraq to fight the Islamic State, Tehran has used its military and financial leverage in Iraq to fortify its regional proxy agenda.

Composed of hundreds of thousands of armed Shiite militia members, Iraq's Popular Mobilization Forces (PMF) are an invaluable coercive force to achieve Iran's regional ambitions. The Iranian-backed PMF have launched rocket and mortar attacks against US forces and killed hundreds of antigov-ernment protesters. Fearing Iranian-backed militias, Iraqi government policy rarely contravenes PMF interests. Failure to permit Tehran's exploitation of Iraq's banking system could have dire security consequences for Baghdad.

Iranian-backed Shiite smuggling networks in Bahrain have been espe-cially active in sending Iranian weapons to Persian Gulf–based regional mi-litias.[69] Iran transfers arms to Bahraini Shiite and Yemeni Houthi insurgents whose caches of weapons have grown in greater sophistication and lethality. Interdicted in international waters by the Yemeni Coast Guard in 2013, the *Jihan I* (a local dhow or fishing vessel) contained over sixteen thousand blocks of Iranian-fabricated C-4 explosives, sixteen thousand rounds of ammunition, hundreds of grenades, and dozens of remote-controlled explosive devices.[70]

The *Jihan I* was followed by the seizure of another fishing vessel by Australian Navy cruiser HMAS *Darwin* in March 2016 off the coast of Oman, which is a sea lane used extensively by the IRGC-QF to send clan-destine arms to its Yemeni Houthi proxy force. The Australian Navy confis-cated thousands of small arms (rifles, rifle-propelled grenades, and mortars), including North Korean Type-73 light machine guns used by the Houthis in the Yemeni conflict.[71]

One UN investigation found that between 2013 and 2018 Iran had become a primary supplier of weapons to Bahraini- and Yemeni-aligned insurgents.[72] Basing their study on weapons caches seized by Bahraini security forces and shipping interdictions in international waters, UN investigators found that 73 percent of the bullets seized were manufactured in Iran and that many of the Chinese-made assault rifles had their serial numbers obliterated. Iran likely acquired these weapons via its connection with North Korea's clandestine weapons sales network that has provided Iran with significant arms caches.

Throughout the Persian Gulf, the IRGC-QF works with local Mafias to transport tons of armaments and dual-use technologies like drones and night-vision goggles to proxy groups. Many of these shipments are concealed in small fishing vessels that navigate across the Iran-Oman-Yemen waterway and the narrow Bab al-Mandeb Strait. On the basis of evidence found in six vessel seizures by international and local navies between 2018 and 2019, the UN study found that Iran had transferred tons of small arms, unmanned aerial vehicle technologies, and surface-to-air missiles to Houthi rebels.[73] Many of these rockets and missiles are based on Scud prototypes likely acquired from North Korea.

Iran has also employed Somali smuggling networks to ferret weapons to Houthi rebels. The IRGC utilized Mohammad Omar Salim's Somali Puntland criminal syndicate to transport Iranian arms to its Yemeni proxies via the Gulf of Aden. Salim's network has historically worked with al-Qaeda and Islamic State groups in Somalia, and its partnership with the IRGC represents a diversification of his weapons-smuggling operations.[74] In June 2020, Saudi Naval Forces seized one of Salim's dhows (the *al-Bari 2*), which was transporting over twelve hundred Chinese assault rifles, dozens of antitank missiles, and thousands of heavy and light machine guns.[75]

Sharing a border with Yemen, Oman has additionally served as a vital IRGC overland supply route for the provision of weapons for the Houthis. Oman's and Iran's economies have historically been intertwined, and past Omani rulers have acted as intermediaries between the Islamic Republic and the West.

Iranian networks in Europe and the Middle East have been especially active in the clandestine smuggling of planes and aviation parts for Iran's sanctioned air carriers Mahan Air and Caspian Airlines. Run by former IRGC commanders, these airlines have smuggled Quds Force and Hezbollah fighters to Syria in service to the Assad regime. America and European countries have sanctioned many Iranian air carriers because of their involvement in Tehran's overseas wars.

This has severely compromised IRGC access to any legitimate channel to purchase jets and aviation parts. Iran, however, has used shell companies and complex third-party transfers to acquire sanctioned materials for its beleaguered aviation industry.[76] It has relied on Turkish and Iraqi front companies and expatriate sympathizers across the world to purchase planes and aviation parts for reexport to sanctioned Iranian air carriers. Concerned over Iran's capacity to get American planes and aviation parts from third-party suppliers, the Clinton administration in 1999 promulgated Executive Order 13059, prohibiting export and reexport of all US-origin goods to Iran, including aviation equipment and planes.[77]

Tighter export or reexport license requirements have forced Iran's reliance on a complex chain of front companies that use multiple transshipment points and middlemen to acquire American-made planes and equipment. One such example involved a Dutch company that purchased planes and equipment for Iran between 2005 and 2007 and then sent the merchandise to Cyprus and UAE to mask final sale and delivery to Mahan Air.

There are other cases. A dual US-Iranian citizen was prosecuted and sent to prison for over two years for sending Iran aviation parts between 1999 and 2007 by routing parts through Malaysia and Singapore and reexporting them without a license to Iran while fraudulently listing Singapore as the end user. In 2012, another US-Iranian dual national was prosecuted for sending aviation parts and equipment to Iran using a UK office and sending the materials to Iran via third countries.

Using front companies and multilevel transshipment points, Mahan Air has acquired planes and aviation parts for decades. Iran's network in Europe has been especially gifted in procuring sanctioned aviation parts and planes for Mahan Air. The United Kingdom is an important conduit for many of these illegal transfer schemes. One Iranian-British expatriate bought Boeing 747s for Mahan Air and fraudulently identified an Armenian air carrier as an end user to mask the planes' reexport to Iran. In 2010, one UK firm paid $15 million in fines to the US Treasury Department for sending three Boeing aircraft to Mahan Air via third parties illegally, without an export license. Yet another Iranian-British expatriate acquired nine European Airbuses for the sanctioned airline, transferring the planes to Iraq and Malta, changing their air registries, and then masking their final transfer to the Islamic Republic.

Hoping to foil the illegal transfer of sanctioned aviation equipment to Iran, the US Treasury Department in 2015 designated al-Nasir Air in Iraq as an Iranian front company and sanctioned entity, precluding it from acquiring American-made aviation merchandise. The resumption of tighter US sanctions after the 2018 American JCPOA pullout, moreover, affected the flow of aviation parts and planes to unsanctioned Iranian airlines because European suppliers feared America's future application of secondary sanctions against their companies.

Iraqi Kurdistan is an important route for smuggling sanctioned materials into Iran.[78] Faced with discrimination against their respective communities, Kurdish groups across the porous Iraq-Iran frontier have for centuries trafficked illicit contraband. Cross-border movement of arms and dual-use technologies as well as drugs has been facilitated by IRGC units and corrupt border guards who get a percentage of the highly lucrative smuggling operations. The Iraq-Iran border is a key transit route for drugs into southern Europe.

Iran has furthermore used its sanctioned energy sector to assist friendly regimes. The Islamic Republic has directed oil-smuggling operations to sanctioned states like Syria and Venezuela.[79] Iranian front companies operating under multiple foreign cargo-shipping registries conceal their navigation routes by turning off their vessels' AIS to hide oil supply at Iranian ports and end user destination points. Forged freight documents and ship-to-ship transfers are also used to conceal the delivery of sanctioned materials to pro-Iranian criminal states.

In 2020, the Islamic Republic sent five tankers flying under different national registries to deliver refined gasoline to shortage-plagued Venezuela in return for a reported $1.5 billion in gold payments.[80] Venezuelan government insider and Colombian criminal superfacilitator Alex Saab was reportedly instrumental in forging the illegal Iranian-gas-for-Venezuelan-gold payment scheme. His later extradition to the United States on money-laundering charges adds credibility to these allegations.[81] Significantly, the gold was flown out of Venezuela by the sanctioned Iranian airline Mahan Air.

The Venezuelan and Iranian regimes have tried to circumvent sanctioned trade in US dollars by erecting a barter system. In September 2021, the agreement between Caracas and Tehran swapped Venezuelan heavy crude oil for Iranian condensate, allowing the beleaguered Bolivarian Republic to facilitate its overseas oil export capacity.[82]

Some Iranian clandestine maritime traffic to sanctioned states like Venezuela has been seized in international waters. The British Royal Navy in 2019 seized a Panamanian-registered tanker carrying 2.1 million barrels of Iranian oil to Syria while in transit in the Strait of Gibraltar.[83] The IRGC-QF has also been instrumental in the shipment of sanctioned petroleum and crude oil to Venezuela's beleaguered regime. Such shipments are unsurprising for Venezuela is Iran's core ally and an important transport node for Iranian and Hezbollah clandestine traffic in Latin America.

Before the 2018 fall of Omar al-Bashir's Islamist regime, Iran used Sudan as a key transit point for clandestine arms shipments to Hamas in the Gaza Strip.[84] Under Bashir's regime, Iranian-financed arms were permitted free transit into Egypt's Sinai Desert and then on to the Gaza Strip, where the weapons were transited through Hamas's underground tunnel network.[85] During Bashir's regime, Israel bombed overland IRGC-QF-directed arms convoys traveling through Sudan to Egypt and even launched naval commando operations against IRGC networks operating along Sudan's coast.[86] Iran is estimated to have provided Hamas and Palestinian Islamic Jihad with $100 million a year in material support and weapons.[87]

Despite regime change in Sudan and the country's 2020 recognition of Israel, Sudan remains an important illicit hub for Iranian arms transfers. Clandestine overland and sea transfers of Iranian-supplied arms to Hamas continued, reinforced by the bribery of border officials and complicit Bedouin criminal networks operating in Egypt's lawless Sinai Peninsula.[88]

As discussed in chapter 7, Iranian and North Korean weapons proliferation networks converge for Tehran has been a conduit for North Korean–designed small arms, rockets, and antitank missiles sent to Hamas. Many of these weapons were shipped via Sudan to Egypt and on to the Gaza Strip. Hamas has also constructed sea tunnels running underneath the Mediterranean to ferret Iranian-supplied arms dropped by "fishing vessels" in the Mediterranean. Here the Palestinian militia has used hundreds of underwater divers to transport arms through sea tunnels that link to its Metro underground system. In 2020, Israel destroyed what it suspects was a Hamas "port" to transfer maritime arms traffic to its underground system.[89]

As stated in chapter 7, Hamas's electrified underground tunnel system (likely built with North Korean technical assistance) has been a vital supply route for criminal contraband and weapons. Described as the Metro by Israel defense experts, this elaborate subterranean network composed of thousands of tunnels is a critical node in Hamas's resistance strategy for it permits Hamas operatives to store, smuggle, and deploy weapons.[90]

North Korea's Sanctions Evasion: Can It Remain Successful?

North Korea has, as we have shown, become highly successful at evading sanctions. This is no accident. Pyongyang has adjusted international sanctions by constantly changing its tactics, techniques, and procedures (TTP). Their proliferation networks have gone from relatively simple operations back in the early 2000s to highly sophisticated, multifaceted entities that work not only with other rogue states, such as Syria and Iran, but with states who are actually American allies, such as Egypt, and groups who use terrorism as a proclaimed aspect of their policy, such as Hezbollah, Hamas, and the Houthis. But it goes further than that. According to a documentary titled *The Mole*, the North Koreans are actively marketing many of their weapons on the open market (even using brochures), often using nefarious middlemen and criminal networks. For example, Scud missiles can be purchased for $5 million each, and antitank weapons were photographed in a brochure as well. This is just another example of North Korea's willingness to go through illicit arms dealers to sell their weapons to anyone who will buy them.[91] Former UN Panel of Experts member Hugh Griffiths called the documentary "highly credible."[92]

In this section, we will describe how the North Korean illicit sanctions evasion network has evolved, morphed, and constantly changed its TTP. We will also describe some of the measures taken by the international community to rein in North Korea, to date often unsuccessfully. We will show how the network—unlike what some analysts have opined—continues to exist and to enhance the North Korean government's ability to arm itself and maintain large amounts of illicit funds in its real budget. We will also talk about how efforts by both Russia and China to protect North Korea from containment by the UN began largely in 2018 and have evolved to the point that both nations are overtly engaging, enabling, and supporting North Korea with both sanctioned activities and activities with other state and nonstate actors that bring funds into the Kim Jong-un regime.

While Russia and China have always been hesitant to enforce sanctions against North Korea, until recent years both nations agreed to most of these sanctions—albeit with watered-down wording in UN documents. But in 2018 this began to change. In fact, both Russia and China began to circumvent efforts by the United States and like-minded states during that year. According to press reports during August 2018, "There is a mounting body of evidence that Pyongyang is evading the restrictions with a combination of subterfuge and lax enforcement by China and Russia, its closest allies, rendering the US plan of 'maximum pressure' increasingly ineffective."[93] During the same time frame, the US Treasury Department sanctioned a Russian bank for knowingly conducting transactions with North Korean operatives.[94]

Continuing the trend of lax sanctions enforcement, more evidence came to light in 2022 when the Treasury Department sanctioned two Russian financial institutions "for conducting transactions on behalf of DPRK entities." These Russian entities allowed North Korea to conduct business that supported the development of their WMD and WMD-related programs. To again quote the document that outlined the sanctions, "Today Treasury is targeting supporters of the DPRK's WMD and ballistic missile programs, as well as foreign financial institutions that have knowingly provided significant financial services to the DPRK government."[95]

On May 26, 2022, in a UN Security Council vote, "the Security Council voted on a draft resolution updating and strengthening the 1718 Democratic People's Republic of Korea (DPRK) sanctions regime. The draft resolution was not adopted because China and Russia both cast a veto. The remaining 13 Council members voted in favour of the resolution."[96] The US ambassador to the UN remarked in a joint statement speaking for Washington, Seoul, and Tokyo, "The vetoes today are dangerous. Those members have taken a stance that not only undermines the Security Council's previous actions to which they've committed, but also undermines our collective security." The Russian ambassador to the UN Vassily Nebenzia stated, "Our Western colleagues are accustomed to blaming North Korean authorities, yet they ignore the fact that Pyongyang's repeated calls to the U.S. to stop its hostile activities, which would unlock dialogue opportunities, were never taken seriously, whereas U.S. colleagues only kept saying over and over again that more sanctions were needed."[97] Clearly the Russian ambassador was taking the side of North Korea, as the only "hostile activities" the United States had engaged in were justifiable sanctions against North Korea for its rogue-state behavior. Thus, Russia, which itself has engaged in rogue-state behavior, has now made it clear that it defends the rogue-state behavior of its ally and arms supplier North Korea.

Also disturbing when it comes to the ongoing cooperation and Russia's and China's protection of North Korea from the containment of its illicit activities and sanctions violations in the international community, reports came out in 2021 outlining North Korea's operations that send soldiers overseas to earn foreign currency for the regime. Included in the list of nations where soldiers were reportedly sent overseas (in violation of sanctions) were both Russia and China. Within North Korea, the Seventh and Eighth General Bureau were said to be organizing these deployments. Also among the nations where North Korean soldiers were traveling to work as laborers were Mongolia, Syria, Qatar, Egypt, Kuwait, Iran, and the UAE.[98]

North Korea has, for a very long time, been able to circumvent international sanctions by illicitly using ships that fly under the flags of other nations. This is a very difficult set of operations to track, and the North Koreans—even now—continue to be quite adept at using this methodology. DPRK merchant ships or those leased illicitly (and in violation of sanctions) from other nations often fall under the flags of states in sub-Saharan Africa or even Pacific Island nations.[99] The bottom line here is that by conducting these operations in this way, North Korea continues to maintain with relative ease a capability of transshipping arms and other illicit material in violation of sanctions.[100] During 2020, the Trump administration issued the Global Maritime Advisory, whose guidelines focused on the illicit maritime activities (and there are many) of Iran, North Korea, and Syria.[101] While this was at the time considered prudent, these roadblocks set up to counter proliferation and illicit economic operations have not made a strong dent in North Korea's maritime sanctions-busting operations.

But "reflagging"—that is to say, sailing illicitly under flags of other nations in violation of sanctions (it appears often without officials from these nations realizing what is happening)—is not the only way that North Korea gets around sanctions using maritime means. North Korea—and Iran—now also avoid their merchant ships being identified and hunted down by evading AIS requirements for international merchant shipping as directed by the International Maritime Organization (IMO). To quote a study conducted by the research group C4ADS, "Vessel identity laundering is a novel tactic in which one or more vessels adopt a different identity on Automatic

Identification System (AIS) transmissions in order to allow 'dirty' (i.e. associated with illicit activities) ships to assume 'clean' identities, and involves at least one vessel in this operation assuming an identity that is obtained by defrauding the IMO. Vessel identity laundering is significantly more sophisticated than previously observed instances of 'vessel identity tampering,' in which vessels modify their physical appearance or broadcast false data on AIS transmissions." The study goes on to say, "In recent years, C4ADS has observed at least 11 ships engaging in elaborate schemes to create fraudulent ship registrations with the IMO, which are subsequently used to 'launder' the identity of vessels that have been associated with illicit activities. In particular, we have seen networks involved in DPRK sanctions evasion and smuggling use these tactics to avoid the heightened scrutiny of the sanctions regime."[102]

In September 2022, it was reported that a technology that allows fake locational transmissions was being used by both criminal elements and rogue nation-states in their international maritime transshipments The technology allows those who use it to actually manipulate GPS coordinates. Reportedly, the technology has largely the same effect as VPN software: ships appear to be in a particular location but are actually physically located elsewhere. This also allows these violators to put out false data making IMO authorities believe that the ship or ships are hundreds of miles away from their actual location. Of course, it is important to state here that key violators of AIS regulations are North Korea and Iran.[103] It also shows that North Korea continues to upgrade, manipulate, and advance its TTP when it comes to sanctions evasion operations.

This plethora of activity that North Korea has engaged in to make money for the regime and to prop up the capabilities of its military (not to mention keeping the elite in a luxurious lifestyle) certainly has evolved over the years, as we have seen in the previous paragraphs. And in fact there is still more, and it is related to cyber. But before getting to that, it is important to note that, for lack of a better term, "getting paid" is only useful to the North Koreans if they actually get the money. The sanctions imposed on North Korea have certainly forced Pyongyang to use methods often used previously by criminal entities. But these sanctions have stopped the flow of money to the regime from illicit and illegal activities.

A 2020 report from the Institute for Science and International Security (an analysis of what were at the time recent UN Panel of Experts reports) found that covert North Korean accounts existed in banks in Austria, Libya, Kuwait, Thailand, and Russia (to name key nations) and that accounts in China were also involved—either knowingly or unknowingly. The report also showed front companies that were operating in the Marshall Islands, Switzerland, Malaysia, Singapore, and Thailand. While their identity may not have been "known," it appears that sanctions violations were also being made through US companies.[104] This spiderweb of front companies, front companies of front companies, phony documents, phony names, and shipments under false vouchers formed (and still often form) such a confusing picture that it is extremely hard to monitor or contain it.

A report in the *Financial Times* from March 2023 that described North Korea's importation of sanctioned oil also outlined the diverse, complex, and often difficult-to-detect illegal financial networks that North Korea has used in recent years to launder its illicit transactions. Many of the financial transactions occurred in Hong Kong and Macau. According to the report, "North Korean Officials, diplomats, spies and assorted operatives have been mobilized in support of this illicit shadow economy, which continues to operate through a network of shell companies, financial institutions and foreign brokers. But Pyongyang also relies on foreign organized criminal groups such as the Triads and Japan's Yakuza to assist in the regime's overseas financing and procurement activities. Hardened criminals offer the North Koreans access to global smuggling, distribution and money laundering networks." The report goes on to say, "The FT and RUSI have identified more than 100 companies, properties, individuals and ships as part of a network connecting North Korea to businesses and individuals across East Asia."[105]

The dizzying activities of illicit networks that North Korea has operated for years (as documented above) allow them to launder the illicit money earned through nefarious activities and get it back to North Korea or banks in China where North Korean operatives can take the money out as needed. But this is no longer the only way that North Korea launders its money. In an interview we conducted in October 2022, the evidence was laid out for us by "David" Choi, a retired South Korean NIS agent who now is an advocate for going after North Korea's illicit funds. This evidence was later documented by Tara O, a North Korean expert. To quote her study, "North Korea launders money via cryptocurrency to circumvent the banking system, according to a former National Intelligence Service (NIS) official who recently left the

NIS." She further expands on what Choi said in his interview by stating, "The former NIS official Mr. Choi stated that North Korea transfers funds using cryptocurrency, which means the banks are not involved in the international transfers. Bank transfers above certain threshold would be scrutinized by the governments, and would be prevented under the international sanctions, but the cryptocurrency bypasses the banking system." She further expands on his statements by articulating the following information he provided:

Here is the process of laundering discovered, as described by Choi:

- Banks are hacked and money stolen
- With the stolen money, cryptocurrency, such as BitCoin or Ethereum, is bought
- Transfers cryptocurrency to Tehran (Iran), Damascus (Syria), Dubai (UAE) via links in email and PayPal
- Within those countries, cryptocurrency is further traded [known as layering]
- After multiple small transactions, the cryptocurrency is transferred to China
- In China, the in-bound cryptocurrency is turned into cash
- The cash is transferred to North Korea[106]

In our interview with Choi, he described operations that laundered money gained from electronic bank theft and the theft of other electronic assets that may have been vulnerable to theft by North Korean hackers. But there is no reason that this same methodology could not be used to launder money gained from military proliferation, technical training or assistance to other rogue states or nonstate actors, and other illicit activities. At least for now, using cyber to launder money appears to be far more difficult to detect and contain than simply running the dirty cash through banks that may not even realize it is from North Korea. This presents a real problem for policymakers in several nations and for international law enforcement.

On March 7, 2024, the UN Panel of Experts reported, "According to one Member State, the malicious cyberactivities of the Democratic People's Republic of Korea generate approximately 50 per cent of its foreign currency income and are used to fund its weapons programmes. A second Member State reported that 40 per cent of the weapons of mass destruction programmes of the Democratic People's Republic of Korea are funded by illicit cybermeans." The report further stated, "Based on industry and media reports, private sector companies and Member State information, the Panel is investigating 17 cryptocurrency heists in 2023 for which the Democratic People's Republic of Korea may be responsible, valued at more than $750 million (see annex 94). The Panel is further investigating a total of 58 suspected cyberattacks by the Democratic People's Republic of Korea on cryptocurrency-related companies between 2017 and 2023, valued at approximately $3 billion."[107]

It is important to note that these illicit networks, money laundering through organized crime and through Bitcoin, and other activities designed to "clean" dirty money and get it back to the regime do not operate in a vacuum. In fact, the power that controls all of these seemingly unconnected (at least on the surface) illicit activities is the party in North Korea, as we addressed earlier. Office 39 (within the party) remains the economic power broker within the regime, even today. Thus, these activities continue to be monitored, supervised, and sometimes interrupted by the now infamous Office 39, which essentially runs and maintains the regime's party-run slush fund.[108] Of course, Office 39 answers directly to Kim Jong-un.[109]

North Korean economic irregularities again showed up during 2020. North Korea had carried out large-scale money laundering for years using several shell companies and the help of Chinese companies, as they filtered the money through prominent banks in New York (Chinese nationals have also been sanctioned for the money-laundering activities). This was all being done even as the North Korean merchant shipping fleet was forced to slow down its operations because of COVID-19—but cyber operations were becoming a high priority. Using multiple shell companies in places all over the world, banks in New York, and other banks, such as Deutsche Bank, the North Koreans were able to successfully launder money through banks that either did not monitor accounts with sufficient rigor or were hoodwinked by multilayered front companies.[110] If they were about to be detected, the front companies simply shut down and formed new companies. This constant shell game made it difficult for both banks and regulators to stop the transactions from going through. The US government did take action; for example, the Justice Department charged several individuals. In fact, a North Korean official in Malaysia (one of the key places where details have occurred) was actually successfully extradited to the United States to stand trial for illicit financial activities, though North Koreans continued to operate in the county even after the Pyongyang Embassy was shut down there because of the extradition. Of interest, according to a senior research fellow at South Korea's Korean Institute for National Unification, North Korea's "methods of evading sanctions have not been enough to offset their impact."[111]

Stopping or even containing the multilayered North Korean sanctions evasion networks remains a daunting task. As stated above, progress has been made, and thus prudent analysis dictates that sanctions need to continue, but they should be adjusted and given higher priority if democratic states want to make illicit activities even more difficult for the North Koreans. There are many issues. UN and European Union sanctions are often poorly enforced by member states. Most UN member states have a weak capacity to support compliance. Sanctions are often passed without thought of enforcement. The UN Security Council and major member states have often been less than skillful at building political will. Sanctions are sometimes not enforced because some governments simply are not willing to do it. North Korea often (but not always) uses smaller banks and is now adjusting by using cyber to launder its money. Every time sanctions are imposed that cannot be reasonably enforced, it creates a negative international perception.[112] The illicit networks infrastructure as controlled by Office 39 continues to exist, but it evolves as geopolitical and international law enforcement changes.[113] North Korean front companies that are well known often use yet more front companies, literally making them front companies for front companies. We particularly see this in the Middle East in places such as Lebanon.[114]

Iran has also benefited from its strategic alliance with North Korea. Pyongyang has used Chinese-, Malaysian-, and Singapore-based front companies to transport weapons and dual-use materials to Iran.[115] The Iran–North Korea partnership is a crucial node in the Islamic Republic's sanctions evasions system and has been pivotal for Tehran's armed support for Syria and proxy groups.

In 2015 (at the height of the Syrian civil war), North Korean expert and longtime Congressional Research Service analyst Larry Niksch testified before Congress that "North Korea may receive from Iran upwards of $2 to $3 billion annually from Iran for the various forms of collaboration between them."[116] Underwritten by the Islamic Republic, North Korea began construction on a $2 billion al-Kibar plutonium nuclear reactor in Deir ez-Zor province that Damascus hoped to use to build an atomic weapon. Derailed by a September 2007 Israeli air strike that obliterated the construction site, the presence of this clandestine facility underscores the depth of the Iran–North Korea partnership.[117] The 2011 Syrian civil war was a magnet for enhanced North Korean arms transfers to Iran and Iran's proxies. For example, a 2018 UN Panel of Experts report stated that between 2012 and 2017 Pyongyang sent at least thirty-nine arms shipments to the Syrian regime, exacerbating the civil wars raging in the region and fortifying Tehran's forward defense system.[118]

North Korean state trading companies (front companies for proliferation) operate in Iran. Pyongyang's notorious Korean Mining Development Corporation (KOMID) supplies the Islamic Republic with a vast cache of small arms, missiles, and rockets through multiple front companies operating across the globe.[119] Despite its success in getting hard currency, Iran has even resorted to the use of cryptocurrencies like Bitcoin to conceal energy and financial transactions. These activities appear to be growing, and as addressed earlier, at least some of them appear to be conducted in cooperation with North Korea.[120] Following the example of its Iranian patron, Hamas military al-Qassam wing is soliciting Bitcoin donations on its websites.[121]

The clandestine activities outlined in this chapter illustrate Iran's unwillingness to abide by its international commitments on antiterrorist financing and money-laundering protocols. Having signed international conventions prohibiting such activities, Iran has failed to abide by its responsibilities. The international advisory board the Financial Action Task Force has designated Iran as a high-risk and noncooperative jurisdiction in the fight against money laundering and terrorist financing.[122] Iran shares this designation with criminalized states like North Korea and Venezuela. Confronted by an obstructionist Iran, the United States and the international community have embarked on a host of measures to curb the Islamic Republic's malign behavior. Given the sanctions evasion system of Iran and its proxies, American and international sanctions authorities have been forced to develop countermeasures.

A Comparative Examination of Tehran's and Pyongyang's Sanctions Evasion Systems

Introduction

In this section, we compare the Iranian and North Korean sanctions evasions systems, noting similarities and differences. These global networks converge in Africa and the Middle East using front and shell companies, third-party intermediaries, criminalized states, and diplomats to circumvent the best efforts of the international community to curb their illicit networks. Tehran and Pyongyang have comparable aims of pairing regime survival with the undermining of their enemies. They have jointly contributed to insecurity and conflict across the Middle East and Africa.

Both systems adapt to exigent circumstances and never hesitate to take advantage of cracks in sanctions regimes that allow them to pursue their respective national interests. In this quest, they depend on the assistance of other revisionist states (Russia, China, and Venezuela, among others) who seek to upend the liberal international order, similarly focused on the propagation of criminal finance to sustain corrupt autocratic regimes.

They complement each other, employing remarkably similar TTP and show a surprising level of resilience and adaptability in the way they manage their illicit trading networks. What follows is an overview of the key constituent actors, convergent TTP, and notable differences in their sanctions evasion systems. Table 8.3 summarizes some of these components, noting some symmetries and discordances in their strategies of sanctions circumvention.

Similarities

Iran and North Korea have created state-directed networks with centralized offices devoted to circumventing global sanctions that for decades have targeted state elites, military officials, companies, and key industries. These offices and the sprawling networks they manage are an extension of the military-industrial deep-state complex that has developed in these countries. Most of the benefits derived from illicit financial transactions enrich the party, military, and political elite.

Iranian and North Korean sanctions evasion allows these states to arm and financially support insurgent-terrorist movements and criminalized states across the Middle East and Africa. Faced with a concerted international campaign to sanction their regimes for human rights abuses, weapons proliferation, money laundering, and support for terrorism, these regimes have erected a complex system of sanctions evasion that includes a maze of front and shell companies and banks, criminal facilitators, rogue states, and third-party intermediaries.

Table 8.3. Iran and North Korea Sanctions Circumvention Strategy

Evasion system	Specialized office to direct and manage sanctions evasion	Tactics, techniques, and procedures	Geographic area of operations and clandestine activities	Asymmetries in the two systems
Iran Threat Network (IRGC and Hezbollah)	IRGC Unit 190, Hezbollah Business Affairs Component (BAC) and Office 108	(1) Front and shell companies and banks	Latin America, West African countries with large Lebanese diaspora communities, some of whom are embedded in money laundering, counterfeiting, drug running, arms smuggling	Uses Latin America extensively for its operations where, beyond the use of Panamanian law, money laundering, and vessel registration, North Korea has little presence
		(2) Concealed cargo in vessels that change national registries frequently and travel under different flags		
		(3) Use of countries with loose tax and financial-reporting regulations	Dubai and use of large Iranian expat community for currency fraud, illegal weapons smuggling, and acquisition of dual-use technologies	Relies on Hezbollah as a key third party in its illicit transfer and procurement of weapons where there is no comparable role for a terror-insurgent-criminal group in the North Korean system
		(4) Use of criminalized states and regional allies for sanctions evasion		
		(5) Clandestine ship-to-ship transfers of sanctioned materials		

Continued

Table 8.3. Iran and North Korea Sanctions Circumvention Strategy (*Continued*)

Evasion system	Specialized office to direct and manage sanctions evasion	Tactics, techniques, and procedures	Geographic area of operations and clandestine activities	Asymmetries in the two systems
North Korean networks	Office 39	(1) Front and shell companies and banks (2) Concealed cargo in vessels that change national registries frequently and travel under different flags (3) Use of countries with loose tax and financial-reporting regulations (4) Use of criminalized states and regional allies for sanctions evasion (5) Use of clandestine ship-to-ship transfers of proscribed materials	(1) Use of lax Asian financial safe havens like Macao, Hong Kong, Singapore, and Malaysia to facilitate weapons procurement, proliferation, drug running, money laundering, and counterfeiting (2) Use of Chinese front companies and banks to facilitate sanctions evasion (3) Export of illegal coal and labor to China (4) Use of African or Middle Eastern networks to assist weapons transfers	Dominant in Asia, an area where Iranian networks have minimal presence Relies on forced labor system to earn hard currency from Russia and China, whereas Tehran has no equivalent system Cybercrime and counterfeiting operations are more extensive than in Iran's system

Sources: John Park and Jim Walsh, "Stopping North Korea, Inc.: Sanctions Effectiveness and Unintended Consequences," The Brookings Institution, November 7, 2016, 18–20, https://www.brookings.edu/wp-content/uploads/2017/05/20161107_north_korea_sanctions_corrected_transcript.pdf; King Mallory, *North Korean Sanctions: Evasion Techniques* (Santa Monica, CA: Rand, 2021), 20–31, https://www.rand.org/content/dam/rand/pubs/research_reports/RRA1500/RRA1537-1/RAND_RRA1537-1.pdf; Matthew Levitt, "Hezbollah's Criminal Networks: Useful Idiots, Henchmen, and Organized Criminal Facilitators," Washington Institute for Near East Policy, October 2016, https://www.washingtoninstitute.org/policy-analysis/hezbollahs-criminal-networks-useful-idiots-henchmen-and-organized-criminal.

Pyongyang's and Tehran's specialized administrative units direct far-flung criminal empires designed to procure and proliferate arms, rockets, missiles, weaponized drones, and dual-use technology for use in their own military-industrial complexes. Iran has used its illicit revenues to empower terrorist-insurgent groups and criminalized states in Middle East and Africa. Described as the regime's elite slush fund, North Korea's Office 39 has historically controlled $4–5 billion in illicit overseas accounts that has historically been used to benefit the financial interests of the Kim family.[123]

For North Korea, state trading companies run by the governmental entities spearhead Pyongyang's sanctions evasion network. Among the most important of these entities are KOMID and the Korean General Corporation for External Construction.[124] The Reconnaissance General Bureau, for example, founded one conglomerate, Malaysia-Korea Partnership Group, with thirty-two companies operating in eighteen African countries and six Middle Eastern ones that was actively involved in the proliferation of weapons, money laundering, and a host of other illicit trades.[125]

For decades, North Korea has created a system of third-party middlemen, many located in China, to operate front and shell companies with access to international markets.[126] Pyongyang has made considerable use of financial safe havens like Macao, Hong Kong, Malaysia, and Singapore with lax financial-reporting laws, using front and shell companies to export sanctioned goods and engage in money laundering.

The convergence between North Korea's and Iran's clandestine sanctions evasion, weapons procurement and proliferation, and money-laundering systems is striking. Run by the IRGC Unit 190 and Hezbollah's BAC, these entities are the equivalent to Pyongyang's Office 39. Working together, Unit 190 and the BAC use front and shell companies in Latin America, West Africa, and the Middle East to procure weapons and dual-use technologies, proliferate arms to proxy forces, launder money, smuggle drugs, and engage in counterfeiting operations. Like its North Korean ally, the Iran Threat Network makes extensive use of cargo vessels (flying under variable national registries), engages in clandestine ship-to-ship transfers of sanctioned goods, conceals navigation routes in sanctioned ports of call by disabling the ship's AIS, and conceals and disguises sanctioned products in large, difficult-to-inspect tankers.

Perhaps the most sanctioned state on earth, North Korea has successfully circumvented sanctions for decades and has made a mockery of international efforts to curb its weapons procurement and proliferation system. The UN Panel of Experts reports have repeatedly documented the regime's successful circumvention of weapons and energy sanctions.[127] North Korea's system is adaptable and resilient and has overcome repeated setbacks. Every effort that US and international officials have made to close the system has led to innovation and adaptation.

This diversification of operations in conjunction with Office 39's international front companies showed the system's capacity for innovation and the dynamic functioning of North Korea's sanctions evasion system.[128] The same is equally true for the Iranian and Hezbollah systems that change front and shell companies with alarming alacrity to offset prosecutorial efforts to curb Tehran's illicit smuggling and money-laundering schemes. To overcome sanctions on weapons procurement and proliferation, Tehran and Pyongyang have created a bewildering network composed of state enterprises, diplomats, criminals, insurgent groups, third-party intermediaries, and corrupt businessmen. North Korea has extensively used its diplomatic corps as cash couriers to open fraudulent bank accounts under multiple identities and bribe third-party intermediaries across Asia, the Middle East, and Africa to facilitate the movement of illicit funds, sanctioned armaments, and weapons.[129]

Tehran has been equally assertive in the use of its diplomats as emissaries of illicit enterprise and terrorism. As seen earlier in this chapter, the Iranian Embassy in Buenos Aires and diplomat Mohsen Rabbani worked with Hezbollah agents in the TBA to illicitly finance and execute terrorist attacks in Argentina against Israeli and Jewish interests. Working with Iranian-backed religious, charitable, and cultural institutions, Iranian embassies throughout Latin America have raised illicit funds to finance terrorist operations throughout the world.

Iran and North Korea have made extensive use of Dubai as a major center for currency transport and illicit exchange. The IRGC regularly sends cash couriers to UAE to take advantage of lax regulatory procedures involving exchange houses where fraudulent accounts to acquire dollars are electronically transferred back or carried to Iran. Many of these currency exchange houses are run by Iranian expatriates who pay IRGC couriers favorable exchange rates and are complicit in arranging the fraudulent transactions.[130]

KOMID's operations in Iran likely intersect with IRGC's flagship consortium GHORB, whose firm specializes in providing energy and public transport infrastructure for the Islamic Republic and has long prospered by its managers' close personal relationship with the government and the Office of the Supreme Leader. Illicit state-to-state relations are also a critical part of North Korea's and Iran's sanctions evasion networks. North Korea, China, Russia, Syria, Sudan, Venezuela, and Iran interface to circumvent US and UN sanctions on energy, weapons, dual-use technologies, and illegal labor practices. China and Russia have used North Korean laborers in energy, fishing, and timber operations where Pyongyang siphons off the bulk of workers' earnings.[131]

Iran and Venezuela actively circumvent global sanctions on energy shipments between the two countries and overcome laws against money laundering. Clandestine Iranian shipments of light crude oil to Venezuela reward the country, which has become a central hub for the Hezbollah-directed narcotics trade and money laundering. Iran and Venezuela circumvent financial restrictions on their dollar-denominated trade by swapping refined oil for gold and uranium. Lax Venezuelan passports allow for easy citizenship so IRGC and Hezbollah agents can engage in their illicit enterprises. Lebanese diaspora communities in parts of the country assist Hezbollah criminal operations, with Margarita Island serving as a central hub for illicit finance and enterprise.[132]

Differences

Despite the similarities, there are some notable differences. Here geographic proximity and the displacement of native diaspora populations matter. North Korea's Asian network is more developed than Iran's operations in the region. North Korean front and shell companies in China, Singapore, Malaysia, Russia, and Macau could be considered the core foundation for Office 39's criminal operations.

Latin America is not prominently featured in Pyongyang's sanctions evasion system. In contrast, that region is a critically important source of illicit finance for the Iran Threat Network. IRGC-Hezbollah criminal networks are well developed in the TBA, Venezuela, and Columbia, aided by the presence of significant Lebanese diaspora communities.

There is, moreover, no North Korean equivalent to Hezbollah, whose criminal operations in Latin America, Europe, and West Africa provide Iran critical material support and allow the Islamic Republic a shield to avoid direct retaliation for terrorist and criminal actions conducted by its surrogates. Pyongyang lacks such a cover, which theoretically makes it more vulnerable to international retribution for its actions.

That said, North Korea's cyber capabilities appear more advanced than Tehran's evolving electronic war-fighting capacity.[133] Armed with at least seven thousand cyber operatives, North Korea has engaged in major denial of service attacks in South Korean and US commercial enterprises. Pyongyang has been especially deft at Bitcoin theft and has siphoned off considerable resources from cryptocurrency accounts. North Korea infamously retaliated against Sony Corporation for its financing and marketing of a *South Park* film spoofing the Kim regime. Though Iran has engaged in cyberattacks against Sunni Gulf States for their military intervention in Yemen and their support for the Abraham Accords, their capacity to inflict considerable harm on the US financial system is considered limited.[134]

The Iranians, moreover, do not have an equivalent to North Korea's overseas forced labor system where they can prosper from institutionalized slavery and gain access to illicit funds. North Korea regularly takes 90 percent of the earnings of its foreign working force, which labors under terrible conditions in Chinese and Russian mineral- and timber-extraction industries.[135] The revenue Pyongyang derives from its forced labor system is considerable. Though Iran has coerced Afghan Shia living illegally in their country to serve in militias fighting in Syria, its capacity to impose conditions of forced servitude on its population is constrained.

As future US administrations look to cut deals with Iran, they should heed how the past implementation of the JCPOA facilitated Iran's missile and militia project.[136] Iran used the cash proceeds attendant to sanctions relief to amplify their axis of resistance strategy.

Though the previous Biden administration sought to include Iran's regional policy as part of a stronger, longer agreement, any attempt to do so is likely to continue to be rebuffed by Iran, which has made Tehran's missile and militia policy nonnegotiable. Iran's progressive violation of the JCPOA enrichment and centrifuge restriction clauses complicated the round of talks held between European and Iranian negotiators in Vienna.

Negotiations have been further complicated by the supply of armed drones Iran provided to Russia in support of its 2022 military campaign in Ukraine. This support, moreover, has been accompanied by IRGC-QF advisers training Russian aviators how to guide these Shahed-136 and 133 drones.[137] In response, the US Department of the Treasury has sanctioned Iranian firms and individuals involved in the clandestine smuggling of loitering munitions to Moscow.[138]

These conditions are exacerbated by Iran's unwillingness to let International Atomic Energy Agency inspectors investigate the origins of uranium traces found at undeclared military sites and its stated intent to develop uranium metals for civilian research purposes; the prognosis for successful talks is not good. Limits on Iran's nuclear and ballistic missile development expired in 2023, so any new JCPOA agreement would not impact the Islamic Republic's missile program. Iran would likely use the augmented trade and investment opportunities under a new interim agreement to advance its missile development and militia project. Under such a scenario, clandestine efforts to sabotage Iran's nuclear program are likely to increase.

North Korea remains unwilling to legitimately negotiate anything about its nuclear and ballistic missile programs. Pyongyang instead continues to be intent on proliferating weapons to rogues states and nonstate actors, working closely with its ally Iran, and conducting sanctions-busting activities that will enable its current regime to survive. Thus, the governments of North Korea and Iran both remain intent on engaging in illicit activities that will gain funds for their respective regimes. Only proactive and robust counterproliferation and countercyber efforts by the international community will contain these efforts.

Conclusions and Policy Implications

Bruce E. Bechtol Jr. and Anthony N. Celso

The Rise of Revisionist Powers

This book is the first comprehensive study of the North Korea–Iran relationship and the damage that partnership has done to Middle Eastern and Asian security. It contributes to academic debate over the insecurity bred by autocratic revisionist powers. The dangers posed by revisionist states for American security interests are a predominant concern in recent US national security policy documents.[1]

Today, great power competition has supplanted the war on terror as the West's key security challenge. Chapter 1 ("Setting the Context: The Strategic Partnership between Iran and North Korea") argues that the Iran–North Korea partnership threatens America and its regional allies. Revisionist powers like Iran and North Korea seek to undermine the military integrity of Washington's military alliances in the Middle East and Asia.

Geo-military rivalry between democratic and revisionist powers, if anything, is rising. Since Russia's February 2022 invasion of Ukraine, American policymakers have intensified the West's commitment to stem Moscow's efforts to broaden its sphere of influence. As Washington fortifies a coalition of nations to arm and finance Ukraine's defensive capacity, Moscow's war is assisted by Chinese, Iranian, and North Korean military resources and economic support. Alliances between revisionist countries have exacerbated conflicts from Syria to Yemen and Ukraine.[2]

Though more foreign policy attention is devoted to Chinese and Russian efforts to weaken US-led alliances, their junior powers (Iran and North Korea) have more directly threatened Western interests. Tehran's and Pyongyang's past actions in the Middle East and Asia have proved more destabilizing and violent than those of their larger patrons in recent years.

This is amplified by the fact that military confrontation between the West and North Korea and Iran is considerably more likely. Iranian-backed militias in Iraq and Lebanon have killed hundreds of American troops. Washington, moreover, fought a major war against North Korea over seventy years ago.

Iran and North Korea have undermined America's regional security interests for over a generation. The significance of the North Korea–Iran strategic partnership, which trades arms for oil and money, has endured since the Cold War. By our reckoning, Iran pays over $1 billion a year for North Korean weapons and technology support.

The interconnection between North Korea's financial enrichment and Iran's regional hegemonic ambitions is growing. We argue that analysts should view Iran and North Korea's partnership as an integrated global threat network—North Korea's supplies of advanced weapon technologies, platforms, and missile systems are provided to Tehran's armed forces in return for Iranian cash and oil. Financial transactions between these two heavily sanctioned nations are maintained by an elaborate system of clandestine criminal finance spearheaded by a global network of front and shell companies.[3]

In recent years, North Korean arms have been transferred by the Islamic Republic (and sometimes sent directly, depending on the arms deal) to Iran's Syrian, Lebanese, Yemeni, and Palestinian proxies, which have destabilized the region with the larger aim of weakening the United States' military position in the Middle East. Tehran and Pyongyang work with other revisionist powers to undermine the Western economic and security global order and enhance sanctions evasion.

Long beneficiaries of Chinese and Russian patronage (North Korea much longer than Iran), Iran and North Korea have reciprocated by supporting Moscow's military campaign in Ukraine with armaments and sanctions evasion. Moscow and Tehran's defense partnership has deepened, with the Islamic Republic providing hundreds of drones for Russian combat operations in Ukraine. Iran has plans to construct drone factories in Russia and Belarus to facilitate Moscow's military campaign.[4]

Though diminished by Israel's weakening of Hezbollah and the collapse of the Syrian regime, Iran's influence stretches across the Persian Gulf and the Levant, allowing it to threaten American, Saudi, and Israeli interests. Iranian-backed Houthi rebels in 2019, for example, launched devastating drone and missile strikes against Saudi Arabia's oil operations, effectively halving the kingdom's export capacity for a day.[5]

Iranian-supported Shia militias in Iraq have attacked American and Israel forces. At the behest of Tehran, the Houthis have attacked maritime shipping and Israel to force a ceasefire in the Gazan conflict.

North Korea's generation-long defense relationship with the Islamic Republic challenges America's military and economic position in Asia. Without Iranian financial patronage, Pyongyang's regime could not maintain its formidable military or export its armaments to Iran and its proxies. The synchronicity between Pyongyang's financial enrichment and Iran's military empowerment has not been comprehensively studied by researchers. This book hopes to help to correct that academic void.

Summary and Analysis of Evidence

We began our analysis by sketching North Korean and Iranian military capabilities. As chapters 2 ("North Korea's Military Capabilities: Building Systems to Threaten and Sell") and 3 ("Iran's Military Capabilities: Becoming a Hegemon Thanks to Acquisition") emphasize, these nations are skilled in asymmetric warfare strategies that prioritize missile strikes, patrol boat swarm attacks, cyber warfare, and special forces. North Korea has exported entire weapons systems to Iran and even built several fabrication facilities there in order to go "offshore."

Tehran's ballistic missile arsenal has benefited from the North Korean technology, advisers, scientific assistance, and infrastructure support that Tehran has progressively shipped to its Shia and terror-insurgent proxies across the Middle East. On the basis of North Korean designs, Iran has developed missile fabrication sites and underground tunnels across the Middle East.[6] Operated by Hezbollah in Lebanon, several of these artisanal weapons factories are concentrated in densely populated areas to shield them from military strikes.

Paid for by Iran, North Korean missile systems, technologies, conventional weapons, and underground tunnels have been transferred to Tehran's regional surrogates. The Islamic Republic's way of war is enabled by Shia and Palestinian proxies allowing it to threaten Israeli and Saudi security and mount lethal attacks against US forces in the region.

Iran's missile arsenal is the Middle East's largest. Improvements in Tehran's ballistic missile capability presage the development of a nuclear weapons program that, like North Korea's, can be used to threaten the global order. Here Pyongyang's technology and scientific assistance has aided Iran's nuclear power program and has been extended to the Islamic Republic's proxies. Financed by Tehran, North Korea's efforts to create a Syrian nuclear reactor were short-circuited by a 2007 Israeli air strike at the planned reactor's construction site.[7]

Pyongyang's nuclear weapons program was developed clandestinely, violating successive efforts by the West to forestall such a development. North Korea's systematic violation of past nuclear accords shows Tehran how such agreements can be exploited. Iranian noncompliance with basic provisions of the JCPOA follows the North Korean precedent.

Since the 2015 agreement, Iran has strengthened its nuclear centrifuge program, building underground bunkers to preserve its uranium enrichment facilities and possibly shield its weapons research from military assaults. Since 2020, Iran's successful launching of space satellites has provided the technological foundation for an intercontinental ballistic missile (ICBM) capable of carrying a nuclear warhead.

Nuclear cooperation between the two regional powers is emblematic of the strategic importance that Tehran and Pyongyang place on their relationship. The ideological, tactical, and strategic drivers of the rogue alliance are detailed in chapter 4 ("The Ideological, Financial, and Environmental Forces Leading to the North Korea–Iran Rogue Alliance"). Totalitarian ideology, mutual enemies, tactical financial interests, and collective survival are pivotal factors in facilitating the alliance.

The Democratic People's Republic of Korea (DPRK) and the Islamic Republic of Iran are ruled by party officials, military elites, and unsavory entrepreneurs whose financial enrichment comes at the expense of their people.[8] Cooperation on weapons development, transfer, and proliferation has proved mutually beneficial. It has generated financial dividends and improved military capability for these rogue regimes.

The trade of North Korean weapons for Iranian oil and money is facilitated by sanctions evasion strategies that these regimes have honed for decades. Their respective military, party, and financial elites are embedded in the global system of front companies involved in clandestine oil, arms, dual-use equipment, money laundering, and technology sales. Without this vast net-work of criminal enterprises, neither regime could survive.

North Korea and Iran present themselves as populist revolutionary states. The juxtaposition between populist regime ideology and elite enrichment is telling. State revolutionary ideology and propaganda in Iran and North Korea provide a convenient cover masking corruption and elite financial enrich-ment.

Chapters 5 ("Rogue Allies and Pyongyang's Military Proliferation to Iran: Russia and China Are Now Key Enablers") and 6 ("Rogue Allies in Action: Proxy Wars in the Middle East") focus on North Korea's arms transfers to Iran, which have enabled the Islamic Republic to engage in asymmetric war-fare using its Shia and Palestinian proxies. Tehran's quest for an arms bridge stretching from Iraq to Lebanon has contributed to the cycle of civil wars and failed states in the Levant and the Persian Gulf.[9]

The Islamic Republic's past four-capitals (Damascus, Beirut, Baghdad, and Sanaa) strategy featured Tehran's efforts to capture and pilfer states and equip their proxies with precision-guided missile systems that aim to destroy Israel and force a US military disengagement from the region. Iranian and Hezbollah military entrenchment in Lebanon and Tehran's patronage of Palestinian resistance groups threaten Israel with a multifront war.

Since Hamas's October 7, 2023, attacks, Jerusalem has dispatched its forces to the Gaza Strip and South Lebanon. The Israeli Defense Forces (IDF) has degraded North Korean–facilitated Hamas and Hezbollah's military in-frastructure and tunnel systems. These facilities will need to be rebuilt if Iran wants to preserve its axis of resistance strategy.

As chapter 7 ("North Korean Support to Iran's Proxy Partners") vividly points out, North Korean transfers of arms, dual-use equipment, and infra-structure support have fortified Iran's proxy forces across the Middle East. Without Pyongyang's provision of technology and weapons, Iran's regional policy would not have presented the severe challenge that it does today.

These weapons systems must be paid for, and Iran has financed the pro-vision of North Korean arms through money, cryptocurrency theft, and oil transfers that require a comprehensive system of sanctions evasion.[10] Chapter 8 ("Rogue Allies and the Criminal Financial Networks That Support the Partnership") details the Iranian–Hezbollah–North Korean sanctions evasion systems designed to circumvent international sanctions on illicit weapons, dollars, oil, arms, cryptocurrency, and coal transfers.

International sanctions have limited but not incapacitated Iranian and North Korean weapons proliferation efforts. Chapter 8 specifies the tactics, techniques, and procedures (TTP) these states employ to erect shell and front companies in financial safe havens and cooperative states.

Iran's 2023 entry into the Shanghai Cooperation Council is emblematic of the revisionist bloc's efforts to circumvent international sanctions. Compliance with international sanctions placed on the DPRK and the Islamic Republic are hindered by Russian and Chinese complicity in Pyongyang's and Tehran's sanctions evasion strategies. North Korea's export of sanctioned coal and slave labor has allowed the Chinese and Russian companies access to valuable human and energy resources.[11] Moscow and Tehran in 2023 planned to integrate their banking systems to circumvent international financial sanctions on dollar transactions.

The Islamic Republic's agreements with Russia and China presage deeper military and economic partnerships within the revisionist bloc. Beijing's signing of a twenty-five-year $400 billion pact with Iran in 2020 is part of its Belt and Road Initiative and is illustrative of the People's Republic's efforts to facilitate a larger military and economic presence in the Middle East.[12]

The West's failure to curtail the weapons proliferation and sanctions evasion programs of the rogue alliance compromises regional and global security. Combating illicit weapons proliferation and sanctions evasion has proved particularly vexing for international policymakers.

For every front and shell company targeted, other clandestine enterprises tied to the DPRK and Islamic Republic weapons proliferation and money-laundering schemes emerge. North Korean and Iranian sanctions evasion techniques constantly evolve and innovate. They work in tandem to underwrite criminal networks across the Middle East and Asia. The illicit oil-money transfers that Iran makes to North Korea pay for weapons and dual-use technologies that directly threaten Middle Eastern regional financial and physical security.

The rogue alliance's relationship also poses significant consequences for peace and stability in North Asia. Enriched by Iranian financial patronage, North Korea's missile tests and improved ICBM capability undermine US, South Korean, and Japanese security. Failure to effectively manage North Korea's missile provocations increases the risk of major military confrontation on the Korean Peninsula and beyond.

The scale of Iran–North Korea weapons proliferation and sanctions evasions requires a recalibration of the international community's efforts to combat their malign impact. Past attempts in the nuclear containment area have failed, and neither Iran nor North Korea has been effectively contained. Diplomacy, economic sanctions, and military threats have not yielded any diminishment of Pyongyang and Tehran's weapons-for-financial-compensation relationship.

Iran's proxy forces have destabilized Lebanon, Iraq, and Yemen and enabled Palestinian terrorism. The growing security challenges require a new approach that treats the North Korea–Iran alliance as a combined challenge and not as separate compartmentalized problems. This will require a global comprehensive strategy to sever the complex financial nodes that link Pyongyang's weapons transfers to Iran and its surrogates.

Combating the Rogue Alliance

Relaxed enforcement of sanctions has often been coupled with diplomatic efforts to coax North Korean and Iranian compliance with nuclear accords. Historically, this approach has failed. Sanctions relief during the 1990s' Agreed Framework and its successors allowed Pyongyang to clandestinely develop and augment its nuclear weapons stockpile. Similarly, the JCPOA's relaxation of sanctions on Iranian financial and oil transactions permitted the Islamic Republic's ability to finance its proxy network across the Middle East and augment its large missile arsenal. With the JCPOA restraints on Iranian ballistic missile sales and development ending in October 2023, urgent action is needed.

Since the 2018 American withdrawal from the JCPOA, Tehran has enhanced its uranium enrichment capacity to 60 percent. Most of the JCPOA violations have occurred during the Biden administration, which used reduced sanctions enforcement to unsuccessfully lure the Iranians back into compliance. Within months, Iran could fabricate enough weapons-grade fissile material to produce a handful of nuclear weapons. The advent of a new 2025 Trump administration presages a more muscular economic and military posture toward Iran.[13]

Diplomacy to prevent North Korea's nuclear weapons program have failed so badly that some analysts advocate for the West to relinquish demands for Pyongyang's atomic disarmament. Iran and North Korea have also successfully exploited cracks in sanctions enforcement. Beijing and Moscow's complicity in enabling the DPRK and the Islamic Republic to circumvent global restrictions suggests that any future nuclear agreement with Chinese and Russian participation is problematic.

This does not mean, however, that the West cannot at least limit the damage the rogue alliance does to the international order. Any systematic effort to rein in this partnership requires looking at it as a holistic network. Excepting a 2006 congressional law that aims to penalize North Korea, Iran, and Syria for their weapons proliferation cooperation, US policymakers have looked at Pyongyang and Tehran as isolated problems.[14]

American intelligence, national security makers, diplomats, and Treasury officials should instead form a task force where every means of US power can be employed to take down Iranian–North Korean weapons proliferation and sanctions evasion networks. Working with the Europeans and the Japanese governments, US policymakers can impose more secondary sanctions (which must be strongly enforced) of Chinese and Russian banks and firms that enable Pyongyang's weapons transfers to the Islamic Republic.

Due to Russia's Ukraine war, American and European powers have tried to isolate Moscow by sanctioning its oil, arms, and financial trades. Whether the international community has the will or capacity to economically penalize Beijing remains to be seen. Even if America gets the Europeans and the Japanese to abide by secondary sanctions on Chinese enterprises and financial institutions, economic measures alone are unlikely to succeed in curtailing North Korean weapons for Iranian oil and money transfers.

Any effective containment effort requires cyber warfare, vessel seizures, and selective military strikes. The United States and Israel, for example, were successful in disrupting Iranian enrichment capabilities through the introduction of computer viruses during the Obama administration. Though only a fraction of North Korean arms shipments to Iran and its proxies have been interdicted in international waters, more robust, rigorous efforts would help.

International navies have also played a role in stemming Iran's export of oil to the Syrian regime and weapons to its proxies. Israel's war between the war has launched thousands of air strikes against IRGC and Hezbollah weapons convoys and factories to prevent Tehran's military entrenchment in Syria.[15] Pyongyang's efforts at raiding cryptocurrency networks need to be stymied by targeting North Korea's cyber operators. Cutting off this lucrative source of financing for the regime is vital.

The global community's failure to prevent North Korea's nuclear weapons breakout cannot be repeated in Iran's case. The Islamic Republic's quest for regional dominance and the ideological character of the regime's leadership require all measures short of conventional war. Israel's cyber and military campaign to disrupt Iran's nuclear weapons development shows the promise of limited kinetic operations short of starting a major military confrontation.

Jerusalem's assassination of Iran's top scientists, drone attacks against its research facilities, and industrial espionage campaign against Tehran's centrifuge program have delayed but not eliminated the Islamic Republic's atomic weapons plans. Retaliating against Iranian missile strikes, IDF warplanes on October 25, 2024, struck twenty Iranian missile and drone production facilities, disabling their defense systems and inflicting damage on these locations.[16]

The Israeli Air Force concentrated its attacks on Iran's Parchin and Khojir military complexes, which featured advanced nuclear weapons research as well as drone and missile production sites.[17] This may presage a future round of Israeli attacks directly against these facilities.

American provision of bunker-busting bombs and refueling tankers for the Israeli Air Force will be vital to the success of a future military strike against Iran's diverse nuclear infrastructure. Even if Jerusalem succeeds in bombing Iran's facilities, such a development will not guarantee that the regime will fail to restart its program.

Military support for regional allies in the Middle East and Northeast Asia is critical to deter Tehran and Pyongyang. US military disengagement from these regional theaters would create a destabilizing power vacuum that should be avoided. America also needs to improve regional missile defense systems.

US-Israeli missile defense research and investment will assist in the development of a regional defensive shield that could include Bahrain, the UAE, and possibly Saudi Arabia. Such a security net could assist in the Abraham Accords' extension to Saudi Arabia to protect the kingdom from Iranian and proxy missile strikes. Only through a comprehensive economic, diplomatic, informational, and military deterrence and containment strategy that treats the Iran–North Korea partnership as an integrated network can the destabilizing activities of these two states be contained.

Notes

1. Setting the Context

1. See Michael Eisenstadt, "The Strategic Culture of the Islamic Republic of Iran: Operational and Policy Implications," MES Monographs, Washington Institute for Near East Policy, August 2011, https://www.washingtoninstitute.org/policy-analysis /view/the-strategic-culture-of-the-islamic-republic-of-iran-religion-expediency-a.

2. See Hanin Ghaddar, "Iran's Foreign Legion: The Impact of Shia Militias on US Foreign Policy," Policy Notes, Washington Institute for Near East Policy, 2018, https://www.washingtoninstitute.org/policy-analysis/view/irans-foreign-legion-the -impact-of-shia-militias-on-u.s.-foreign-policy.

3. See Sebastien Roblin, "Iran Just Struck U.S. Bases in Iraq with Ballistic Missiles. Here's Why They're Tehran's Favored Weapon," *Forbes*, January 7, 2020, https:// www.forbes.com/sites/sebastienroblin/2020/01/07/iran-just-struck-us-bases-in-iraq -with-ballistic-missiles-heres-why-theyre-tehrans-favored-weapon/#27c432c3136c.

4. Eisenstadt, "Strategic Culture of the Islamic Republic of Iran."

5. Matthew Levitt, "Major Beneficiaries of the Iran Deal: IRGC and Hezbollah," Washington Institute for Near East Policy, September 17, 2015, https://www .washingtoninstitute.org/policy-analysis/view/major-beneficiaries-of-the-iran-deal -irgc-and-hezbollah.

6. Suzanne Maloney, "The Roots of Iran's Regional Strategy," Atlantic Council, September 2017, https://www.atlanticcouncil.org/in-depth-research-reports/issue-brief /the-roots-drivers-and-evolution-of-iran-s-regional-strategy/.

7. Vali Nasr, *The Shia Revival: How Conflicts within Islam Will Shape the Future* (New York: W. W. Norton, 2006).

8. See Michael Eisenstadt, "Rumors of War: Responding to Iranian Pushback in the Gulf," Washington Institute for Near East Policy, May 2019, https://www .washingtoninstitute.org/policy-analysis/view/rumors-of-war-responding-to-iranian -pushback-in-the-gulf.

9. Michael Herzog, "Contextualizing Israeli Concerns over the Iranian Nuclear Deal," Washington Institute for Near East Policy, June 2015, https://www .washingtoninstitute.org/policy-analysis/view/contextualizing-israeli-concerns -about-the-iran-nuclear-deal.

10. Robin Hughes, "Tehran Takes Steps to Protect Nuclear Facilities," *Jane's Defence Weekly*, January 25, 2006, 4–5.

11. Eisenstadt, "Strategic Culture of the Islamic Republic of Iran," 3.

12. Ibid.

13. Patrick McEachern and Jaclyn O'Brien McEachern, *North Korea, Iran and the Challenge to International Order: A Comparative Perspective* (Milton Park: Routledge, 2017).

14. Bruce Cumings, Ervand Abrahamian, and Moshe Ma'oz, *Inventing the Axis of Evil: The Truth about North Korea, Iran, and Syria* (New York: New Press, 2006).

15. See Nicholas Blanford, *Warriors of God: Inside Hezbollah's Thirty-Year Struggle against Israel* (New York: Random House, 2011), 20–219.

16. Larry Niksch, "North Korea Terrorism List Removal," Congressional Research Service, January 6, 2010, http://fpc.state.gov/documents/organization/137273.pdf.

2. North Korea's Military Capabilities

1. See Bruce E. Bechtol Jr., *North Korean Military Proliferation in the Middle East and Africa: Enabling Violence and Instability* (Lexington: University Press of Kentucky, 2018), chap. 2.

2. For analysis of the weaponization of North Korea's plutonium and HEU programs, see Mary Beth Nikitin, "North Korea's Nuclear Weapons: Technical Issues," RL34256, Congressional Research Service, April 3, 2013, https://www.fas.org/sgp/crs/nuke/RL34256.pdf.

3. Robert L. Gallucci, "North Korea, Iran, and the Proliferation of Nuclear Weapons: The Threat, U.S. Policy, and the Prescription . . . and the India Deal," in *How to Make America Safe: New Policies for National Security*, ed. Stephen Van Evera (Cambridge, MA: Tobin Project, 2006), https://www.tobinproject.org/sites/tobinproject.org/files/assets/Make_America_Safe_North_Korea_Iran_Nuclear_Proliferation.pdf.

4. For more information about North Korea's first two nuclear tests, see Mark Fitzpatrick, "North Korean Proliferation Challenges: The Role of the European Union," Non-proliferation Papers 18, EU Non-proliferation Consortium, June 2012, https://www.sipri.org/research/disarmament/eu-consortium/publications/nonproliferation-paper-18.

5. "N. Korea Resumes Tests for Smaller Missile Warheads," *Chosun Ilbo*, February 26, 2015, https://english.chosun.com/site/data/html_dir/2015/02/26/2015022601825.html.

6. "Iranian Nuke Chief Was in N. Korea for Atomic Test," *Times of Israel*, February 17, 2013, https://www.timesofisrael.com/iranian-nuke-chief-was-in-n-korea-for-atomic-test/.

7. See Jack Liu, "North Korea's Yongbyon Nuclear Facility: New Activity at the Plutonium Production Complex," *38 North*, September 8, 2015, https://38north

.org/2015/09/yongbyon090815/; "N. Korea Digging New Tunnel at Its Nuke Test Site: Official," Yonhap, October 30, 2015, https://english.yonhapnews.co.kr/news /2015/10/30/0200000000AEN20151030002800315.html; Andrea Shalal, David Brunnstrom, and Jonathan Landay, "North Korea Nuclear Test Did Not Increase Technical Capability: U.S.," Reuters, January 19, 2016, https://www.reuters.com /article/us-northkorea-nuclear-usa-idUSKCN0UY042; "North Korea Nuclear Blast Shows 'Uncanny Resemblance' to Last Test—Analyst," Reuters, January 8, 2016, https://in.reuters.com/article/northkorea-nuclear-seismic-idINKBN0UM0K Y20160108; Nick Hansen, Robert Kelley, and Allison Puccioni, "North Korean Nuclear Programme Advances," *Janes Intelligence Review*, March 30, 2016, https:// www.janes.com/article/59118/north-korean-nuclear-programme-advances; "North Korea's Nuclear Programme: How Advanced Is It?," BBC, January 6, 2016, https:// www.bbc.com/news/world-asia-pacific-11813699.

8. See Foster Klug and Kim Tong-Hyung, "Rhetoric or Real? N. Korea Nuclear Test May Be a Bit of Both," Associated Press, September 11, 2016, https://bigstory .ap.org/article/f9234cbd0efa4d3caafcbecb88e16576/rhetoric-or-real-n-korea-nuclear -test-may-be-bit-both; Kang Jin-kyu and Kang Chan-su, "North Korea's Fifth Nuclear Test Strongest Yet," *Joongang Ilbo*, September 10, 2016, https://mengnews.joins .com/view.aspx?aId=3023659.

9. For detailed analysis that supports the assessments described in this paragraph about North Korea's sixth nuclear test, see Vladimir Khrustalev, "Thermonuclear Shock: A Detailed Analysis of the Explosion of the DPRK's Hydrogen Bomb and Its Consequences," Defcon Warning System, September 8, 2017, https://defcon warningsystem.com/2017/09/08/thermonuclear-shock-detailed-analysis-explosion -dprks-hydrogen-bomb-consequences/; Choe Sang-hun and David E. Sanger, "North Korean Nuclear Test Draws U.S. Warning of 'Massive Military Response,'" *New York Times*, September 2, 2017, https://www.nytimes.com/2017/09/03/world/asia/north -korea-tremor-possible-6th-nuclear-test.html?mcubz=3; James Griffiths and Angela Dewan, "Hydrogen Bomb: What Is It and Can North Korea Deliver One?," CNN, September 3, 2017, https://www.cnn.com/2017/09/03/asia/hydrogen-bomb-north -korea-explainer/index.html; NORSAR, "The Nuclear Explosion in North Korea on 3 September 2017: A Revised Magnitude Assessment," September 12, 2017, https:// www.norsar.no/press/latest-press-release/archive/the-nuclear-explosion-in-north-korea -on-3-september-2017-a-revised-magnitude-assessment-article1548-984.html.

10. American Geophysical Union, "2017 North Korean Nuclear Test Order of Magnitude Larger Than Previous Tests, New Study Finds," press release, June 3, 2019, https://news.agu.org/press-release/2017-north-korean-nuclear-test-order-of -magnitude-larger-than-previous-tests-new-study-finds/.

11. See Lee Haye-ah, "Key N.K. Uranium Plant Continues to Be Updated: U.S. Monitor," Yonhap, May 30, 2020, https://en.yna.co.kr/view/AEN202005 30000200325; Ankit Panda, "Exclusive: Revealing Kangson, North Korea's First Covert Uranium Enrichment Site," *Diplomat*, July 13, 2018, https://thediplomat

.com/2018/07/exclusive-revealing-kangson-north-koreas-first-covert-uranium-en richment-site/; "NK Has Built Uranium Enrichment Facilities," *Donga Ilbo*, February 18, 2009, https://www.donga.com/en/article/all/20090218/261399.

12. See Joseph S. Bermudez Jr., Victor Cha, and Jennifer Jun, "Yongbyon Update: New Activity at Building 500 and Rising Waters," Beyond Parallel: Center for Strategic and International Studies, July 11, 2022, https://beyondparallel.csis.org /yongbyon-update-new-activity-at-building-500-and-rising-waters/.

13. See "North Korea's Military Capabilities," Council on Foreign Relations, June 28, 2022, https://www.cfr.org/backgrounder/north-korea-nuclear-weapons-missile -tests-military-capabilities; Michael Lee, "North Seems to Be Restoring Punggye -ri Tunnel," *Joongang Ilbo*, June 29, 2022, https://koreajoongangdaily.joins.com/2022 /03/29/national/northKorea/North-Korea-nuclear-test/20220329182231013.html; "U.S. Charges N. Koreans with Laundering $2.5 Bln to Support Nuclear Program," Yonhap, May 29, 2020, https://en.yna.co.kr/view/AEN20200529000351325; Byun Duk-kun, "N. Korea Continues to Develop Nuclear Capability While Evading UN Sanctions: Report," Yonhap, April 2, 2022, https://en.yna.co.kr/view /AEN20220402000500325; Jordan King, "North Korea 'Working Prisoners to Death to Rebuild Banned Nuclear Testing Site,'" *Metro News*, May 18, 2022, https://metro.co.uk/2022/05/18/north-korea-working-prisoners-to-death-to-re build-banned-nuclear-testing-site-16669601/; Lee Haye-ah, "N. Korea Tests Nuclear Detonation Device: Presidential Office," Yonhap, May 25, 2022, https://en.yna.co.kr /view/AEN20220525008952315.

14. See Oh Seok-min, "N. Korea Beefs Up Missile Units, Special Forces over Past Years: Defense Ministry," Yonhap, February 2, 2021, https://en.yna.co.kr/view /AEN20210202003000325.

15. See Lim Hui Jie, "Missiles Aren't the Only Threat from North Korea. Its Conventional Arms Are Just as Deadly," CNBC, August 16, 2023, https://www.cnbc .com/2023/08/17/missiles-arent-only-threat-from-north-korea-conventional-arms -as-deadly.html.

16. See "KN-09 (KN-SS-9)," Missile Threat: CSIS Missile Defense Project, July 31, 2021, https://missilethreat.csis.org/missile/kn-09-kn-ss-x-9/.

17. See "Update on the DPRK's 600 mm Multiple Launch Rocket System," Open Nuclear Network, February 13, 2023, https://opennuclear.org/publication /update-dprks-600-mm-multiple-launch-rocket-system; Jeong Tae Joo, "N. Korea's Latest Launches of Short-Range Ballistic Missiles Were Final Pre-deployment Tests," *Daily NK*, May 16, 2022, https://www.dailynk.com/english/n-koreas-latest-launch es-of-short-range-ballistic-missiles-were-final-pre-deployment-tests/; Jung Da-min, "North Korea's Missile Capability: How Far It Has Come and Its Implications in Denuclearization Talks," *Korea Times*, December 3, 2019, https://www.koreatimes. co.kr/www/nation/2023/09/103_279661.html; Choi Si-young, "NK Hails Successful Test of Advanced Rockets," *Korea Herald*, March 3, 2020, https://www.koreaher ald.com/view.php?ud=20200303000773.

18. See Kyle Mizokami, "No, North Korea's Tank Isn't the Best in the World. Not Even Close," *Popular Mechanics*, June 23, 2021, https://www.popularmechanics .com/military/weapons/a36805563/north-korea-storm-tiger-tank/.

19. "The Mysterious Origins of a New North Korean Howitzer," 21st Century Asian Arms Race, October 26, 2018, https://21stcenturyasianarmsrace.com /2018/10/26/the-mysterious-origins-of-a-new-north-korean-howitzer/.

20. See Josh Smith and Soo-Hyang Choi, "North Korea Unveils First Tactical, Nuclear-Armed Submarine," Reuters, September 8, 2023, https://www.reuters.com /world/asia-pacific/north-korea-launches-new-tactical-nuclear-attack-submarine -kcna-2023-09-07/.

21. See Eric Talmadge, "Experts See Russia Fingerprints on North Korea's New Missile," Associated Press, May 10, 2019, https://apnews.com/general-news-20afeea 785634442b8300ba2fab0c002; Michael S. Repass and Nicole Wolkov, "Contrary to Previous Claims, Evidence Shows Iskander Missiles in the Second Nagorno-Kara bakh War," Caspian Policy Center, April 15, 2021, https://www.caspianpolicy.org /research/security-and-politics-program-spp/contrary-to-previous-claims-evidence -shows-iskander-missiles-in-the-second-nagorno-karabakh-war.

22. See "Iskander-M (SS-26)," Missile Defense Advocacy Alliance, August 12, 2019, https://missiledefenseadvocacy.org/missile-threat-and-proliferation/todays-missile -threat/russia/iskander-m-ss-26/; Vann H. Van Diepen, "Initial Analysis of North Korea's March 25 SRBM Launches," *38 North*, March 30, 2021, https://www .38north.org/2021/03/initial-analysis-of-north-koreas-march-25-srbm-launches /#:~:text=That%20these%20launches%20involved%20SRBMs,conduct%20(if%20 not%20gearing%20up; Geoff Brumfiel, "North Korea's Newest Missile Appears Similar to Advanced Russian Design," National Public Radio, May 8, 2019, https://www .npr.org/2019/05/08/721135496/north-koreas-newest-missile-appears-similar-to -advanced-russian-design; Michael Elleman, "Preliminary Assessment of the KN-24 Missile Launches," *38 North*, March 25, 2020, https://www.38north.org/2020/03 /melleman032520/; "KN-23 at a Glance," Missile Threat: CSIS Missile Defense Project, Center for Strategic and International Studies, 2020, https://missilethreat.csis .org/missile/kn-23/; "KN-24 [Hwasong-11] Tactical Missile System," GlobalSecurity. org, August 5, 2022, https://www.globalsecurity.org/wmd/world/dprk/kn-24.htm.

23. See Song Sang-ho, "N. Korea Announces Firing of 2 Train-Borne Guided Missiles into East Sea," Yonhap, January 15, 2022, https://en.yna.co.kr/view /AEN20220115000352325; "North Korea Tests Railway-Borne Missile in Latest Launch amid Rising Tension with U.S.," Reuters, January 15, 2022, https://www .nbcnews.com/news/north-korea/north-korea-tests-railway-borne-missile-latest -launch-amid-rising-n1287561.

24. See Jeong Eun Lee, Jaeduk Seo, and Dukin Han, "North Korea Raises Stakes with New Mach-10 Hypersonic Missile Test," Radio Free Asia, January 11, 2022, https:// www.rfa.org/english/news/korea/missile-01112022204855.html; "North Korea Yet to Fully Develop Hypersonic Missile, but Its Tests Raise Concerns: US Official," *Korea*

Times, May 19, 2022, https://www.koreatimes.co.kr/www/nation/2023/10/103
_329419.html; Sungwon Baik and Christy Lee, "Analysis: Why North Korea's Hypersonic Missile Test Is Troubling," Voice of America, January 19, 2022, https://
www.voanews.com/a/analysis-why-north-korea-s-hypersonic-missile-test-is
-troubling/6404637.html#:~:text=Despite%20the%20focus%20of%20atten
tion,change%20its%20course%20of%20flight; Ross Niebergall, "North Korean
Hypersonic Threat Is an Alarming Wake-Up Call for How We Innovate," *Defense
News*, January 21, 2022, https://www.defensenews.com/opinion/commentary/2022
/01/21/north-korean-hypersonic-threat-is-an-alarming-wake-up-call-for-how-we
-innovate/; Ralph Savelsberg and Tomohiko Kawaguchi, "North Korea's Hypersonic
Missile Claims Are Credible, Exclusive Analysis Shows," *Breaking Defense*, February
16, 2022, https://breakingdefense.com/2022/02/north-koreas-hypersonic-missile
-claims-are-credible-exclusive-analysis-shows/.

25. See Hyonhee Shin, "Explainer: Why Is North Korea Testing Hypersonic
Missiles and How Do They Work?," Reuters, April 3, 2024, https://www.reuters
.com/world/asia-pacific/why-is-north-korea-testing-hypersonic-missiles-how-do
-they-work-2024-04-03/?utm.

26. See Joseph Trevithick, "North Korea's Latest Hypersonic Missile System Is
One Sinister-Looking Weapon," *War Zone*, April 3, 2024, https://www.twz.com
/land/north-koreas-latest-hypersonic-missile-system-is-one-sinister-looking-weap
on?mc_cid=6d464456ba&mc_eid=70bf478f36.

27. See Joyce Lee and Josh Smith, "Update 5: North Korea Aims to Adopt Solid-Fuel Missiles for Faster Launches," Reuters, April 3, 2024, https://sg.finance
.yahoo.com/news/3-north-korea-aims-switch-212436627.html.

28. See Vann H. Van Diepen, "Second Flight of North Korea's Solid IRBM Also
Second Flight of HGV," *38 North*, April 5, 2024, https://www.38north.org/2024/04
/second-flight-of-north-koreas-solid-irbm-also-second-flight-of-hgv/.

29. See Kim Tong-Hyung, "South Korean Defense Chief Says North Korea Has
Supplied 7,000 Containers of Munitions to Russia," Associated Press, March 18,
2024, https://apnews.com/article/north-korea-russia-arms-transfers-ukraine-a37b
c290ed3ee59cfbbafdc2a994dc58.

30. The writing for the previous five paragraphs came from a piece I wrote for the
National Interest, published here with the permission of the editor. The authors would
like to thank Harry Kazianis for granting us permission to restate these important
issues in this forum. See Bruce E. Bechtol, "The North Korea Hypersonic Missile
Threat Is Real," *National Interest*, April 12, 2024, https://nationalinterest.org/blog
/korea-watch/north-korea-hypersonic-missile-threat-real-210544.

31. See Bechtol, *North Korean Military Proliferation*, chap. 2.

32. See Chaewon Chung and Jeongmin Kim, "North Korea Shows Off Apparent
New Solid Fuel Missile," *NK News*, April 26, 2022, https://www.nknews.org/2022/04
/north-korea-rolls-out-long-range-hwasong-17-nuclear-missiles-at-military-parade/;
Song Sang-ho, "N. Korea Fires What Seems to Be SLBM toward East Sea: S. Korea,"
Yonhap, October 19, 2021, https://en.yna.co.kr/view/AEN20211019002958325;

Yu Yong-weon, "N. Korea Fires Missile from Submarine," *Chosun Ilbo*, May 9, 2022, https://english.chosun.com/m/news/article.amp.html?contid=2022050900668; Daehan Lee, "North Korea Fires Possible Pukguksong-5 SLBM," *Naval News*, October 19, 2021, https://www.navalnews.com/naval-news/2021/10/north-korea-fires -possible-pukguksong-ballistic-missile/; Joyce Lee, "North Korea Says It Successfully Tested New Submarine-Launched Ballistic Missile," Reuters, October 19, 2019, https://www.reuters.com/article/us-northkorea-missiles/north-korea-says-it-success fully-tested-new-submarine-launched-ballistic-missile-idUSKBN1WH2GS; "Factbox: North Korea's Submarine-Launched Missiles," Reuters, October 19, 2021, https://news.yahoo.com/factbox-north-koreas-submarine-launched-072807688. html?guccounter=1&guce_referrer=aHR0cHM6Ly93d3cuZ29vZ2xlLmNvbS88& guce_referrer_sig=AQAAACbQAPa_qczR-2Tn-qA7147UiNYDTqBdA5ZdhjE vR7F34_EsQ8GLbO4zY8TBJBivLQYTqoAozTl1wF7umCeOUUWmZW3bHf 5g0c2-gRlpa415p5EkV5scYyRkWHqBZU8J72XRIWLuUY6-0f4RqgQTRhaai L7VAscSSEgFyVIX9kLZ; "N. Korea Fires Apparent SLBM off East Coast: S. Korean Military," *Korea Herald*, May 7, 2022, https://www.koreaherald.com/view.php? ud=20220507000050; H. I. Sutton, "Unusual Submarine Likely to Increase Threat from North Korea," *Naval News*, October 2, 2020, https://www.navalnews.com /naval-news/2020/10/unusual-submarine-likely-to-increase-threat-from-north -korea/.

33. See Theodore A. Postol, "North Korean Missiles and US Missile Defense," *Physics and Society* 47, no. 2 (April 2018), https://higherlogicdownload.s3.ama zonaws.com/APS/a05ec1cf-2e34-4fb3-816e-ea1497930d75/UploadedImages /Newsletter_PDF/April18.pdf; Choi Jae-hee, "N. Korea Confirms Missile Test of Intermediate Range Hwasong-12," *Korea Herald*, January 31, 2022, https://www .koreaherald.com/view.php?ud=20220131000100; "North's ICBMs May Have Re-entry Ability, Says Report," *Joongang Ilbo*, November 18, 2020, https://korea joongangdaily.joins.com/2020/11/18/national/northKorea/ICBM-Heritage-Foun dation-CIA/20201118192200453.html; Michelle Nichols, "North Korea Has 'Probably' Developed Nuclear Devices to Fit Ballistic Missiles, U.N. Report Says," *Guardian*, August 3, 2020, https://www.theguardian.com/world/2020/aug/04 /north-korea-has-probably-developed-nuclear-devices-to-fit-ballistic-missiles-un #:~:text=In%202017%20a%20leaked%20US,targets%20including%20the%20 US%20mainland; "N. Korea Missing 'Last 2 Pieces' of Technology to Perfect ICBMs: U.S. General," *Korea Herald*, August 11, 2018, https://www.koreaherald .com/view.php?ud=20180811000022; Jeffrey Lewis, "DPRK RV Video Analysis," Arms Control Wonk, November 9, 2018, https://www.armscontrolwonk.com /archive/1206084/dprk-rv-video-analysis/.

34. See Dasi Yoon, "North Korea's Powerful New Missile Has Shortcomings as a Weapon," *Wall Street Journal*, December 4, 2022, https://www.wsj.com/articles /north-koreas-powerful-new-missile-has-shortcomings-as-a-weapon-11670123155; "N.K. Leader Inspects Hwasong-17 ICBM Test Launch, Declares Resolute Nuclear Response to Threats," Yonhap, November 19, 2022, https://en.yna.co.kr/view

/AEN20221119000552325; Colin Zwirko, "North Korea Test-Launched New 'Hwasong-17' ICBM for First Time, State Media Says," *NK News*, March 25, 2022, https://www.nknews.org/2022/03/north-korea-test-launched-new-hwasong-17 -icbm-for-first-time-state-media-says/; "North Korea Showcases Its Biggest ICBM Yet as Kim Vows to Hasten Development of North's Nuclear Arsenal," *CBS News*, April 26, 2022, https://www.cbsnews.com/news/north-korea-nuclear-icbm-kim -jong-un/; "N. Korea Tests New ICBM System, US to Impose Additional Sanctions," Yonhap, March 11, 2022, https://en.yna.co.kr/view/AEN20220311000400325; "N. Korea's Hwasong-17 ICBM Launch Seems to Have Ended in Failure: Source," *Korea Times*, November 3, 2022, https://www.koreatimes.co.kr/www/na tion/2023/10/103_339102.html.

35. See Hyung-jin Kim, Tong Kim, and Mari Yamaguchi, "N. Korea Fires Missile That May Have Been New Type of Weapon," Associated Press, April 13, 2023, https://apnews.com/article/north-korea-missile-launches-us-drills-55e946567117c 176b027ee7c4253483e.

36. See Theodore Postol, "The Transfer of a Russian ICBM to North Korea?," Beyond Parallel: CSIS, August 17, 2023, https://beyondparallel.csis.org/the-transfer -of-a-russian-icbm-to-north-korea/.

37. See Richard Engel and Kennett Werner, "North Korea's New Missile Technology May Have Soviet Roots," *NBC News*, March 2, 2018, https://www.nbcnews.com /news/world/north-korea-s-new-missile-technology-may-have-soviet-roots-n852231.

38. The writing for the previous seven paragraphs came from a piece I wrote for *1945*, published here with the permission of the editor. The authors would like to thank Harry Kazianis for granting us permission to restate these important issues in this forum. See Bruce E. Bechtol, "Hwasong-18: The North Korean ICBM with 'Russian DNA'?," *1945*, August 21, 2023, https://www.19fortyfive.com/2023/08 /hwasong-18-the-north-korean-icbm-with-russian-dna/?fbclid=IwAR3doiynF _r6HlG4DHtUXc1zj9sA4yFBtMSdJ3eFavnPuGOY0gRoFJCszVs.

39. See Bechtol, "Hwasong-18."

40. See Antony J. Blinken, "United States Designates Entities and Individuals Linked to the Democratic People's Republic of Korea's (DPRK) Weapons Programs," US Department of State, January 12, 2022, https://www.state.gov/united-states-des ignates-entities-and-individuals-linked-to-the-democratic-peoples-republic-of-ko reas-dprk-weapons-programs/.

41. See ibid.

42. See Minnie Chan, "North Korea Using Russian Satellite Navigation System Instead of GPS for Missile Launches, Observers Say," *South China Morning Post*, January 18, 2022, https://www.scmp.com/news/china/military/article /3163727/north-korea-using-russian-satellite-navigation-system-instead#:~:tex t=ChinaMilitary ,North%20Korea%20using%20Russian%20satellite%20naviga tion%20system%20instead,for%20missile%20launches%2C%20observers%20 say&text=North%20Korea%20has%20been%20launching,navigation%20net work%2C%20according%20to%20observers.

43. For an excellent example of this, See Jack Kim and James Pearson, "North Korea Appeared to Use China Truck in Its First Claimed ICBM Test," Reuters, July 4, 2017, https://www.reuters.com/article/us-northkorea-missiles-china-truck /north-korea-appeared-to-use-china-truck-in-its-first-claimed-icbm-test-idUSKBN 19P1J3.

44. Bill Gertz, "Secret Document Reveals China Covertly Offering Missiles, Increased Aid to North Korea," *Washington Free Beacon*, January 2, 2018, https://free beacon.com/national-security/secret-document-reveals-china-covertly-offering-mis siles-increased-aid-north-korea/.

45. See Catalin Cimpanu, "Hackers Breach and Steal Data from South Korea's Defense Ministry," ZDNet, January 16, 2019, https://www.zdnet.com/article/hackers -breach-and-steal-data-from-south-koreas-defense-ministry/; Duncan Riley, "North Korea Suspected in Attack That Delayed Printing of Major Newspapers," *SiliconAN-GLE*, December 30, 2018, https://siliconangle.com/2018/12/30/north-korea-sus pected-behind-attack-delayed-printing-major-newspapers/; Ian Talley and Dustin Volz, "U.S. Targets North Korean Hacking as Rising National-Security Threat," *Wall Street Journal*, September 15, 2019, https://www.wsj.com/articles/u-s-targets -north-korean-hacking-as-rising-national-security-threat-11568545202; William Suberg, "North Korea Launched Cryptocurrency Attacks in Response to Sanc-tions, Says FBI," Cointelegraph, May 30, 2019, https://cointelegraph.com/news /north-korea-launched-cryptocurrency-attacks-in-response-to-sanctions-says-fbi; Park Han-na, "North Korea–Backed Hackers Intensify Information Warfare, Fi-nancial Theft," *Korea Herald*, March 26, 2019, https://www.koreaherald.com/view .php?ud=20190326000616.

46. See Ravie Lakshmanan, "North Korean Hackers Are Targeting ATMs in India with New Data-Stealing Malware," Next Web, September 14, 2019, https:// thenextweb.com/news/north-korean-hackers-are-targeting-atms-in-india-with-new -data-stealing-malware; Anthony Cuthbertson, "North Korea Using Cryptocur-rency to Fund Nuclear Weapons Development, Report Warns," *Independent*, April 22, 2019, https://www.Independent.co.uk/tech/north-korea-bitcoin-cryptocurrency -nuclear-weapons-sanctions-rusi-a8872056.html; Mun Dong Hui, "N. Korean Hackers Mount Phishing Attack on NKHR Groups," *Daily NK*, December 30, 2019, https://www.dailynk.com/english/north-korean-hackers-mount-phishing-attack -nkhr-groups/#:~:text=Korean%20hackers%20mount%20phishing%20at tack%20on%20NKHR%20groups,-Experts%20suggest%20that&text=On%20 Dec.,North%20Korea%27s%20human%20rights%20violations; Jeff Stone, "Goo-gle Catches North Korean, Iranian Hackers Impersonating Journalists in Phishing Efforts," *CyberScoop*, March 26, 2020, https://cyberscoop.com/google-phishing -warning-hacking-campaign-iran-north-korea/.

47. See Jamie Redman, "3 Reports Look at North Korea's Lazarus Group, Iran's Farhad Exchange, and the Crypto Ponzi Futurenet," Bitcoin.com, May 6, 2020, https://news.bitcoin.com/3-reports-look-at-north-koreas-lazarus-group-irans-farhad -exchange-and-crypto-ponzi-futurenet/.

48. Jason Bartlett, "Why Is North Korea So Good at Cybercrime?," *Diplomat*, November 13, 2020, https://thediplomat.com/2020/11/why-is-north-korea-so-good -at-cybercrime/.

49. See Kelsey Atherton, "North Korea's Hackers Target Tech Secrets," *Breaking Defense*, October 30, 2020, https://breakingdefense.com/2020/10/north-koreas -hackers-target-tech-secrets/.

50. See Andrew Salmon, "Cyber Warrior's Glimpse into Kim's Operation Chaos," *Asia Times*, February 27, 2021, https://asiatimes.com/2021/02/cyber-warriors -glimpse-into-kims-operation-chaos/.

51. See Andrew Salmon, "North Korea's Cyber Commandos Range Far, Strike Deep," *Asia Times*, March 2, 2021, https://asiatimes.com/2021/03/kims-cyber-com mandos-range-far-strike-deep/#:~:text=These%20realities%20force%20Pyong yang%20to,web%20and%20across%20the%20globe; Elizabeth Shim, "North Korea Stole $1B during Cyber Heists over Past Decade, Study Says," UPI, April 8, 2021, https://www.upi.com/Top_News/World-News/2021/04/08/nkorea-North-Korea -cyber-attack-crypto/5451617891625/.

52. See Tory Newmyer and Jeremy B. Merrill, "U.S. Hasn't Stopped N. Korean Gang from Laundering Its Crypto Haul," *Washington Post*, April 23, 2022, https:// www.washingtonpost.com/business/2022/04/23/north-korea-hack-crypto-access/; Byun Duk-kun, "N. Korea Increasingly Relies on Cyber Crimes to Fund Weapons Programs: U.N. Expert," Yonhap, April 21, 2022, https://en.yna.co.kr/view /AEN20220421000200325; Tory Newmyer, "Treasury Sanctions Crypto Service That Helped North Koreans Launder Funds," *Washington Post*, March 6, 2022, https://www.washingtonpost.com/technology/2022/05/06/treasury-crypto-sanc tions/; Charlie Bradley, "North Korea's Major Weakness Exposed: 'Take It Away, Everything Collapses," *Express*, April 4, 2022, https://www.express.co.uk/news/world /1650212/north-korea-news-weakness-office-39-kim-jong-un-spt; Michael Lee, "Pyongyang Starts Liking Crypto a Bit Too Much," *Joongang Ilbo*, July 6, 2022, https://koreajoongangdaily.joins.com/2022/07/06/national/northKorea/Korea -North-Korea-cryptocurrency/20220706174357557.html.

53. See Seulkee Jang, "Inside N. Korea's Internet-Based Foreign Currency-Earning Activities," *Daily NK*, December 20, 2022, https://www.dailynk.com/english /inside-north-korea-internet-based-foreign-currency-earning-activities/.

54. See Ji Da-gyum, "Tale of North Korea's Cyberterrorists: How They Break into 'Unhackable' Crypto Platforms and Cash Out," *Korea Herald*, December 12, 2022, https://www.koreaherald.com/view.php?ud=20221212000714#:~:text=Tale%20 of%20North%20Korea%27s%20cyberterrorists,crypto%20platforms%20and%20 cash%20out&text=This%20is%20the%20second%20installment,hermit%20 regime%E2%80%99s%20nuclear%20ambitions; Christian Encila, "Hackers from North Korea Seen as Culprits in DeBridge Finance Cyberattack," Bitcoinist, August 5, 2022, https://bitcoinist.com/hackers-suspects-in-debridge-attack/; US Federal Bureau of Investigation, "FBI Confirms Lazarus Group Cyber Actors Responsible for Harmony's Horizon Bridge Currency Theft," press release, January 23, 2023,

https://www.fbi.gov/news/press-releases/fbi-confirms-lazarus-group-cyber-actors
-responsible-for-harmonys-horizon-bridge-currency-theft; Phil Rosen, "North Korean
Hackers Are Posing as VC Firms to Steal Crypto—and a Blockchain Expert Says
2023 Could Bring More Cyberattacks Than Ever," *Business Insider*, January 2, 2023,
https://markets.businessinsider.com/news/currencies/north-korea-hackers-lazarus
-crypto-crime-venture-capital-firms-trm-2023-1; Nate Nelson, "North Korea's Top
APT Swindled $1B From Crypto Investors in 2022," *Dark Reading*, January 25,
2023, https://www.darkreading.com/remote-workforce/north-korea-apt-swindled-1b
-crypto-investors-2022; Kim Eun-joong, "N.Korea Stole Billions Worth of Crypto
from S.Korea," *Chosun Ilbo*, February 27, 2023, https://www.chosun.com/english
/north-korea-en/2023/02/07/UA3WJKRM3D7PYYWHMRTFVZBIKI/;
Song Sang-ho, "N. Korea's Cybertheft Last Year Estimated at $1.7 Billion: U.N. Panel
Report," Yonhap, October 28, 2023, https://en.yna.co.kr/view/AEN20231028000
500315.

3. Iran's Military Capabilities

1. Ali Ansari, "The Myth of the White Revolution: Mohammad Reza Shah, Modernization and the Consolidation of Power," *Middle East Studies* 37, no. 3 (2010): 1–24.

2. William Goldstein, "Secularization and the Iranian Revolution," *Journal of Islamic Perspectives*, no. 3 (2020): 50–67.

3. Defense Intelligence Agency, "Iran Military Power: Ensuring Regime Survival and Securing Regional Dominance," 2019, 2, https://www.dia.mil/News-Features /Articles/Article-View/Article/2020456/.

4. Ansari, "Myth of the White Revolution," 20.

5. Defense Intelligence Agency, "Iran Military Power," 2.

6. Goldstein, "Secularization and the Iranian Revolution," 58.

7. Vali Nasr, *The Shia Revival: How Conflicts within Islam Will Shape the Future* (New York: W. W. Norton, 2007), 119–45.

8. Kim Ghattas, *Black Wave: Saudi Arabia, Iran, and the Forty-Year Rivalry That Unraveled Culture, Religion, and Collective Memory in the Middle East* (New York: Henry Holt, 2020).

9. Nasr, *Shia Revival*.

10. Goldstein, "Secularization and the Iranian Revolution," 65–66.

11. Erik Olson, "Iran's Path Dependent Military Doctrine," *Strategic Studies Quarterly* 10, no. 2 (Summer 2016), https://www.airuniversity.af.edu/Portals/10 /SSQ/documents/Volume-10_Issue-2/Olson.pdf.

12. Nasr, *Shia Revival*, 141.

13. Alex Vatanka, "Whither the IRGC of the 2020s: Is Iran's Proxy War Strategy Sustainable?," *New America*, January 2021, https://d1y8sb8igg2f8e.cloudfront.net /documents/Whither_the_IRGC_of_the_2020s_.pdf.

14. Kasra Aarabi, "Beyond Borders: The Expansionist Ideology of Iran's Islamic Revolutionary Guard Corps," Tony Blair Institute for Global Change, February 2020, https://institute.global/insights/geopolitics-and-security/beyond-borders-expansionist-ideology-irans-islamic-revolutionary-guard-corps.

15. Michael Eisenstadt, "The Strategic Culture of the Islamic Republic of Iran: Religion, Expediency, and Soft Power in an Era of Disruptive Change," Policy Analysis/Monograph, Washington Institute for Near East Policy, November 23, 2015, https://www.washingtoninstitute.org/policy-analysis/strategic-culture-islamic-republic-iran-religion-expediency-and-soft-power-era; Reuel Marc Gerecht, "Iran: The Shi'ite Imperial Power," Foundation for Defense of Democracies, May 2018, https://www.fdd.org/analysis/2018/05/20/iran-the-shiite-imperial-power/; Mehdi Khalaji, "Apocalyptic Politics: On the Rationality of Iranian Politics," Washington Institute for Near East Policy, January 2008, https://www.washingtoninstitute.org/policy-analysis/apocalyptic-politics-rationality-iranian-policy.

16. Ali Ansari and Kasra Aarabi, "Ideology and Iran's Revolution: How 1979 Changed the World," Tony Blair Institute for Global Change, February 2019, https://institute.global/policy/ideology-and-irans-revolution-how-1979-changed-world.

17. Farzin Nadimi, "Iran and Russia's Growing Defense Ties," Washington Institute for Near East Policy, February 2015, https://www.washingtoninstitute.org/policy-analysis/iran-and-russias-growing-defense-ties.

18. Christopher Kozak, "The Strategic Convergence of Russia and Iran," *Institute for the Study of War Blog*, February 2017, https://understandingwar.org/backgrounder/strategic-convergence-russia-and-iran.

19. Defense Intelligence Agency, "Iran Military Power," 46, 54.

20. Nadimi, "Iran and Russia's Growing Defense Ties."

21. Farzin Nadimi, "Iran and China Are Strengthening Their Military Ties," Washington Institute for Near East Policy, November 2016, https://www.washingtoninstitute.org/pdf/view/3176/en; Farnaz Fassihi and Steven Lee Myers, "China with $400 Billion Deal with Iran Could Deepen Its Influence in the Mideast," *New York Times*, March 29, 2021, https://www.nytimes.com/2021/03/27/world/middleeast/china-iran-deal.html.

22. John Hardie, "Iran Aids Russia's Imperialist War against Ukraine," *Algemeiner*, Foundation for Defense of Democracies, November 22, 2022, https://www.fdd.org/analysis/2022/11/22/iran-aids-russias-imperialist-war; Nicholas Car, Kitaneh Fitzpatrick, and Katherine Lawlor, "Russia and Iran Double Down on their Strategic Partnership," Institute for the Study of War/American Enterprise Institute Critical Threats Project, August 11, 2022, https://www.understandingwar.org/backgrounder/russia-and-iran-double-down-their-strategic-partnership.

23. Michael Doran and Peter Rough, "China's Emerging Middle East Kingdom," *Tablet Magazine*, August 2020, https://www.tabletmag.com/sections/israel-middle-east/articles/china-middle-eastern-kingdom.

24. Nadimi, "Iran and China Are Strengthening Their Military Ties."

NOTES TO PAGES 41–43   199

25. Bruce E. Bechtol Jr., *North Korean Military Proliferation in the Middle East and Africa: Enabling Violence and Instability* (Lexington: University Press of Kentucky, 2018), 94–95.

26. Farzin Nadimi, "Iran's New Ballistic Missile May Have North Korean ICBM Links," Washington Institute for Near East Policy, September 2017, https://www .washingtoninstitute.org/policy-analysis/irans-new-ballistic-missile-may-have-north -korean-icbm-links.

27. Paul Kerr and Steven Hildreth, "Iran–North Korea–Syria Ballistic Missile and Nuclear Cooperation," Congressional Research Service, February 2016, https://crsre ports.congress.gov/product/pdf/R/R43480; Dany Shoham, "The Quadruple Threat: North Korea, China, Pakistan, and Iran," Perspectives Paper 1795, BESA Center, November 2020, https://besacenter.org/wp-content/uploads/2020/11/1795-Con tiguous-Quartet-Shoham-final.pdf.

28. International Atomic Energy Agency, *Board of Governors Report*, March 2020, https://www.iaea.org/iaea-director-generals-introductory-statement-to-the-board -of-governors-1-march-2021.

29. US Department of the Treasury, "Treasury Targets Actors Involved in Production and Transfer of Iranian Unmanned Arial Vehicles to Russia for Use in Ukraine," press release, November 15, 2022, https://home.treasury.gov/news/press-releases /jy1104.

30. Ansari, "Myth of the White Revolution."

31. "Iran's Nuclear Program: Status," Congressional Research Service, December 2019, https://www.iranwatch.org/sites/default/files/irans-nuclear-program-may-10 -2019.pdf.

32. Michael Eisenstadt and Mehdi Khalaji, "Nuclear Fatwa: Religion and Politics in Iran's Proliferation Strategy," Washington Institute for Near East Policy, September 2011, https://www.washingtoninstitute.org/policy-analysis/nuclear-fatwa-religion -and-politics-irans-proliferation-strategy; "Iran's Nuclear Program: Status," Congressional Research Service.

33. Michael Eisenstadt, "What Iran's Chemical Past Tells Us about Its Nuclear Future," Washington Institute for Near East Policy, April 2014, https://www.wash ingtoninstitute.org/policy-analysis/what-irans-chemical-past-tells-us-about-its-nu clear-future.

34. David Albright, "The Iranian Nuclear Archive: Implications and Recommendations," Foundation for Defense of Democracies, February 2019, https://www.fdd .org/analysis/2019/02/25/the-iranian-nuclear-archive-implications-and-recommen dations/.

35. Yehezkel Dror, "An Integrationist Imperative: Attack Iran and Launch a Regional Peace Initiative," BESA Center, May 2012, https://besacenter.org/wp-con tent/uploads/2012/05/iran.pdf.

36. Tony Badran, Matthew Brodsky, and Jonathan Schanzer, "Controlled Chaos: The Escalation of Conflict between Israel and Iran in War-Torn Syria," Foundation

for Defense of Democracies, July 2018, https://www.fdd.org/wp-content/uploads/2018/07/REPORT_ControlledChaos.pdf.

37. Dennis Ross, "The Coming Iran Nuclear Talks: Openings and Obstacles," Transition 2021: Policy Notes for the Biden Administration, Washington Institute for Near East Policy, January 2021, https://www.washingtoninstitute.org/policy-analysis/coming-iran-nuclear-talks-openings-and-obstacles.

38. Ofira Seliktar, "The End of the JCPOA Road?," *Middle East Quarterly* 27, no. 5 (Summer 2020): 1–18; Arvin Khoshnood, "The Dangers of Lifting Sanctions on the Islamic Republic of Iran," Perspectives Paper 1907, BESA Center, January 2020, https://besacenter.org/lifting-iran-sanctions/; Mark Dubowitz, Reuel Marc Gerecht, and Behnam Ben Taleblu, "What Yes with Iran Looks Like," Foundation for Defense of Democracies, June 2019, https://www.fdd.org/analysis/memos/2019/06/26/what-yes-with-iran-looks-like/.

39. Ross, "Coming Iran Nuclear Talks," 3–4.

40. Colm Quinn, "Talks over Iran Deal Enter Fourth Round in Vienna," *Foreign Policy*, May 2, 2021, https://foreignpolicy.com/2021/05/07/iran-nucelar-vienna-jcpoa/.

41. David Albright, Sarah Burkhard, and Andrea Stricker, "Analysis of IAEA Verification and Monitoring Report—September 2021," Institute for Science and International Security, September 13, 2021, https://isis-online.org/isis-reports/detail/analysis-of-iaea-iran-verification-and-monitoring-report-september-2021/.

42. Michael Eisenstadt, "Iran's Nuclear Hedging Strategy: Shaping the Islamic Republic's Proliferation Calculus," Policy Focus 178, Washington Institute for Middle East Policy, November 2022, 6–8, https://www.washingtoninstitute.org/policy-analysis/irans-nuclear-hedging-strategy-shaping-islamic-republics-proliferation-calculus.

43. Ibid., 14–17.

44. Michael Eisenstadt, "Working in the Gray Zone: Countering Iran's Asymmetric Way of War," Washington Institute for Near East Policy, January 2021, https://www.washingtoninstitute.org/policy-analysis/operating-gray-zone-counter-iran; Hal Brands, "Paradoxes of the Gray Zone," FPRI, February 2016, https://www.fpri.org/article/2016/02/paradoxes-gray-zone/.

45. Katerina Oskarsson, "DIMEFIL Instruments of Power in the Gray Zone," *Open Publications* 1 (Winter 2017): 21, https://www.academia.edu/32325460/The_Effectiveness_of_DIMEFIL_Instruments_of_Power_in_the_Gray_Zone.

46. Farzin Nadimi, "Iran's Military Establishment Doubles Down on the Revolution," Policy Watch 3482, Washington Institute for Near East Policy, May 2021, https://www.washingtoninstitute.org/pdf/view/2546/en.

47. Oula Alrifai, "In the Service of Ideology: Iran's Religious and Socio-economic Activities in Syria," Policy Note 100, Washington Institute for Near East Policy, March 2021, https://www.washingtoninstitute.org/policy-analysis/service-ideology-irans-religious-and-socioeconomic-activities-syria.

48. "Iranian Foreign and Defense Policies," Congressional Research Service, January 2021, https://crsreports.congress.gov/product/pdf/R/R44017.

49. "Iran: Internal Politics and US Policy and Options," Congressional Research Service, December 2020, https://crsreports.congress.gov/product/pdf/RL/RL32048.

50. Hesam Forozan and Afshin Shahi, "The Military and the State in Iran: The Economic Rise of the Revolutionary Guards," *Middle East Journal* 71, no. 1 (Winter 2017): 67–86.

51. Hossein Rassam and Sanam Vakil, "The Iranian Deep State: Understanding the Politics of Transition in the Islamic Republic," Hoover Institute Essay, October 12, 2020, 3–4, https://www.hoover.org/sites/default/files/research/docs/rassam_and_vakil_webready.pdf.

52. Aarabi, "Beyond Borders."

53. Farzan Nadimi, "Iran's Evolving Approach to Asymmetric Naval War: Strategies and Capabilities in the Persian Gulf," Washington Institute for Near East Policy, April 2020, https://www.washingtoninstitute.org/policy-analysis/irans-evolving-approach-asymmetric-naval-warfare-strategy-and-capabilities-persian.

54. Rassam and Vakil, "The Iranian Deep State," 7–8.

55. "Iran Missile Program: Past and Present," Iran Watch, June 2020, https://www.iranwatch.org/sites/default/files/iran-missile-program-past-present.pdf.

56. Nadimi, "Iran's Military Establishment Doubles Down," 1.

57. Farzin Nadimi, "Iran's National Army Reorganizes," Washington Institute for Near East Policy, August 2017, https://www.washingtoninstitute.org/policy-analysis/irans-national-army-reorganizes.

58. Paul Bucala and Marie Donovan, "A New Era in Iran's Military Leadership," Critical Threats, December 2016, https://www.criticalthreats.org/analysis/a-new-era-for-irans-military-leadership.

59. Olson, "Iran's Path Dependent Military Doctrine," 83.

60. Michael Eisenstadt, "Deterring Iran in the Gray Zone: Insights from Four Decades of Conflict," Policy Notes 103, Washington Institute for Near East Policy, April 2021, https://www.washingtoninstitute.org/policy-analysis/deterring-iran-gray-zone-insights-four-decades-conflict; Farzin Nadimi, "Iran's Latest Missile Launch: Scenarios and Implications for the New Administration," Washington Institute for Near East Policy, February 2017, https://www.washingtoninstitute.org/policy-analysis/irans-latest-missile-test-scenarios-and-implications-new-administration.

61. Eisenstadt, "Deterring Iran in the Gray Zone," 14.

62. Congressional Research Service, "Iran Foreign and Defense Policies," 7.

63. Shimon Shapira and Daniel Diker, "The Second Islamic Revolution: Strategic Implications for the West," in *Iran, Hizbullah, Hamas and the Global Jihad: A New Conflict Paradigm* (Jerusalem: Jerusalem Center for Public Affairs, 2007), 33–54, https://www.jcpa.org/text/iran-hizbullah-hamas.pdf.

64. Yossi Mansharof, "The Relationship between Iran and Palestinian Islamic Jihad," Jerusalem Institute for Strategy and Security, February 27, 2020, https://jiss.org.il/wp-content/uploads/2020/02/mansharof-yossi-relationship-between-iran-and-pij-jiss-english-27-02-2020.pdf.

65. Ibid., 19.

66. Ronen Bergman, "Live Updates: Hopes for Israel-Hamas Ceasefire as International Pressure Grows," *New York Times*, May 20, 2021, https://www.nytimes.com /live/2021/05/20/world/israel-palestine-gaza.

67. Yoaz Hendel, "Iran's Nukes and Israel's Dilemma," *Middle East Quarterly* 19, no. 1 (Winter 2012): 31–38.

68. Nader Uskowi, "The Evolving Iranian Strategy in Syria: A Looming Conflict with Israel," Atlantic Council, Scowcroft Center, September 2018, https://www .atlanticcouncil.org/wp-content/uploads/2019/09/The_Evolving_Iranian_Strategy _in_Syria.pdf.

69. Michael Eisenstadt and Michael Knights, "Beyond Worst-Case Analysis: Iran's Likely Response to an Israeli Preventive Strike," Washington Institute for Near East Policy, June 2012, https://www.washingtoninstitute.org/media/3274?disposition= inline.

70. Hendel, "Iran's Nukes and Israel's Dilemma," 31.

71. Ibid., 34–36.

72. Farzin Nadimi, "New Iranian Bill Aims to Officialize a Policy of Avenging Soleimani and Destroying Israel," Washington Institute for Near East Policy, January 2021, https://www.washingtoninstitute.org/policy-analysis/new-iranian-bill-aims-offi cialize-policy-avenging-soleimani-and-destroying-israel.

73. Farzin Nadimi, "Iran and Israel's Undeclared War at Sea (Part II): The Potential for Military Escalation," Washington Institute for Near East Policy, April 2021, https://www.washingtoninstitute.org/policy-analysis/iran-and-israels-undeclared -war-sea-part-2-potential-military-escalation.

74. Matthew Levitt, "Breaking Hezbollah's Golden Rule: An Inside Look at the Modus Operandi of Hezbollah's Islamic Jihad Organization," *Perspectives on Terrorism* 14, no. 4 (2020): 21–42.

75. Michael Eisenstadt, "Were Iran and the United States Really 'on the Brink'? Observations on Gray Zone Conflict," Washington Institute for Near East Policy, September 2020, https://www.washingtoninstitute.org/policy-analysis/were-iran-and -united-states-really-brink-observations-gray-zone-conflict; Farzin Nadimi, "Iran's Potential Military Reaction to New US Sanctions," Washington Institute for Near East Policy, November 2017, https://www.washingtoninstitute.org/policy-analysis /irans-potential-military-reactions-new-us-sanctions; Ilan Goldberg et al., "Countering Iran in the Gray Zone: What the US Should Learn from Israeli Operations in Syria," Center for a New American Security, April 2020, https://www.cnas.org/pub lications/reports/countering-iran-gray-zone.

76. Michael Knights, "Yemen's Southern Hezbollah: Implementing Houthi Missile and Drone Improvements," Policy Watch 3463, Washington Institute for Near East Policy, April 2021, https://www.washingtoninstitute.org/pdf/view/16639/en; Michael Rubin, "A Short History of the Iranian Drone Program," American Enterprise Institute, August 2020, https://www.aei.org/research-products/report/a-short -history-of-the-iranian-drone-program/.

77. Michael Knights, Adnan al-Gabarni, and Casey Coombs, "The Houthi Jihad Council: Command and Control in 'the Other Hezbollah,'" *CTC Sentinel* 15 (October 2022): 1–23, 10, https://ctc.usma.edu/the-houthi-jihad-council-command-and -control-in-the-other-hezbollah/.

78. Annie Fixler and Frank Cilluffo, "Evolving Menace: Iran's Use of Cyber-Enabled Warfare," Foundation for Defense of Democracies, November 2018, https:// www.fdd.org/analysis/2018/11/06/evolving-menace/.

4. The Ideological, Financial, and Environmental Forces Leading to the North Korea–Iran Rogue Alliance

1. See Liudmila Zakharova, "Economic Cooperation between Russia and North Korea: New Goals and New Approaches," *Journal of Eurasian Studies* 7, no. 2 (July 2016), https://www.sciencedirect.com/science/article/pii/S1879366516300124.

2. See "How Did the North Korean Famine Happen?," Wilson Center, April 30, 2002, https://www.wilsoncenter.org/article/how-did-the-north-korean-famine -happen.

3. See Claudia Rosset, "Kim Jong-Il's Cashbox," *Forbes*, April 15, 2010, https:// www.forbes.com/2010/04/15/kim-jong-il-north-korea-opinions-columnists-clau dia-rosett.html?sh=38e0104d79a4.

4. See Dana Kennedy, "Inside 'Office 39': North Korea's Illicit Global Smuggling Network," *New York Post*, June 27, 2020, https://nypost.com/2020/06/27/inside-of fice-39-north-koreas-illicit-global-smuggling-network/.

5. For more background on Office 39, see Iñigo Camilleri De Castanedo, "Office 39: North Korea's Secret Slush Funds," *Grey Dynamics*, November 8, 2021, https:// greydynamics.com/office-39-north-koreas-secret-slush-fund/.

6. See Matthew Carney, "Defector Reveals Secrets of North Korea's Office 39, Raising Cash for Kim Jong-un," *ABC News*, January 5, 2018, https://www.abc.net .au/news/2018-01-06/north-korea-defector-reveals-secrets-of-office-39/9302308.

7. See *Final Report of the Panel of Experts Submitted Pursuant to Resolution 1874 (2009)*, UN Security Council, November 5, 2010, https://www.undocs.org /S/2010/571.

8. *Final Report of the Panel of Experts Submitted Pursuant to Resolution 2515 (2020)*, UN Security Council, March 4, 2021, https://undocs.org/S/2021/211.

9. See Evelyn Cheng, "Five Ways North Korea Gets Money to Build Nuclear Weapons," CNBC, April 18, 2017, https://www.cnbc.com/2017/04/18/how-does -north-korea-get-money-to-build-nuclear-weapons.html.

10. For examples of this, see Samuel Ramani, "North Korea's Enduring Economic and Security Presence in Africa," *38 North*, June 24, 2021, https://www.38north .org/2021/06/north-koreas-enduring-economic-and-security-presence-in-africa/.

204 NOTES TO PAGES 67–70

11. For an example of a subsidized North Korea supporting Third World nations in Africa during the Cold War, see Benjamin R. Young, "North Korea in Africa: Historical Solidarity, China's Role, and Sanctions Evasion," US Institute of Peace, February 2021, https://www.usip.org/publications/2021/02/north-korea-africa -historical-solidarity-chinas-role-and-sanctions-evasion.

12. See Cheng, "Five Ways."

13. See Anthony Cordesman, "The Lessons of Modern War: Chapter 8," Center for Strategic and International Studies, May 1990, https://csis-website-prod.s3 .amazonaws.com/s3fs-public/legacy_files/files/media/csis/pubs/9005lessonsirani raqii-chap08.pdf.

14. See Morse Tan, "The North Korean Nuclear Crisis: Past Failures, Present Solutions," *Saint Louis University Law Journal* 50, no. 2 (2006), https://scholarship .law.slu.edu/cgi/viewcontent.cgi?article=1711&context=lj.

15. See Suzanne Maloney, "Major Beneficiaries of the Iran Deal: The IRGC and Hezbollah," Testimony, Brookings Institution, September 17, 2015, https://www .brookings.edu/testimonies/major-beneficiaries-of-the-iran-deal-the-irgc-and -hezbollah/; Ashley Lane, "Iran's Islamist Proxies in the Middle East," Wilson Center, December 5, 2022, https://www.wilsoncenter.org/article/irans-islamist-proxies.

16. See Gary J. Schmidt, *Rise of the Revisionists: Russia, China and Iran* (Washington, DC: AEI Press, 2018); Reuel Marc Gerecht, "Iran: The Shi'ite Imperial Power," in Schmidt, *Rise of the Revisionists*, 69–91; Mehdi Khalaji, "Apocalyptic Politics: On the Rationality of Iranian Politics," Washington Institute for Near East Policy, January 2008, https://www.washingtoninstitute.org/policy-analysis/apocalyptic-politics -rationality-iranian-policy; Ali Ansari and Kasra Aarabi, "Ideology and Iran's Revolution: How 1979 Changed the World," Tony Blair Institute for Global Change, February 2019, https://institute.global/policy/ideology-and-irans-revolution-how -1979-changed-world.

17. See Saeid Golkar and Kasra Aarabi, "The View from Tehran: Iran's Militia Doctrine," Tony Blair Institute for Global Change, February 2021, https://institute .global/sites/default/files/2021-02/Tony%20Blair%20Institute%2C%20The%20 View%20From%20Tehran%2C%20Iran%27s%20Militia%20Doctrine%20 %28February%202020%29.pdf.

18. See Vali Nasr, *The Shia Revival: How Conflicts within Islam Will Shape the Future* (New York: W. W. Norton, 2006).

19. Golkar and Aarabi, "View from Tehran," 11–20.

20. Gerecht, "Iran."

21. David Rapoport, "The Four Waves of Modern Terror: International Dimensions and Consequences," UCLA Geneva, September 2011, https://international .ucla.edu/media/files/Rapoport-Four-Waves-of-Modern-Terrorism.pdf.

22. "Hezbollah: A North Korea–Type Guerilla Force," *Intelligence Online*, August 25, 2006, https://www.intelligenceonline.com/political-intelligence/2006/08/25 /hezbollah-a-north-korea-type-guerilla-force,21788114-EVE.

23. Fabrice Balanche, "Sectarianism in Syria's Civil War: A Geopolitical Study," Washington Institute for Near East Policy, February 2018, https://www.washington institute.org/pdf/view/2442/en.

24. Farzin Nadimi, "Iran's Afghan and Pakistani Proxies: Syria and Beyond," Washington Institute for Near East Policy, August 2016, https://www.washingtonin stitute.org/pdf/view/3341/en.

25. Anthony Celso, "Sectarianism, Failed States and the Radicalization of Sunni Jihadist Groups," *International Journal of Political Science* 4, no. 2 (2018): 22–35.

26. Aaron Zelin and Phillip Smyth, "The Vocabulary of Sectarianism," Washington Institute for Near East Policy, January 2014, https://www.washingtoninstitute.org/pdf/view/4879/en.

27. Anthony Cordesman and Bryan Gold, *The Gulf Military Balance: The Missile and Nuclear Connections* (Washington, DC: Center for Strategic and International Studies, 2014), 60–61.

28. "National Security Strategy of the United States," White House, December 2017, https://trumpwhitehouse.archives.gov/wp-content/uploads/2017/12/NSS-Final -12-18-2017-0905.pdf.

29. Robert Hamilton, Chris Miller, and Aaron Stein, eds., *Russia's War in Syria: Assessing Russian Military Capabilities and Lessons Learned* (Philadelphia: FPRI, 2020), https://www.fpri.org/research/eurasia/russias-war-in-syria-assessing-russian -military-capabilities-and-lessons-learned/.

30. Farnaz Fassihi and Steven Lee Myers, "China with $400 Billion Deal with Iran Could Deepen Its Influence in the Mideast," *New York Times*, March 29, 2021, https://www.nytimes.com/2021/03/27/world/middleeast/china-iran-deal.html.

31. Farzin Nadimi, "Iran and Russia's Growing Defense Ties," Washington Institute for Near East Policy, February 2015, https://www.washingtoninstitute.org /policy-analysis/iran-and-russias-growing-defense-ties.

32. Farzin Nadimi, "Iran and China Are Strengthening Their Military Ties," Washington Institute for Near East Policy, November 2016, https://www.washing toninstitute.org/policy-analysis/iran-and-china-are-strengthening-their-military-ties.

33. For an excellent example of North Korea reflagging ships for proliferation purposes, see Niharika Mandhana, "Fake Signals and Illegal Flags: How North Korea Uses Clandestine Shipping to Fund Regime," *Wall Street Journal*, November 28, 2018, https://www.wsj.com/articles/fake-signals-and-illegal-flags-how-north-korea -uses-clandestine-shipping-to-fund-regime-1543402289.

34. Larry Niksch, "The Iran–North Korea Strategic Relationship," Institute for Corean-American Studies, July 28, 2015, https://www.icasinc.org/2015/2015l/2015l lan.html.

35. "Shahab 3," Missile Threat: CSIS Missile Defense Project, July 31, 2021, https://missilethreat.csis.org/missile/shahab-3/.

36. Farzin Nadimi, "Iran's New Ballistic Missile May Have North Korean ICBM Links," Washington Institute for Near East Policy, September 2017, https://www

.washingtoninstitute.org/policy-analysis/irans-new-ballistic-missile-may-have-north-korean-icbm-links; Kasra Aarabi, "Beyond Borders: The Expansionist Ideology of Iran's Islamic Revolutionary Guard Corp," Tony Blair Institute for Global Change, February 2020, https://institute.global/sites/default/files/2020-01/IRGC%20Report%2027012020.pdf.

37. Bruno Gomes Guimarães, "North Korea: Ideology, War and Violence," *Revista Conjunto Austral* 5 (2014): 23, 71, https://www.academia.edu/23681889/North_Korea_ideology_war_and_violence.

38. Takashi Sakai, "North Korea's Political System," Japan Digital Library, March 2016, https://www2.jiia.or.jp/en/pdf/digital_library/korean_peninsula/160331_Takashi_Sakai.pdf.

39. Robert Collins, *Marked for Life: Songbun, North Korea's Social Classification System* (Washington DC: Committee for Human Rights in North Korea, 2012).

40. "Iran: Human Rights I Review 2020/2021," Amnesty International, April 7, 2021, 1–5, https://www.amnesty.org/en/wp-content/uploads/2021/05/MDE1339642021ENGLISH.pdf.

41. Seong-Chang Cheong, "Stalinism and Kimilsungism: A Comparative Analysis of Ideology and Power," *Asian Perspective* 24, no. 1 (2000): 133–61, https://www.yumpu.com/en/document/view/5474328/stalinism-and-kimilsungism-columbia-law-school.

42. Guimarães, "North Korea," 70–72.

43. Aarabi, "Beyond Borders."

44. Saeed Ghasseminejad and Mohammad R. Jahan-Parvar, "The Impact of Financial Sanctions: The Case of Iran 2011–2016," International Financial Discussion Papers, Board of Governors of the Federal Reserve System, May 2020, 8.

45. Nasr, *Shia Revival*, 119–46.

46. Alex Vatanka, "Iran's Use of Shia Militant Proxies: Ideological and Practical Expediency versus Uncertain Sustainability," Middle East Institute, June 2018, https://www.mei.edu/sites/default/files/publications/Vatanka_PolicyPaper.pdf.

47. See "Report: Iran Offered North Korea Oil for Nuclear Weapons Assistance," *Haaretz*, November 26, 2005, https://www.haaretz.com/2005-11-26/ty-article/report-iran-offered-north-korea-oil-for-nuclear-weapons-assistance/0000017f-db6f-df9c-a17f-ff7f6e5f0000.

48. Seth Jones, "War by Proxy: Iran's Growing Footprint in the Middle East," Center for Strategic and International Studies, March 2019, https://www.csis.org/war-by-proxy.

49. "Background Briefing with Senior Intelligence Officials on Syria's Covert Nuclear Reactor and North Korea's Involvement," Office of the Director of National Intelligence, April 24, 2008, https://irp.fas.org/news/2008/04/odni042408.pdf.

50. "The United States Assessment of the Assad Regime's Use of Chemical Weapons," White House, April 2018, https://dod.defense.gov/portals/1/features/2018/0418_syria/img/United-States-Assessment-of-the-Assad-Regime%E2%80%99s-Chemical-Weapons-Use.pdf.

51. Adam Garfinkle, "The Chemistry of Syrian Lies and US Credulity Revealed," Foreign Policy Research Institute, October 2016, https://www.fpri.org/article /2016/10/chemistry-syrian-lies-u-s-credulity-revealed/.

52. Guimarães, "North Korea," 72–75.

53. Michael Herzog, "The Growing Risk of an Israel-Iran Confrontation in Syria," Washington Institute for Near East Policy, December 2017, https://www.wash ingtoninstitute.org/policy-analysis/growing-risk-israel-iran-confrontation-syria.

54. Nader Uskowi, "The Evolving Iranian Strategy in Syria: A Looming Conflict with Israel," Atlantic Council, Scowcroft Center for Strategy and Security, September 2018, https://www.atlanticcouncil.org/wp-content/uploads/2019/09/The_Evolving _Iranian_Strategy_in_Syria.pdf.

55. Farzan Nadimi, "Iran's Evolving Approach to Asymmetric Naval War: Strategies and Capabilities in the Persian Gulf," Washington Institute for Near East Policy, April 2020, https://www.washingtoninstitute.org/policy-analysis/irans-evolving -approach-asymmetric-naval-warfare-strategy-and-capabilities-persian.

56. Michael Knights, "Yemen's 'Southern Hezbollah': Implications of Houthi Missile and Drone Improvements," Washington Institute for Near East Policy, April 2021, https://www.washingtoninstitute.org/policy-analysis/yemens-southern-hezbollah -implications-houthi-missile-and-drone-improvements.

57. Ibid., 1–2.

58. Ibid., 4–7.

5. Rogue Allies and Pyongyang's Military Proliferation to Iran

1. See "What's Driving Iran to Build a Better Missile," *Real Clear Defense*, February 19, 2020, https://www.realcleardefense.com/articles/2020/02/19/whats_driving _iran_to_build_a_better_missile_115054.html.

2. For an excellent example of analysis claiming that ballistic missile cooperation between North Korea and Iran has "slowed," please refer to an online webinar from May 2020. The Brookings Institution expert Jung H. Pak stated that ballistic missile cooperation between North Korea and Iran had largely "petered out" since the mid-1990s. Clearly she was unaware of the large-scale proliferation from North Korea to Iran after that time frame of missiles such as the Musudan; North Korean assistance to Syrian and Iranian engineers working on upgrades to systems such as the Scud C, Scud D, and extended-range No Dong; the North Korean assistance to the Iranians with a booster rocket with four No Dong engines (a near duplicate of the booster rocket for North Korea's Unha system); or the missile cooperation between North Korea and Iran on advanced IRBM and ICBM technology (including missile components flowing from North Korea to Iran), which began as early as 2013 and continues today. This continued largely unabated until the COVID-19 virus temporarily put a damper on maritime shipments of military systems and parts. See

"International Seminar: Tunnels, Missiles, Reactors: Understanding North Korea's Role in the Middle East," Brookings Institution and Institute for National Security Studies (Israel), May 20, 2020, https://www.brookings.edu/events/webinar-tun nels-missiles-reactors-understanding-north-koreas-role-in-the-middle-east/. Another example of misguided analysis is a May 30, 2013, statement in which Stephan Haggard of the University of California San Diego said, "Opportunities for weapons sales have also clearly been on a downward slide since their heyday in the 1980s, and more recently as a result of the combination of PSI and UN sanctions." One hopes that the numerous reports of the UN Panel of Experts and unclassified data that was available at the time—and now—have enlightened Haggard to the point that he understands that proliferation to Iran can also mean proliferation or payments through Iran that affect Syria, another major customer to which sales have not been on a "downward slide" (until the collapse of the Assad regime in 2024) from North Korea and were not at the time. See Stephan Haggard, "Sources: New Books from Bechtol and Lankov," North Korea Witness to Transformation, Peterson Institute for International Economics, May 30, 2013, https://www.piie.com/blogs/north-korea-witness-trans formation/sources-new-books-bechtol-and-lankov.

3. See Donald Kirk, "The Military Relationship between Iran and North Korea," InsideSources, January 20, 2020, https://insidesources.com/the-military-relation ship-between-iran-and-north-korea/.

4. See Tamir Eshel, "Simorgh First Launch—an Iranian Success or Failure?," *Defense Update*, April 24, 2016, https://defense-update.com/20160424_simorgh.html.

5. "Iran Missile Milestones: 1984–2023," Iran Watch, March 29, 2023, https://www.iranwatch.org/our-publications/weapon-program-background-report /iran-missile-milestones-1985-2020.

6. Much of the writing for the first two paragraphs of this chapter came from a piece I wrote for the *National Interest*, published here with the permission of the editor. The authors would like to thank Harry Kazianis for granting us permission to restate these important issues in this forum. See Bruce E. Bechtol, "Why the Iran–North Korea Missile Alliance Is Pure Trouble," *National Interest*, May 24, 2020, https://nationalinterest.org/blog/korea-watch/why-iran-north-korea-missile -alliance-pure-trouble-157351.

7. See Bill Gertz, "Iran, North Korea Secretly Developing New Long-Range Rocket Booster for ICBMs," *Washington Free Beacon*, November 26, 2013, https:// freebeacon.com/national-security/iran-north-korea-secretly-developing-new-long -range-rocket-booster-for-icbms/.

8. See Marcus Noland and Sherman Robinson, "Rigorous Speculation: The Collapse and Revival of the North Korean Economy," Working Papers 99-1, Peterson Institute for International Economics, January 1999, https://www.piie.com/publica tions/working-papers/rigorous-speculation-collapse-and-revival-north-korean-econ omy.

9. See Anthony Cordesman, *The Lessons of Modern War*, vol. 2, *The Iran-Iraq War* (Washington, DC: Center for Strategic and International Studies, 1990), https://

csis-website-prod.s3.amazonaws.com/s3fs-public/legacy_files/files/media/csis/pubs/9005lessonsiraniraqii-chap10.pdf.

10. See Kevin Woods, Williamson Murray, and Thomas Holaday, "Saddam's War: An Iraqi Military Perspective of the Iran-Iraq War," with Mounir Elkhamri, McNair Paper 70, National Defense University, 2009, https://ndupress.ndu.edu/Portals/68/Documents/Books/saddams-war.pdf.

11. Chad O'Carroll and John G. Grisafi, "North Korea's Million Man Army: Potential Mercenary Force?," *NK News*, May 15, 2015, https://www.nknews.org/2015/05/north-koreas-million-man-army-potential-mercenary-force/.

12. Central Intelligence Agency, "Unclassified Report to Congress on the Acquisition of Technology Relating to Weapons of Mass Destruction and Advanced Conventional Munitions, 1 July through 31 December 2001," 2002, https://2001-2009.state.gov/p/sca/rls/16476.htm.

13. Daniel Dolan, "The North Korean Connection," *USNI News*, June 17, 2012, https://news.usni.org/2012/06/17/north-korean-connection.

14. See Ahmad Majidyar, "U.S. Officials: Iran's Latest Missile Launch Hints Tehran-Pyongyang Cooperation," Middle East Institute, May 5, 2017, https://www.mei.edu/content/io/us-officials-iran-s-latest-missile-launch-hints-tehran-pyongyang-cooperation; Alex Hollings, "Could China Be Funneling Missile Technology to North Korea through Iran?," *SOFREP: Special Forces News*, May 6, 2017, https://sofrep.com/80694/china-funneling-missile-technology-north-korea-iran/; "Yono Class / Ghadir Class Midget Submarine," GlobalSecurity.org, 2017, https://www.globalsecurity.org/military/world/iran/ghadir.htm; "Yono Class (Ghadir)," Military Edge, Foundation for Defense of Democracies, 2017, https://militaryedge.org/armaments/ghadir/; Lucas Tomlinson, "Iran Attempted Missile Launch from Submarine, US Officials Say," *Fox News*, May 3, 2017, https://www.foxnews.com/world/2017/05/03/iran-attempted-missile-launch-from-submarine-us-officials-say.html https://militaryedge.org/armaments/ghadir/; Ariel Zilber, "Iran 'Conducts Failed Missile Test from Same Submarine Used by North Korea' Just Days after Near Incident with US Warship in the Strait of Hormuz," *Daily Mail*, May 3, 2017, https://www.dailymail.co.uk/news/article-4471140/Iran-conducts-failed-missile-test-submarine.html; Kenneth Katzman, "Iran's Long-Range Missile Capabilities," Iran Watch, July 15, 1998, https://www.iranwatch.org/library/government/united-states/congress/legislation-reports/irans-long-range-missile-capabilities; "North Korea Modernises Submarine Fleet," *Janes Intelligence Review*, May 10, 2016, https://www.janes360.com/images/assets/463/57463/North_Korea_modernises_submarine_fleet1.pdf.

15. See Andrea Berger, "North Korea, Hamas, and Hezbollah: Arm in Arm?," *38 North*, August 5, 2014, https://www.38north.org/2014/08/aberger080514/.

16. For an example of the Iranian funding of groups such as Hezbollah, see Ashley Lane, "Iran's Islamist Proxies in the Middle East," Wilson Center, August 16, 2023, https://www.wilsoncenter.org/article/irans-islamist-proxies.

17. See Amatzia Baram, "Iran's Stakes in Syria," Geopolitical Intelligence Services, October 28, 2021, https://www.gisreportsonline.com/r/iran-syria/.

18. See Michael Elleman, "Iran's Ballistic Missile Program," Iran Primer, US Institute of Peace, January 13, 2021, https://iranprimer.usip.org/resource/irans-ballistic-missile-program.

19. See Jonathan McLaughlin, "North Korea Missile Milestones, 1969–2017," Wisconsin Project, January 23, 2018, https://www.wisconsinproject.org/north-korea-missile-milestones/.

20. See "Safir," Missile Threat: CSIS Missile Defense Project, August 2, 2021, https://missilethreat.csis.org/missile/safir/.

21. See "Will Iran's Simorgh Space Launcher Appear in North Korea?," Nuclear Threat Initiative, July 8, 2016, https://www.nti.org/analysis/articles/will-irans-simorgh-space-launcher-appear-north-korea/.

22. See "Iran Missile Milestones: 1984–2023," Iran Watch, March 29, 2023, https://www.iranwatch.org/our-publications/weapon-program-background-report/iran-missile-milestones-1985-2020.

23. Tal Inbar, interview by Bruce E. Bechtol Jr., Tel Aviv, August 22, 2022.

24. Some of the writing for this paragraph came from a piece I wrote for the *National Interest*, published here with the permission of the editor. The authors would like to thank Harry Kazianis for granting us permission to restate these important issues in this forum. See Bechtol, "Why the Iran."

25. See Mikhaila Friel, "Half of the Missiles Iran Fired at Israel Failed on Launch or Malfunctioned and Crashed, Reports Say," *Business Insider*, April 15, 2024, https://www.businessinsider.com/half-of-iran-missiles-fired-israel-failed-reports-2024-4.

26. "Emad, Ghadr (Shahab-3 Variants)," Missile Threat: CSIS Missile Defense Project, January 31, 2023, https://missilethreat.csis.org/missile/emad/.

27. See Gary Milhollin, "Ballistic Missiles: Who Are the Future Suppliers?," Iran Watch, March 2, 1999, https://www.iranwatch.org/our-publications/speech/ballistic-missiles-who-are-future-suppliers.

28. Michael Elleman, "North Korea–Iran Missile Cooperation," *38 North*, September 22, 2016, https://www.38north.org/2016/09/melleman092216/.

29. "Emad," Missile Defense Advocacy Alliance, June 5, 2018, https://missiledefenseadvocacy.org/missile-threat-and-proliferation/todays-missile-threat/iran/emad/.

30. A. B. Abrams, "The North Korean Origins of Iran's Rocket Strike Capability against Israel," *Daily NK*, April 15, 2024, https://www.dailynk.com/english/north-korean-origins-iran-rocket-strike-capability-against-israel/.

31. Much of the writing for the past four paragraphs of this chapter came from a piece I wrote for the *National Interest*, published here with the permission of the editor. The authors would like to thank Harry Kazianis for granting us permission to restate these important issues in this forum. See Bruce E. Bechtol, "Iran's Attack on Israel Was Enabled by North Korean Missile Technology," *National Interest*, April 18, 2024, https://nationalinterest.org/blog/buzz/irans-attack-israel-was-enabled-north-korean-missile-technology-210647.

32. See David Gritten, Matt Murphy, and Patrick Jackson, "What We Know about Iran's Missile Attack on Israel," BBC, October 3, 2024, https://www.bbc.com/news/articles/c70w1j0l488o.

33. Douglas Frantz, "Iran Closes In on Ability to Build a Nuclear Bomb," *Los Angeles Times*, April 4, 2003, https://www.latimes.com/archives/la-xpm-2003-aug-04-fg-nuke4-story.html.

34. "North Korea Back on the Terrorism List?," Congressional Research Service, June 29, 2010, https://www.everycrsreport.com/reports/RL30613.html.

35. See "North Korea Supplied Nuclear Software to Iran: German Report," Reuters, April 24, 2011, https://www.reuters.com/article/us-nuclear-northkorea-iran/north-korea-supplied-nuclear-software-to-iran-german-report-idUSTRE77N2FZ20110824.

36. See Joby Warrick, "IAEA Says Foreign Expertise Has Brought Iran to Threshold of Nuclear Capability," *Washington Post*, November 6, 2011, https://www.washingtonpost.com/world/national-security/iaea-says-foreign-expertise-has-brought-iran-to-threshold-of-nuclear-capability/2011/11/05/gIQAc6hjtM_story.html.

37. See Gertz, "Iran, North Korea."

38. See Bill Gertz, "North Korea Transfers Missile Goods to Iran during Nuclear Talks," *Washington Free Beacon*, April 15, 2015, https://freebeacon.com/national-security/north-korea-transfers-missile-goods-to-iran-during-nuclear-talks/.

39. See US Department of the Treasury, "Treasury Sanctions Those Involved in Ballistic Missile Procurement for Iran," press release, January 17, 2016, https://home.treasury.gov/news/press-releases/jl0322.

40. See William J. Broad and David E. Sanger, "North Korea's Missile Success Is Linked to Ukrainian Plant, Investigators Say," *New York Times*, April 14, 2017, https://www.nytimes.com/2017/08/14/world/asia/north-korea-missiles-ukraine-factory.html.

41. For an excellent analysis of the design and capabilities of the Hwasong-12, 14, and 15, see Theodore A. Postol, "North Korean Missiles and US Missile Defense," *Physics and Society* 47, no. 2 (April 2018), https://higherlogicdownload.s3.amazonaws.com/APS/a05ec1cf-2e34-4fb3-816e-ea1497930d75/UploadedImages/Newsletter_PDF/April18.pdf.

42. Much of the writing for the past three paragraphs of this chapter came from a piece I wrote for the *National Interest*, published here with the permission of the editor. The authors would like to thank Harry Kazianis for granting us permission to restate these important issues in this forum. See Bechtol, "Why the Iran."

43. See "North Korean Foreign Minister Visits Iran as US Sanctions Take Effect," *Times of Israel*, August 7, 2018, https://www.timesofisrael.com/north-korean-foreign-minister-visits-iran-as-us-sanctions-take-effect/.

44. See Dan De Luce, "U.N. Investigating Suspected North Korean Arms Dealers in Iran," *NBC News*, March 12, 2019, https://www.nbcnews.com/news/north-korea/u-n-investigating-suspected-north-korean-arms-dealers-iran-n982016.

45. See US Department of the Treasury, "Treasury Sanctions Key Actors in Iran's Nuclear and Ballistic Missile Programs," press release, September 21, 2020, https://home.treasury.gov/news/press-releases/sm1130.

46. See "Iran and North Korea Resumed Cooperation on Missiles, U.N. Says," Iran Watch, February 8, 2021, https://www.iranwatch.org/news-brief/iran-north-korea-resumed-cooperation-missiles-un-says.

47. See Abhishek Kumar, "Revisiting the Nuclear Nexus between Pakistan, China, and North Korea," Institute for Security and Development Policy, January 5, 2023, https://isdp.se/revisiting-the-nuclear-nexus-between-pakistan-china-and-north-korea/.

48. See Michael Weisskopf, "China Sells Arms to Iran via N. Korea," *Washington Post*, April 3, 1984, https://www.washingtonpost.com/archive/politics/1984/04/03/china-sells-arms-to-iran-via-n-korea/c425f361-4e38-4b92-bba5-b8bd5cf22fb0/.

49. See Shirzad Azad, *Iran and China: A New Approach to Their Bilateral Relations* (Lanham, MD: Lexington Books, 2017), 7.

50. See Simon Watkins, "Iran to Import North Korean Missiles in 25-Year Military Deal with China," OilPrice.com, October 19, 2020, https://oilprice.com/Energy/Energy-General/Iran-To-Import-North-Korean-missiles-In-25-Year-Military-Deal-With-China.html.

51. Much of the writing for the past four paragraphs of this chapter came from a piece I wrote for the *National Interest*, published here with the permission of the editor. The authors would like to thank Harry Kazianis for granting us permission to restate these important issues in this forum. See Bruce E. Bechtol, "North Korea, China and Iran: The Axis of Missiles?," *National Interest*, October 25, 2020, https://nationalinterest.org/blog/korea-watch/north-korea-china-and-iran-axis-missiles-171367.

52. See Chad O'Carroll, "UN Panel of Experts: How Cold War Squabbling Hinders North Korea Sanctions," *NK News*, October 1, 2020, https://www.nknews.org/pro/panel-of-experts-how-cold-war-squabbling-hinders-north-korea-sanctions/; Andrea Stricker, "Russia and China Obstruct UN Reporting on North Korea," Foundation for Defense of Democracies, October 21, 2020, https://www.fdd.org/analysis/2020/10/21/russia-and-china-obstruct-un-reporting-on-north-korea/.

53. See "Pyongyang in Talks with Moscow on Access to Donbass," *Intelligence Online*, June 20, 2022, https://www.intelligenceonline.com/government-intelligence/2022/06/20/pyongyang-in-talks-with-moscow-on-access-to-donbass,109793254-art.

54. See Seulkee Jang, "N. Korea Has Selected Workers to Be Dispatched to Eastern Ukraine," *Daily NK*, August 5, 2022, https://www.dailynk.com/english/north-korea-selected-workers-dispatched-eastern-ukraine/; Evan Simko-Bednarski, "Russian State TV: North Korea Offering Kremlin 100,000 'Volunteers,'" *New York Post*, August 5, 2022, https://nypost.com/2022/08/05/russian-state-tv-north-korea-offers-kremlin-100000-troops/.

55. See Julian Barnes, "Russia Is Buying North Korean Artillery, According to U.S. Intelligence," *New York Times*, September 5, 2022, https://www.nytimes.com/2022/09/05/us/politics/russia-north-korea-artillery.html#:~:text=WASHINGTON%20%E2%80%94%20Russia%20is%20buying%20millions,pariah%20states%20for%20military%20supplies.

56. See Alan Rappeport, "North Korea Secretly Shipped Munitions to Russia through the Middle East and North Africa, the U.S. Says," *New York Times*, November 2, 2022, https://www.nytimes.com/2022/11/02/world/europe/russia-ukraine-north-korea-ammunition.html#:~:text=Black%20Sea%20Matters-,North%20Korea%20secretly%20shipped%20munitions%20to%20Russia%20through%20the%20Middle,the%20course%20of%20the%20war.%E2%80%9D.

57. See Martyn Williams and Peter Makowsky, "A North Korean Rail Yard near Russia Springs to Life," *38 North*, December 12, 2022, https://www.38north.org/2022/12/a-north-korean-rail-yard-near-russia-springs-to-life/#:~:text=Recent%20commercial%20satellite%20imagery%20indicates,alongside%20trains%20at%20least%20twice.

58. "North Korea Sold Arms to Russia's Wagner Group, US Says," BBC, December 22, 2022, https://www.bbc.com/news/world-europe-64072570.

59. "N. Korea Continues to Provide Ammunition to Russia in Violation of UNSC Sanctions: White House," Yonhap, January 21, 2023, https://en.yna.co.kr/view/AEN20230121000300325.

60. See Dasi Yoon, "North Korean–Russian Trade Rebounds, Satellite Images Show," *Wall Street Journal*, February 17, 2023, https://www.wsj.com/articles/north-korean-russian-trade-rebounds-satellite-images-show-8423f37b.

61. Khang Vu, "Why North Korea Is Denying Its Involvement in Russia's War in Ukraine," *Interpreter*, February 14, 2023, https://www.lowyinstitute.org/the-interpreter/why-north-korea-denying-its-involvement-russia-s-war-ukraine#:~:text=This%20explains%20why%20Pyongyang%20has,being%20seen%20as%20supplying%20mercenaries.

62. "US Slaps Sanctions on Entities over Alleged Arms Deals between NK, Russia," *Korea Times*, August 17, 2023, https://www.koreatimes.co.kr/www/nation/2023/08/103_357205.html.

63. See Aamer Madhani, "US Says North Korea Delivered 1,000 Containers of Equipment and Munitions to Russia for Ukraine War," Associated Press, October 13, 2023, https://apnews.com/article/north-korea-russia-us-munitions-ukraine-war-7091eaba254b680888a9b1ec8a68135f.

64. See James Byrne, Joseph Byrne, and Gary Somerville, "The Orient Express: North Korea's Clandestine Supply Route to Russia," Royal United Services Institute, October 16, 2023, https://rusi.org/explore-our-research/publications/commentary/report-orient-express-north-koreas-clandestine-supply-route-russia.

65. See Jon Herskovitz, "Ghost Ships at Reawakened North Korea Port Put Ukraine in Peril," Bloomberg, December 26, 2023, https://www.bloomberg.com

/news/articles/2023-12-26/ghost-ships-at-reawakened-north-korea-port-put
-ukraine-in-peril?sref=hhjZtX76.

66. See Micah McCartney, "Russia May Have Collected More Weapons from North Korea," *Newsweek*, March 28, 2024, https://www.newsweek.com/russia-may -have-collected-more-weapons-north-korea-1884404.

67. See US Department of State, "Imposing Additional Sanctions on Those Supporting Russia's War against Ukraine," press release, July 20, 2023, https://www .state.gov/imposing-additional-sanctions-on-those-supporting-russias-war-against -ukraine/.

68. *Report of the Panel of Experts Established Pursuant to Resolution 1874 (2009)*, UN Security Council, March 5, 2019, https://www.securitycouncilreport.org /atf/cf/%7B65BFCF9B-6D27-4E9C-8CD3-CF6E4FF96FF9%7D/s_2019_171 .pdf.

69. Some of the writing for this paragraph came from a piece I wrote for *1945*, published here with the permission of the editor. The authors would like to thank Harry Kazianis for granting us permission to restate these important issues in this forum. See Bruce E. Bechtol, "The North Korea–Russia Alliance Is a Dangerous Threat," *1945*, September 1, 2023, https://www.19fortyfive.com/2023/09/the-north -korea-russia-alliance-is-a-dangerous-threat/?fbclid=IwAR1m-TzA_W4j4r9p juX-3ZJM1mP37S3UQawqMTAOVsJ34DMPfaCYFH0fINo.

70. For examples of reports stating that some of the ammunition North Korea supplied to Russia appears to be of low quality, see "Russia's Own Troops Are Being Blown Up by Low Quality Artillery Ammo from North Korea," *Kyiv Post*, December 23, 2023, https://www.kyivpost.com/post/25872; Alexander Fabino, "Russia Hurt-ing Own Troops with Low-Quality Artillery: Ukraine," *Newsweek*, December 23, 2023, https://www.newsweek.com/russia-low-quality-artillery-north-korea-supply -ukraine-war-1855204.

71. See Colleen Long and Aamer Madhani, "Russia Has Used North Kore-an Ballistic Missiles in Ukraine and Is Seeking Iranian Missiles, US Says," Asso-ciated Press, January 4, 2024, https://apnews.com/article/russia-ballistic-missile -ukraine-iran-us-intelligence-3601a979e91d19c94e7d0fe27a398669; "Iranian and North Korean Missiles Do Not Pose a New Challenge for Ukrainian Air Defense, Says Air Force," *New Voice of Ukraine*, January 5, 2024, https://english.nv.ua /nation/iran-and-north-korea-missiles-for-russia-very-similar-to-russia-produced -design-50381769.html; Song Sang-ho, "N. Korera Recently Sent Several Doz-en Ballistic Missiles to Russia:: U.S. Official," Yonhap, January 5, 2024, https:// www.koreaherald.com/view.php?ud=20240105000092#:~:text=N.%20Korea%20 recently%20sent%20several,missiles%20to%20Russia%3A%20US%20official& text=North%20Korea%20recently%20provided%20Russia,its%20protracted%20 war%20in%20Ukraine; Parisa Hafezi, John Irish, Tom Balmforth, and Jonathan Landay, "Exclusive: Iran Sends Russia Hundreds of Ballistic Missiles," Reuters, Feb-ruary 21, 2024, https://www.reuters.com/world/iran-sends-russia-hundreds-ballistic -missiles-sources-say-2024-02-21/#:~:text=DUBAI%2C%20Feb%2021%20

(Reuters),the%20two%20U.S.%2Dsanctioned%20countries; "NATO Chief Warns about Iranian, North Korean Arms for Russia," *Iran International*, April 3, 2024, https://www.iranintl.com/en/202404037107.

72. See "North Korea Has Sent 6,700 Containers of Munitions to Russia, South Korea Says," *Straits Times*, February 27, 2024, https://www.straitstimes.com/asia /north-korea-has-sent-6700-containers-of-munitions-to-russia-south-korea-says.

73. See Song Sang-ho, "N. Korea Has Sent More Than 10,000 Containers of Munitions, Materials to Russia since Sept.: State Dept.," Yonhap, February 24, 2024, https://en.yna.co.kr/view/AEN20240224000352315?section=nk/nk.

74. See US Department of State, "Responding to Two Years of Russia's Full-Scale War on Ukraine and Navalny's Death," press release, February 23, 2024, https:// www.state.gov/imposing-measures-in-response-to-navalnys-death-and-two-years-of -russias-full-scale-war-against-ukraine/.

75. See George Grylls, "North Korea 'Supplies Half of the Shells Used by Russia in Ukraine,'" *The Times*, October 4, 2024, https://www.thetimes.com/world /russia-ukraine-war/article/north-korea-supplies-half-of-the-shells-used-by-russia -in-ukraine-d3fkhppjs.

76. See Chris York, "This Is How North Korean Troops Could Be Used in Russia's War in Ukraine," *Kyiv Independent*, October 15, 2024, https://kyivindependent.com /this-is-how-north-korean-troops-could-be-used-in-russias-war-in-ukraine/?utm _source=flipboard&utm_content=topic/moscowrussia.

77. See Josh Smith, "North Korean Weapons Extending Russian Stockpiles, German General Says," *Reuters*, September 9, 2024, https://www.reuters.com /world/north-korean-weapons-extending-russian-stockpiles-german-general-says -2024-09-09/.

78. See Chang Dong-woo, "N. Korea Decides to Send around 10,000 Soldiers to Support Russia in Ukraine War: Seoul," *Yonhap*, October 18, 2024, https://en.yna .co.kr/view/AEN20241018006856315.

79. See Lee Sang-Min, "Former U.S. Officials: Sending North Korean Troops to Russia Won't Be a 'Game Changer,'" *Radio Free Asia*, October 18, 2024.

80. See "North Korea Got Over $6 Billion in Payment for Weapons and Troops from Russia: It's Alarmingly Cheap," *Defense Express*, December 26, 2024, https:// en.defence-ua.com/analysis/north_korea_got_over_6_billion_in_payment_for _weapons_and_troops_from_russia_its_alarmingly_cheap-12983.html.

81. See Joseph DeThomas, "UN Panel of Experts: The Final Act," *38 North*, April 11, 2024, https://www.38north.org/2024/04/un-panel-of-experts-the-final-act/.

6. Rogue Allies in Action

1. Michael Knights, "Soleimani Is Dead: The Road Ahead for Iranian-Backed Militias," *CTC Sentinel* 13, no. 1 (2020): 1–10; Ariane M. Tabatabai, "After Soleimani: What Is Next for the Quds Force?," *CTC Sentinel* 13, no. 1 (2020): 33–38.

2. Michael Eisenstadt, "Operating in the Gray Zone: Countering Iran's Asymmetric Way of War," Policy Focus 162, Washington Institute for Near East Policy, 2020, https://www.washingtoninstitute.org/policy-analysis/view/operating-in-the-gray-zone-countering-irans-asymmetric-way-of-war; Hassan Mneimneh, "Washington Should Recognize the Russian Strategic Achievement in Syria," Washington Institute for Near East Policy, May 29, 2018, https://www.washingtoninstitute.org/fikraforum/view/washington-should-recognize-the-russian-strategic-achievement-in-syria.

3. Eisenstadt, "Operating in the Gray Zone," 19.

4. Suzanne Maloney, "The Roots and Evolution of Iran's Regional Policy," Atlantic Council, September 2017, https://www.atlanticcouncil.org/in-depth-research-reports/issue-brief/the-roots-drivers-and-evolution-of-iran-s-regional-strategy/.

5. Ibid.

6. Vali Nasr, *The Shia Revival: How Conflicts within Islam Will Shape the Future* (New York: W. W. Norton, 2006), 130–32.

7. Ibid., 119–20.

8. Ibid., 132–33.

9. Jean-Pierre Filiu, *Apocalypse in Islam* (Berkley: University of California Press, 2011), 23–29.

10. Mohammad Ali Kadivar, "Ayatollah and the Republic: The Religious Establishment in Iran and Its Interactions with the Islamic Republic," *Project on Middle East Political Science Studies: New Analysis of Shia Politics*, December 2017, 6–9; Roozbeh Safshekan and Farzan Sabet, "The Source of Legitimacy in the Guardianship of the Jurist: Historical Genealogy and Political Implications," *Project on Middle East Political Science Studies: New Analysis of Shia Politics*, December 2017, 15–19, https://pomeps.org/wp-content/uploads/2017/12/POMEPS_Studies_28_NewAnalysis_Web.pdf.

11. Anthony Celso, "Sectarianism and State Failure: The Radicalization of Sunni Jihadist Groups," *International Journal of Political Science* 4, no. 3 (2018): 22–35; Hanin Ghaddar, "Iran's Foreign Legion: The Impact of Shia Militias on U.S. Foreign Policy," Policy Note 46 Washington Institute for Near East Policy, 2018, https://www.washingtoninstitute.org/policy-analysis/view/irans-foreign-legion-the-impact-of-shia-militias-on-u.s.-foreign-policy.

12. Phillip Smyth, "The Shi'ite Jihad in Syria: The Regional Effects," Policy Focus 138, Washington Institute for Near East Policy, 2015, https://www.washingtoninstitute.org/policy-analysis/view/the-shiite-jihad-in-syria-and-its-regional-effects.

13. Nakissa Jahanbani and Suzanne Weedon Levy, "Iran Entangled: Iran and Hezbollah's Support to Proxies Operating in Syria," Combatting Terrorism Center at West Point, April 2022, 30–33, https://ctc.westpoint.edu/iran-entangled-iran-and-hezbollahs-support-to-proxies-operating-in-syria/.

14. Michael Eisenstadt, "The Strategic Culture of the Islamic Republic of Iran," MES Monographs 1, The Washington Institute for Near East Policy, August 2011,

https://www.washingtoninstitute.org/policy-analysis/view/the-strategic-culture
-of-the-islamic-republic-of-iran-religion-expediency-a.

15. Behnam Ben Taleblu, "Arsenal: Assessing the Islamic Republic of Iran's Ballistic Missile Program," Foundation for Defense of Democracies, February 2023, 12, https://www.fdd.org/analysis/2023/02/15/arsenal-assessing-the-islamic-republic
-of-irans-ballistic-missile-program/.

16. Ibid., 14.

17. Ibid., 25–31.

18. Joshua Giles, *Withdrawing under Fire: Lessons Learned from Islamist Insurgencies* (Washington: Potomac Books, 2011), 79–122.

19. Kenneth Katzman, "Iran's Foreign and Defense Policies," Congressional Research Service, April 29, 2020, https://fas.org/sgp/crs/mideast/R44017.pdf.

20. Seth G. Jones, "War by Proxy: Iran's Growing Footprint in the Mideast," Center for Strategic and International Studies, March 2020, https://www.csis.org/war-by-proxy.

21. Eisenstadt, "Strategic Culture of the Islamic Republic of Iran."

22. Nasr, *Shia Revival*, 184.

23. Ibid., 183.

24. Ibid., 171–72.

25. Jackson Doering., "Washington's Militia Problem in Syria Is an Iran Problem," Policy Watch 2932, Washington Institute for Near East Policy, February 2018, https://www.washingtoninstitute.org/policy-analysis/view/washingtons-militia
-problem-in-syria-is-an-iran-problem.

26. Knights, "Soleimani Is Dead," 1.

27. Phillip Smyth, "Beware of Muqtada al-Sadr," Washington Institute for Near East Policy, October 19, 2016, https://www.washingtoninstitute.org/policy-analysis/view/beware-of-muqtada-al-sadr.

28. Ibid.

29. Council on Foreign Relations and Foreign Affairs, *New Arab Revolt: What Happened, What It Means, and What Happens Next?* (New York: Council on Foreign Relations and Foreign Affairs, 2011), https://www.cfr.org/book/new-arab-revolt.

30. Natalie Schreffler, "North Korea and Hezbollah: A Nexus Worth Fearing?," *Penn State International Affairs Review*, April 8, 2013, https://sites.psu.edu/psiareview/2013/04/08/north-korea-and-hezbollah-a-nexus-worth-fearing/.

31. Yoko Kubota, "Israel Says Seized North Korean Arms Were for Hamas, Hezbollah," Reuters, May 12, 2020, https://www.reuters.com/article/2010/05/12/us-israel-korea-north-idUSTRE64B18520100512.

32. Amos Harel and Avi Issacharoff, *34 Days: Israel, Hezbollah, and the War in Lebanon* (New York: Palgrave McMillian, 2008).

33. Michael Herzog, "Iran across the Border: Israel's Pushback in Syria," Policy Note 66, Washington Institute for Near East Policy, July 2019, https://www.washingtoninstitute.org/policy-analysis/view/iran-across-the-border-israels-pushback-in-syria.

34. Ibid.

35. "Israel and Hezbollah: Deterrence and the Threat of Miscalculation," Council on Foreign Relations, September 11, 2017, https://www.cfr.org/report/israel-and-hezbollah-deterrence-and-threat-miscalculation.

36. Ibid.

37. Ehud Yaari, "Bracing for an Israel-Iran Confrontation in Syria," *American Interest*, April 2018, https://www.washingtoninstitute.org/policy-analysis/view/bracing-for-an-israel-iran-confrontation-in-syria.

38. Taleblu, "Arsenal," 30.

39. "Why Is There a War in Syria?," *BBC News*, March 15, 2018, https://www.bbc.co.uk/news/world-middle-east-355806229.

40. Aymenn al-Tamimi, "The Evolution in Islamic State Administration: The Documentary Evidence," *Perspectives on Terrorism* 9, no. 4 (2019): 117–29.

41. Anthony Celso, "Superpower Hybrid Warfare in Syria," *Marine Corps University Journal* 9, no. 2 (2018): 92–116.

42. Ibid., 110.

43. Paul Bucala, "Iran's New Way of War in Syria," Institute for the Study of War, February 2017, https://www.understandingwar.org/sites/default/files/Iran%20New%20Way%20of%20War%20in%20Syria_FEB%202017.pdf.

44. Katzman, "Iran's Foreign and Defense Policies."

45. Ghaddar, "Iran's Foreign Legion."

46. Jeffery White, "Hizb Allah at War in Syria: Report, Operations, Effects, and Implications," *CTC Sentinel* 7, no. 1 (2014): 14–18.

47. Hugo Spalding et al., "Russia's Deployment to Syria: Putin's Middle East Game Changer," Warning Intelligence Update, Institute for the Study of War, September 17, 2015, https://www.understandingwar.org/backgrounder/russian-deployment-syria-putin%E2%80%99s-middle-east-game-changer.

48. Ibid.

49. Anna Borshchevskaya, "Moscow's Middle East Resurgence: Russia's Goals Go Beyond Damascus," *Middle East Quarterly* (Winter 2018): 1–13, https://www.washingtoninstitute.org/sites/default/files/pdf/Borshchevskaya20171204-MiddleEastQuarterly-MEQ.pdf.

50. Hugo Spalding, "Russia's False Narrative in Syria," Backgrounder, Institute for the Study of War, December 1, 2015, https://www.understandingwar.org/backgrounder/russias-false-narrative-syria-december-1-2015

51. Michael Eisenstadt, "Has the Assad Regime 'Won' Syria's Civil War?," Washington Institute for Near East Policy, May 15, 2016, https://www.washingtoninstitute.org/policy-analysis/view/has-the-assad-regime-won-syrias-civil-war.

52. Aaron Lund, "Red Line Redux: How Putin Tore Up Obama's 2013 Syria Deal," Century Foundation, February 3, 2017, https://tcf.org/content/report/red-line-redux-putin-tore-obamas-2013-syria-deal/?agreed=1.

53. *BBC News*, "Why Is There a War in Syria?"

54. See Michael Schwirtz, "U.N. Links North Korea to Syria's Chemical Weapons Program," *New York Times*, February 27, 2018, https://www.nytimes.com /2018/02/27/world/asia/north-korea-syria-chemical-weapons-sanctions.html.

55. Fabrice Balanche, "Latest Battle in Idlib Could Send Another Wave of Refugees into Europe," Policy Watch 3259, Washington Institute for Near East Policy, February 2020, https://www.washingtoninstitute.org/policy-analysis/view/latest -battle-for-idlib-could-send-another-wave-of-refugees-to-europe; Aymenn Jawad al-Tamimi, "Idlib and Its Environs: The Narrowing Prospect for a Rebel Holdout," Policy Note 75, Washington Institute for Near East Policy, February 2020, https:// www.washingtoninstitute.org/policy-analysis/view/idlib-and-its-environs-narrow ing-prospects-for-a-rebel-holdout.

56. Michael A. Reynolds, "Outfoxed by the Bear? America's Losing Game in the Near East," Russia Foreign Policy Papers, Foreign Policy Research Institute of Philadelphia, April 25, 2018, https://www.fpri.org/article/2018/04/outfoxed-by-the-bear -americas-losing-game-against-russia-in-the-near-east/.

57. Jones, "War by Proxy," 4.

58. Knights, "Soleimani Is Dead," 1–2.

59. Herzog, "Iran across the Border," 4.

60. Nicolas Carl, "The Reshaping of Iran's Axis of Resistance," The Institute for the Study of War, December 10, 2024, https://www.understandingwar.org/back grounder/reshaping-iran%E2%80%99s-axis-resistance.

61. Jones, "War by Proxy", 8.

62. Michael Knights, Hamdi Malik, and Crispin Smith, "Iraq's New Regime Change: How Tehran Backed Terrorist Organizations and Milia's captured the Iraqi State," *CTC Sentinel* 16, no. 11(December 2023): 1–24, https://ctc.westpoint.edu /iraqs-new-regime-change-how-tehran-backed-terrorist-organizations-and-militias -captured-the-iraqi-state/.

63. Ibid.

64. *Report of the Panel of Experts established pursuant to resolution 1874 (2009)*, UN Document S2019171, UN Security Council, March 5, 2019, 44–45, https:// documents-dds-ny.un.org/doc/UNDOC/GEN/N19/028/82/PDF/N1902882.pdf? OpenElement.

65. Jones, "War by Proxy," 7.

66. Michael Knights, Adnan al-Gabarni, and Casey Coombs, "The Houthi Jihad Council: Command and Control in 'the Other Hezbollah,'" *CTC Sentinel* 15 (October 2022): 1–23, 10, https://ctc.usma.edu/the-houthi-jihad-council-command-and -control-in-the-other-hezbollah/.

67. Taleblu, "Arsenal," 27–29.

68. Congressional Research Service, "Iran Foreign and Defense Policies," 7.

69. Shimon Sahpira and Daniel Diker, "The Second Islamic Revolution: Strategic Implications for the West," in *Iran, Hizbullah, Hamas and the Global Jihad: A New Conflict Paradigm for the West*, ed. Dore Gold (Jerusalem: Jerusalem Center for Public

Affairs, 2007), 33–54, https://jcpa.org/book/iran-hizbullah-hamas-and-the-global -jihad-a-new-conflict-paradigm-for-the-west/.

70. Joe Truzman, "Iran and Its Network of Nineteen Terrorist Organizations on Israel's Border," Foundation for the Defense for Democracies, 2022, https://www .fdd.org/wp-content/uploads/2023/07/fdd-visual-iran-and-its-network-of-nine teen-terrorist-organizations-on-israels-borders.pdf.

71. Moath al-Amoudi, "Is North Korea Supplying Arms to Palestinian Factions?" *Al Monitor*, August 22, 2016, https://www.al-monitor.com/originals/2016/08/pal estinian-resistance-factions-weapons-deals-black-market.html; "Hamas Acquires North Korean Laser Guided Missiles," *Virtual Jerusalem*, January 24, 2017, http:// virtualjerusalem.com/newsphp?Itemid=25124.

72. Ben-David, "Hamas Advanced Weaponry," 8.

73. Emanuel Ottolenghi, "A Formula for Strife," *Longitude* 116, June 1, 2021, 50, https://www.fdd.org/analysis/2021/06/01/a-formula-for-strife.

74. Yossi Mansharot, "The Relationship between Iran and Palestinian Islamic Jihad," Jerusalem Institute for Strategy and Security, February 27, 2020, https:// jiss.org.il/wp-content/uploads/2020/02/mansharof-yossi-relationship-between -iran-and-pij-jiss-english-27-02-2020.pdf.

75. Ibid., p. 19.

76. Ibid.

77. Jeffrey Genttlemann, Anat Schwarts, and Adam Sella, "'Screams without Words' How Hamas Weaponized Sexual Violence on October 7," *New York Times*, December 28, 2023, https://www.nytimes.com/2023/12/28/world/middleeast/oct -7-attacks-hamas-israel-sexual-violence.html; Isabel Kershner "Israel Shows Raw Footage of October 7 Attacks," *New York Times*, October 23, 2023, https://www .nytimes.com/2023/10/23/world/middleeast/israel-hamas-attack-video.html; Eitan Shamir, "The Iron Swords War: The Strategic Balance so Far and What's Next," Begin-Sadat Center for Strategic Studies, July 14, 2024, https://besacenter.org/the -iron-swords-war-the-strategic-balance-so-far-and-whats-next/.

78. Shamir, "The Iron Swords War"; Anthony Celso, "Hamas's Unholy Jihad," *Israel Affairs*, last modified September 11, 2024, https://www.tandfonline.com/doi /full/10.1080/13537121.2024.2394286.

79. Ido Levy, "Hamas is Weakened, but a Prolonged Guerilla Conflict Looms," *The Washington Institute*, September 12, 2024, https://www.washingtoninstitute.org /policy-analysis/hamas-weakened-prolonged-guerrilla-conflict-looms.

80. Emanuel Fabian, "Gallant: IDF Razed 150 Tunnels on Egypt-Gaza Border, Defeated Hamas's Rafah Brigade," *Times of Israel*, August 21, 2024, https://www .timesofisrael.com/gallant-idf-razed-150-tunnels-on-egypt-gaza-border-defeated -hamass-rafah-brigade.

81. Matthew Levitt, "Hezbollah Is Weakened, but Still Dangerous," *The Prospect*, October 2, 2024, https://www.prospectmagazine.co.uk/world/middle-east/68078 /hezbollah-is-weakened-but-still-dangerous.

82. Kathleen Magramo et al., "October 3, 2024: Israeli Strikes on Hezbollah Targets Continue in Beirut, Lebanon," CNN, last modified October 4, 2024, https://edition.cnn.com/world/live-news/israel-iran-attack-war-lebanon-10-03-24-intl-hnk/index.html?t=1727987948468.

83. Alexandra Braverman et al., "Iran Update, October 1, 2024," Institute for the Study of War, last modified October 1, 2024, https://www.understandingwar.org/backgrounder/iran-update-october-1-2024.

84. Annika Ganzeveld, "The Consequences of the IDF Strikes into Iran," Institute for the Study of War, last modified November 12, 2024, https://www.understandingwar.org/backgrounder/consequences-idf-strikes-iran.

85. Nicholas Carl, "Israeli Retaliatory Strikes on Iran," Institute for the Study of War, October 26, 2024, https://www.understandingwar.org/backgrounder/israeli-retaliatory-strikes-iran.

86. Matthew Levitt, "Fighters without Borders: Forecasting New Trends in the Iran Threat," *CTC Sentinel* 13, no. 2 (2020): 1–8.

87. David Albright, Spencer Faragasso, and Andrea Stricker, "Analysis of IAEA Iran Verification and Monitoring Report—August 2024," Foundation for Defense of Democracies (FDD), last modified September 9, 2024, https://www.fdd.org/analysis/2024/09/09/analysis-of-iaea-iran-verification-and-monitoring-report-august-2024.

88. Orde F. Kittrie, Bradley Bowman, and Benham Ben-Taleblu, "Deterring Iran's Dash to the Bomb," Foundation for Defense of Democracies (FDD), last modified August 2024, https://www.fdd.org/wp-content/uploads/2024/08/fdd-monograph-deterring-irans-dash-to-the-bomb.pdf.

7. North Korean Support to Iran's Proxy Partners

1. See Hassan Hassan, "The Middle Eastern Problem Soleimani Figured Out," *Politico*, January 12, 2020, https://www.politico.com/news/magazine/2020/01/12/iran-middle-eastern-problem-soleimani-figured-out-097350.

2. See Jay Solomon, "North Korea's Alliance with Syria Reveals a Wider Proliferation Threat," Washington Institute, November 2, 2017, https://www.washingtoninstitute.org/policy-analysis/view/north-koreas-alliance-with-syria-reveals-a-wider-proliferation-threat.

3. For an example of this, see R. James Woolsey, "Breaking the Iran, North Korea, and Syria Nexus," Joint Hearing before the House Committee on Foreign Affairs, April 11, 2013, https://www.fdd.org/analysis/2013/04/11/breaking-the-iran-north-korea-and-syria-nexus/.

4. For an example of this, see Gavriel D. Ra'anan, "The Evolution of the Soviet Use of Surrogates in Military Relations with the Third World, with Particular Emphasis on Cuban Participation in Africa," Rand, December 1979, https://www.rand.org/pubs/papers/P6420.html.

5. See Keith B. Richburg, "Beyond a Wall of Secrecy, Devastation," *Washington Post*, October 19, 1997, https://www.washingtonpost.com/wp-srv/inatl/longterm /korea/stories/function.htm.

6. See "Syria Missile Development," Wisconsin Project, March 1, 1997, https:// www.wisconsinproject.org/syria-missile-development/.

7. See Andrea Berger, "North Korea, Hamas, and Hezbollah: Arm in Arm?," *38 North*, August 5, 2014, https://www.38north.org/2014/08/aberger080514/.

8. See "Assad Planning to Visit North Korea: Report," *Middle East Eye*, June 4, 2018, https://www.middleeasteye.net/news/assad-planning-visit-north-korea -report.

9. For more on the Soviet sphere of influence in the Middle East, see Ehsan M. Ahrari, *The Islamic Challenge and the United States: Global Security in an Age of Uncertainty* (Montreal: McGill-Queens University Press, 2017), 26–42.

10. For an excellent analysis of how the Soviet Union subsidized nations in the Third World during the Cold War, see Henry Trofimenko, "The Third World and the U.S.-Soviet Competition: A Soviet View," *Foreign Affairs*, June 1, 1981, https://www .foreignaffairs.com/articles/russian-federation/1981-06-01/third-world-and-us-sovi et-competition.

11. Alexandre Mansourov, "North Korea: Entering Syria's Civil War," *38 North*, November 24, 2013, https://www.38north.org/2013/11/amansourov112513/# _edn13.

12. Ibid.

13. See Franz-Stefan Gady, "Is North Korea Fighting for Assad in Syria?," *Diplomat*, March 24, 2016, https://thediplomat.com/2016/03/is-north-korea-fighting -for-assad-in-syria/.

14. Matthew Levitt, "Hezbollah Finances: Funding the Party of God," Washington Institute, February 2005, https://www.washingtoninstitute.org/policy-analysis /view/hezbollah-finances-funding-the-party-of-god.

15. Carl Anthony Wege, "The Hizballah–North Korea Nexus," *Small Wars Journal*, January 23, 2011, https://smallwarsjournal.com/blog/journal/docs-temp/654 -wege.pdf.

16. For an excellent example of the types of deals that are cut to get arms to Hezbollah, often using Iran or Syria as a go-between, see "Bulsae-3 in South Lebanon: How Hezbollah Upgraded its Anti-Armour Capabilities with North Korean Assistance," *Military Watch*, September 2, 2019, https://militarywatchmagazine.com /article/bulsae-3-in-south-lebanon-how-hezbollah-upgraded-its-anti-armour-capa bilities-with-north-korean-assistance.

17. See Arshad Mohammed, "North Korea May Have Aided Hezbollah: U.S. Report," Reuters, December 12, 2007, https://www.reuters.com/article/us -korea-north-terrorism/north-korea-may-have-aided-hezbollah-u-s-report-idUSN 126891920071213.

18. See Seth J. Frantzman, "Can Iron Dome Cut It for Indirect Fire Protection? US Army Is Buying a Couple Systems to Find Out," *Defense News*, February 6, 2019,

https://www.defensenews.com/global/mideast-africa/2019/02/06/can-iron-dome-cut-it-for-indirect-fire-protection-us-army-is-buying-a-couple-systems-to-find-out/.

19. "Hezbollah: A North Korea–Type Guerilla Force," *Intelligence Online*, August 25, 2006, https://www.intelligenceonline.com/political-intelligence/2006/08/25/hezbollah-a-north-korea-type-guerilla-force,21788114-EVE.

20. For an example of Hamas rocket attacks into Israel, see Isabel Kershner, "Gaza Militants Fire 250 Rockets, and Israel Responds with Airstrikes," *New York Times*, May 4, 2019, https://www.nytimes.com/2019/05/04/world/middleeast/gaza-rock ets-israel.html.

21. See Ariel Natan Pasko, "North Korea: There Is an Israel Connection," *Arutz Sheva*, March 2016, https://www.israelnationalnews.com/Articles/Article.aspx/20887.

22. See Joanna Paraszczuk, "Lawsuit: Kim Jong-il's Regime Sponsored Terror," *Jerusalem Post*, December 20, 2011, https://www.jpost.com/international/lawsuit-kim-jong-ils-regime-sponsored-terror; "Revealed: N. Korea Hideout of Red Army Faction Fugitives," *Japan Times*, May 17, 2014, https://www.japantimes.co.jp/news/2014/05/17/national/revealed-n-korea-hideout-of-red-army-faction-fugi tives/#page.

23. "North Korea: Relations with the Third World," Congressional Research Service, June 1993, https://web.archive.org/web/20090917120827/http://www.coun try-data.com/cgi-bin/query/r-9642.html.

24. See Nack An and Rose An, "North Korean Military Assistance," in *Communist Nations' Military Assistance*, ed. John F. Copper and Daniel S. Papp (New York: Routledge, 2018).

25. For an example of proxy warfare in the Middle East during the Cold War, see Doyle McManus, "Syria and the Perils of Proxy War," *Los Angeles Times*, January 11, 2014, https://www.latimes.com/opinion/op-ed/la-oe-mcmanus-column-proxy-war -syria-20140112-column.html.

26. See Stephanie G. Newman, "Arms, Aid, and the Superpowers," *Foreign Affairs*, June 1, 1988, https://www.foreignaffairs.com/articles/russian-federation /1988-06-01/arms-aid-and-superpowers.

27. See "Syria: Missile," Nuclear Threat Initiative, January 3, 2024, https://www .nti.org/countries/syria/.

28. See Scott Neuman, "North Korea Reportedly Sending Missile, Chemical Weapons Parts to Syria," *Two-Way*, National Public Radio, February 28, 2018, https://www.npr.org/sections/thetwo-way/2018/02/28/589401924/north-korea -reportedly-sending-missile-chemical-weapons-parts-to-syria.

29. Iran's contributions to Syria were big even before the civil war—but after it started, they got much bigger. See Jubin Goodarzi, "Iran and Syria," Iran Primer, US Institute of Peace, October 11, 2020, https://iranprimer.usip.org/resource/iran-and -syria.

30. See Bruce E. Bechtol Jr., *North Korean Military Proliferation in the Middle East and Africa: Enabling Instability and Violence* (Lexington: University Press

of Kentucky, 2018), chap. 5; Michael V. Hayden, "The CIA's Counterprolifera-
tion Efforts" (address, Los Angeles World Affairs Council, September 16, 2008),
https://www.lawac.org/speech/2008-09/hayden,michael2008.pdf;   "Background
Briefing with Senior Intelligence Officials on Syria's Covert Nuclear Reactor and
North Korea's Involvement," Office of the Director of National Intelligence, April
24, 2008, https://www.dni.gov/files/documents/Newsroom/Speeches%20and%20
Interviews/20080424_interview.pdf; Mark Mazzetti and Helene Cooper, "Israeli
Nuclear Suspicions Linked to Raid in Syria," *New York Times*, September 17, 2007,
https://www.nytimes.com/2007/09/18/world/asia/18korea.html; Michael Sheridan,
"Kim Jong-il Builds 'Thunderbirds' Runway for War in North Korea," *Sunday Times*,
April 27, 2008, https://www.timesonline.co.uk/tol/news/world/asia/article3822538
.ece; "North Korea Provided Raw Uranium to Syria in 2007: Sources," *Kyodo News*,
February 28, 2010, https://www.istockanalyst.com/article/viewiStockNews/arti
cleid/3903101; Kim So-hyun, "Worries Surface Over N.K.-Iranian Nuclear Deals,"
Korea Herald, March 18, 2010, https://www.koreaherald.co.kr/national/Detail
.jsp?newsMLId=20100318000038.

31. "North Korea Sent Syria Missile and Chemical Weapon Items, Says UN
Report," *Guardian*, February 28, 2018, https://www.theguardian.com/world/2018
/feb/28/north-korea-sent-syria-missile-and-chemical-weapon-items-says-un-report.

32. For an example of Iranian support for Syria, see "Iran's Foreign and Defense
Policies," Congressional Research Service, December 11, 2018, https://crsreports
.congress.gov/product/pdf/R/R44017/57.

33. See "North Korean HT-16PGJ MANPADS in Syria," *Oryx*, March 22, 2016,
https://www.bellingcat.com/news/mena/2016/03/22/north-korean-ht-16pgj-man
pads-in-syria/.

34. See "N. Korean Army Units Fighting for Syria Regime: Al-Zubi," Anadolu
Agency, April 2, 2016, https://www.aa.com.tr/en/world/n-korean-army-units-fight
ing-for-syria-regime-al-zubi/544517.

35. A shipment to Egypt with conventional weapons was assessed to be worth
$23 million in 2016. Between 2012 and 2017, the UN Panel of Experts detect-
ed forty shipments from North Korea to Syria. Several of the shipments were of
WMD-related cargo (largely chemical weapons or related materials), which would be
more valuable (and thus worth more money) than conventional shipments. Thus, it
is actually a conservative estimate to say that during Syria's civil war North Korea was
making hundreds of millions of dollars a year, just from its arms shipments to Syria.
See Michael Schwirtz, "U.N. Links North Korea to Syria's Chemical Weapons Program," *New York Times*, February 27, 2018, https://www.nytimes.com/2018/02/27
/world/asia/north-korea-syria-chemical-weapons-sanctions.html.

36. For more information about North Korean proliferation and training to and
for the Syrians, during and after the Yom Kippur War, see Michael Freund, "Funda-
mentally Freund: When Israel Fought North Korea," *Jerusalem Post*, October 7, 2014,
https://www.jpost.com/opinion/fundamentally-freund-when-israel-fought-north
-korea-378346.

37. Chad O'Carroll, "UN: Syria Invited at Least 800 North Koreans to Work in Military, Construction," *NK News*, August 6, 2020, https://www.nknews.org /2020/08/un-syria-invited-at-least-800-north-koreans-to-work-in-military-con struction/.

38. Shreyas Reddy, "With Assad's Ouster, North Korea Loses a Key Partner in the Middle East," NK News, December 9, 2024, https://www.nknews.org/2024/12 /with-assads-ouster-north-korea-loses-a-key-partner-in-the-middle-east/.

39. See: Mick Krever, "Israel Strikes Syria 480 Times and Seizes Territory as Netanyahu Pledges to Change Face of the Middle East," CNN, December 11, 2024, https://www.cnn.com/2024/12/10/middleeast/israel-syria-assad-strikes-intl/index .html.

40. For an example of this, see David Daoud, "Hezbollah Considers the United States, Not Israel, Its Greatest Enemy," Atlantic Council, April 30, 2020, https://www .atlanticcouncil.org/blogs/iransource/hezbollah-considers-the-united-states-not -israel-its-greatest-enemy/.

41. See Goodarzi, "Iran and Syria."

42. Intelligence Online, "Hezbollah a North Korea-Type Guerilla Force," last modified August 25 2006, https://www.intelligenceonline.com/political-intelli gence/2006/08/25/hezbollah-a-north-korea-type-guerilla-force,21788114-eve.

43. Lenny Ben-David, "Mining for Trouble in Lebanon," *Jerusalem Post*, October 29, 2007, https://www.jpost.com/opinion/op-ed-contributors/mining-for-trouble -in-lebanon.

44. "Iranian Officer: Hezbollah Has a Commando Naval Unit," *Asharq Al-Awsat*, last modified July 29, 2006, https://eng-archive.aawsat.com/theaawsat/news-middle -east/iranian-officer-hezbollah-has-a-commando-naval-unit.

45. Tal Beeri, "Hezbollah's 'Land of Tunnels'—the North Korean-Iranian Connection," Alma Researchand Education Center, last modified August 12, 2021, https://israel-alma.org/hezbollahs-land-of-tunnels-the-north-korean-iranian -connection/.

46. Some of the articulations in the four paragraphs above were originally published as a piece in *National Interest*. Republished here with permission of the editor. The author would like to thank Mr. Harry Kazianis, the editor of *National Interest*. See: Bruce E. Bechtol, "North Korea's Hezbollah Connection," *National Interest*, October 2, 2024, https://nationalinterest.org/blog/korea-watch/north -korea%E2%80%99s-hezbollah-connection-213046.

47. See Yoko Kubota, "Israel Says Seized North Korean Arms Were for Hamas, Hezbollah," Reuters, May 12, 2020, https://www.reuters.com/article/2010/05/12 /us-israel-korea-north-idUSTRE64B18520100512.

48. See Marisa Sullivan, "Hezbollah in Syria," Institute for the Study of War, April 2014, https://www.understandingwar.org/sites/default/files/Hezbollah_Sullivan _FINAL.pdf.

49. "Israel Says 90 Pct of Syria's Ballistic Missiles Used Up on Rebels," Reuters, November 15, 2015, https://www.reuters.com/article/mideast-crisis-syria-missiles

/israel-says-90-pct-of-syrias-ballistic-missiles-used-up-on-rebels-idUSL8N13 D4M220151118.

50. See Gideon Kouts, "Former Syrian General: Hezbollah Is in Possession of Chemical Weapons," *Jerusalem Post*, March 8, 2018, https://www.jpost.com/middle -east/former-syrian-official-to-maariv-hezbollah-has-chemical-weapons-544567.

51. See Tzvi Joffre, "Hezbollah Transporting Hundreds of Chemical Weapons to Lebanon—Report," *Jerusalem Post*, November 20, 2022, https://www.jpost.com /middle-east/article-722921.

52. For more on the Hezbollah-Hamas relationship, see Levitt, "Hezbollah Finances."

53. See Daniel Levin, "Iran, Hamas and Palestinian Islamic Jihad," Iran Primer, United States Institute of Peace, July 9, 2018, https://iranprimer.usip.org/blog/2018 /jul/09/iran-hamas-and-palestinian-islamic-jihad.

54. Bruce E. Bechtol, "Are the Rockets Fired by Hamas into Israel Coming from North Korea?," *National Interest*, March 21, 2021, https://nationalinterest.org/blog /korea-watch/are-rockets-fired-hamas-israel-coming-north-korea-185729.

55. See Berger, "North Korea, Hamas, and Hezbollah."

56. See Con Coughlin, "Hamas and North Korea Are Working on a Secret Arms Deal," *Telegraph*, July 26, 2014, https://www.businessinsider.com/hamas-north-korea -arms-deal-2014-7.

57. See Hannah Beech and Ronen Bergman, "Behind a Roadside Hit in Malaysia, Israeli-Palestinian Intrigue," *New York Times*, April 25, 2018, https://www .nytimes.com/2018/04/25/world/asia/hamas-mossad-malaysia.html.

58. See Lee Ho-Jeong, "South's Military Alarmed by North's Apparent Involvement in Hamas Attack," *Joongang Ilbo*, October 17, 2023, https://koreajoongangdaily .joins.com/news/2023-10-17/national/northKorea/Souths-military-alarmed-by -Norths-apparent-involvement-in-Hamas-attack/1891975.

59. Kim Soo-yeon, "S. Korea's Spy Agency Confirms Hamas' Suspected Use of N. Korean Weapons," *Yonhap*, January 8, 2024, https://en.yna.co.kr/view /AEN20240108002351315?section=nk/nk; Hyung-Jin Kim, Kim Tong-Hyung, and Jon Gambrell, "Evidence Shows Hamas Militants Likely Used Some North Korean Weapons in Attack on Israel," Associated Press, October 19, 2023, https://apnews .com/article/israel-palestinians-hamas-north-korea-weapons-703e33663e a299f920d0d14039adfbb8.

60. See Coughlin, "Hamas and North Korea."

61. See Daphné Richemond-Barak, "Tunnel Warfare Expert on What She Sees in Newly-Discovered Tunnel in Gaza," interview by Erin Burnett, CNN, December 19, 2023, https://www.cnn.com/videos/world/2023/12/19/gaza-tunnel-warfare-expert -sot-ebof-vpx.cnn.

62. See Samuel Ramani, "Could North Korea Benefit from Middle East Shifts?," *Diplomat*, August 24, 2015, https://thediplomat.com/2015/08/could-north-korea -benefit-from-middle-east-shifts/.

63. See Elizabeth Shim, "Report: North Korea Supplying Missiles to Yemen rebels," UPI, August 3, 2015, https://www.upi.com/Top_News/World-News/2015/08/03 /Report-North-Korea-supplying-missiles-to-Yemen-rebels/3021438619655/.

64. See *Final Report of the Panel of Experts Submitted Pursuant to Resolution 2407 (2018)*, UN Security Council, March 5, 2019, https://www.undocs.org/S/2019/171.

65. See Bruce Riedel, "Why Are Yemen's Houthis Attacking Riyadh Now?," Council on Foreign Relations, March 30, 2020, https://www.brookings.edu/blog /order-from-chaos/2020/03/30/why-are-yemens-houthis-attacking-riyadh-now/.

66. Paul Rogers, "North Korea Is Selling Arms and Breaking Sanctions: Does Anyone Care?," Open Democracy, March 25, 2019, https://www.opendemocracy .net/en/north-korea-is-selling-arms-and-breaking-sanctions-does-anyone-care/.

67. See Ji-ha Ham, "'Hangul' on Houthi Rebel Missile Fragments . . . Hamas Rockets Are Emblazoned with 'Visger-7 Class,'" Voice of America, last modified January 5, 2024, https://www.voakorea.com/a/7427146.html.

68. For more on the surrogate role the Houthis play for Iran, see "US Gives Evidence Iran Supplied Missiles That Yemen Rebels Fired at Saudi Arabia," *Guardian*, December 14, 2017, https://www.theguardian.com/world/2017/dec/14/us-gives-ev idence-iran-supplied-missiles-that-yemen-rebels-fired-at-saudi-arabia.

69. Most of the information in the section on Hamas and in the concluding paragraph of this chapter was originally published as a piece in *1945*. Republished here with permission of the editor. The author would like to thank Harry Kazianis, the editor of *1945*. See Bruce E. Bechtol Jr., "Hamas Is Using North Korean Weapons against Israel," *1945*, October 24, 2023, https://www.19fortyfive.com/2023/10 /hamas-is-using-north-korean-weapons-against-israel/.

8. Rogue Allies and the Criminal Financial Networks That Support the Partnership

1. "Iran Sanctions," Congressional Research Service, April 2021, https://sgp.fas .org/crs/mideast/RS20871.pdf.

2. Ibid., 37–41.

3. Ibid., 58.

4. Eric Lorber, "Impact of Sanctions in Africa," Congressional Statement for the House Committee on Financial Services, Foundation for Defense of Democracies, May 25, 2021, https://www.fdd.org/wp-content/uploads/2021/05/2021.05.25-Lorber -Testimony.pdf.

5. *Report of the Panel of Experts Report Pursuant to Resolution 11874 S/2018/171*, UN Security Council, March 5, 2018, 44–45, https://www.securitycouncilreport.org /atf/cf/%7B65BFCF9B-6D27-4E9C-8CD3-CF6E4FF96FF9%7D/s_2018_171.pdf.

6. Emanuele Ottolenghi, "An Examination of Iran's Threat Network," Congressional Testimony before the House Homeland Security Committee, Foundation

for Defense of Democracies, April 2017, https://www.fdd.org/analysis/2018/04/17/state-sponsors-of-terrorism-an-examination-of-irans-global-terrorism-network-2/; Omer Carmi, "Deconstructing and Countering 'Iran's Threat Network,'" Washington Institute for Near East Policy, October 16, 2017, https://www.washingtoninstitute.org/policy-analysis/deconstructing-and-countering-iran-threat-network.

7. "The Biden Administration Refuses to Rule Out Sanctions Relief for Iran," Flash Brief, Foundation for Defense of Democracies, December 12, 2022, https://www.fdd.org/analysis/2022/12/12/biden-administration-sanctions-relief-iran/; Michael Eisenstadt, "Iran's Nuclear Hedging Strategy: Shaping the Islamic Republic's Proliferation Calculus," Policy Focus 178, Washington Institute for Near East Policy, November 2022, 6–8, https://www.washingtoninstitute.org/policy-analysis/irans-nuclear-hedging-strategy-shaping-islamic-republics-proliferation-calculus.

8. Matthew Levitt, "Hezbollah's Procurement Channels: Leveraging Criminal Networks Partnering with Iran," *CTC Sentinel* 12, no. 3 (March 2019): 1–9.

9. Emanuele Ottolenghi, "The Role of Iranian Dual Nationals in Sanctions Evasion," Congressional Testimony before House Committee on Oversight and Government Reform, Foundation for Defense of Democracies, February 2016, https://republicans-oversight.house.gov/wp-content/uploads/2016/02/2016-02-10-Ottolenghi-Testimony-Bio.pdf.

10. Michael Eisenstadt, "The Strategic Culture of the Islamic Republic of Iran: Religion, Expediency, and Soft Power in an Era of Disruptive Change," Washington Institute for Near East Policy, November 2015, https://www.washingtoninstitute.org/policy-analysis/strategic-culture-islamic-republic-iran-religion-expediency-and-soft-power-era.

11. Kasra Aarabi, "Beyond Borders: The Expansionist Ideology of Iran's Islamic Revolutionary Guard Corps," Tony Blair Institute for Global Change, February 2020, https://institute.global/sites/default/files/2020-01/IRGC%20Report%202701 2020.pdf.

12. Matthew Levitt, "Hezbollah's Criminal Networks: Useful Idiots, Henchmen, and Organized Criminal Facilitators," Washington Institute for Near East Policy, October 2016, https://www.washingtoninstitute.org/policy-analysis/hezbollahs-criminal-networks-useful-idiots-henchmen-and-organized-criminal.

13. Emanuele Ottolenghi, "Role of Iranian Dual Nationals in Sanctions Evasion," 2–20.

14. Matthew Levitt, "Iranian and Hezbollah Operations in South America: Then and Now," *Prism* 5, no. 4 (April 2016): 119–33, https://cco.ndu.edu/Portals/96/Documents/prism/prism_5-4/Iranian%20and%20Hezbollah.pdf; Matthew Levitt, "On Bombing Anniversary, Iran Still Engaged in Illicit Activity," *Hill*, July 2017, https://www.washingtoninstitute.org/policy-analysis/bombing-anniversary-iran-still-engaged-illicit-activity.

15. Todd Benson, "Where Is the Promised Investigation of the Hezbollah-Iran Plane Bombing in Panama?," *Townhall*, September 2019, https://townhall.com

/columnists/toddbensman/2019/09/03/where-is-the-promised-investigation
-of-the-hezbollahiran-plane-bombing-in-panama-n2552441.

16. Matthew Levitt, "Hizb Allah Resurrected: The Party of God's Return to Tradecraft," *CTC Sentinel* 6, no. 4 (April 2013): 1–5.

17. Matthew Levitt, "Breaking Hezbollah's Golden Rule: An Inside Look and the Modus Operandi of Hezbollah's Islamic Jihad Organization," *Perspectives of Terrorism* 14, no. 4 (August 2014): 21–42.

18. Matthew Levitt, "Hizbollah and the Qods Force in Iran's Shadow War with the West," Washington Institute for Near East Policy, January 2013, https://www.washingtoninstitute.org/policy-analysis/hizballah-and-qods-force-irans-shadow-war-west.

19. Matthew Levitt, "Hezbollah's International Presence and Operations," AJC Global Jewish Advocacy, August 2018, https://www.ajc.org/news/hezbollahs-international-presence-and-operations.

20. *Hearing before the House Committee on Financial Services: Task Force to Investigate Terrorism Financing*, 114th Cong. (2016) (statement of Emanuele Ottolenghi, "The Enemy in Our Backyard: Examining Terror Funding Schemes in South America"), https://docs.house.gov/meetings/BA/BA00/20160608/105051/HHRG-114-BA00-Wstate-OttolenghiE-20160608.pdf.

21. Douglas Farah, "Terrorist-Criminal Pipelines and Criminalized States: Emerging Alliances," *Prism* 2, no. 3 (January 2013): 1–32; Robert Killebrew, "Criminal Insurgency in the Americas and Beyond," *Prism* 2, no. 3 (January 2013): 33–52.

22. Colin P. Clarke, "Drugs and Thugs: Funding Terrorism through Narcotics Trafficking," *Journal of Strategic Security* 3, no. 4 (Fall 2016): 1–15; Chris Dishman, "The Leaderless Nexus: When Crime and Terror Converge," *Studies in Conflict and Terrorism* 28 (2005): 237–52.

23. Assaf Moghadam, *The Nexus of Global Jihad: Understanding Cooperation between Terrorist Actors* (New York: Columbia University Press, 2019).

24. Douglas Farah, "Terrorist-Criminal Pipelines," 18–24.

25. Emanuele Ottolenghi, *The Laundromat: Hezbollah's Money Laundering and Drug Trafficking Operations in Latin America*, Mideast Security and Policy Studies 194 (Ramat Gan: Begin-Sadat Center for Strategic Studies, Bar-Ilan University, 2021), https://besacenter.org/wp-content/uploads/2021/07/194web.pdf.

26. Levitt, "Hezbollah's Criminal Networks," 168.

27. Levitt, "Hezbollah's Procurement Channels," 1.

28. Ottolenghi, *Laundromat*, 22–26.

29. Ibid.

30. Levitt, "Hezbollah's Criminal Networks," 166–70.

31. Ottolenghi, "Enemy in Our Backyard," 3–7.

32. Ottolenghi, *Laundromat*, 23–24.

33. Ibid.

34. Levitt, "Hezbollah's Criminal Networks," 160.

35. Emanuele Ottolenghi, "From Latin America to West Africa, Hezbollah's Complex Web of Connections Is Fueling Terrorist Activity," *National*, August 2019, https://www.fdd.org/analysis/2019/08/29/from-latin-america-to-west-africa-hezbol lahs-complex-web-of-connections-is-fuelling-its-terrorist-activity/.

36. Tony Badran and Emanuele Ottolenghi, "Hezbollah Finance in Lebanon: A Primary Source Review," Foundation for Defense of Democracies, August 2020, 4; Matthew Levitt, "Hezbollah's Corruption Crisis Runs Deep," Washington Institute for Near East Policy, July 2018, https://www.washingtoninstitute.org/pdf /view/2158/en.

37. United States District East New York Bartlett et al. v. Sociétié Générale Banque au Liban et al., Defendants Case 19-cv-7 (CBA) (VMS); James Rickards, "Crisis in Lebanon: Anatomy of a Financial Collapse," Foundation for Defense of Democracies, August 2020, https://libnanews.com/wp-content/uploads/2020/08/fdd-mono graph-crisis-in-lebanon.pdf.

38. Rickards, "Crisis in Lebanon," 27.

39. Ibid., 25–27.

40. Levitt, "Hezbollah's Criminal Networks," 157–58, 160–61.

41. Matthew Levitt, "In Search of Nuance in the Debate over Hezbollah's Criminal Operations and the U.S. Response," *Lawfare Research Paper Series* 5, no. 3 (March 2018): 1–34.

42. Joseph Humire, "The Maduro-Hezbollah Nexus: How Iran-Backed Networks Prop Up the Venezuelan Regime," *Atlantic Council*, October 2020, https://www.at lanticcouncil.org/in-depth-research-reports/issue-brief/the-maduro-hezbollah-nex us-how-iran-backed-networks-prop-up-the-venezuelan-regime/.

43. "Kingpins of Corruption: Targeting Transnational Organized Crime in Latin America," American Enterprise Institute, June 2017, 18–21, https://www.aei.org /wp-content/uploads/2017/06/Kingpins-and-Corruption.pdf.

44. Ibid., 21.

45. Humire, "Maduro-Hezbollah Nexus," 8.

46. Farah, "Terrorist-Criminal Pipelines and Criminalized States," 22–24.

47. Rickards, "Crisis in Lebanon," 25–27.

48. Badran and Ottolenghi, "Hezbollah Finance in Lebanon," 8.

49. Peter Kirechu, "Iran's Currency Laundromats in the Emirates," *CTC Sentinel* 14, no. 5 (June 2021): 26–31; "Under the Shadow of Illicit Economies in Iran," Global Initiative against Transnational Organized Crime, October 2020, https://glo balinitiative.net/analysis/under-the-shadow-illicit-economies-in-iran/.

50. Behnam Ben Taleblu, "The Sanctioned Cabinet of Ebrahim Raisi," Foundation for Defense of Democracies, September 30, 2021, https://www.fdd.org/analy sis/2021/09/30/the-sanctioned-cabinet-of-ebrahim-raisi/.

51. Saeed Ghasseminejad and Mohammad R. Jahan-Parvar, "The Impact of Financial Sanctions: The Case of Iran 2011–2016," International Financial Discussion Papers, Board of Governors of the Federal Reserve System, May 2020, https://www .federalreserve.gov/econres/ifdp/files/ifdp1281.pdf; Nader Habibi, "The Impact of

Sanctions on Iran-GCC Economic Relations," Middle East Brief, Brandeis University Middle East Studies, November 2010, https://www.brandeis.edu/crown/publica tions/middle-east-briefs/pdfs/1-100/meb45.pdf.

52. Ghasseminejad and Jahan-Parvar, "Impact of Financial Sanctions," 8.

53. Ibid., 8–9.

54. Emanuel Ottolenghi et al., "How the Nuclear Deal Enriches Iran's Revolutionary Guard Corps," Foundation for Defense of Democracies, Center on Sanctions and Illicit Finance, October 2016, 11–26, https://www.fdd.org/analysis/2016/10/04 /how-the-nuclear-deal-enriches-irans-revolutionary-guard-corps/.

55. Ibid., 16.

56. Levitt, "Hezbollah's Procurement Channels."

57. Ibid., 1–2.

58. Ibid., 4–7.

59. Lorber, "How Targets of Sanctions Undermine and Evade Sanctions," 7.

60. Ibid., 7–9.

61. Ibid., 11–12.

62. Ibid., 12–13.

63. Ottolenghi, "Role of Iranian Dual Nationals in Sanctions Evasion," 12.

64. Habibi, "Impact of Sanctions on Iran-GCC Economic Relations," 7.

65. Kirechu, "Iran's Currency Laundromats in the Emirates."

66. Ibid.

67. John P. Caves and Meghan Peri Crimmins, "Major Turkish Bank Prosecuted in Unprecedented Iran Sanctions Case," Wisconsin Project on Nuclear Arms Control, March 2020, https://www.iranwatch.org/our-publications/articles-reports/ma jor-turkish-bank-prosecuted-unprecedented-iran-sanctions-evasion-case.

68. US Department of State, "Outlaw Regime," 23–24.

69. Tim Michetti, "A Guide to Illicit Iranian Weapons Transfers: The Bahraini File," Atlantic Council, December 2020, https://www.atlanticcouncil.org/in-depth -research-reports/report/a-guide-to-illicit-iranian weapon-transfers-the-bahrain-file/.

70. Ibid., 58–66.

71. "HMAS Darwin Seizes Large Weapons Haul as Part of Counter-Terrorism Operation in Middle East," ABC News, March 8, 2016, https://www.abc.net.au /news/2016-03-08/hmas-darwin-seizes-large-weapons-cache/7228308.

72. Report of the Panel of Experts Established Pursuant to Resolution 1874, UN Security Council S/ 2019/171, March 5, 2019, https://www.ncnk.org/sites/default /files/UN_POE_March2019_Final_Report.pdf.

73. UN Panel of Experts on Yemen to the president of the UN Security Council, January 22, 2021, https://digitallibrary.un.org/record/3898851.

74. Jay Bahadur, "Snapping Back against Iran: The Case of Al-Bari 2 and the UN Arms Embargo," Global Initiative against Transnational Organized Crime, December 2020, https://globalinitiative.net/wp-content/uploads/2020/11/Snapping-back -against-Iran-The-case-of-the-Al-Bari-2-and-the-UN-arms-embargo_GITOC.pdf.

75. Ibid., 3.

76. Emanuel Ottolenghi, Ann Fixler, and Yaya J. Fanusie, "Flying under the Radar: Evasion in the Iranian Aviation Sector," Foundation for Defense of Democracies, July 2016, https://s3.us-east-2.amazonaws.com/defenddemocracy/uploads/documents/Ottolenghi_Fixler_Fanusie_Aviation_Sanctions_Evasion.pdf.

77. Ibid., 5.

78. Tom Westcott and Afshin Ismaeli, "Sanctions and Smuggling: The Role of Iraqi Kurdistan and Iran's Border Economies," Global Initiative against Transnational Organized Crime, April 2019, https://globalinitiative.net/wp-content/uploads/2019/04/TGIATOC-Report-Sanctions-Iraq-Iran-05Apr1300-Web.pdf.

79. Farzin Nadimi, "Iran's Atlantic Voyage: Implications of Naval Deployments to Venezuela or Syria," Washington Institute for Near East Policy, June 2021, https://www.washingtoninstitute.org/policy-analysis/irans-atlantic-voyage-implications-naval-deployments-venezuela-or-syria.

80. Humire, "Maduro-Hezbollah Nexus," 11.

81. James Bosworth, "Venezuela's Relations with Iran: Maduro's Lifesaver in 2020," in Venezuela's Authoritarian Allies: The Ties that Bind?, ed. Cynthia J. Arnson (Washington, DC: Wilson Center, 2021), 212.

82. Deisy Buitrago, Marianna Parraga, and Matt Spetalnick, "Under US Sanctions, Iran and Venezuela Strike Oil Export Deal," Reuters, September 25, 2021, https://www.reuters.com/business/energy/exclusive-under-us-sanctions-iran-venezuela-strike-oil-export-deal-sources-2021-09-25/.

83. Nadimi, "Iran's Atlantic Voyage," 1.

84. Terrence G. Lichtenwald and Frank S. Perri, "Terrorist Use of Smuggling Tunnels," International Journal of Criminology and Sociology 2 (2013):210–26; Ido Levy, "How Iran Fuels Hamas Terrorism," Washington Institute for Near East Policy, July 2021, https://www.washingtoninstitute.org/policy-analysis/how-iran-fuels-hamas-terrorism; Jonathan Schanzer, "Hamas' Benefactors: A Network of Terror," Congressional Testimony before the Foreign Affairs Committee, Foundation for Defense of Democracies, September 2014, https://docs.house.gov/meetings/FA/FA13/20140909/102629/HHRG-113-FA13-Wstate-SchanzerJ-20140909.pdf.

85. Levy, "How Iran Fuels Hamas Terrorism," 2–3.

86. Schanzer, "Hamas' Benefactors," 14–15.

87. US Department of State, "Outlaw Regime," 10.

88. Lenny Ben-David, "Hamas' Advanced Weaponry: Rockets, Artillery, Drones, Cyber," no. 651, Jerusalem Center for Security and Foreign Affairs, August 2021, 17, https://jcpa.org/article/hamas-advanced-weaponry-rockets-artillery-drones-cyber/.

89. See "The Flow of Arms into the Gaza Strip," Australian Institute of International Affairs, 2015, https://www.internationalaffairs.org.au/the-flow-of-arms-into-the-gaza-strip/.

90. Bertil Lintner, "North Korea's Link to Hamas," Global Asia 18, no. 4 (December 2023), https://www.globalasia.org/v18no4/feature/north-koreas-link-to-hamas_bertil-lintner.

91. See Chad O'Carroll, "Gold, Drugs, Missiles: North Korea's Attempted Illegal Sales through the KFA," *NK News*, October 11, 2020, https://www.nknews.org/2020/10/gold-drugs-missiles-north-koreas-attempted-illegal-sales-through-the-kfa/.

92. See Paul Adams, "Documentary Claims to Expose North Korea Trying to Dodge Sanctions," BBC, October 11, 2020, https://www.bbc.com/news/world-asia-54464581.

93. See Benjamin Haas, "North Korea Frustrates US as 'Maximum Pressure' Eases on Sanctions," *Guardian*, August 6, 2018, https://www.theguardian.com/world/2018/aug/06/north-korea-frustrates-us-maximum-pressure-eases-sanctions.

94. See US Department of the Treasury, "Treasury Targets Russian Bank and Other Facilitators of North Korean United Nations Security Council Violations," press release, August 3, 2018, https://home.treasury.gov/news/press-releases/sm454.

95. See US Department of the Treasury, "Treasury Sanctions Individual, Banks, and Trading Company for Supporting North Korea's WMD and Ballistic Missile Programs," press release, May 27, 2022, https://home.treasury.gov/news/press-releases/jy0801.

96. "DPRK (North Korea): Yesterday's Vote on a Sanctions Resolution," UN Security Council Report, May 27, 2022, https://www.securitycouncilreport.org/whatsinblue/2022/05/dprk-north-korea-yesterdays-vote-on-a-sanctions-resolution.php.

97. See Lee Sung-Eun, "China, Russia Veto New UN Sanctions on North Korea," *Joongang Ilbo*, May 27, 2022, https://koreajoongangdaily.joins.com/2022/05/27/national/northKorea/korea-north-north-korea/20220527160545751.html.

98. See Seulkee Jang, "N. Korea Expands the Number of Soldiers Going Abroad to Earn Foreign Currency," *Daily NK*, May 13, 2021, https://www.dailynk.com/english/north-korea-expands-number-soldiers-going-abroad-earn-foreign-currency/#:~:text=In%20fact%2C%2090%25%20of%20the,compared%20to%20ordinary%20civilian%20workers.

99. For an excellent example of this, see Michelle Wiese Bockmann, "US Seizes Cameroon-Flagged Tanker for North Korea Sanctions Evasion," *Lloyd's List*, April 27, 2021, https://lloydslist.com/LL1136600/US-seizes-Cameroon-flagged-tanker-for-North-Korea-sanctions-evasion.

100. See Oh Taek-sung, "International Cooperation Called Key to Curbing North Korea's Sanctions Evasion," Voice of America, September 19, 2019, https://www.voanews.com/a/east-asia-pacific_more-international-cooperation-called-key-curbing-north-koreas-sanction-evasion/6176138.html.

101. See Humeyra Pamuk, Jonathan Saul, and Timothy Gardner, "Trump Administration Issues Global Maritime Advisory on Sanctions, with Industry Input," Reuters, May 14, 2020, https://www.reuters.com/article/idUSKBN22Q2LC/.

102. See Andrew Boling et al., "Unmasked Vessel Identity Laundering and North Korea's Maritime Sanctions Evasion," C4ADS, September 9, 2021, https://c4ads.org/reports/unmasked/.

103. See Anatoly Kurmanaev, "High Seas Deception: How Shady Ships Use GPS to Evade International Law, Sanctions," *New York Times*, September 3, 2022, https:// buffalonews.com/high-seas-deception-how-shady-ships-use-gps-to-evade-interna tional-law-sanctions/article_72f963ff-14f8-5883-89c9-bb25f901b642.html#:~: text=The%20vessels%20carry%20out%20the,place%20while%20physically%20 being%20elsewhere.

104. See David Albright, Sarah Burkhard, and Spencer Faragasso, "Alleged Sanctions Violations of UNSC Resolutions on North Korea for 2019/2020: The Number Is Increasing," Institute for Science and International Security, July 1, 2020, https:// isis-online.org/isis-reports/detail/alleged-north-korea-sanctions-violations-2020/.

105. Christian Davies et al., "Inside North Korea's Oil Smuggling: Triads, Ghost Ships and Underground Banks," *Financial Times*, March 29, 2023, https://ig.ft.com /north-korea-oil-smuggling/.

106. See Tara O, "How North Korea Launders Money Using Cryptocurrency to Evade Sanctions," East Asia Research Center, October 8, 2022, https://eastasiare search.org/2022/10/08/how-north-korea-launders-money-using-cryptocurrency-to -evade-sanctions/.

107. See *Final Report of the Panel of Experts Submitted Pursuant to Resolution 2680 (2023)*, United Nations Security Council, March 7, 2024, https://main.un.org/secu ritycouncil/en/sanctions/1718/panel_experts/reports.

108. See Morgan Dunn, "Inside Room 39, North Korea's Mysterious State-Run Slush Fund," *All That's Interesting*, June 10, 2021, URL: https://allthatsinteresting .com/room-39.

109. See John Walcott, "Cash, Yachts, and Cognac: Kim Yo-Jong's Links to the Secretive Office Keeping North Korea's Elites in Luxury," *Time*, April 29, 2020, https://time.com/5829508/kim-yo-jong-money-office-39/.

110. See Matthew Goldstein, "The Fed Slaps Deutsche Bank with a $186 Million Fine," *New York Times*, July 19, 2023, https://www.nytimes.com/2023/07/19/busi ness/federal-reserve-deutsche-bank-fine.html.

111. See Elizabeth Shim, "Sanctions on North Korea Effective Despite Illicit Activity, Analyst Says," UPI, April 13, 2021, https://www.upi.com/Top _News/World-News/2021/04/13/nkorea-North-Korea-sanctions-effective-analy sis/9821618323241/; Seulkee Jang, "North Korea Neglects to Recall Malaysia-Based Officials Focused on Smuggling," *Daily NK*, April 1, 2021, https://www.dailynk .com/english/north-korea-neglects-recall-malaysia-officials-focused-smuggling/; "Defendants and Front Companies Named in DOJ Indictment Operate Additional Active Companies and Trade with North Korea," Sayari, June 11, 2020, https:// sayari.com/resources/defendants-and-front-companies-named-in-doj-indictment -operate-additional-active-companies-and-trade-with-north-korea/; Andrew W. Lehren and Dan De Luce, "Secret Documents Show How North Korea Launders Money through U.S. Banks," *NBC News*, September 20, 2020, https://www.nbc news.com/news/world/secret-documents-show-how-north-korea-launders-money -through-u-n1240329; Katie Benner, "North Koreans Accused of Laundering $2.5

Billion for Nuclear Program," *New York Times*, May 28, 2020, https://www.nytimes
.com/2020/05/28/us/politics/north-korea-money-laundering-nuclear-weapons
.html; "Rickety Anchor: North Korea Calls Its Illicit Shipping Fleet Home amid
Coronavirus Fears," Royal United Services Institute, March 26, 2020, https://rusi
.org/explore-our-research/publications/commentary/rickety-anchor-north-korea
-calls-its-illicit-shipping-fleet-home-amid-coronavirus-fears; Lee Haye-ah, "U.S.
Sanctions 2 Chinese Nationals Linked to N.K. Cyber Group," Yonhap, March 3,
2020, https://en.yna.co.kr/view/AEN20200303000100325; US Department of Justice, "Department of Justice Announces Charges of North Korean and Malaysia Nationals for Bank Fraud, Money Laundering and North Korea Sanctions Violations,"
press release, September 11, 2020, https://www.justice.gov/opa/pr/department-jus
tice-announces-charges-north-korean-and-malaysia-nationals-bank-fraud-money.

112. See Enrico Carisch, former UNSC financial and natural resources sanctions
monitor, interview by Bruce E. Bechtol Jr., March 27, 2022.

113. See Hyun-Seung Lee, prominent North Korean defector and son of a former high-ranking official from Office Number 39 (now also a defector), interview
by Bruce E. Bechtol Jr., February 14, 2022; Lee, interview by Bruce E. Bechtol Jr.,
March 27, 2022.

114. See David Asher, senior fellow, Hudson Institute, interview by Bruce E.
Bechtol Jr., February 17, 2022.

115. For important examples of this, see Kathrin Kranz, "North Korean Conglomerates: Their Arms Connection, and Sanction Busting Activities," Compliance
and Capacity Skills International, 2023, https://ccsi.global/north-korean-conglom
erates/.

116. Larry Niksch, "Iran–North Korea Strategic Relationship," Testimony to the
House Committee on Foreign Affairs, July 28, 2015, https://docs.house.gov/meet
ings/FA/FA18/20150728/103824/HHRG-114-FA18-Wstate-NikschL-20150728
.pdf.

117. See "Report: Iran Financed Syrian Nuke Plans," *NBC News*, March 19,
2009, https://www.nbcnews.com/id/wbna29777355.

118. UN Security Council, *Report of the Panel of Experts Report Pursuant to Resolution 11874 S/2018/171*, 48–53.

119. Samuel Ramani, "North Korea–Iran Relations Post-JCPOA," *38 North*,
November 9, 2023, https://www.38north.org/2023/11/north-korea-iran-relations
-post-jcpoa/.

120. See Eric Lob, "Iran and Cryptocurrency: Opportunities and Obstacles for
the Regime," Middle East Institute, December 27, 2022, https://www.mei.edu/pub
lications/iran-and-cryptocurrency-opportunities-and-obstacles-regime.

121. See Gianluca Pacchiani, "Terrorists Raised $130m in Crypto since 2021;
Sought More via Social Media after Attack," *Times of Israel*, October 23, 2023,
https://www.timesofisrael.com/gazan-terror-groups-raised-over-130-million-in
-crypto-to-fund-attack/#:~:text=Hamas%27s%20military%20arm%2C%20
the%20al,the%20US%20Department%20of%20Justice.

122. See Levitt et al., "Can Bankers Fight Terrorism?," *Foreign Affairs*, October 2017, https://www.foreignaffairs.com/articles/2017-10-16/can-bankers-fight-terrorism.

123. Bruce E. Bechtol Jr., "North Korean Illicit Activities and Sanctions: A National Security Dilemma," *Cornell International Law Journal* 51 (2018), https://ww3 .lawschool.cornell.edu/research/ILJ/upload/Bechtol-final.pdf.

124. John Park and Jim Walsh, "Stopping North Korea, Inc.: Sanctions Effectiveness and Unintended Consequences," MIT Security Studies, August, 2016, https://www.belfercenter.org/sites/default/files/legacy/files/Stopping%20North%20 Korea%20Inc%20Park%20and%20Walsh%20.pdf.

125. King Mallory, *North Korean Sanctions: Evasion Techniques* (Santa Monica, CA: Rand, 2021), https://www.rand.org/content/dam/rand/pubs/research_reports /RRA1500/RRA1537-1/RAND_RRA1537-1.pdf.

126. Park and Walsh, "Stopping North Korea, Inc."

127. UN Security Council, *Report of the Panel of Experts Pursuant to Resolution 1874 S/2019/17*.

128. Seongjin "Spencer" Park, "Evading, Hacking and Laundering for Nukes: North Korea's Financial Cybercrimes and the Missing Silver Bullet for Countering Them," *Fordham International Law Journal* 45, no. 4 (2022): 675–716, https:// ir.lawnet.fordham.edu/cgi/viewcontent.cgi?article=2843&context=ilj.

129. For a key example of this, see US Department of the Treasury, "Treasury Targets DPRK's International Agents and Illicit Cyber Intrusion Group," press release, November 30, 2023, https://home.treasury.gov/news/press-releases/jy1938.

130. For an excellent example of this, see "Tracking an Iran-DPRK Gold Smuggling Scheme with Public Records," Sayari, July 7, 2021, https://sayari.com/resourc es/tracking-an-iran-dprk-gold-smuggling-scheme-with-public-records/.

131. Robert Rook, "Arts of Evasion: North Korea, Sanctions and the World," *Towson University Journal of International Affairs* 1, no. 2 (Spring 2018): 69–82, 77, https://cpb-us-w2.wpmucdn.com/wp.towson.edu/dist/b/55/files/2018/05/SPRING -2018-ROOK-ARTICLE-1t27fhc.pdf.

132. For an excellent example of Iran-Venezuela-Hezbollah illicit activities, see "Israel Reveals Secret Iranian Gold Smuggling Trade to Finance Hezbollah," *Asharq al-Awsat*, February 27, 2023, https://english.aawsat.com/home/article/4182031/israel -reveals-secret-iranian-gold-smuggling-trade-finance-hezbollah.

133. S. Park, "Evading, Hacking and Laundering for Nukes."

134. Annie Fixler, "The Cyber Threat from Iran after the Death of Soleimani," *CTC Sentinel* 13, no. 2 (February 2020): 20, https://ctc.westpoint.edu/cyber-threat -iran-death-soleimani/.

135. Rook, "Arts of Evasion," 77.

136. Brian O'Toole, "Rejoining the Iran Nuclear Deal: Not So Easy?," Atlantic Council, January 2021, https://www.atlanticcouncil.org/in-depth-research-reports /issue-brief/rejoining-the-iran-nuclear-deal-not-so-easy/.

137. John Hardie, "Iran Aids Russia's Imperialist War against Ukraine," *Algemeiner*, Foundation for Defense of Democracies, November 22, 2022, https://www.fdd

.org/analysis/2022/11/22/iran-aids-russias-imperialist-war; Nicholas Car, Kitaneh Fitzpatrick, and Katherine Lawlor, "Russia and Iran Double Down on Their Strategic Partnership," Institute for the Study of War/American Enterprise Institute Critical Threats Project, August 11, 2022, https://www.understandingwar.org/backgrounder /russia-and-iran-double-down-their-strategic-partnership.

138. US Department of the Treasury, "Treasury Iranian Persons Involved in the Production of Unmanned Arial Vehicles and Weapons Shipment to Russia," press release, September 9, 2022, https://home.treasury.gov/news/press-releases/jy0940.

9. Conclusions and Policy Implications

1. See "National Security Strategy of the United States," White House, December 2017, https://au.usembassy.gov/2017-national-security-strategy-new-national-secu rity-strategy-new-era/; "National Security Strategy of the United States," White House, October 2022, https://www.whitehouse.gov/wp-content/uploads/2022/10 /Biden-Harris-Administrations-National-Security-Strategy-10.2022.pdf.

2. See Dany Shoham, "The Quadruple Threat: North Korea, China, Pakistan, and Iran," Perspectives Paper 1795, BESA Center, November 2020, https://besa center.org/wp-content/uploads/2020/11/1795-Contiguous-Quartet-Shoham-final .pdf; Claudia Rosett, "The Iran–North Korea Strategic Alliance," In *House Hearing, 114 Congress (From the US Government Publishing Office)*. Testimony before the House Foreign Affairs Subcommittee Hearing, Foundation for Defense of Democracies, July 28, 2015, https://docs.house.gov/meetings/FA/FA18/20150728/103824 /HHRG-114-FA18-Wstate-RosettC-20150728.pdf; Maya Carlin, "North Korea and Iran: The Military Alliance That America Fears," *1945*, May 2022, https://www .19fortyfive.com/2022/05/iran-north-korea-cooperation-submarines-icbm/.

3. See John Park and Jim Walsh, "Stopping North Korea, Inc.: Sanctions Effectiveness and Unintended Consequences," MIT Security Studies, August 2016, 18–20, https://www.belfercenter.org/sites/default/files/legacy/files/Stopping%20North%20 Korea%20Inc%20Park%20and%20Walsh%20.pdf; King Mallory, *North Korean Sanctions: Evasion Techniques* (Santa Monica, CA: Rand, 2021), 20–31, https:// www.rand.org/content/dam/rand/pubs/research_reports/RRA1500/RRA1537-1 /RAND_RRA1537-1.pdf; Saeed Ghasseminejad and Mohammad R. Jahan-Parvar, "The Impact of Financial Sanctions: The Case of Iran 2011–2016," International Finance Discussion Papers 1281, Federal Reserve Board of Governors, November 2020, https://www.federalreserve.gov/econres/ifdp/files/ifdp1281.pdf; Daniel Wertz, "The Evolution of Financial Sanctions on North Korea," *North Korea Review* 9, no. 3 (Fall 2013): 69–82.

4. See John Hardie, "Iran Aids Russia's Imperialist War against Ukraine," *Algemeiner*, Foundation for Defense of Democracies, November 22, 2022, https:// www.fdd.org/analysis/2022/11/22/iran-aids-russias-imperialist-war; Nicholas Car, Kitaneh Fitzpatrick, and Katherine Lawlor, "Russia and Iran Double Down on Their

Strategic Partnership," Institute for the Study of War/American Enterprise Institute Critical Threats Project, August 11, 2022, https://www.understandingwar.org/back grounder/russia-and-iran-double-down-their-strategic-partnership.

5. See Michael Knights, Adnan al-Gabarni, and Casey Coombs, "The Houthi Jihad Council: Command and Control in 'the Other Hezbollah,'" *CTC Sentinel* 15 (October 2022): 1–23, 10, https://ctc.usma.edu/the-houthi-jihad-council-com mand-and-control-in-the-other-hezbollah/.

6. See Behnam Ben Taleblu, "Arsenal: Assessing the Islamic Republic of Iran's Ballistic Missile Program," Foundation for Defense of Democracies, February 2023, 12, https://www.fdd.org/analysis/2023/02/15/arsenal-assessing-the-islamic-repub lic-of-irans-ballistic-missile-program/; "Iran Missile Program: Past and Present," Iran Watch, June 2020, https://www.iranwatch.org/sites/default/files/iran-missile-pro gram-past-present.pdf.

7. See Paul Kerr and Steven Hildreth, "Iran–North Korea–Syria Ballistic Missile and Nuclear Cooperation," Congressional Research Service Report, February 2016, https://crsreports.congress.gov/product/pdf/R/R43480.

8. See Park and Walsh. "Stopping North Korea, Inc.," 18–20; Kasra Aarabi, "Beyond Borders: The Expansionist Ideology of Iran's Islamic Revolutionary Guard Corps," Tony Blair Institute for Global Change, February 2020, https://institute .global/sites/default/files/2020-01/IRGC%20Report%2027012020.pdf.

9. See Seth G. Jones, "War by Proxy: Iran's Growing Footprint in the Mideast," CSIS Brief, Center for Strategic and International Studies, March 2020, https:// www.csis.org/war-by-proxy.

10. See Emanuele Ottolenghi, "The Role of Iranian Dual Nationals in Sanctions Evasion," Congressional Testimony before House Committee on Oversight and Gov ernment Reform, Foundation for Defense of Democracies, February 2016, https:// republicans-oversight.house.gov/wp-content/uploads/2016/02/2016-02-10-Otto lenghi-Testimony-Bio.pdf; Matthew Levitt, "Hezbollah's Procurement Channels: Le veraging Criminal Networks Partnering with Iran," *CTC Sentinel* 12, no. 3 (March 2019): 1–9; Emanuele Ottolenghi, *The Laundromat: Hezbollah's Money Laundering and Drug Trafficking Operations in Latin America*, Mideast Security and Policy Stud ies 194 (Ramat Gan: Begin-Sadat Center for Strategic Studies, Bar-Ilan University, 2021), https://besacenter.org/wp-content/uploads/2021/07/194web.pdf; Peter Kire chu, "Iran's Currency Laundromats in the Emirates," *CTC Sentinel* 14, no. 5 (June 2021): 26–31; "Under the Shadow of Illicit Economies in Iran," Global Initiative against Transnational Organized Crime, October 2020, https://globalinitiative.net /analysis/under-the-shadow-illicit-economies-in-iran/; Emanuel Ottolenghi, Ann Fixler, and Yaya J. Fanusie, "Flying under the Radar: Evasion in the Iranian Aviation Sector," Foundation for Defense of Democracies, July 2016, https://s3.us-east-2.am azonaws.com/defenddemocracy/uploads/documents/Ottolenghi_Fixler_Fanusie _Aviation_Sanctions_Evasion.pdf.

11. See Choe Sang-Hun, "North Koreans Trapped in 'State Sponsored Slavery' in Russia," *New York Times*, April 3, 2023, https://www.nytimes.com/2023/04/03/world/asia/north-korea-human-rights.html.

12. See Grant Rumley, "China's Security Presence in the Middle East: Redlines and Guidelines for the United States," Washington Institute for Near East Policy, October 2022, https://www.washingtoninstitute.org/pdf/view/17676/en.

13. See Dennis Ross, "A New Iran Deal Might Be on the Horizon," Washington Institute for Near East Policy, June 23, 2023, https://www.washingtoninstitute.org/policy-analysis/new-iran-nuclear-deal-might-be-horizon.

14. See Kerr and Hildreth, "Iran–North Korea–Syria."

15. See Tony Badran, Matthew Brodsky, and Jonathan Schanzer, "Controlled Chaos: The Escalation of Conflict between Israel and Iran in War-Torn Syria," Foundation for Defense of Democracies, July 2018, https://www.fdd.org/wp-content/uploads/2018/07/REPORT_ControlledChaos.pdf.

16. Annika Ganzeveld, "The Consequences of the IDF Strikes into Iran," Institute for the Study of War, last modified November 12, 2024, https://www.understandingwar.org/backgrounder/consequences-idf-strikes-iran.

17. Nicholas Carl, "Israeli Retaliatory Strikes on Iran," Institute for the Study of War, October 26, 2024, https://www.understandingwar.org/backgrounder/israeli-retaliatory-strikes-iran.

Selected Bibliography

Aarabi, Kasra. "Beyond Borders: The Expansionist Ideology of Iran's Islamic Revolutionary Guard Corps." Tony Blair Institute for Global Change, February 2020. https://institute.global/insights/geopolitics-and-security/beyond-borders-expansionist-ideology-irans-islamic-revolutionary-guard-corps.

Aarabi, Kasra, and Jemima Shelley. "Insights from the Streets of Iran: How Removal of the Hijab Became a Symbol of Regime Change." Tony Blair Institute for Global Change, November 2022. https://institute.global/policy/protests-and-polling-insights-streets-iran-how-removal-hijab-became-symbol-regime-change.

Adesnik, David, and Behnam Ben Taleblu. "Burning Bridge: The Iranian Land Corridor to the Mediterranean." Foundation for Defense of Democracies, June 2019. https://www.fdd.org/wp-content/uploads/2019/06/fdd-report-burning-bridge.pdf.

Ahrari, Ehsan M. *The Islamic Challenge and the United States: Global Security in an Age of Uncertainty*. Montreal: McGill-Queens University Press, 2017.

Alaaldin, Ranj. "Post-election Iraq and the Intra-Shiite War." Hudson Institute. Current Trends in Islamist Ideology, September 26, 2022. https://www.hudson.org/node/45283.

Albright, David. "The Iranian Nuclear Archive: Implications and Recommendations." Foundation for Defense of Democracies, February 25, 2019. https://www.fdd.org/analysis/2019/02/25/the-iranian-nuclear-archive-implications-and-recommendations/.

Albright, David, Sarah Burkhard, and Spencer Faragasso. "Alleged Sanctions Violations of UNSC Resolutions on North Korea for 2019/2020: The Number Is Increasing." Institute for Science and International Security, July 1, 2020. https://isis-online.org/isis-reports/detail/alleged-north-korea-sanctions-violations-2020/.

Albright, David, Sarah Burkhard, and Andrea Stricker. "Analysis of IAEA Verification and Monitoring Report—September 2021." Institute for Science and International Security, September 13, 2021. https://isis-online.org/isis-reports/detail/analysis-of-iaea-iran-verification-and-monitoring-report-september-2021/.

Alrifai, Oula. "In the Service of Ideology: Iran's Religious and Socio-economic Activities in Syria." Policy Note 100. Washington Institute for Near East Policy, March 2021. https://www.washingtoninstitute.org/policy-analysis/service-ideology-irans-religious-and-socioeconomic-activities-syria.

al-Tamimi, Aymenn. "The Evolution in Islamic State Administration: The Documentary Evidence." *Perspectives on Terrorism* 9, no. 4 (2019): 117–29.

al-Tamimi, Aymenn Jawad. "Idlib and Its Environs: The Narrowing Prospect for a Rebel Holdout Policy." Note 75. Washington Institute for Near East Policy, February 2020. https://www.washingtoninstitute.org/policy-analysis/view/idlib-and-its-environs-narrowing-prospects-for-a-rebel-holdout.

American Enterprise Institute. "Kingpins of Corruption: Targeting Transnational Organized Crime in Latin America." June 2017. https://www.aei.org/wp-content/uploads/2017/06/Kingpins-and-Corruption.pdf.

American Geophysical Union. "2017 North Korean Nuclear Test Order of Magnitude Larger Than Previous Tests, New Study Finds." June 3, 2019. https://news.agu.org/press-release/2017-north-korean-nuclear-test-order-of-magnitude-larger-than-previous-tests-new-study-finds/.

An, Nack, and Rose An. "North Korean Military Assistance." In *Communist Nations' Military Assistance*, edited by John F. Copper and Daniel S. Papp. New York: Routledge, 2018.

Anadolu Agency. "N. Korean Army Units Fighting for Syria Regime: Al-Zubi." April 2, 2016. https://www.aa.com.tr/en/world/n-korean-army-units-fighting-for-syria-regime-al-zubi/544517.

Ansari, Ali. "The Myth of the White Revolution: Mohammad Reza Shah, Modernization and the Consolidation of Power." *Middle East Studies* 37, no. 3 (2010): 1–24.

Ansari, Ali, and Kasra Aarabi. "Ideology and Iran's Revolution: How 1979 Changed the World." Tony Blair Institute for Global Change, February 2019. https://institute.global/policy/ideology-and-irans-revolution-how-1979-changed-world.

Asharq al-Awsat. "Israel Reveals Secret Iranian Gold Smuggling Trade to Finance Hezbollah." February 27, 2023. https://english.aawsat.com/home/article/4182031/israel-reveals-secret-iranian-gold-smuggling-trade-finance-hezbollah.

Asher, David. Interview by Bruce E. Bechtol Jr., February 17, 2022.

Atherton, Kelsey. "North Korea's Hackers Target Tech Secrets." *Breaking Defense*, October 30, 2020. https://breakingdefense.com/2020/10/north-koreas-hackers-target-tech-secrets/.

Australian Institute of International Affairs. "The Flow of Arms into the Gaza Strip." 2015. https://www.internationalaffairs.org.au/the-flow-of-arms-into-the-gaza-strip/.

Azad, Shirzad. *Iran and China: A New Approach to Their Bilateral Relations*. Lanham, MD: Lexington Books, 2017.

Badran, Tony, Matthew Brodsky, and Jonathan Schanzer. "Controlled Chaos: The Escalation of Conflict between Israel and Iran in War-Torn Syria." Foundation for Defense of Democracies, July 2018. https://www.fdd.org/wp-content/up loads/2018/07/REPORT_ControlledChaos.pdf.

Badran, Tony, and Emanuele Ottolenghi. "Hezbollah Finance in Lebanon: A Primary Source Review." Foundation for Defense of Democracies, August 2020. https://www.fdd.org/analysis/2020/09/23/hezbollah-finance-in-lebanon/.Baha dur, Jay. "Snapping Back against Iran: The Case of Al-Bari 2 and the UN Arms Embargo." Global Initiative against Transnational Organized Crime, December 2020. https://globalinitiative.net/wp-content/uploads/2020/11/Snapping-back -against-Iran-The-case-of-the-Al-Bari-2-and-the-UN-arms-embargo_GITOC.pdf.

Balanche, Fabrice. "Latest Battle in Idlib Could Send Another Wave of Refugees into Europe." Policy Watch 3259. Washington Institute for Near East Policy, February 2020. https://www.washingtoninstitute.org/policy-analysis/view/latest-battle -for-idlib-could-send-another-wave-of-refugees-to-europe.

———. "Sectarianism in Syria's Civil War: A Geopolitical Study." Washington Institute for Near East Policy, February 2018. https://www.washingtoninstitute.org /pdf/view/2442/en.

Baram, Amatzia. "Iran's Stakes in Syria." Geopolitical Intelligence Services, October 28, 2021. https://www.gisreportsonline.com/r/iran-syria/.Bartlett, Jason. "Why Is North Korea So Good at Cybercrime?" *Diplomat*, November 13, 2020. https:// thediplomat.com/2020/11/why-is-north-korea-so-good-at-cybercrime/.

Bechtol, Bruce E. "Are the Rockets Fired by Hamas into Israel Coming from North Korea?" *National Interest*, March 21, 2021. https://nationalinterest.org/blog /korea-watch/are-rockets-fired-hamas-israel-coming-north-korea-185729.

———. "Hwasong-18: The North Korean ICBM with 'Russian DNA'?" *1945*, August 21, 2023. https://www.19fortyfive.com/2023/08/hwasong-18-the-north -korean-icbm-with-russian-dna/?fbclid=IwAR3doiynF_r6HlG4DHtUXc1zj 9sA4yFBtMSdJ3eFavnPuGOY0gRoFJCszVs.

———. "North Korea, China and Iran: The Axis of Missiles?" *National Interest*, October 25, 2020. https://nationalinterest.org/blog/korea-watch/north-korea-china -and-iran-axis-missiles-171367.

———. "The North Korea–Russia Alliance Is a Dangerous Threat." *1945*, September 1, 2023. https://www.19fortyfive.com/2023/09/the-north-korea-russia-alliance -is-a-dangerous-threat/?fbclid=IwAR1m-TzA_W4j4r9pjuX-3ZJM1mP 37S3UQawqMTAOVsJ34DMPfaCYFH0fINo.

———. "Why the Iran–North Korea Missile Alliance Is Pure Trouble." *National Interest*, May 24, 2020. https://nationalinterest.org/blog/korea-watch/why-iran -north-korea-missile-alliance-pure-trouble-157351.

Bechtol, Bruce E., Jr. "Hamas Is Using North Korean Weapons against Israel." *1945*, October 24, 2023. https://www.19fortyfive.com/2023/10/hamas-is-using -north-korean-weapons-against-israel/.

———. "North Korean Illicit Activities and Sanctions: A National Security Dilemma." *Cornell International Law Journal* 51 (2018). https://ww3.lawschool.cor nell.edu/research/ILJ/upload/Bechtol-final.pdf.

————. *North Korean Military Proliferation in the Middle East and Africa: Enabling Violence and Instability*. Lexington. University Press of Kentucky, 2018.

Beeri, Tal. "Hezbollah's 'Land of Tunnels': The North Korean–Iranian Connection." Alma Research Center, July, 2021. https://israel-alma.org/wp-content/uploads/2021/08/Hezbollah-Land-of-Tunnels-the-North-Korean-Iranian-Connection.pdf.

Ben-David, Lenny. "Hamas' Advanced Weaponry: Rockets, Artillery, Drones, Cyber." No. 651. Jerusalem Center for Security and Foreign Affairs, August 2021, https://jcpa.org/article/hamas-advanced-weaponry-rockets-artillery-drones-cyber/.

Berger, Andrea. "North Korea, Hamas, and Hezbollah: Arm in Arm?" *38 North*, August 5, 2014. https://www.38north.org/2014/08/aberger080514/.

Bergman, Ronen. "Live Updates: Hopes for Israel-Hamas Ceasefire as International Pressure Grows." *New York Times*, May 20, 2021. https://www.nytimes.com/live/2021/05/20/world/israel-palestine-gaza.

Bermudez, Joseph S., Jr., Victor Cha, and Jennifer Jun. "Yongbyon Update: New Activity at Building 500 and Rising Waters." Beyond Parallel: Center for Strategic and International Studies, July 11, 2022. https://beyondparallel.csis.org/yongbyon-update-new-activity-at-building-500-and-rising-waters/.

Blanford, Nicholas. *Warriors of God: Inside Hezbollah's Thirty-Year Struggle against Israel*. New York: Random House, 2011.

Blinken, Antony J. "United States Designates Entities and Individuals Linked to the Democratic People's Republic of Korea's (DPRK) Weapons Programs." US Department of State, January 12, 2022. https://www.state.gov/united-states-designates-entities-and-individuals-linked-to-the-democratic-peoples-republic-of-koreas-dprk-weapons-programs/.

Bockmann, Michelle Wiese. "US Seizes Cameroon-Flagged Tanker for North Korea Sanctions Evasion." *Lloyd's List*, April 27, 2021. https://lloydslist.com/LL1136600/US-seizes-Cameroon-flagged-tanker-for-North-Korea-sanctions-evasion.

Boling, Andrew, Lucas Kuo, Luke Snyder, and Lauren Sung. "Unmasked Vessel Identity Laundering and North Korea's Maritime Sanctions Evasion." C4ADS, September 9, 2021. https://c4ads.org/reports/unmasked/.

Borshchevskaya, Anna. "Russia's Goals Go Beyond Damascus: Moscow's Middle East Resurgence." *Middle East Quarterly*, Winter 2018. https://www.meforum.org/middle-east-quarterly/russia-goals-go-beyond-damascus.

Bosworth, James. "Venezuela's Relations with Iran: Maduro's Lifesaver in 2020." In *Venezuela's Authoritarian Allies: The Ties That Bind?*, edited by Cynthia J. Arnson, 192–213. Washington, DC: Wilson Center, 2021.

Brands, Hal. "Paradoxes of the Gray Zone." FPRI, February 2016. https://www.fpri.org/article/2016/02/paradoxes-gray-zone/.

Brookings Institution and Institute for National Security Studies (Israel). "International Seminar: Tunnels, Missiles, Reactors: Understanding North Korea's Role in the Middle East." May 20, 2020. https://www.brookings.edu/events/webinar-tunnels-missiles-reactors-understanding-north-koreas-role-in-the-middle-east/.

Brumfiel, Geoff. "North Korea's Newest Missile Appears Similar to Advanced Russian Design." National Public Radio, May 8, 2019. https://www.npr.org/2019/05 /08/721135496/north-koreas-newest-missile-appears-similar-to-advanced -russian-design.

Bucala, Paul. "Iran's New Way of War in Syria." Institute for the Study of War, February 2017. https://www.understandingwar.org/sites/default/files/Iran%20 New%20Way%20of%20War%20in%20Syria_FEB%202017.pdf.

Bucala, Paul, and Marie Donovan. "A New Era in Iran's Military Leadership." Critical Threats, December 2016. https://www.criticalthreats.org/analysis/a-new-era-for -irans-military-leadership.

Byrne, James, Joseph Byrne, and Gary Somerville. "The Orient Express: North Korea's Clandestine Supply Route to Russia." Royal United Services Institute, October 16, 2023. https://rusi.org/explore-our-research/publications/commentary /report-orient-express-north-koreas-clandestine-supply-route-russia.

Car, Nicholas, Kitaneh Fitzpatrick, and Katherine Lawlor. "Russia and Iran Double Down on Their Strategic Partnership." Institute for the Study of War/American Enterprise Institute Critical Threats Project, August 11, 2022. https://www .understandingwar.org/backgrounder/russia-and-iran-double-down-their-strate gic-partnership.

Carisch, Enrico. Interview by Bruce E. Bechtol Jr., March 27, 2022.

Carlin, Maya. "North Korea and Iran: The Military Alliance That America Fears." 1945, May 2022. https://www.19fortyfive.com/2022/05/iran-north-korea-co operation-submarines-icbm/.

Carmi, Omer. "Deconstructing and Countering 'Iran's Threat Network.'" Washington Institute for Near East Policy, October 16, 2017. https://www.washingtonin stitute.org/policy-analysis/deconstructing-and-countering-iran-threat-network.

Carney, Matthew. "Defector Reveals Secrets of North Korea's Office 39, Raising Cash for Kim Jong-un." ABC News, January 5, 2018. https://www.abc .net.au/news/2018-01-06/north-korea-defector-reveals-secrets-of-office-39 /9302308.

Caves, John P., and Meghan Peri Crimmins. "Major Turkish Bank Prosecuted in Unprecedented Iran Sanctions Case." Wisconsin Project on Nuclear Arms Control, March 2020. https://www.iranwatch.org/our-publications/articles-reports/major -turkish-bank-prosecuted-unprecedented-iran-sanctions-evasion-case.

Celso, Anthony. "Sectarianism, Failed States and the Radicalization of Sunni Jihadist Groups." International Journal of Political Science 4. no. 2 (2018): 22–35.

———. "Superpower Hybrid Warfare in Syria." Marine Corps University Journal 9, no. 2 (2018): 92–116.

Center for Strategic and International Studies. "KN-09 (KN-SS-9)." Missile Threat: CSIS Missile Defense Project, July 31, 2021. https://missilethreat.csis.org/missile /kn-09-kn-ss-x-9/.

———. "KN-23 at a Glance." Missile Threat: CSIS Missile Defense Project, 2020. https://missilethreat.csis.org/missile/kn-23/.

———. "Safir." Missile Threat: CSIS Missile Defense Project, August 2, 2021. https://missilethreat.csis.org/missile/safir/.

———. "Shahab 3." Missile Threat: CSIS Missile Defense Project, July 31, 2021. https://missilethreat.csis.org/missile/shahab-3/.

Central Intelligence Agency. "Unclassified Report to Congress on the Acquisition of Technology Relating to Weapons of Mass Destruction and Advanced Conventional Munitions, 1 July through 31 December 2001." 2002. https://2001-2009.state.gov/p/sca/rls/16476.htm.

Cheong, Seong-Chang. "Stalinism and Kimilsungism: A Comparative Analysis of Ideology and Power." *Asian Perspective* 24, no. 1 (2000): 133–61. https://www.yumpu.com/en/document/view/5474328/stalinism-and-kimilsungism-columbia-law-school.

Chung, Chaewon, and Jeongmin Kim. "North Korea Shows Off Apparent New Solid Fuel Missile." *NK News*, April 26, 2022. https://www.nknews.org/2022/04/north-korea-rolls-out-long-range-hwasong-17-nuclear-missiles-at-military-parade/.

Cimpanu, Catalin. "Hackers Breach and Steal Data from South Korea's Defense Ministry." ZD Net, January 16, 2019. https://www.zdnet.com/article/hackers-breach-and-steal-data-from-south-koreas-defense-ministry/.

Clarke, Colin P. "Drugs and Thugs: Funding Terrorism through Narcotics Trafficking." *Journal of Strategic Security* 3, no. 4 (Fall 2016): 1–15.

Collins, Robert. *Marked for Life: Songbun, North Korea's Social Classification System.* Washington, DC: Committee for Human Rights in North Korea, 2012.

Congressional Research Service. "Iran: Internal Politics and US Policy and Options." December 2020. https://crsreports.congress.gov/product/pdf/RL/RL32048.

———. "Iranian Foreign and Defense Policies." January 2021. https://crsreports.congress.gov/product/pdf/R/R44017.

———. "Iran's Foreign and Defense Policies." December 11, 2018. https://crsreports.congress.gov/product/pdf/R/R44017/57t.

———. "North Korea: Relations with the Third World." June 1993. https://web.archive.org/web/20090917120827/http://www.country-data.com/cgi-bin/query/r-9642.html.

Cordesman, Anthony, and Bryan Gold. *The Gulf Military Balance: The Missile and Nuclear Connections.* Washington, DC: Center for Strategic and International Studies, 2014.

Cordesman, Anthony, and Abraham Wagner. *Lessons of Modern War: the Arab-Israeli Conflicts, 1973–1989.* New York: Westview Press, 1991.

Council on Foreign Relations. "Israel and Hezbollah: Deterrence and the Threat of Miscalculation." September 11, 2017. https://www.cfr.org/report/israel-and-hezbollah-deterrence-and-threat-miscalculation.

———. "North Korea's Military Capabilities." June 28, 2022. https://www.cfr.org/backgrounder/north-korea-nuclear-weapons-missile-tests-military-capabilities.

Cumings, Bruce, Ervand Abrahamian, and Moshe Ma'oz, *Inventing the Axis of Evil: The Truth about North Korea, Iran, and Syria.* New York: New Press, 2006.

Daoud, David. "Hezbollah Considers the United States, Not Israel, Its Greatest Enemy." Atlantic Council, April 30, 2020. https://www.atlanticcouncil.org/blogs /iransource/hezbollah-considers-the-united-states-not-israel-its-greatest-enemy/.

Defense Intelligence Agency. "Iran Military Power: Ensuring Regime Survival and Securing Regional Dominance." 2019. https://www.dia.mil/News-Features /Articles/Article-View/Article/2020456/ .

Dishman, Chris. "The Leaderless Nexus: When Crime and Terror Converge." *Studies in Conflict and Terrorism* 28 (2005): 237–52.

Doering, Jackson. "Washington's Militia Problem in Syria Is an Iran Problem." Policy Watch 2932. Washington Institute for Near East Policy, February 2018. https:// www.washingtoninstitute.org/policy-analysis/view/washingtons-militia-prob lem-in-syria-is-an-iran-problem.

Dolan, Daniel. "The North Korean Connection." *USNI News*, June 17, 2012. https:// news.usni.org/2012/06/17/north-korean-connection.

Doran, Michael, and Peter Rough. "China's Emerging Middle East Kingdom." *Tablet Magazine*, August 2020. https://www.tabletmag.com/sections/israel-middle-east /articles/china-middle-eastern-kingdom.

Dror, Yehezkel. "An Integrationist Imperative: Attack Iran and Launch a Regional Peace Initiative." BESA Center, May 2012. https://besacenter.org/wp-content /uploads/2012/05/iran.pdf.

Dubowitz, Mark, Reuel Marc Gerecht, and Behnam Ben Taleblu. "What Yes with Iran Looks Like." Foundation for Defense of Democracies, June 2019. https:// www.fdd.org/analysis/memos/2019/06/26/what-yes-with-iran-looks-like/.

Dunn, Morgan. "Inside Room 39, North Korea's Mysterious State-Run Slush Fund." *All That's Interesting*, June 10, 2021. https://allthatsinteresting.com/room-39.

Eisenstadt, Michael. "Has the Assad Regime 'Won' Syria's Civil War?" Washington Institute for Near East Policy, May 15, 2016. https://www.washingtoninstitute .org/policy-analysis/view/has-the-assad-regime-won-syrias-civil-war.

———. "Iran's Nuclear Hedging Strategy: Shaping the Islamic Republic's Proliferation Calculus." Policy Focus 178. Washington Institute for Near East Policy, November 2022. https://www.washingtoninstitute.org/policy-analysis/irans -nuclear-hedging-strategy-shaping-islamic-republics-proliferation-calculus.

———. "Operating in the Gray Zone: Countering Iran's Asymmetric Way of War." Policy Focus 162. Washington Institute for Near East Policy, 2020. https://www .washingtoninstitute.org/policy-analysis/view/operating-in-the-gray-zone-coun tering-irans-asymmetric-way-of-war.

———. "Rumors of War: Responding to Iranian Pushback in the Gulf." Washington Institute for Near East Policy, May 2019. https://www.washingtoninstitute .org/policy-analysis/view/rumors-of-war-responding-to-iranian-pushback-in-the -gulf.

————. "The Strategic Culture of the Islamic Republic of Iran." MES Monographs 1. Washington Institute for Near East Policy,. November 23, 2015 https://www.washingtoninstitute.org/policy-analysis/strategic-culture-islamic-repub lic-iran-religion-expediency-and-soft-power-era.

————. "The Strategic Culture of the Islamic Republic of Iran: Religion, Expediency, and Soft Power in an Era of Disruptive Change." Washington Institute for Near East Policy, November 2015. https://www.washingtoninstitute.org/policy-analy sis/strategic-culture-islamic-republic-iran-religion-expediency-and-soft-power-era.

————. "Were Iran and the United States Really 'on the Brink'? Observations on Gray Zone Conflict." Washington Institute for Near East Policy, September 2020. https://www.washingtoninstitute.org/policy-analysis/were-iran-and-united -states-really-brink-observations-gray-zone-conflict.

————. "What Iran's Chemical Past Tells Us about Its Nuclear Future." Washington Institute for Near East Policy, April 2014. https://www.washingtoninstitute.org /policy-analysis/what-irans-chemical-past-tells-us-about-its-nuclear-future.

————. "Working in the Gray Zone: Countering Iran's Asymmetric Way of War." Washington Institute for Near East Policy, January 2021. https://www.washing toninstitute.org/policy-analysis/operating-gray-zone-counter-iran.

Eisenstadt, Michael, and Mehdi Khalaji. "Nuclear Fatwa: Religion and Politics in Iran's Proliferation Strategy." Washington Institute for Near East Policy, September 2011. https://www.washingtoninstitute.org/policy-analysis/nuclear-fatwa-religion -and-politics-irans-proliferation-strategy.

Eisenstadt, Michael, and Michael Knights. "Beyond Worst-Case Analysis: Iran's Like- ly Response to an Israeli Preventive Strike." Washington Institute for Near East Pol- icy, June 2012. https://www.washingtoninstitute.org/media/3274?disposition= inline.

Elleman, Michael. "Iran's Ballistic Missile Program." Iran Primer. US Institute of Peace, January 13, 2021. https://iranprimer.usip.org/resource/irans-ballistic-missile -program.

————. "Preliminary Assessment of the KN-24 Missile Launches." *38 North*, March 25, 2020. https://www.38north.org/2020/03/melleman032520/.

Encila, Christian. "Hackers from North Korea Seen as Culprits in DeBridge Fi- nance Cyberattack." Bitcoinist, August 5, 2022. https://bitcoinist.com/hackers -suspects-in-debridge-attack/.

Eshel, Tamir. "Simorgh First Launch—an Iranian Success or Failure?" *Defense Update*, April 24, 2016. https://defense-update.com/20160424_simorgh.html.

Fabino, Alexander. "Russia Hurting Own Troops with Low-Quality Artillery: Ukraine." *Newsweek*, December 23, 2023. https://www.newsweek.com/russia -low-quality-artillery-north-korea-supply-ukraine-war-1855204.

Farah, Douglas. "Terrorist-Criminal Pipelines and Criminalized States: Emerging Alliances." *Prism* 2, no. 3 (January 2013): 1–32.

Filiu, Jean-Pierre. *Apocalypse in Islam*. Berkley: University of California Press, 2011.

Fitzpatrick, Mark. "North Korean Proliferation Challenges: The Role of the European Union." Non-proliferation Papers 18. EU Non-proliferation Consortium, June 2012. https://www.sipri.org/research/disarmament/eu-consortium/publications/nonproliferation-paper-18.

Fixler, Annie. "The Cyber Threat from Iran after the Death of Soleimani." *CTC Sentinel* 13, no. 2 (February 2020). https://ctc.westpoint.edu/cyber-threat-iran-death-soleimani/.

———. "Iran: Dangers of Iran's Cyber Ambitions." In "The Attack on America's Future," by Samantha F. Ravich and Annie Fixler, 50–61. Foundation for Defense of Democracies, November 2022. https://www.fdd.org/analysis/2022/10/28/the-attack-on-americas-future-cyber-enabled-economic-warfare/.

Fixler, Annie, and Frank Cilluffo. "Evolving Menace: Iran's Use of Cyber-Enabled Warfare." Foundation for Defense of Democracies, November 2018. https://www.fdd.org/analysis/2018/11/06/evolving-menace/.

Forozan, Hesam, and Afshin Shahi. "The Military and the State in Iran: The Economic Rise of the Revolutionary Guards." *Middle East Journal* 71, no. 1 (Winter 2017): 67–86.

Foundation for Defense of Democracies. "Yono Class (Ghadir)." Military Edge, 2017. https://militaryedge.org/armaments/ghadir/.

Frantzman, Seth J. "Can Iron Dome Cut It for Indirect Fire Protection? US Army Is Buying a Couple Systems to Find Out." *Defense News*, February 6, 2019. https://www.defensenews.com/global/mideast-africa/2019/02/06/can-iron-dome-cut-it-for-indirect-fire-protection-us-army-is-buying-a-couple-systems-to-find-out/.

Gady, Franz-Stefan. "Is North Korea Fighting for Assad in Syria?" *Diplomat*, March 24, 2016. https://thediplomat.com/2016/03/is-north-korea-fighting-for-assad-in-syria/.

Gallucci, Robert L. "North Korea, Iran, and the Proliferation of Nuclear Weapons: The Threat, U.S. Policy, and the Prescription . . . and the India Deal." In *How to Make America Safe: New Policies for National Security*, edited by Stephen Van Evera. Cambridge, MA: Tobin Project, 2006. https://www.tobinproject.org/sites/tobinproject.org/files/assets/Make_America_Safe_North_Korea_Iran_Nuclear_Proliferation.pdf.

Garfinkle, Adam. "The Chemistry of Syrian Lies and US Credulity Revealed." Foreign Policy Research Institute, October 2016. https://www.fpri.org/article/2016/10/chemistry-syrian-lies-u-s-credulity-revealed/.

Gerecht, Reuel Marc. "Iran: The Shi'ite Imperial Power." Foundation for Defense of Democracies, May 2018. https://www.fdd.org/analysis/2018/05/20/iran-the-shiite-imperial-power/.

Ghaddar, Hanin. "Iran Occupies Lebanon via Proxy, but the Lebanese Still Have Agency." Caravan. Hoover Institution, October 13, 2022. https://www.hoover.org/research/iran-occupies-lebanon-proxy-lebanese-still-have-agency.

————. "Iran's Foreign Legion: The Impact of Shia Militias on U.S. Foreign Policy." Policy Notes. Washington Institute for Near East Policy, 2018. https://www
.washingtoninstitute.org/policy-analysis/view/irans-foreign-legion-the-impact
-of-shia-militias-on-u.s.-foreign-policy.

Ghasseminejad, Saeed, and Mohammad R. Jahan-Parvar. "The Impact of Financial Sanctions: The Case of Iran, 2011–2016." International Financial Discussion Papers. Board of Governors of the Federal Reserve System, May 2020. https://
www.federalreserve.gov/econres/ifdp/files/ifdp1281.pdf.

Ghattas, Kim. *Black Wave: Saudi Arabia, Iran, and the Forty-Year Rivalry That Unraveled Culture, Religion, and Collective Memory in the Middle East*. New York: Henry Holt, 2020.

Giles, Joshua. *Withdrawing under Fire: Lessons Learned from Islamist Insurgencies*. Washington, DC: Potomac Books, 2011.

Global Initiative against Transnational Organized Crime. "Under the Shadow of Illicit Economies in Iran." October 2020. https://globalinitiative.net/analysis
/under-the-shadow-illicit-economies-in-iran/.

GlobalSecurity.org. "KN-24 [Hwasong-11] Tactical Missile System." August 5, 2022. https://www.globalsecurity.org/wmd/world/dprk/kn-24.htm.

————. "Yono Class / Ghadir Class Midget Submarine." 2017. https://www
.globalsecurity.org/military/world/iran/ghadir.htm.

Goldberg, Ilan, Nicholas Heras, Kaleigh Thomas, and Jennie Matuschak, "Countering Iran in the Gray Zone: What the US Should Learn from Israeli Operations in Syria." Center for a New American Security, April 2020, https://www.cnas.org
/publications/reports/countering-iran-gray-zone.

Goldstein, William. "Secularization and the Iranian Revolution." *Journal of Islamic Perspectives*, no. 3 (2020): 50–67.

Golkar, Saeid, and Kasra Aarabi. "The View from Tehran: Iran's Militia Doctrine." Tony Blair Institute for Global Change, February 2021. https://institute.global
/insights/geopolitics-and-security/view-tehran-irans-militia-doctrine.

Goodarzi, Jubin. "Iran and Syria." Iran Primer. United States Institute of Peace, October 11, 2020. https://iranprimer.usip.org/resource/iran-and-syria.

Guimarães, Bruno Gomes. "North Korea: Ideology, War, and Violence." *Revista Conjunto Austral* 5 (2014). https://www.academia.edu/23681889/North_Korea_ide
ology_war_and_violence.

Habibi, Nader. "The Impact of Sanctions on Iran-GCC Economic Relations." Middle East Brief. Brandeis University Middle East Studies, November 2010. https://
www.brandeis.edu/crown/publications/middle-east-briefs/pdfs/1-100/meb45
.pdf.

Hamilton, Robert, Chris Miller, and Aaron Stein, eds. *Russia's War in Syria: Assessing Russian Military Capabilities and Lessons Learned*. Philadelphia: FPRI, 2020. https://www.fpri.org/research/eurasia/russias-war-in-syria-assessing-russian
-military-capabilities-and-lessons-learned/.

Hansen, Nick, Robert Kelley, and Allison Puccioni. "North Korean Nuclear Programme Advances." *Janes Intelligence Review*, March 30, 2016. https://www.janes.com/article/59118/north-korean-nuclear-programme-advances.

Hardie, John. "Iran Aids Russia's Imperialist War against Ukraine." *Algemeiner*. Foundation for Defense of Democracies, November 22, 2022. https://www.fdd.org/analysis/2022/11/22/iran-aids-russias-imperialist-war.

Harel, Amos, and Avi Issacharoff. *34 Days: Israel, Hezbollah, and the War in Lebanon*. New York: Palgrave McMillian, 2008.Hayden, Michael V. "The CIA's Counterproliferation Efforts." Address to the Los Angeles World Affairs Council, September 16, 2008. https://www.lawac.org/speech/2008-09/hayden,michael2008.pdf.

Hendel, Yoaz. "Iran's Nukes and Israel's Dilemma." *Middle East Quarterly* 19, no. 1 (Winter 2012): 31–38.

Herzog, Michael. "Contextualizing Israeli Concerns over the Iranian Nuclear Deal." Washington Institute for Near East Policy, June 2015. https://www.washingtoninstitute.org/policy-analysis/view/contextualizing-israeli-concerns-about-the-iran-nuclear-deal.

———. "The Growing Risk of an Israel-Iran Confrontation in Syria." Washington Institute for Near East Policy, December 2017. https://www.washingtoninstitute.org/policy-analysis/growing-risk-israel-iran-confrontation-syria.

———. "Iran across the Border: Israel's Pushback in Syria." Policy Note 66. Washington Institute for Near East Policy, July 2019. https://www.washingtoninstitute.org/policy-analysis/view/iran-across-the-border-israels-pushback-in-syria.

Hollings, Alex. "Could China Be Funneling Missile Technology to North Korea through Iran?" *SOFREP: Special Forces News*, May 6, 2017. https://sofrep.com/80694/china-funneling-missile-technology-north-korea-iran/.

Hughes, Robin. "Tehran Takes Steps to Protect Nuclear Facilities." *Jane's Defence Weekly*, January 25, 2006, 4–5.

Humire, Joseph. "The Maduro-Hezbollah Nexus: How Iran-Backed Networks Prop Up the Venezuelan Regime." Atlantic Council, October 2020. https://www.atlanticcouncil.org/in-depth-research-reports/issue-brief/the-maduro-hezbollah-nexus-how-iran-backed-networks-prop-up-the-venezuelan-regime/.

Inbar, Tal. Interview by Bruce E. Bechtol Jr., Tel Aviv, August 22, 2022.

Intelligence Online. "Hezbollah: A North Korea–Type Guerilla Force." August 25, 2006. https://www.intelligenceonline.com/political-intelligence/2006/08/25/hezbollah-a-north-korea-type-guerila-force,21788114-EVE.

———. "Pyongyang in Talks with Moscow on Access to Donbass." June 20, 2022. https://www.intelligenceonline.com/government-intelligence/2022/06/20/pyongyang-in-talks-with-moscow-on-access-to-donbass,109793254-art.

International Atomic Energy Agency. *Board of Governors Report*, March 2020. https://www.iaea.org/iaea-director-generals-introductory-statement-to-the-board-of-governors-1-march-2021.

Iran Watch. "Iran and North Korea Resumed Cooperation on Missiles, U.N. Says." February 8, 2021. https://www.iranwatch.org/news-brief/iran-north-korea-resumed -cooperation-missiles-un-says.

———. "Iran Missile Milestones: 1984–2023." March 29, 2023. https://www .iranwatch.org/our-publications/weapon-program-background-report/iran -missile-milestones-1985-2020.

———. "Iran Missile Program: Past and Present." June 2020. https://www.iranwatch .org/sites/default/files/iran-missile-program-past-present.pdf.

Jahanbani, Nakissa, and Suzanne Weedon Levy. "Iran Entangled: Iran and Hezbollah's Support to Proxies Operating in Syria." Combatting Terrorism Center at West Point, April 2022. https://ctc.westpoint.edu/iran-entangled-iran-and-hezbol lahs-support-to-proxies-operating-in-syria/.

Janes Intelligence Review. "North Korea Modernises Submarine Fleet." May 10, 2016. https://www.janes360.com/images/assets/463/57463/North_Korea_modernises _submarine_fleet1.pdf.

Jang, Seulkee. "Inside N. Korea's Internet-Based Foreign Currency-Earning Activities." *Daily NK*, December 20, 2022. https://www.dailynk.com/english/inside -north-korea-internet-based-foreign-currency-earning-activities/.

———. "N. Korea Expands the Number of Soldiers Going Abroad to Earn Foreign Currency." *Daily NK*, May 13, 2021. https://www.dailynk.com/english /north-korea-expands-number-soldiers-going-abroad-earn-foreign-curren cy/#:~:text=In%20fact%2C%2090%25%20of%20the,compared%20to%20or dinary%20civilian%20workers.

———. "N. Korea Has Selected Workers to Be Dispatched to Eastern Ukraine." *Daily NK*, August 5, 2022. https://www.dailynk.com/english/north-korea-select ed-workers-dispatched-eastern-ukraine/.

———. "North Korea Neglects to Recall Malaysia-Based Officials Focused on Smuggling." *Daily NK*, April 1, 2021. https://www.dailynk.com/english/north-korea -neglects-recall-malaysia-officials-focused-smuggling/.

Jones, Seth. "War by Proxy: Iran's Growing Footprint in the Middle East." Center for Strategic and International Studies, March 2019. https://www.csis.org /war-by-proxy.

Kadivar, Mohammad Ali. "Ayatollah and the Republic: The Religious Establishment in Iran and Its Interactions with the Islamic Republic." *Project on Middle East Political Science Studies: New Analysis of Shia Politics*, December 2017, 6–9.

Katzman, Kenneth. "Iran's Foreign and Defense Policies." Congressional Research Service, April 29, 2020. https://fas.org/sgp/crs/mideast/R44017.pdf.

———. "Iran's Long-Range Missile Capabilities." Wisconsin Project on Nuclear Arms Control. Iran Watch, July 15, 1998. https://www.iranwatch.org/library /government/united-states/congress/legislation-reports/irans-long-range-mis sile-capabilities.

Kennedy, Dana. "Inside 'Office 39': North Korea's Illicit Global Smuggling Network." *New York Post*, June 27, 2020. https://nypost.com/2020/06/27/inside-office-39-north-koreas-illicit-global-smuggling-network/.

Kerr, Paul, and Steven Hildreth. "Iran–North Korea–Syria Ballistic Missile and Nuclear Cooperation." Congressional Research Service, February 2016. https://crsreports.congress.gov/product/pdf/R/R43480.

Khalaji, Mehdi. "Apocalyptic Politics: On the Rationality of Iranian Politics." Washington Institute for Near East Policy, January 2008. https://www.washingtoninstitute.org/policy-analysis/apocalyptic-politics-rationality-iranian-policy.

Khoshnood, Arvin. "The Dangers of Lifting Sanctions on the Islamic Republic of Iran." Perspectives Paper 1907. BESA Center, January 2020. https://besacenter.org/lifting-iran-sanctions/.

Khrustalev, Vladimir. "Thermonuclear Shock: A Detailed Analysis of the Explosion of the DPRK's Hydrogen Bomb and Its Consequences." Defcon Warning System, September 8, 2017. https://defconwarningsystem.com/2017/09/08/thermonuclear-shock-detailed-analysis-explosion-dprks-hydrogen-bomb-consequences/.

Killebrew, Robert. "Criminal Insurgency in the Americas and Beyond." *Prism* 2, no. 3 (January 2013): 33–52.

Knights, Michael. "Soleimani Is Dead: The Road Ahead for Iranian-Backed Militias." *CTC Sentinel* 13, no. 1 (2020): 1–10.

———. "Yemen's Southern Hezbollah: Implementing Houthi Missile and Drone Improvements." Policy Watch 3463. Washington Institute for Near East Policy, April 2021. https://www.washingtoninstitute.org/pdf/view/16639/en.

Knights, Michael, Adnan al-Gabarni, and Casey Coombs. "The Houthi Jihad Council: Command and Control in 'the Other Hezbollah.'" *CTC Sentinel* 15 (October 2022). https://ctc.usma.edu/the-houthi-jihad-council-command-and-control-in-the-other-hezbollah/.

Kozak, Christopher. "The Strategic Convergence of Russia and Iran." Institute for the Study of War, February 2017. https://understandingwar.org/backgrounder/strategic-convergence-russia-and-iran.

Kranz, Kathrin. "North Korean Conglomerates: Their Arms Connection, and Sanction Busting Activities." Compliance and Capacity Skills International, 2023. https://ccsi.global/north-korean-conglomerates/.

Kumar, Abhishek. "Revisiting the Nuclear Nexus between Pakistan, China, and North Korea." Institute for Security and Development Policy, January 5, 2023. https://isdp.se/revisiting-the-nuclear-nexus-between-pakistan-china-and-north-korea/.

Lakshmanan, Ravie. "North Korean Hackers Are Targeting ATMs in India with New Data-Stealing Malware." Next Web, September 14, 2019. https://thenextweb.com/news/north-korean-hackers-are-targeting-atms-in-india-with-new-data-stealing-malware.

Lane, Ashley. "Iran's Islamist Proxies in the Middle East." Wilson Center, December 5, 2022. https://www.wilsoncenter.org/article/irans-islamist-proxies.

Lee, Daehan. "North Korea Fires Possible Pukguksong-5 SLBM." *Naval News*, October 19, 2021. https://www.navalnews.com/naval-news/2021/10/north-korea-fires-possible-pukguksong-ballistic-missile/.

Lee, Hyun-Seung. Interview by Bruce E. Bechtol Jr., February 14, 2022.

———. Interview by Bruce E. Bechtol Jr., March 27, 2022.

Lee, Joyce. "North Korea Says It Successfully Tested New Submarine-Launched Ballistic Missile." Reuters, October 19, 2019. https://www.reuters.com/article/us-northkorea-missiles/north-korea-says-it-successfully-tested-new-submarine-launched-ballistic-missile-idUSKBN1WH2GS.

Levin, Daniel. "Iran, Hamas and Palestinian Islamic Jihad." Iran Primer. United States Institute of Peace, July 9, 2018. https://iranprimer.usip.org/blog/2018/jul/09/iran-hamas-and-palestinian-islamic-jihad.

Levitt, Matthew. "Breaking Hezbollah's Golden Rule: An Inside Look at the Modus Operandi of Hezbollah's Islamic Jihad Organization." *Perspectives on Terrorism* 14, no. 4: (2020) 21–42.

———. "Fighters without Borders: Forecasting New Trends in the Iran Threat." *CTC Sentinel* 13, no. 2 (2020): 1–8.

———. "Hezbollah Finances: Funding the Party of God." Washington Institute, February 2005. https://www.washingtoninstitute.org/policy-analysis/view/hezbollah-finances-funding-the-party-of-god.

———. "Hezbollah Prioritizes Its Own Interests: Putting Lebanon at Risk." Washington Institute for Near East Policy, October 2019. https://www.washingtoninstitute.org/policy-analysis/hezbollah-prioritizes-its-own-interests-putting-lebanon-risk.

———. "Hezbollah's Corruption Crisis Runs Deep." Washington Institute for Near East Policy, July 2018. https://www.washingtoninstitute.org/pdf/view/2158/en.

———. "Hezbollah's Criminal Networks: Useful Idiots, Henchmen, and Organized Criminal Facilitators." Washington Institute for Near East Policy, October 2016. https://www.washingtoninstitute.org/policy-analysis/hezbollahs-criminal-networks-useful-idiots-henchmen-and-organized-criminal.

———. "Hezbollah's Procurement Channels: Leveraging Criminal Networks Partnering with Iran." *CTC Sentinel* 12, no. 3 (March 2019): 1–9.

———. "Hizbollah and the Qods Force in Iran's Shadow War with the West." Washington Institute for Near East Policy, January 2013. https://www.washingtoninstitute.org/policy-analysis/hizballah-and-qods-force-irans-shadow-war-west.

———. "In Search of Nuance in the Debate over Hezbollah's Criminal Operations and the U.S. Response." *Lawfare Research Paper Series* 5, no. 3 (March 2018): 1–34.

———. "Iranian and Hezbollah Operations in South America: Then and Now." *Prism* 5 (April 2016). https://cco.ndu.edu/Portals/96/Documents/prism/prism_5-4/Iranian%20and%20Hezbollah.pdf.

———. "Major Beneficiaries of the Iran Deal: IRGC and Hezbollah." Washington Institute for Near East Policy, September 17, 2015. https://www.washington

institute.org/policy-analysis/view/major-beneficiaries-of-the-iran-deal-irgc-and -hezbollah.

———. "On Bombing Anniversary, Iran Still Engaged in Illicit Activity." *Hill*, July 2017. https://www.washingtoninstitute.org/policy-analysis/bombing-anniversary -iran-still-engaged-illicit-activity.

Levitt, Matthew, Katherine Bauer, Danielle Camner Lindholm, Celina Realuyo, Jodi Vittori and Peter Neuman. "Can Bankers Fight Terrorism?" *Foreign Affairs*, October 2017. https://www.foreignaffairs.com/articles/2017-10-16/can-bankers -fight-terrorism.

Levy, Ido. "How Iran Fuels Hamas Terrorism." Washington Institute for Near East Policy, July 2021. https://www.washingtoninstitute.org/policy-analysis/how-iran -fuels-hamas-terrorism.

Lewis, Jeffrey. "DPRK RV Video Analysis." Arms Control Wonk, November 9, 2018. https://www.armscontrolwonk.com/archive/1206084/dprk-rv-video-analysis/.

Lintner, Bertil. "North Korea's Link to Hamas." *Global Asia* 18, no. 4 (December 2023). https://www.globalasia.org/v18no4/feature/north-koreas-link-to-hamas _bertil-lintner.

Liu, Jack. "North Korea's Yongbyon Nuclear Facility: New Activity at the Plutonium Production Complex." *38 North*, September 8, 2015. https://38north.org /2015/09/yongbyon090815/.

Lob, Eric. "Iran and Cryptocurrency: Opportunities and Obstacles for the Regime." Middle East Institute, December 27, 2022. https://www.mei.edu/publications /iran-and-cryptocurrency-opportunities-and-obstacles-regime.

Lorber, Eric. "Schemes and Subversion: How Bad Actors and Foreign Governments Undermine and Evade Sanctions Regimes." Congressional Testimony for the House Committee on Financial Services. Foundation for Defense of Democracies, June 16, 2021. https://www.fdd.org/analysis/2021/06/16/schemes-and-sub version/.

Lund, Aaron. "Red Line Redux: How Putin Tore Up Obama's 2013 Syria Deal." Century Foundation, February 3, 2017. https://tcf.org/content/report/red-line -redux-putin-tore-obamas-2013-syria-deal/?agreed=1.

Majidyar, Ahmad. "U.S. Officials: Iran's Latest Missile Launch Hints Tehran-Pyongyang Cooperation." Middle East Institute, May 5, 2017. https://www.mei.edu /content/io/us-officials-iran-s-latest-missile-launch-hints-tehran-pyongyang-co operation.

Mallory, King. *North Korean Sanctions: Evasion Techniques*. Santa Monica, CA: RAND, 2021. https://www.rand.org/content/dam/rand/pubs/research_reports /RRA1500/RRA1537-1/RAND_RRA1537-1.pdf.

Maloney, Suzanne. "Major Beneficiaries of the Iran Deal: The IRGC and Hezbollah." Testimony. Brookings Institution, September 17, 2015. https://www .brookings.edu/testimonies/major-beneficiaries-of-the-iran-deal-the-irgc-and -hezbollah/.

————. "The Roots and Evolution of Iran's Regional Strategy." Atlantic Council, September 2017. https://www.atlanticcouncil.org/in-depth-research-reports/issue -brief/the-roots-drivers-and-evolution-of-iran-s-regional-strategy/.

Mansharof, Yossi. "The Relationship between Iran and Palestinian Islamic Jihad." Jerusalem Institute for Strategy and Security, February 27, 2020. https://jiss .org.il/wp-content/uploads/2020/02/mansharof-yossi-relationship-between -iran-and-pij-jiss-english-27-02-2020.pdf.

Mansourov, Alexandre. "North Korea: Entering Syria's Civil War." 38 North, November 24, 2013. https://www.38north.org/2013/11/amansourov112513/#_edn13.

McEachern, Patrick, and Jaclyn O'Brien McEachern. North Korea, Iran and the Challenge to International Order: A Comparative Perspective. Milton Park: Routledge, 2017.

McLaughlin, Jonathan. "North Korea Missile Milestones, 1969–2017." Wisconsin Project, January 23, 2018. https://www.wisconsinproject.org/north-korea-missile -milestones/.

Michetti, Tim. "A Guide to Illicit Iranian Weapons Transfers: The Bahraini File." Atlantic Council, December 2020. https://www.atlanticcouncil.org/in-depth -research-reports/report/a-guide-to-illicit-iranian-weapon-transfers-the-bahrain -file/.

Middle East Eye. "Assad Planning to Visit North Korea: Report." June 4, 2018. https:// www.middleeasteye.net/news/assad-planning-visit-north-korea-report.

Military Watch. "Bulsae-3 in South Lebanon: How Hezbollah Upgraded Its Anti -Armour Capabilities with North Korean Assistance." September 2, 2019. https://militarywatchmagazine.com/article/bulsae-3-in-south-lebanon-how -hezbollah-upgraded-its-anti-armour-capabilities-with-north-korean-assistance.

Missile Defense Advocacy Alliance. "Iskander-M (SS-26)." August 12, 2019. https:// missiledefenseadvocacy.org/missile-threat-and-proliferation/todays-missile -threat/russia/iskander-m-ss-26/.

Mizokami, Kyle. "No, North Korea's Tank Isn't the Best in the World. Not Even Close." Popular Mechanics, June 23, 2021. https://www.popularmechanics.com /military/weapons/a36805563/north-korea-storm-tiger-tank/.

Mneimneh, Hassan. "Washington Should Recognize the Russian Strategic Achievement in Syria." Washington Institute for Near East Policy, May 29, 2018. https://www.washingtoninstitute.org/fikraforum/view/washington-should -recognize-the-russian-strategic-achievement-in-syria.

Moghadam, Assaf. The Nexus of Global Jihad: Understanding Cooperation between Terrorist Actors. New York: Columbia University Press, 2019.

Mun Dong Hui. "N. Korean Hackers Mount Phishing Attack on NKHR Groups." Daily NK, December 30, 2019. https://www.dailynk.com/english/north-korean -hackers-mount-phishing-attack-nkhr-groups/#:~:text=Korean%20hackers%20 mount%20phishing%20attack%20on%20NKHR%20groups,-Experts% 20suggest%20that&text=On%20Dec.,North%20Korea%27s%20human%20 rights%20violations.

Murray, Lori Esposito. "Can Syria's Chemical Weapons Be Stopped?" Interview by Robert McMahon. Council on Foreign Relations, April 16, 2018. https://www .cfr.org/interview/can-syrias-chemical-weapons-be-stopped.

Nadimi, Farzin. "Iran and China Are Strengthening Their Military Ties." Washington Institute for Near East Policy, November 2016. https://www.washingtoninsti tute.org/pdf/view/3176/en.

———. "Iran and Israel's Undeclared War at Sea (Part II): The Potential for Military Escalation." Washington Institute for Near East Policy, April 2021. https://www.washingtoninstitute.org/policy-analysis/iran-and-israels-unde clared-war-sea-part-2-potential-military-escalation.

———. "Iran and Russia's Growing Defense Ties." Washington Institute for Near East Policy, February 2015. https://www.washingtoninstitute.org/policy-analysis /iran-and-russias-growing-defense-ties.

———. "Iran's Afghan and Pakistani Proxies: Syria and Beyond." Washington Institute for Near East Policy, August 2016. https://www.washingtoninstitute.org /pdf/view/3341/en.

———. "Iran's Atlantic Voyage: Implications of Naval Deployments to Venezuela or Syria." Washington Institute for Near East Policy, June 2021. https://www .washingtoninstitute.org/policy-analysis/irans-atlantic-voyage-implications -naval-deployments-venezuela-or-syria.

———. "Iran's Evolving Approach to Asymmetric Naval War: Strategies and Capabilities in the Persian Gulf." Washington Institute for Near East Policy, April 2020. https://www.washingtoninstitute.org/policy-analysis/irans-evolving-approach -asymmetric-naval-warfare-strategy-and-capabilities-persian.

———. "Iran's Latest Missile Launch: Scenarios and Implications for the New Administration." Washington Institute for Near East Policy, February 2017. https:// www.washingtoninstitute.org/policy-analysis/irans-latest-missile-test-scenari os-and-implications-new-administration.

———. "Iran's Military Establishment Doubles Down on the Revolution." Policy Watch 3482. Washington Institute for Near East Policy, May 2021. https://www .washingtoninstitute.org/pdf/view/2546/en.

———. "Iran's National Army Reorganizes." Washington Institute for Near East Policy, August 2017. https://www.washingtoninstitute.org/policy-analysis/irans-na tional-army-reorganizes.

———. "Iran's New Ballistic Missile May Have North Korean ICBM Links." Washington Institute for Near East Policy, September 2017. https://www.washington institute.org/policy-analysis/irans-new-ballistic-missile-may-have-north-korean -icbm-links.

———. "Iran's Potential Military Reaction to New US Sanctions." Washington Institute for Near East Policy, November 2017. https://www.washingtoninstitute.org /policy-analysis/irans-potential-military-reactions-new-us-sanctions.

———. "New Iranian Bill Aims to Officialize a Policy of Avenging Soleimani and Destroying Israel." Washington Institute for Near East Policy, January 2021.

https://www.washingtoninstitute.org/policy-analysis/new-iranian-bill-aims-offi
cialize-policy-avenging-soleimani-and-destroying-israel.

Nasr, Vali. *The Shia Revival: How Conflicts within Islam Will Shape the Future*. New
York: W. W. Norton, 2006.

Nelson, Nate. "North Korea's Top APT Swindled $1B from Crypto Investors in 2022."
Dark Reading, January 25, 2023. https://www.darkreading.com/remote-work
force/north-korea-apt-swindled-1b-crypto-investors-2022.

Neuman, Scott. "North Korea Reportedly Sending Missile, Chemical Weapons Parts
to Syria." *Two-Way*. National Public Radio, February 28, 2018. https://www.npr
.org/sections/thetwo-way/2018/02/28/589401924/north-korea-reportedly
-sending-missile-chemical-weapons-parts-to-syria.

Newman, Stephanie G. "Arms, Aid, and the Superpowers." *Foreign Affairs*, June 1, 1988.
https://www.foreignaffairs.com/articles/russian-federation/1988-06-01/arms
-aid-and-superpowers.

Niebergall, Ross. "North Korean Hypersonic Threat Is an Alarming Wake-Up Call for
How We Innovate." *Defense News*, January 21, 2022. https://www.defensenews
.com/opinion/commentary/2022/01/21/north-korean-hypersonic-threat-is-an
-alarming-wake-up-call-for-how-we-innovate/.

Nikitin, Mary Beth. "North Korea's Nuclear Weapons: Technical Issues." RL34256.
Congressional Research Service, April 3, 2013. https://www.fas.org/sgp/crs/nuke
/RL34256.pdf.

Niksch, Larry. "The Iran–North Korea Strategic Relationship." Institute for
Corean-American Studies, July 28, 2015. https://www.icasinc.org/2015/2015l
/2015llan.html.

———. "North Korea Terrorism List Removal." Congressional Research Service, January 6, 2010. https://fpc.state.gov/documents/organization/137273.pdf.

Noland, Marcus, and Sherman Robinson. "Rigorous Speculation: The Collapse and
Revival of the North Korean Economy." Working Papers 99-1. Peterson Institute for International Economics, January 1999. https://www.piie.com/publi
cations/working-papers/rigorous-speculation-collapse-and-revival-north-korean
-economy.

NORSAR. "The Nuclear Explosion in North Korea on 3 September 2017: A Revised
Magnitude Assessment." September 12, 2017. https://www.norsar.no/i-fokus
/summing-up-the-nuclear-test-in-north-korea-on-3-september-2017.

Nuclear Threat Initiative. "Arms Control and Proliferation Profile: Syria." 2022.
https://www.armscontrol.org/factsheets/arms-control-and-proliferation-pro
file-syria#Missiles.

———. "Will Iran's Simorgh Space Launcher Appear in North Korea?" July 8, 2016.
https://www.nti.org/analysis/articles/will-irans-simorgh-space-launcher-appear
-north-korea/.

O, Tara. "How North Korea Launders Money Using Cryptocurrency to Evade Sanctions." East Asia Research Center, October 8, 2022. https://eastasiaresearch

.org/2022/10/08/how-north-korea-launders-money-using-cryptocurrency-to
-evade-sanctions/.

O'Carroll, Chad. "Gold, Drugs, Missiles: North Korea's Attempted Illegal Sales through
the KFA." *NK News*, October 11, 2020. https://www.nknews.org/2020/10/gold
-drugs-missiles-north-koreas-attempted-illegal-sales-through-the-kfa/.

———. "UN: Syria Invited at Least 800 North Koreans to Work in Military, Construction." *NK News*, August 6, 2020. https://www.nknews.org/2020/08/un-syria
-invited-at-least-800-north-koreans-to-work-in-military-construction/.

———. "UN Panel of Experts: How Cold War Squabbling Hinders North Korea
Sanctions." *NK News*, October 1, 2020. https://www.nknews.org/pro/panel-of
-experts-how-cold-war-squabbling-hinders-north-korea-sanctions/.

O'Carroll, Chad, and John G. Grisafi. "North Korea's Million Man Army: Potential
Mercenary Force?" *NK News*, May 15, 2015. https://www.nknews.org/2015/05
/north-koreas-million-man-army-potential-mercenary-force/.

Office of the Director of National Intelligence. "Background Briefing with Senior
Intelligence Officials on Syria's Covert Nuclear Reactor and North Korea's Involvement." April 24, 2008. https://irp.fas.org/news/2008/04/odni042408.pdf.

Oh Taek-sung. "International Cooperation Called Key to Curbing North Korea's
Sanctions Evasion." Voice of America, September 19, 2019. https://www.voan
ews.com/a/east-asia-pacific_more-international-cooperation-called-key-curbing
-north-koreas-sanction-evasion/6176138.html.

Olson, Erik. "Iran's Path Dependent Military Doctrine." *Strategic Studies Quarterly*
10, no. 2 (Summer 2016). https://www.airuniversity.af.edu/Portals/10/SSQ/doc
uments/Volume-10_Issue-2/Olson.pdf.

Open Nuclear Network. "Update on the DPRK's 600 mm Multiple Launch Rocket
System." February 13, 2023. https://opennuclear.org/publication/update-dprks
-600-mm-multiple-launch-rocket-system.

Oryx. "North Korean HT-16PGJ MANPADS in Syria." March 22, 2016. https://
www.bellingcat.com/news/mena/2016/03/22/north-korean-ht-16pgj-manpads
-in-syria/.

Oskarsson, Katerina. "The Effectiveness of DIMEFIL Instruments of Power in the
Gray Zone." *Open Publications* 1 (Winter 2017): 21. https://www.academia.edu
/32325460/The_Effectiveness_of_DIMEFIL_Instruments_of_Power_in_the
_Gray_Zone.

O'Toole, Brian. "Rejoining the Iran Nuclear Deal: Not So Easy?" Atlantic Council,
January 2021. https://www.atlanticcouncil.org/in-depth-research-reports/issue
-brief/rejoining-the-iran-nuclear-deal-not-so-easy/.

Ottolenghi, Emanuele. "The Enemy in Our Backyard: Examining Terror Funding
Schemes in South America." In *Hearing before the House Committee on Financial Services: Task Force to Investigate Terrorism Financing*, 114th Cong. 2016. https://docs
.house.gov/meetings/BA/BA00/20160608/105051/HHRG-114-BA00-Wstate
-OttolenghiE-20160608.pdf.

———. "An Examination of Iran's Threat Network." Congressional Testimony before the House Homeland Security Committee, April 2017. https://www.fdd.org/analysis/2018/04/17/state-sponsors-of-terrorism-an-examination-of-irans-global-terrorism-network-2/.

———. "From Latin America to West Africa, Hezbollah's Complex Web of Connections Is Fueling Terrorist Activity." *National,* August 2019. https://www.fdd.org/analysis/2019/08/29/from-latin-america-to-west-africa-hezbollahs-complex-web-of-connections-is-fuelling-its-terrorist-activity/.

———. *The Laundromat: Hezbollah's Money-Laundering and Drug-Trafficking Operations in Latin America.* Mideast Security and Policy Studies 194. Ramat Gan: Begin-Sadat Center for Strategic Studies, Bar-Ilan University, 2021. https://besacenter.org/wp-content/uploads/2021/07/194web.pdf.

———. "The Role of Iranian Dual Nationals in Sanctions Evasion." Congressional Testimony before the House Committee on Oversight and Government Reform, February 2016. https://republicans-oversight.house.gov/wp-content/uploads/2016/02/2016-02-10-Ottolenghi-Testimony-Bio.pdf.

Ottolenghi, Emanuel, Ann Fixler, and Yaya J. Fanusie. "Flying under the Radar: Evasion in the Iranian Aviation Sector." Foundation for Defense of Democracies, July 2016. https://s3.us-east-2.amazonaws.com/defenddemocracy/uploads/documents/Ottolenghi_Fixler_Fanusie_Aviation_Sanctions_Evasion.pdf.

Ottolenghi, Emanuel, Saeed Ghasseminejad, Anne Fixler, and Amir Toumaj. "How the Nuclear Deal Enriches Iran's Revolutionary Guard Corps." Foundation for Defense of Democracies, Center on Sanctions and Illicit Finance, October 2016. https://www.fdd.org/analysis/2016/10/04/how-the-nuclear-deal-enriches-irans-revolutionary-guard-corps/.

Panda, Ankit. "Exclusive: Revealing Kangson, North Korea's First Covert Uranium Enrichment Site." *Diplomat,* July 13, 2018. https://thediplomat.com/2018/07/exclusive-revealing-kangson-north-koreas-first-covert-uranium-enrichment-site/.

Park, John, and Jim Walsh. "Stopping North Korea, Inc: Sanctions Effectiveness and Unintended Consequences." MIT Security Studies, August 2016. https://www.belfercenter.org/sites/default/files/legacy/files/Stopping%20North%20Korea%20Inc%20Park%20and%20Walsh%20.pdf.

Park, Seongjin "Spencer." "Evading, Hacking and Laundering for Nukes: North Korea's Financial Cybercrimes and the Missing Silver Bullet for Countering Them." *Fordham International Law Journal* 45, no. 4 (2022). https://ir.lawnet.fordham.edu/cgi/viewcontent.cgi?article=2843&context=ilj.

Postol, Theodore A. "North Korean Missiles and US Missile Defense." *Physics and Society* 47, no. 2 (April 2018). https://higherlogicdownload.s3.amazonaws.com/APS/a05ec1cf-2e34-4fb3-816e-ea1497930d75/UploadedImages/Newsletter_PDF/April18.pdf.

———. "The Transfer of a Russian ICBM to North Korea?" Beyond Parallel: Center for Strategic and International Studies, August 17, 2023. https://beyondparallel.csis.org/the-transfer-of-a-russian-icbm-to-north-korea/.

Quinn, Colm. "Talks over Iran Deal Enter Fourth Round in Vienna." *Foreign Policy*, May 2021. https://foreignpolicy.com/2021/05/07/iran-nucelar-vienna-jcpoa/.

Ra'anan, Gavriel D., "The Evolution of the Soviet Use of Surrogates in Military Relations with the Third World, with Particular Emphasis on Cuban Participation in Africa." RAND, December 1979. https://apps.dtic.mil/dtic/tr/fulltext/u2/a095442.pdf.

Ramani, Samuel. "Could North Korea Benefit from Middle East Shifts?" *Diplomat*, August 24, 2015. https://thediplomat.com/2015/08/could-north-korea-benefit-from-middle-east-shifts/.

———. "North Korea–Iran Relations Post-JCPOA." *38 North*, November 9, 2023. https://www.38north.org/2023/11/north-korea-iran-relations-post-jcpoa/.

———. "North Korea's Enduring Economic and Security Presence in Africa." *38 North*, June 24, 2021. https://www.38north.org/2021/06/north-koreas-enduring-economic-and-security-presence-in-africa/.

Rapoport, David. "The Four Waves of Modern Terror: International Dimensions and Consequences." UCLA Geneva, September 2011. https://international.ucla.edu/media/files/Rapoport-Four-Waves-of-Modern-Terrorism.pdf.

Real Clear Defense. "What's Driving Iran to Build a Better Missile." February 19, 2020. https://www.realcleardefense.com/articles/2020/02/19/whats_driving_iran_to_build_a_better_missile_115054.html.

Repass, Michael S., and Nicole Wolkov. "Contrary to Previous Claims, Evidence Shows Iskander Missiles in the Second Nagorno-Karabakh War." Caspian Policy Center, April 15, 2021. https://www.caspianpolicy.org/research/security-and-politics-program-spp/contrary-to-previous-claims-evidence-shows-iskander-missiles-in-the-second-nagorno-karabakh-war.

Reynolds, Michael A. "Outfoxed by the Bear? America's Losing Game in the Near East." Russia Foreign Policy Papers. Foreign Policy Research Institute of Philadelphia, April 25, 2018. https://www.fpri.org/article/2018/04/outfoxed-by-the-bear-americas-losing-game-against-russia-in-the-near-east/.

Rickards, James. "Crisis in Lebanon: Anatomy of a Financial Collapse." Foundation for Defense of Democracies, August 2020. https://libnanews.com/wp-content/uploads/2020/08/fdd-monograph-crisis-in-lebanon.pdf.

Riedel, Bruce. "Why Are Yemen's Houthis Attacking Riyadh Now?" Council on Foreign Relations, March 30, 2020. https://www.brookings.edu/blog/order-from-chaos/2020/03/30/why-are-yemens-houthis-attacking-riyadh-now/.

Riley, Duncan. "North Korea Suspected in Attack That Delayed Printing of Major Newspapers." SiliconANGLE, December 30, 2018. https://siliconangle.com/2018/12/30/north-korea-suspected-behind-attack-delayed-printing-major-newspapers/.

Roblin, Sebastien. "Iran Just Struck U.S. Bases in Iraq with Ballistic Missiles. Here's Why They're Tehran's Favored Weapon." *Forbes*, January 7, 2020. https://www.forbes.com/sites/sebastienroblin/2020/01/07/iran-just-struck-us-bases-in

-iraq-with-ballistic-missiles-heres-why-theyre-tehrans-favored-weapon/#27c
432c3136c.

Rogers, Paul. "North Korea Is Selling Arms and Breaking Sanctions: Does Anyone
Care?" Open Democracy, March 25, 2019. https://www.opendemocracy.net/en
/north-korea-is-selling-arms-and-breaking-sanctions-does-anyone-care/.

Rook, Robert. "Arts of Evasion: North Korea, Sanctions and the World." *Towson
University Journal of International Affairs* 1, no. 2 (Spring 2018). https://cpb
-us-w2.wpmucdn.com/wp.towson.edu/dist/b/55/files/2018/05/SPRING-2018
-ROOK-ARTICLE-1t27fhc.pdf.

Rosett, Claudia. "The Iran–North Korea Strategic Alliance." In *House Hearing,
114 Congress (From the US Government Publishing Office)*. Testimony before
the House Foreign Affairs Subcommittee Hearing, July 28, 2015. https://docs
.house.gov/meetings/FA/FA18/20150728/103824/HHRG-114-FA18-Wstate
-RosettC-20150728.pdf.

———. "Kim Jong-Il's Cashbox." *Forbes*, April 15, 2010. https://www.forbes.com
/2010/04/15/kim-jong-il-north-korea-opinions-columnists-claudia-rosett.html?
sh=38e0104d79a4.

Ross, Dennis. "The Coming Iran Nuclear Talks: Openings and Obstacles." Washington Institute for Near East Policy, January 2021. https://www.washingtoninsti
tute.org/policy-analysis/coming-iran-nuclear-talks-openings-and-obstacles.

———. "A New Iran Deal Might Be on the Horizon." Washington Institute for Near
East Policy, June 23, 2023. https://www.washingtoninstitute.org/policy-analysis
/new-iran-nuclear-deal-might-be-horizon.

Royal United Services Institute. "Rickety Anchor: North Korea Calls Its Illicit Shipping Fleet Home amid Coronavirus Fears." March 26, 2020. https://rusi.org
/explore-our-research/publications/commentary/rickety-anchor-north-korea
-calls-its-illicit-shipping-fleet-home-amid-coronavirus-fears.

Rubin, Michael. "A Short History of the Iranian Drone Program." American Enterprise Institute, August 2020. https://www.aei.org/research-products/report/a
-short-history-of-the-iranian-drone-program/.

Rumley, Grant. "China's Security Presence in the Middle East: Redlines and Guidelines for the United States." Washington Institute for Near East Policy, October
2022. https://www.washingtoninstitute.org/policy-analysis/chinas-security-pres
ence-middle-east-redlines-and-guidelines-united-states.

Safshekan, Roozbeh, and Farzan Sabet. "The Source of Legitimacy in the Guardianship of the Jurist: Historical Genealogy and Political Implications." *Project on
Middle East Political Science Studies: New Analysis of Shia Politics*, December 2017.
https://pomeps.org/wp-content/uploads/2017/12/POMEPS_Studies_28_New
Analysis_Web.pdf.

Sakai, Takashi. "North Korea's Political System." Japan Digital Library, March
2016. https://www2.jiia.or.jp/en/pdf/digital_library/korean_peninsula/160331
_Takashi_Sakai.pdf.

Savelsberg, Ralph, and Tomohiko Kawaguchi. "North Korea's Hypersonic Missile Claims Are Credible, Exclusive Analysis Shows." *Breaking Defense*, February 16, 2022. https://breakingdefense.com/2022/02/north-koreas-hypersonic-missile-claims-are-credible-exclusive-analysis-shows/.

Sayari. "Defendants and Front Companies Named in DOJ Indictment Operate Additional Active Companies and Trade with North Korea." June 11, 2020. https://sayari.com/resources/defendants-and-front-companies-named-in-doj-indictment-operate-additional-active-companies-and-trade-with-north-korea/.

———. "Tracking an Iran-DPRK Gold Smuggling Scheme with Public Records." July 7, 2021. https://sayari.com/resources/tracking-an-iran-dprk-gold-smuggling-scheme-with-public-records/.

Schanzer, Jonathan. "Hamas' Benefactors: A Network of Terror." Foundation for the Defense of Democracies (FDD), September 2014. https://www.fdd.org/analysis/2014/09/12/hamass-benefactors-a-network-of-terror-2/

———. "The Quiet War between Israel and Iran: Iran's Hegemonic Drive." Middle East Forum, December 1, 2022. https://www.fdd.org/analysis/2022/12/02/quiet-war-israel-iran/.

Schmidt, Gary J. *Rise of the Revisionists: Russia, China and Iran*. Washington, DC: AEI Press, 2018.

Schreffler, Natalie. "North Korea and Hezbollah: A Nexus Worth Fearing?" *Penn State International Affairs Review*, April 8, 2013. https://sites.psu.edu/psiareview/2013/04/08/north-korea-and-hezbollah-a-nexus-worth-fearing/.

Seliktar, Ofira. "The End of the JCPOA Road?" *Middle East Quarterly* 27, no. 5 (Summer 2020): 1–18.

Shapira, Shimon, and Daniel Diker. "The Second Islamic Revolution: Strategic Implications for the West." In *Iran, Hizbullah, Hamas and the Global Jihad: A New Conflict Paradigm* edited by Dore Gold, 44–61. Jerusalem: Jerusalem Center for Public Affairs, 2007. https://jcpa.org/book/iran-hizbullah-hamas-and-the-global-jihad-a-new-conflict-paradigm for-the-west/.

Shoham, Dany. "The Quadruple Threat: North Korea, China, Pakistan, and Iran." Perspectives Paper 1795. BESA Center, November 2020. https://besacenter.org/wp-content/uploads/2020/11/1795-Contiguous-Quartet-Shoham-final.pdf.

Smyth, Phillip. "Beware of Muqtada al-Sadr." Washington Institute for Near East Policy, October 19, 2016. https://www.washingtoninstitute.org/policy-analysis/view/beware-of-muqtada-al-sadr.

———. "The Shi'ite Jihad in Syria: The Regional Effects." Policy Focus 138. Washington Institute for Near East Policy, 2015. https://www.washingtoninstitute.org/policy-analysis/view/the-shiite-jihad-in-syria-and-its-regional-effects.

Solomon, Jay. "North Korea's Alliance with Syria Reveals a Wider Proliferation Threat." Washington Institute, November 2, 2017. https://www.washingtoninstitute.org/policy-analysis/view/north-koreas-alliance-with-syria-reveals-a-wider-proliferation-threat.

Spalding, Hugo. "Russia's False Narrative in Syria." Backgrounder. Institute for the Study of War, December 1, 2015. https://www.understandingwar.org/back grounder/russias-false-narrative-syria-december-1-2015.

Spaulding, Hugo, Christopher Kozak Christopher Harmer, Daniel Urchick, Jessica Lewis McFate, Jennifer Cafarella, Harleen Gambhir, and Kimberly Kagan. "Russia's Deployment to Syria: Putin's Middle East Game Changer." Warning Intelligence Update. Institute for the Study of War, September 17, 2015. https://www.understandingwar.org/backgrounder/russian-deployment-syria -putin%E2%80%99s-middle-east-game-changer.

Stone, Jeff. "Google Catches North Korean, Iranian Hackers Impersonating Journalists in Phishing Efforts." *CyberScoop*, March 26, 2020. https://cyberscoop.com /google-phishing-warning-hacking-campaign-iran-north-korea/.

Stricker, Andrea. "Russia and China Obstruct UN Reporting on North Korea." Foundation for Defense of Democracies, October 21, 2020. https://www.fdd.org /analysis/2020/10/21/russia-and-china-obstruct-un-reporting-on-north-korea/.

Suberg, William. "North Korea Launched Cryptocurrency Attacks in Response to Sanctions, Says FBI." Cointelegraph, May 30, 2019. https://cointelegraph.com /news/north-korea-launched-cryptocurrency-attacks-in-response-to-sanctions -says-fbi.

Sullivan, Marisa. "Hezbollah in Syria." Institute for the Study of War, April 2014. https://www.understandingwar.org/sites/default/files/Hezbollah_Sullivan_FI NAL.pdf.

Sutton, H. I. "Unusual Submarine Likely to Increase Threat from North Korea." *Naval News*, October 2, 2020. https://www.navalnews.com/naval-news/2020/10 /unusual-submarine-likely-to-increase-threat-from-north-korea/.

Tabatabai, Ariane M. "After Soleimani: What Is Next for the Quds Force?" *CTC Sentinel* 13, no. 1 (2020): 33–38.

Taleblu, Behnam Ben. "Arsenal: Assessing the Islamic Republic of Iran's Ballistic Missile Program." Foundation for Defense of Democracies, February 2023. https://www.fdd.org/analysis/2023/02/15/arsenal-assessing-the-islamic-republic -of-irans-ballistic-missile-program/.

———. "The Sanctioned Cabinet of Ebrahim Raisi." Foundation for Defense of Democracies, September 30, 2021. https://www.fdd.org/analysis/2021/09/30 /the-sanctioned-cabinet-of-ebrahim-raisi/.

Tan, Morse. "The North Korean Nuclear Crisis: Past Failures, Present Solutions." *Saint Louis University Law Journal* 50, no. 2 (2006). https://scholarship.law.slu .edu/cgi/viewcontent.cgi?article=1711&context=lj.

Taylor, Edwin. "Room 39: Shadow Funds Powering North Korea's Elite." *Grey Dynamics*, August 25, 2024. https://greydynamics.com/office-39-north-koreas-secret -slush-fund/.

Thayer, Nate. "The Front Companies Facilitating North Korean Arms Exports." *NK News*, May 30, 2013. https://www.nknews.org/2013/05/the-front-companies -facilitating-north-korean-arms-exports/.

Trofimenko, Henry. "The Third World and the U.S.-Soviet Competition: A Soviet View." *Foreign Affairs*, June 1, 1981. https://www.foreignaffairs.com/articles/russian-federation/1981-06-01/third-world-and-us-soviet-competition.

21st Century Asian Arms Race. "The Mysterious Origins of a New North Korean Howitzer." October 26, 2018. https://21stcenturyasianarmsrace.com/2018/10/26/the-mysterious-origins-of-a-new-north-korean-howitzer/.

UN Panel of Experts on Yemen. Letter to the President of the UN Security Council, January 22, 2021. https://digitallibrary.un.org/record/3898851.

UN Security Council. *Final Report of the Panel of Experts Submitted Pursuant to Resolution 1874 (2009)*. November 5, 2010. https://www.undocs.org/S/2010/571.

———. *Final Report of the Panel of Experts Submitted Pursuant to Resolution 2407 (2018)*. March 5, 2019. https://www.undocs.org/S/2019/171.

———. *Final Report of the Panel of Experts Submitted Pursuant to Resolution 2515 (2020)*. March 4, 2021. https://undocs.org/S/2021/211.

———. *Final Report of the Panel of Experts Submitted Pursuant to Resolution 2680 (2023)*. March 7, 2024. https://main.un.org/securitycouncil/en/sanctions/1718/panel_experts/reports.

UN Security Council Report. "DPRK (North Korea): Yesterday's Vote on a Sanctions Resolution." May 27, 2022. https://www.securitycouncilreport.org/whatsinblue/2022/05/dprk-north-korea-yesterdays-vote-on-a-sanctions-resolution.php.

US Department of Justice. "Department of Justice Announces Charges of North Korean and Malaysia Nationals for Bank Fraud, Money Laundering and North Korea Sanctions Violations." Press release, September 11, 2020. https://www.justice.gov/opa/pr/department-justice-announces-charges-north-korean-and-malaysia-nationals-bank-fraud-money.

US Department of the Treasury. "Treasury Sanctions Individual, Banks, and Trading Company for Supporting North Korea's WMD and Ballistic Missile Programs." Press release, May 27, 2022. https://home.treasury.gov/news/press-releases/jy0801.

———. "Treasury Sanctions Iranian Persons Involved in the Production of Unmanned Aerial Vehicles and Weapons Shipment to Russia." Press release, September 9, 2022. https://home.treasury.gov/news/press-releases/jy0940.

———. "Treasury Sanctions Key Actors in Iran's Nuclear and Ballistic Missile Programs." Press release, September 21, 2020. https://home.treasury.gov/news/press-releases/sm1130.

———. "Treasury Sanctions Those Involved in Ballistic Missile Procurement for Iran." Press release, January 17, 2016. https://home.treasury.gov/news/press-releases/jl0322.

———. "Treasury Targets Actors Involved in Production and Transfer of Iranian Unmanned Arial Vehicles to Russia for Use in Ukraine." Press release, November 15, 2022. https://home.treasury.gov/news/press-releases/jy1104.

———. "Treasury Targets DPRK's International Agents and Illicit Cyber Intrusion Group." Press release, November 30, 2023. https://home.treasury.gov/news/press-releases/jy1938.

————. "Treasury Targets Russian Bank and Other Facilitators of North Korean United Nations Security Council Violations." Press release, August 3, 2018. https://home.treasury.gov/news/press-releases/sm454.

US Department of State. "Imposing Additional Sanctions on Those Supporting Russia's War against Ukraine." Press release, July 20, 2023. https://www.state.gov/imposing-additional-sanctions-on-those-supporting-russias-war-against-ukraine/.

————. "Responding to Two Years of Russia's Full-Scale War on Ukraine and Navalny's Death." Press release, February 23, 2024. https://www.state.gov/imposing-measures-in-response-to-navalnys-death-and-two-years-of-russias-full-scale-war-against-ukraine/.

US Federal Bureau of Investigation. "FBI Confirms Lazarus Group Cyber Actors Responsible for Harmony's Horizon Bridge Currency Theft." Press release, January 23, 2023. https://www.fbi.gov/news/press-releases/fbi-confirms-lazarus-group-cyber-actors-responsible-for-harmonys-horizon-bridge-currency-theft.

Uskowi, Nader. "The Evolving Iranian Strategy in Syria: A Looming Conflict with Israel." Atlantic Council, Scowcroft Center, September 2018. https://www.atlanticcouncil.org/wp-content/uploads/2019/09/The_Evolving_Iranian_Strategy_in_Syria.pdf.

Van Diepen, Vann H. "Initial Analysis of North Korea's March 25 SRBM Launches." *38 North*, March 30, 2021. https://www.38north.org/2021/03/initial-analysis-of-north-koreas-march-25-srbm-launches/#:~:text=That%20these%20launches%20involved%20SRBMs,conduct%20(if%20not%20gearing%20up.

Vatanka, Alex. "Iran's Use of Shia Militant Proxies: Ideological and Practical Expediency versus Uncertain Sustainability." Middle East Institute, June 2018. https://www.mei.edu/sites/default/files/publications/Vatanka_PolicyPaper.pdf.

————. "Whither the IRGC of the 2020s: Is Iran's Proxy Warfare Strategy of Forward Defense Sustainable"? *New America*, January 2021. https://d1y8sb8igg2f8e.cloudfront.net/documents/Whither_the_IRGC_of_the_2020s_.pdf.

Walcott, John. "Cash, Yachts, and Cognac: Kim Yo-Jong's Links to the Secretive Office Keeping North Korea's Elites in Luxury." *Time*, April 29, 2020. https://time.com/5829508/kim-yo-jong-money-office-39/.

Watkins, Simon. "Iran to Import North Korean Missiles in 25-Year Military Deal with China." OilPrice.com, October 19, 2020. https://oilprice.com/Energy/Energy-General/Iran-To-Import-North-Korean-missiles-In-25-Year-Military-Deal-With-China.html.

Wege, Carl Anthony. "The Hizballah-North Korea Nexus." *Small Wars Journal*, January 23, 2011. https://smallwarsjournal.com/blog/journal/docs-temp/654-wege.pdf.

Wertz, Daniel. "The Evolution of Financial Sanctions on North Korea." *North Korea Review* 9, no. 3 (Fall 2013): 69–82.

Westcott, Tom, and Afshin Ismaeli. "Sanctions and Smuggling: The Role of Iraqi Kurdistan and Iran's Border Economies." Global Initiative against Transnational

Organized Crime, April 2019. https://globalinitiative.net/wp-content/uploads /2019/04/TGIATOC-Report-Sanctions-Iraq-Iran-05Apr1300-Web.pdf.

White House. "National Security Strategy of the United States." December 2017. https://trumpwhitehouse.archives.gov/wp-content/uploads/2017/12/NSS-Final -12-18-2017-0905.pdf.

———. "National Security Strategy of the United States." October 2022. https:// www.whitehouse.gov/wp-content/uploads/2022/10/Biden-Harris-Administra tions-National-Security-Strategy-10.2022.pdf.

———. "The United States Assessment of the Assad Regime's Use of Chemical Weapons." April 2018. https://dod.defense.gov/portals/1/features/2018/0418_syria /img/United-States-Assessment-of-the-Assad-Regime%E2%80%99s-Chemical -Weapons-Use.pdf.

Williams, Martyn, and Peter Makowsky. "A North Korean Rail Yard near Russia Springs to Life." *38 North*, December 12, 2022. https://www.38north.org/ 2022/12/a-north-korean-rail-yard-near-russia-springs-to-life/#:~:text=Re cent%20commercial%20satellite%20imagery%20indicates,alongside%20 trains%20at%20least%20twice.

Wilson Center. "How Did the North Korean Famine Happen?" April 30, 2002. https://www.wilsoncenter.org/article/how-did-the-north-korean-famine -happen.

Wisconsin Project. "Syria Missile Development." March 1, 1997. https://www.wis consinproject.org/syria-missile-development/.

Woods, Kevin, Williamson Murray, and Thomas Holaday. "Saddam's War: An Iraqi Military Perspective of the Iran-Iraq War." With Mounir Elkhamri. McNair Paper 70. National Defense University, 2009. https://ndupress.ndu.edu/Portals/68 /Documents/Books/saddams-war.pdf.

Woolsey, R. James. "Breaking the Iran, North Korea, and Syria Nexus." Joint Hearing before the House Committee on Foreign Affairs, April 11, 2013 https://www .fdd.org/analysis/2013/04/11/breaking-the-iran-north-korea-and-syria-nexus/.

Yaari, Ehud. "Bracing for an Israel-Iran Confrontation in Syria." *American Interest*, April 2018. https://www.washingtoninstitute.org/policy-analysis/view/bracing-for -an-israel-iran-confrontation-in-syria.

Young, Benjamin R. "North Korea in Africa: Historical Solidarity, China's Role, and Sanctions Evasion." US Institute of Peace, February 2021. https://www .usip.org/publications/2021/02/north-korea-africa-historical-solidarity-chinas -role-and-sanctions-evasion.

Zakharova, Liudmila. "Economic Cooperation between Russia and North Korea: New Goals and New Approaches." *Journal of Eurasian Studies* 7, no. 2 (July 2016). https://www.sciencedirect.com/science/article/pii/S1879366516300124.

Zelin, Aaron, and Phillip Smyth. "The Vocabulary of Sectarianism." Washington Institute for Near East Policy, January 2014. https://www.washingtoninstitute.org /pdf/view/4879/en.

Zwirko, Colin. "North Korea Test-Launched New 'Hwasong-17' ICBM for First Time, State Media Says." *NK News*, March 25, 2022. https://www.nknews .org/2022/03/north-korea-test-launched-new-hwasong-17-icbm-for-first-time -state-media-says/.

Index

Page numbers in *italics* refer to tables.